C. WRIGHT MILLS

Letters and Autobiographical Writings

C. WRIGHT MILLS

Letters and

Autobiographical Writings

Edited by Kathryn Mills

with Pamela Mills

Introduction by

Dan Wakefield

University of California Press

Berkeley

Los Angeles

London

Epigraphs from "C. Wright Mills: Islander Exploring Main
Street," *Columbia Alumni News* 42, no. 3 (December 1950): 18.

"On Intellectual Craftsmanship," in *The Sociological Imagination* by
C. Wright Mills (New York: Oxford University Press, 1959), 226.

University of California Press
Berkeley and Los Angeles, California

University of California Press, Ltd.
London, England

Library of Congress Cataloging-in-Publication Data

Mills, C. Wright (Charles Wright), 1916–1962.

[Selections.   2000]

Letters and autobiographical writings / C. Wright Mills ;
edited by Kathryn Mills with Pamela Mills.
p.   cm.
Includes bibliographical references and index.

ISBN 0-520-21106-5 (alk. paper)

1. Mills, C. Wright (Charles Wright), 1916–1962—
Correspondence.   2. Mills, C. Wright (Charles Wright),
1916–1962.   3. Sociologists—United States—Biography.   I.
Mills, Kathryn, 1955– .   II. Mills, Pamela, 1943– .   III. Title.
HM479.M55A3   2000
301'.092—dc21
[B]   99-29106
                                                 CIP

Manufactured in the United States of America

08   07   06   05   04   03   02   01   00

10   9   8   7   6   5   4   3   2   1

The paper used in this publication meets the minimum
requirements of ANSI/NISO Z39.48-1992 (R 1997)
(*Permanence of Paper*). ♾

For C. Wright Mills's son, Nikolas,

and for Mills's grandchildren,

Carlos, Paulo, Pedro, and Eric

Mills strides excitedly up and down the room. . . . He pauses to glare at his towering bookcase. "It's a writer's responsibility to orient modern publics to the catastrophic world in which they live," he says. "But he cannot do this if he remains a mere specialist. To do it at all, he's got to do it *big!*"

—*Columbia Alumni News*

Do not allow public issues as they are officially formulated, or troubles as they are privately felt, to determine the problems that you take up for study. Above all, do not give up your moral and political autonomy by accepting in somebody else's terms the illiberal practicality of the bureaucratic ethos or the liberal practicality of the moral scatter. Know that many personal troubles cannot be solved merely as troubles, but must be understood in terms of public issues—and in terms of the problems of history-making. Know that the human meaning of public issues must be revealed by relating them to personal troubles—and to the problems of the individual life.

Know that the problems of social science, when adequately formulated, must include both troubles and issues, both biography and history, and the range of their intricate relations. Within that range the life of the individual and the making of societies occur; and within that range the sociological imagination has its chance to make a difference in the quality of human life in our time.

—*C. Wright Mills*
The Sociological Imagination

CONTENTS

Photographs follow page 204

PREFACE

In the decades since the death of our father, C. Wright Mills, critics and admirers have written about him and his work with wildly varying degrees of factual accuracy as well as the expected divergence of opinions. In 1995, after we received copies of letters he had written to one correspondent over a twenty-year period, we decided that the time had come to allow his own words to speak for themselves.

This volume includes approximately 150 letters selected from more than 600 that Mills wrote to his parents, friends, and colleagues; several autobiographical essays from one of his unfinished manuscripts; and a number of other writings of interest. We chose material for its liveliness, current relevance, and ability to show Mills's point of view, presenting a broad scope of subject matter and mood: from anger to affection, self-doubt to fearless exuberance, the social sciences to motorcycles, the writing life to international politics, from Texas to New York, Denmark to Cuba. Our sources of information for the annotations to this collection range from newspaper articles of the day and other published works to the now-declassified FBI file on Mills and our own interviews with family members and friends.

When we started work on the manuscript for this book, we had to decide how to refer to our father. Like a character in a Russian novel, he went by many names. He was Charleswright to his mother; Charlie to his old friends; C. Wright to his first wife; Wright to his second and third wives and many friends and colleagues; Daddy to his children; the "subject" to the FBI; and simply Mills to his readers. He often signed his letters as Mills, and that is the name we use.

This book is not an exhaustive reference work; even if we had wanted to produce such a tome, we would have been prevented from doing so by the limitations of the available letters. For instance, although we have obtained a good number of letters to most of Mills's closest friends—including Hans Gerth, Ralph Miliband, Bill Miller, and Harvey Swados—we have only one letter to Dick Hofstadter, who was Mills's close friend in Maryland. Mills's friendships with Ian Ballantine, Lewis A. Coser, Hazel Gaudet Erskine, Leo Lowenthal, and Dan Wakefield are represented here with at least one letter to each person, and his friendship with Saul Landau is mentioned in the head notes; but the collection does not include letters to all Mills's colleagues. For example, it includes no letters from Mills to Robert Lynd, whom he frequently mentioned. (No substantial correspondence to Lynd from Mills was available in the archives with their papers.) However, we do have substantive letters from (or about) the various phases of Mills's associations with Daniel Bell, Paul Lazarsfeld, and Dwight Macdonald, as well as letters from Mills's long correspondence and association with Robert K. Merton. We have reason to believe that Mills corresponded with Eric Fromm, but to our knowledge no letters from Mills survived from those exchanges. Fortunately, we do have letters from his exchanges with Saul Alinsky, Frank Freidel, Carlos Fuentes, David Riesman, and E. P. Thompson.

Letter writing played different roles in different relationships. Mills's friendship with Hans Gerth was largely sustained by correspondence after Mills left Wisconsin. Their collaboration led to much letter writing. Luckily, Gerth was a careful archivist; Mills was not. For this reason, we were able to refer to Gerth's side of the correspondence for only about half the selected letters from Mills to Gerth. At the other end of the spectrum is Mills's long and enduring friendship with Harvey Swados, which is not fully reflected in their letters since they saw each other so frequently. Mills moved to Rockland County, New York, partly because the Swadoses were already there. The Mills and Swados families shared family events in the 1950s, and Mills dedicated *The Sociological Imagination* to Harvey and Bette Swados.

As a cautionary note, we'd like to remind readers that letters are simply what the letter writer chose to commit to paper that happened to survive. For example, Mills's family and close friends know that he had an ambivalent relationship with his mother, but as you will see, the letters to her in this book (and all the letters she donated to the Center for American History at the University of Texas at Austin) express only the positive side of his relationship with her.

Mills's special affinity for letter writing is clear from his published work as well as from his correspondence. One example is his article "Letter to the New Left," which was signed "Yours truly, C. Wright Mills" in the British version. Also, Mills wrote his mass market paperback book about Cuba *(Listen, Yankee)* as a series of letters from an imaginary Cuban revolutionary trying to communicate with his U.S. neighbors. Similarly, almost all of Mills's unpublished autobiographical writings took the form of letters to an imaginary Russian colleague whom he called Tovarich,[1] the Russian word for comrade or friend. These autobiographical writings were the more well-developed sections of an unfinished manuscript; other sections sketched some of Mills's impressions about his two visits to the Soviet Union.

What is the importance of Tovarich? Mills's writings to an imaginary Russian friend during the Cold War were a political statement, an effort to foster improved communication between people whose governments were hostile to each other. At the same time, although Mills referred to Russian literature and culture occasionally, his intended audience was naturally much broader than Russian readers or readers of any single nationality. Mills was writing the Tovarich letters to you, the person holding this book, because you are part of his reading public.

In a letter to Tovarich, Mills admitted that he was also writing to himself—using the figure of Tovarich in efforts at self-scrutiny. His datelines show that he wrote these narratives—a political intellectual's "Dear Diary"—from 1956 to 1960, when he was between forty and forty-four years old. His health was not yet a problem for him (although a military physical exam had diagnosed hypertension when he was in his twenties). *White Collar* and *The Power Elite* had already been published; Mills's reputation as a writer was well established.

With the unfinished manuscript "Contacting the Enemy: Tovarich," we found an unmailed letter to his agent, in which Mills wrote, "I send you now a book-length manuscript of which I am quite uncertain. Perhaps it is a book, perhaps it isn't. Perhaps it is part of a book in search of a co-author." Mills asked for help finding a publisher, a good editor, and perhaps a Russian coauthor who would contribute letters too. He wrote that, if good letters from a Russian writer could not be found, his own side of the cor-

---

1. We have kept the spelling used by Mills, which is one of the versions considered correct; other accepted transliterations include "Tovarishch," "Tovarish," and "Tovarisch."

respondence should be published alone. We believe that Mills would be pleased by the publication of the autobiographical portions of that manuscript within this volume.

On the topic of the editorial treatment of the text, we annotated the letters and other writings to supply contexts and explanations for a wide audience. We also tried to make explanations as unobtrusive as possible for those already familiar with the cast of characters, the history, and Mills's books.

We deleted several references to purely private aspects of Mills's life out of respect for family and friends still living. In a few letters in which privacy was not an issue, we made deletions to avoid unnecessarily offending living people. We also made a number of deletions to avoid repetition and to eliminate obscure, insignificant references. All deletions from the original letters are marked by ellipses within brackets. Ellipses without brackets are Mills's. When we inserted identifying information in his letters or writings, we used brackets to mark the additional words.

Written before the days of word processors, personal computers, and spell-checking software, Mills's letters were often riddled with spelling, punctuation, and typographical errors. We corrected these errors along with the rare grammatical slip, except when the nonstandard usage seemed to be intentional, for emphasis or effect, or when Mills used a variant spelling of a person's name. We added paragraph breaks when they were needed. We added punctuation only when it was necessary for comprehension; we preserved various inconsistencies of discretionary punctuation, and we did not add salutations when Mills provided none. Our approach was to make the letters as clear as possible, by cleaning up errors, while preserving the letters' authenticity by minimizing editorial intrusion.

Mills's cover letter to his agent made it clear that he wanted the Tovarich writings to be edited before they were published, partly to avoid self-indulgence, as he put it; and his handwritten marginal notes provided guideposts for that work. For instance, his marginal comments included these instructions: "very good, use it," "can't use this," "cut somewhat." Mills included a chapter-opening epigraph for one letter to Tovarich, so we added other epigraphs, written by authors Mills mentioned with admiration in his letters or elsewhere. As usual our additional text is within brackets.

In the Tovarich writings we did not mark deletions with ellipses and we occasionally changed the location of paragraphs, shortened a heading, or replaced a heading with a phrase that Mills had written in the text. Although we usually left the original references to men, boys, women, and girls in these essays, we occasionally changed "men" to "people."

With the exception of the Texas section on Mills's ancestry and youth, his letters and other writings are presented here in chronological order according to the time they were written. In some of Mills's letters to Tovarich he discussed events covered in his letters to real people, and in some letters to real people he discussed his project of writing to the imaginary Tovarich. Reading these materials in tandem will allow the reader to shuttle between the personal and the public Mills. We hope that this volume will foster insight into Mills's intellectual development and a sense of who he was at the various stages of his life.

We should add a word on our editorial collaboration. Kate Mills took primary responsibility for this volume—visiting eight archives and conducting the other research and most of the correspondence to collect the letters, selecting text from the original Tovarich manuscript, and selecting almost all the letters. Kate researched and drafted the headnotes and nearly all the footnotes, as well as this preface, the chronology, and the acknowledgments. Pam Mills provided editorial advice and did close editing work on the several versions of the manuscript; she also drafted the "Notes on Selected Correspondents" and a number of annotations to the text. We both contributed to the editorial treatment of the writings within the parameters we've described.

Working on this collection of our father's words has been both exhilarating and saddening to us. In the short essays that follow we describe some of our personal memories and experiences related to our father.

REMEMBRANCE

KATHRYN MILLS

I'm writing this in the month of March. It's usually March when I write about my memories of my father—clear memories I'm fortunate to have, since I was not quite seven years old the March he died. I was probably the only child in my nursery school whose father delivered her there on his motorcycle and also let her honk the horn.

I remember my father building our house after his marriage to Yaroslava—a cinder-block house they designed. The back of the house is covered with large, east-facing windows that frame views of a sparkling lake and a field. I loved to pick the wildflowers that grew there.

I remember watching the sweat pour down my father's face as he worked on the construction site of the house, a few months before my fourth birthday. He stood there in the hot sun, squinting into the distance as he paused to rest or think; the sweat traveled down his face in rivulets. I remember other men hauling cinder blocks, and my father must have carried cinder blocks too; but what I can picture is his face as he squinted off into the distance.

Later in that house I visited him in his study. It was morning and he was sitting at his desk in the room where file drawers covered two whole walls. He was writing books. I came in to show him a long word I'd made up, and he said the nonsensical, nonexistent word with great sweeping drama; I laughed so hard I could barely stand up. Then I went to another room to write another word for my father to pronounce. When I returned, he put down his pencil again, so he could repeat our hilarity with full effect.

And I remember my father standing at the stove, stirring a culinary monstrosity that some would call stew. It had large chunks of cheese in it along with the meat; I liked to stretch out this cheese in strings the length of my arm.

My half-sister, Pamela, came to visit us in the house when she was a teenager. She stayed with us the summer Nik—Yara and Wright's son—was born. And Pam and Yara told me about the times we danced after dinner. My father took turns twirling me and Pam across the room, and he and Yara danced with baby Nik held in their arms.

My father didn't want me to watch cartoons on television because he said they had too much violence in them, but *Rawhide* was a different story; we watched that together. And the cattlemen in the West shouted, "Round 'em up and head 'em out!"

I remember being afraid of the dark; I liked my father's attempt to cure me of this fear. He took me on a daytime tour of our house, armed with a flashlight, which he used to light up the far corners of every single closet, every single dark storage place—showing me that there was nothing frightening hiding in the darkness.

On a small personal scale, working on this book turned out to be one way to cut through the darkness—the scarcity of firsthand knowledge—that results from loss. Coming home from my work at a publishing company, I'd find packages of my father's letters in my mailbox. It seems fitting that letters provided me with a way toward a better understanding of my father. When I was in my midtwenties, in 1981, I wrote several rambling "father poems," mostly in the form of letters to him.

One of the anecdotes I wrote down in March 1981 was from my morning visits with my father in his study. It's difficult to describe the way I felt fourteen years later, in 1995, when I was reading one of his unpublished manuscripts in a beat-up, black notebook with a handwritten label and I discovered that my father had also written about those visits (letter to Tovarich, summer 1960, "Specimen Days of My Life," in part 5 of this book).

Another poignant moment came when Yara handed me a long letter addressed to Pam, Nik, and me, which Grandmother Mills had penned just one year after the people at the Oak Hill Cemetery buried her only son, her beloved Charleswright. Holding Grandmother Mills's letter many years after her own death, I was standing amid stacks of papers; I was in the midst of searching out and piecing together letters from my father's life, and Pam was already committed to helping work on the manuscript. We wanted to give readers something authentic, complex, and true on the topic of C. Wright Mills's life and credo—to help ensure that his work and his humanity would be appreciated fully and remembered well. I felt as if Grandmother Mills had anticipated that moment and this project in her letter when she wrote: "As you children become older, your pride and memory of your own wonderful, brilliant father will increase and it is good that his memory will be forever green" (part 1 of this book).

I remember when I first started reading my father's books. I was sixteen years old and my mother, Ruthie, and I were spending Christmas vacation in a seaside town in Mexico. On the beach it was really hot, but it was wonderfully cool within the stone walls and shade of the courtyard in which I first read *The Power Elite*. This was the book my mother had seen from its conception to its publication, providing much of the statistical underpinning, insisting on clarity, precision, and a logical presentation, helping Wright strengthen his arguments and make his ideas accessible to the rest of us.

The book was no substitute for talking about the world with a living father, but it was better than nothing. At least *The Power Elite, The Causes of World War Three* (a softcover about ending the nuclear arms race, which he dedicated to me), *White Collar,* and my father's other books are physically present and intellectually alive. They were there for me when I was ready to go to them.

Sitting with my elbows on the stone tabletop in that Mexican courtyard, I was absorbed in reading *The Power Elite*. I learned about the importance of simultaneously maintaining a healthy respect for complexity and a great capacity for outrage. Some intellectuals seemed to use their analytical skills to erect barriers against decisive action—a form of political paralysis. My father did not have this affliction of the will. For him it was possible—indeed necessary—to be at once energetically analytical, skeptical, and deeply engaged.

I spent a decade of my life engaged in political projects: volunteering for George McGovern's presidential campaign and for public interest research groups, testifying against nuclear power plants while in school, and later working as a full-time community organizer in the Mission Hill section of Boston. There I joined ongoing efforts for affordable housing, equitable city services, and clean air. We talked and planned—in the basement of Mission Church, in our office behind the pizza shop, and in people's homes—and we spent time on the picket line. "Like a tree that's standing by the water, we shall not be moved," we sang.

In my mind's eye I can still see my father standing by the closet door shining his flashlight into the darkness. Yes, it was possible to light up the far corners. No, we should not be afraid to confront what we find there. I believe that my father's lesson for me was also his message to the world. His was the light of reason, humane purpose, and moral passion, and he struggled to dispel the darkness of apathy, confusion, and irresponsibility.

My father did not have the chance to finish building his house of theory, and many years have passed since he labored on that intellectual construction site; but his commitment to craftsmanship, the intensity of his efforts, and the largeness and complexity of his vision are there for us as a source of inspiration.

MY FATHER HAUNTS ME

PAMELA MILLS

I was watching Judith Anderson in a production of *Medea* at Oberlin College on March 20, 1962, when I was called to the phone to learn that my forty-five-year-old father had died. Was it an exaggeration to feel that the tragedy, like that in the play, was public as well as private?

In the decades since then, the ghost of my father has made many appearances, often provoked by gratifying references to his work. Besides the more expected citations in texts directly connected to the social sciences, there have been surprising contexts in which he has suddenly leapt into the present. From my base in Rio de Janeiro, I have observed the ongoing Latin American appreciation of his views. For example, on several occasions during the 1980s, he was quoted by an admirer on the editorial page of the newspaper *Jornal do Brasil*. More recently, in October 1997, just when my ghost-hungry mind had been most receptive to striking appearances, two colleagues came across unexpected references to my father. The first, a student in a master's program in applied linguistics, excitedly told me that she had seen a quotation by Mills in a reading assignment. It was from a 1940 article entitled "Situated Actions and Vocabularies of Motive," one of his first professional publications. The second reference was even more unusual. Another colleague found a comment about my father in Marcia Muller's mystery novel *Pennies on a Dead Woman's Eyes* (1992). In an interview about California in the 1950s, the detective-narrator observes that the intellectuals of the Cold War were a fairly conservative breed. The character being interviewed replies, "Yes, with the exception of a few household names— C. Wright Mills . . . for example" (217). However, one of the greatest surprises came from the first edition of *The Reader's Catalog* (1989). After appreciating the choices in the literature section, I flipped to sociology. Not only did I see *The Power Elite, The Sociological Imagination,* and *White Collar* listed as works of special interest, but I found myself staring at the only photograph in the section—of my father on his motorcycle. In the second, 1997, edition, the photograph has been removed, but *From Max Weber: Essays in Sociology,* the book of translations by Hans H. Gerth and Mills, has been added to the list.

Almost inevitably, as I have worked with the letters in this book, my father has haunted me more than usual. Large and vibrant, he has appeared on the small stage in my mind when I expect him and when I don't, occupying my consciousness with a vividness peculiar to dreams and memories.

In one string of apparitions, he performs in scenes in my childhood, assuming the fatherly form I remember during the summer of 1949, which we spent on Lake Temagami in Canada. He protects me from choppy waters on the trip from the mainland to the islands by putting my six-year-old self in the covered bow of our motorboat. Later, at our destination, I see him standing tall near the simple wooden dock, on the few yards of ground between the house he helped build and the usually calm strip of water that separated this larger piece of land from the other small island he had purchased. Maybe we are about to go for a ride in a kayak, paddling for some minutes to a pool-like cove where we drift among pastel water lilies, delighting in the honking loons that skim the water in the distance. In the house, he reads *David Copperfield* to me, which I do not understand; but I like to lie next to him, listening to his voice. Suddenly, the scene switches to New York City. I am no older than seven, and I see his hazel eyes behind horned-rimmed glasses intently focused on my face, teaching me always to look people straight in the eye when I talk with them. He wants me to be like he is—self-confident, straightforward, no-nonsense.

A second cluster of scenes comes from my adolescent years, when I was sixteen and seventeen. In 1959, after not seeing my father for several years, I renewed contact with an author-father who both intimidated and fascinated me. I especially remember the summer of 1960, which I spent in his house with Yara, Katie, and newborn Niki. By this time, I had lost the child's unthinking adoration of the parent. With the critical spirit typical of my age, I perceived his faults, perhaps the most obvious being what was also responsible for his great intellectual productivity—his self-absorption regarding his work. In this act of my memories, the boat rides give way to motorcycle rides, as I sit behind him feeling the wind on my face and, on one occasion, listen to him explain the difference between the established wealthy and the nouveaux riches. Sometimes he becomes almost my peer, once showing me the wonders of his BMW by suddenly turning off the road to climb a steep wooded hill, and then capsizing the bike, fortunately with no harmful consequence other than a small cut on his ankle. But it is not examples of his love of throbbing motors that most appear on my mind-stage. The image that most impressed me then and that rises before me now is that of a muscular figure of energy and determination, overflowing with ambitious plans for the future, envisioning books that would cut through official distortions to produce uncompromising versions of the truth as his logical mind perceived it. His most comprehensive project would be to divide the world into five areas in order to do a comparative study. That summer, he was working on *Listen, Yankee*, in which he defended the Cuban revolution with unswerving moral conviction. The house was filled with correspondence from well-known, international intellectuals and the electricity of his ideas.

May his words haunt you too.

ACKNOWLEDGMENTS

We would like to thank the following libraries and archives for their assistance and for providing copies of letters in their collections:

Boston College: Archives, Burns Library

Columbia University: Rare Book and Manuscripts, Central Records, and the Council for Research in the Social Sciences

Harcourt Brace and Company: Archives

Harvard University: the Arthur and Elizabeth Schlesinger Library on the History of Women in America, Radcliffe College, and courtesy of the Harvard University Archives

London School of Economics and Political Science: the British Library of Political and Economic Science

New York University: Robert F. Wagner Labor Archives of the Tamiment Institute Library

Northwestern University Archives

Oxford University Press: Trade Editorial Department

Princeton University: Department of Rare Books and Special Collections, Manuscript Division (Carlos Fuentes collection)

State Historical Society of Wisconsin in Madison

University of Illinois at Chicago: Saul Alinsky/Industrial Areas Foundation Records, Special Collections, the University Library

University of Massachusetts at Amherst: Special Collections and Archives

University of Michigan at Ann Arbor: Michigan Historical Collections, Bentley Historical Library, Papers of Read Bain, Boxes 2 and 3

University of Texas at Austin: the Center for American History, Charles Wright Mills Papers, and the Harry Ransom Humanities Research Center

Yale University Library: Manuscripts and Archives, Dwight Macdonald Papers

We give special thanks to Ralph Elder, Assistant Director of the Center for American History at the University of Texas at Austin, which holds the Charles Wright Mills Papers. Mr. Elder answered many questions by mail, and he was very helpful and gracious during Kate's visit to Austin.

We are grateful to the following individuals who gave us copies of letters from their private collections: Daniel Bell, Nobuko Gerth, Richard Gillam, Justin Kaplan, Walter Klink, Susanne H. Lowenthal, Robert K. Merton, Marion Miliband, Virginia Miller, Ruth Harper Mills, Yaroslava Surmach Mills, Dorothy Thompson, Arthur Vidich, Dan Wakefield, and Dennis Wrong.

We are glad that Richard Gillam, in the course of his research on Mills, collected many of Mills's letters; the ones he provided from Mills to Hazel Gaudet Erskine and Ian Ballantine are the only letters to these correspondents in our possession, and we thank Dr. Gillam for sharing them with us. We are also grateful for his sending us letters to Bill Miller, some of which we had not seen. Nobuko Gerth's work to assemble Mills's many letters to Hans Gerth is also appreciated.

Although we did not publish letters from all the collections listed above, all the letters were helpful in researching the context of the letters we did publish; all were valuable to the project in some way or another.

We would like to thank Yaroslava Surmach Mills for giving her permission to publish selections from the Tovarich manuscript and the letters that appear in this volume. Yaroslava also loaned us other documents and files, as well as photographs and negatives. We also thank our mothers, Ruth Harper Mills and Freya James, as well as Yaroslava, for their patience in answering our questions while we worked on this project. We thank Ruth for showing us the passage in Simone de Beauvoir's memoirs in which de

Beauvoir describes her meeting with our father; a quotation from that passage is in this book.

Michael Moore, Kate's husband, read parts of the manuscript and helped with some of the research to locate correspondents, news articles, and death certificates, advising Kate and helping collect information. For this and for accommodating the letter book as a long-term presence in his home, thanks go to Michael.

Thanks also go to Boris Milman, Pam's significant other, for helping to translate words from foreign languages and for providing Pam with frequent computer assistance as well as a constantly sympathetic ear.

We would like to credit Steven Dandaneau, Professor of Sociology at the University of Dayton, for obtaining a copy of the declassified FBI file on Mills. He shared a copy with Arthur Vidich, Senior Lecturer and Professor Emeritus at the New School for Social Research, who mailed us a copy, and we thank them both.

Guy Oakes of Monmouth University was very helpful in providing copies of surviving relevant correspondence from Hans Gerth to Mills; we appreciate his generosity and time.

Robert K. Merton, University Professor Emeritus at Columbia University, thought of obtaining a copy of Mills's original application for a Guggenheim Memorial Foundation grant; when asked about a reference to the application, Professor Merton asked G. Thomas Tanselle of the Guggenheim Foundation to supply a copy of the whole file for us. A portion of this application, in which Mills discussed his mentors and intellectual development, is included in this volume, and we appreciate Professor Merton's thoughtfulness and Mr. Tanselle's responsiveness in helping make this possible.

Timothy Chester, candidate for a Ph.D. in Sociology at the Texas Agricultural and Mechanical University, shared information from his research concerning the year Mills spent at Texas A & M and provided copies of Mills's letters to the editor of that school's paper. We've included those two letters in this volume, with thanks to Mr. Chester.

We thank Andreas Hess, Lecturer at the University of Sussex in Brighton, England, who provided information about the German translation of *White Collar,* which was difficult for us non-German speakers to obtain and decipher.

We thank Brandon Trissler at Oxford University Press for his assistance in marshaling Mills's letters and internal documents in the Oxford editorial files on *White Collar, The Power Elite,* and Mills's unfinished, unpublished project on intellectuals, tentatively entitled "The Cultural Apparatus." The files were an invaluable source of background information, as well as several letters included in this volume.

Naomi Schneider, our editor at the University of California, was insightful and encouraging, and we were fortunate to have her involvement and excellent editorial eye.

We are very grateful to those who read and commented on the complete preliminary manuscript, some of whom also saw parts of the manuscript at other stages as well: Norman Birnbaum, Lewis A. Coser, Richard Robbins, Donald Sabo, Milton Yinger, and, as always, Dan Wakefield.

Many thanks go to the following people who read a part, or parts of, the manuscript and gave us comments and encouragement along the way: Peter Davison, Darcy Dumont, Ellen W. Faran, Steve Fraser, Diane Gold, Mike Gorkin, Janet Greenblatt, Ruth Hapgood, Dominic Hodgkin, Liz Kubik, Saul Landau, Bonnie Lass, Robert K. Merton, Virginia Miller, Nancy Naro, Glenn Kaye Novarr, Shaun O'Connell, John Radziewicz, Pam Rogers, and Felice Swados.

The comments and suggestions of those who saw all or part of the manuscript before we finalized it were indispensable to us. Needless to say, we take full responsibility for any errors or awkwardness that may remain.

Liz Borkowski, of Reliable Business Services in Boston, Massachusetts, was invaluable and tireless in her contribution of word-processing skill in manuscript preparation. Her work went beyond the call of duty on a number of occasions.

INTRODUCTION
by Dan Wakefield

In all eras there are a few figures in every field—the arts, academia, science, entertainment—who not only speak to and for their own time but whose work and message also resonate in future periods, making an impact on life and thought in generations to come. Such a figure was C. Wright Mills.

A sociologist whose vision and objectives often overflowed the boundaries of that discipline (and often riled those within it), Mills was also a powerful and controversial social critic, teacher, writer, humanist, and individualist. A Texas-bred maverick, Mills transplanted himself to New York City and addressed the world through his books and ideas, which shook up and energized the gray flannel 1950s and gave grounding and voice to the radicals of the 1960s. His work continues to illuminate, inspire, and challenge those who hope to understand and even to ameliorate the circumstances in which we live.

The core of Mills's classic study of American society at midcentury (which is only one part of his contribution) is composed of three volumes: on labor (*The New Men of Power*), the middle class (*White Collar*), and the upper class of decision makers (*The Power Elite*). These books "stand relatively alone as a comprehensive corpus of social criticism in the decades following the Second World War," according to Andrew Jamison and Ron Eyerman in *Seeds of the Sixties*.[1] They go on to say that these three volumes are sociology in the classic sense of "the study of society" rather than the compressed and jargon-ridden approaches of the profession that Mills brilliantly analyzed (and dismissed) in *The Sociological Imagination*.

Not surprisingly for one who had his own personal vision, Mills became increasingly impatient with the technical, impersonal, statistical side of sociology. But first he proved he could master those techniques exactingly and efficiently, directing studies for unions and government, leading research teams like one that produced a book Mills coauthored, *The Puerto Rican Journey*. The book was a solid one and valuable in its field, but it could have been written by any number of research teams; it is hardly recognizable as Mills. He later wrote me that "my own slight experience with them [the Puerto Ricans] was disappointing, especially in PR itself. . . . But I don't really know them. My stuff was at a great distance and necessarily statistical in nature." A journalist I knew who interviewed Mills a few years before his death said that when he brought up the old controversy about Mills's relation to his academic profession, Mills waved his hand, as if brushing the matter away, and said, "What the hell, *I* take polls."

It was with *White Collar* that Mills really first broke free from the constrictions of formal academic sociology, in terms of both style and audience. He began to reach a wider public that was hungry for the kind of interpretation that illuminates life concerns, the kind of analysis affirming Mills's basic belief that "neither the life of an individual nor the history of a society can be understood without understanding both." As Mills later elaborated this idea in *The Sociological Imagination,* what people need, and "what they feel they need," from "the sociological imagination" is help seeing "what is going on in the world and what may be happening within themselves [as a result]."

How successfully Mills delivered such insights can be seen in his readers' response to *White Collar* and *The Power Elite,* as well as to later, shorter works that were a kind of high-level "pamphleteering," as Mills himself described them: *The Causes of World War Three,* his impassioned plea for an end to the nuclear arms race, and *Listen, Yankee,* his early argument for the Cuban revolution from the viewpoint of a Cuban revolutionary. Mills began to receive a growing amount of mail from people who wanted to know what they should or could do not only about the issues of war and peace, foreign policy, and the social sciences but also about their own lives. They seemed

---

1. Andrew Jamison and Ron Eyerman, *Seeds of the Sixties* (Berkeley and Los Angeles: University of California Press, 1994), 16.

to feel that Mills, like some all-knowing combination of Dear Abby and Carl Jung, would be able to tell them.

The personal nature of the response to Mills and his work can be seen in the homage of people like Dick Flacks, a graduate student in social psychology at the University of Michigan, and his wife, Mickey, when they named their son "C. Wright." After Mills's premature death of a heart attack in 1962 at age forty-five, strangers who knew him only from his writing joined his family and friends at his funeral. As part of the Quaker service (Mills professed himself an atheist or, as he liked to put it more dramatically, a "pagan"), some of them spoke up, prefacing their tributes with "I didn't know C. Wright Mills personally" and then reading a favorite passage from one of his books, much as if reciting from a sacred text. I think the kind of personal response Mills's work elicited was best explained by his longtime friend and neighbor Harvey Swados, a distinguished novelist of the era. Swados wrote in *Dissent* magazine after Mills's death that "the best of the young academics" as well as "many thousands of plain readers" here and abroad were drawn to his work because

all these people were responding to what was at bottom not merely a logical indictment which could be upheld or attacked, but a poetic vision of America: an unlovely vision perhaps, expressed with a mixture of awkwardness and brilliance, but one that did not really need statistical buttressing or the findings of research teams in order to be apprehended by sensitive Americans as corresponding to their own sense of what was going on about them, more truly and unflinchingly than any other contemporary statement. They were responding in that unlovely decade, the fat and frightened fifties, to one who refused to compromise or to make the excuses that others were making— excuses mislabeled descriptions or analyses—for what was happening to their country. They sensed correctly that, faulty and flawed as it was, the vision of Wright Mills cut through the fog and lighted their lives for them.[2]

Affirming the impact of Mills's work in that era from a scholarly viewpoint, Jamison and Eyerman contend that "almost single-handedly in the 1950s, Mills would try to keep alive what he later called the sociological imagination in countering the drift toward conformity, homogenization, and instrumental rationality; in short, mass society."[3]

Nor was it only the readers of "the fat and frightened fifties" who were

2. Harvey Swados, "C. Wright Mills: A Personal Memoir," *Dissent* (winter 1963): 40.
3. Jamison and Eyerman, *Seeds of the Sixties,* 30.

influenced by Mills's work. If his books illuminated the 1950s, they even more powerfully and directly motivated and inspired the youthful radical movements of the 1960s. Tom Hayden, a national leader of the most important student radical group of the era (Students for a Democratic Society, or SDS) and now a California state representative, writes in his memoir, *Reunion,* that "the two writers who had the most influence on us [the founders of the SDS] were Albert Camus and C. Wright Mills." Hayden began reading Mills when he was editor of the student newspaper at the University of Michigan, the *Michigan Daily,* and felt that the Columbia University sociology professor

> defied the drabness of academic life and quickly became the oracle of the New Left, combining the rebel life style of James Dean and the moral passion of Albert Camus, with the comprehensive portrayal of the American condition we were all looking for. Mills died in his early forties . . . during the very spring I was drafting the *Port Huron Statement,* before any of us had a chance to meet him, making him forever a martyr to the movement. . . .
>
> He seemed to be speaking to us directly when he declared in his famous letter to "The New Left" that all over the world young radical intellectuals were breaking the old molds, leading the way out of apathy.
>
> Mills's analysis validated us not only personally, but as a generation and as activist-organizers, the political identity we were beginning to adopt.[4]

In *The Making of a Counter Culture,* Theodore Roszak explains Mills's cultural as well as political influence on the 1960s, pointing out that "Ginsberg and the beatniks can be associated chronologically with the aggressively activist sociology of C. Wright Mills. . . . Mills was by no means the first postwar figure who sought to tell it like it is about the state of American public life and culture. . . . But it was Mills who caught on. His tone was more blatant; his rhetoric, catchier. He was the successful academic who suddenly began to cry for action in a lethargic profession, in a lethargic society."[5]

Nor was Mills's influence limited to culture and politics in the United States; if anything, he was more appreciated abroad, where his books have been translated into twenty-three languages, including Croat and Flemish. Perhaps the most striking example of that appreciation abroad can be traced to the time when a young revolutionary in the mountains of Cuba's Orien-

---

4. Tom Hayden, *Reunion: A Memoir* (New York: Random House, 1988), 78, 80, 81.

5. Theodore Roszak, *The Making of a Counter Culture* (Garden City, N.Y.: Doubleday, 1968), 24–25.

te province was reading *The Power Elite*. Later that year, after Fidel Castro's revolution ousted the dictator Batista and the young revolutionary came to power, he welcomed the author of that book when he came to Cuba. Mills wanted to see and report on the revolution firsthand. The result was a short, highly controversial work in Mills's "pamphleteering" style called *Listen, Yankee* (1960) that attempted to describe the Cuban revolution from the viewpoint of a Cuban revolutionary.

It's largely forgotten now that Mills was not the only American intellectual to pin great hopes on Castro in the early days of his regime. Just after the Bay of Pigs invasion in April 1961, the *Village Voice* published an "Open Letter to Castro" by Norman Mailer, who wrote, "I have said nothing in public about you or your country since I signed a statement last year in company with Baldwin, Capote, Sartre, and Tynan that we believe in 'Fair Play for Cuba.' But now I am old enough to believe that one must be ready to be faithful to one's truth. So, Fidel Castro, I announce to the City of New York that you gave all of us who are alone in this country, and usually not speaking to one another, some sense that there were heroes left in the world."[6]

Listen, Yankee was a best-seller, and it brought down the ire of not only critics and reviewers but also the FBI, which began actively tracking Mills and his work and activities. The book was popular in much of Latin America and was hailed by the Mexican novelist Carlos Fuentes and other leading Latin American intellectuals, but in the United States the resulting furor led to mounting pressures that clearly contributed to Mills's early death by heart attack.

I had the good fortune of knowing Mills personally, first as a student of his at Columbia, then as an assistant on a research project, and later as a friend. I make no pretense of detachment in commenting on the life and work of a man I knew to be as great in generosity and kindness as in talent and dedication. My first conversation with him occurred in the most inappropriate of places: an elevator. Riding in an elevator with Mills was rather like riding in a Volkswagen with an elephant, not so much because of the reality of his size (at a little over six feet and weighing two hundred pounds, he was bigger than average) but because of the terrific sense of restlessness and ready-to-burst energy about him; and perhaps it was also because he came to work in a rather bulky getup suggestive of a guerrilla warrior going to meet the

6. Norman Mailer, "An Open Letter to JFK and Castro: The Letter to Castro," *Village Voice* 6, no. 27 (27 April 1961).

enemy (which in a way he took the situation to be in regard to himself and academia). Even his wardrobe was a subject of controversy.

In that era of cautious professors in gray flannel suits, Mills came roaring into Morningside Heights on his BMW motorcycle, wearing plaid shirts, old jeans, and work boots, carrying his books in a duffel bag strapped across his broad chest. At the time of my first encounter with him in 1954, Mills was an already legendary professor at Columbia College, and I was an undergraduate recently inspired by reading *White Collar* and anxious to see its author in action. My only chance was to get permission from Mills himself to take his limited-enrollment seminar in liberalism.

I waited for my quarry in the cold, cheerless lobby of Hamilton Hall, ambushed him on the way to the elevator, and squeezed in beside him to make my pitch. He fired the requisite questions at me in a rather aggressive, discouraging tone, and I think my answers made it obvious that I had little qualification and a lot of enthusiasm for taking the course. When the elevator ejected the crowd at the floor of his office, I had the feeling Mills glanced back at me and said "OK" mainly to rid himself of a temporary nuisance.

In the classroom as well as in the pages of his widely read books, Mills was a great teacher. His lectures matched the flamboyance of his personal image, as he managed to make entertaining the heavyweight social theories of Karl Mannheim, Max Weber, and José Ortega y Gasset. He shocked us out of our "silent generation" student torpor by pounding his desk and proclaiming that each man should build his own house (as he did himself) and that, by God, with the proper study, we should each be able to build our own *car!*

"Nowadays men often feel that their private lives are a series of traps," Mills wrote in the opening sentence of *The Sociological Imagination,* and I can hear him saying it as he paced in front of the class, speaking not loudly now but with a compelling sense of intrigue, as if he were letting you in on a powerful secret. Against the awful image of Willy Loman's wasted life, which haunted our dreams of the future in the 1950s, against the lockstep fate of *The Lonely Crowd* and *The Organization Man,* which seemed to lie in wait for us after graduation, Mills offered more hopeful possibilities. His withering critique of the stifling elements he saw in our society and reported in his books and articles was not simply negative. The very audacity of Mills's attacks on the status quo carried with it a promise of something better.

In the undergraduate classes he taught back in the 1950s, Mills surprised and enthralled us with calls to "abandon" the cities, which he felt were already hopelessly dehumanizing, and set up small, self-governing units around the country. There people could develop crafts and skills and work with their hands, as he was already doing, building houses and learning to repair his beloved German motors.

All this was more than a decade before the first communes were established and before *Zen and the Art of Motorcycle Maintenance* became a best-seller and a kind of Bible to a whole subculture. At the time of his death, Mills was working on (among other things, five books either just completed or in various stages of progress) a proposal for a book about a political consciousness that was just emerging in this country; he called it "the New Left."

The vitality and continuing value of Mills's work spring partly from the fact that as an inveterate teacher he told us not only how things were but how they might be, and sometimes how each of us might make them better. His stand was that as intellectuals we have a *responsibility* to make them better. He labeled and excoriated "the rise of the cheerful robot, of the technological idiot, of the crackpot realist" both in this country as well as in totalitarian societies.

Mills originally took an interest in me because of an offbeat paper I wrote for his course comparing Ortega's *The Rise of the Masses* with a short story by Hemingway called "Banal Story." He called me in after class, and instead of berating me for frivolousness as I had feared, calmly stoked his pipe, observed me with a detached curiosity, and said he'd enjoyed the paper—not so much for its eloquence as its novelty. He said it was a relief from the usual student reports, which bored him. He urged me to "do some more like that," which led to a growing number of discussions between us, and eventually to his offer of a temporary job.

When I finished his course and graduated soon after, in February of 1955, I told Mills I was taking a job as a reporter on a weekly newspaper in New Jersey. He took a knowing puff on his pipe and said, "Small-town stuff, you'll be back"—and I was, courtesy of the job Mills offered me that summer doing research on intellectuals in America (one of several projects he didn't live to complete). Another former student, Walter Klink, who had done research on *The Power Elite,* also worked on the intellectuals project that summer, and Mills took a genuine and fatherly interest in both of us. As a "boss" and a mentor and friend, he was, to each of us, patient, kind, and helpful, both personally and professionally.

"Now Dan," Mills counseled me during that summer of '55—long before the dawn of women's liberation—"you're not married yet and you're living alone. You must get one of your girlfriends to come over every Sunday night and cook a big stew that will last a week. You bottle it up in seven Mason jars and take one out each day, and you have a good, healthy meal instead of that bachelor stuff." He was full of advice that was often valuable and always entertaining, from books I should read (he thrust James Agee's *Let Us Now Praise Famous Men* on me when it was out of print and not yet in vogue) to hints on work habits ("Set up a file"—and he showed me how). Running through all his advice was one grand theme, which served as his own motto: an approach to life he called "Taking it big," which he not only advocated but applied to everything from eating and drinking to scholarship and writing. Almost any advice he gave ended with the exhortation "Take it big, boy!"

Mills introduced me to the Homestead, a restaurant famous for serving the biggest pieces of beef at the best prices anywhere in New York City. It was over in the meat-packing district, on the western fringe of Greenwich Village, and supposedly its proximity to the fresh meat coming in accounted for the great deals that this popular, plain-style restaurant offered its customers. Mills was known to go there and, after the meal, say to the waiter, "That was good—I'll have the same thing again." He'd eat a second helping of everything, including the sirloin steak, and pie for dessert. He practiced what he preached. (Another example of his "double dinners" is described firsthand in his letters.)

In his efforts to help me in my own career I learned a good deal about his. He had urged me at first to go into sociology, and when I said I was more interested in writing than in doing scholarly research or compiling statistics, he said that didn't matter; if you wanted to write about the world you had to have a "handle," and sociology could provide that. That's how he used it himself. He thought of himself primarily as a writer and devoted his most intense efforts to the difficult discipline of English prose. Ideas and theories came rather easily to him, but writing did not, and he sweated over it, seeking advice and criticism, often from Swados, who respected Mills's "unending and humble desire to learn how to commit to paper with precision and fluency all that he believed."[7] That desire was so great that it was, as far as I know, one of the few things Mills was humble about.

He attached an almost magical quality to the power of writing; after all, hadn't it brought him, with academic whistle-stops along the way, out

7. Swados, "C. Wright Mills."

of Texas to New York City and national—even worldwide—prominence? It was in this spirit that Mills explained to me once how he managed to escape what he considered a less than desirable academic post at the University of Maryland: "I wrote my way out of there."

It was not academic positions but his personal vision that absorbed and obsessed him, and *White Collar* was the first book he was able to express it in. He later wrote that creation of this book was "a task primarily motivated by the desire to articulate my own experience in New York City since 1945." He put it more dramatically when he slyly told me he had met a woman at a party who "really understands me. She told me 'I know you, Mills—I read *White Collar* and I know what it's all about.' I asked her to tell me and she said, 'That's the story of a Texas boy who came to New York.'" Mills paused, frowning, and then broke into a giant grin as he said with delight, "And my God, she was right!"

Certainly there were elements in Mills—that big, gruff, motorcycle-mounted scholar who had burst out of Texas—of a kind of intellectual Gatsby. He mentioned once that the first books he remembered reading were a series of little volumes on "Success" that were owned by his father, a white-collar businessman. Like all boys from the provinces in those days, Mills identified New York City as the citadel or headquarters of success, and as one who had come there myself from Indiana I understood the feeling. I think the sense we shared of escape from province to city was one of the things that informed our friendship. I remember once driving with Mills from his house in Rockland County to Columbia on a bright winter morning, and as we crossed over the George Washington Bridge he pointed to the dazzling skyline and, with a sweeping gesture, said, "Take that one, boy!" I shivered and smiled, imagining that in other crossings he had said the same thing to himself.

During my summer of research for Mills, I worked mainly in the Columbia library and my own apartment, and every week or so spent a day at his house, reporting, discussing, and listening as Mills paced back and forth, thinking out loud, the puffs of smoke from his pipe reminding me of the steam from an engine, for his mind in high gear seemed like a dynamo. When classes resumed in the fall, I moved my notes and typewriter into Mills's office in Hamilton Hall and worked out of there. But his real office was at home. The Columbia office simply contained old student papers, files of finished projects, a hot plate for warming up soup, and an electric espresso machine. Neither his stomach nor his mind operated with its usual gargantuan appetite at the college office, and our talks there were disjointed and disappointing. Mills always seemed subdued when he came in, said very little, and stalked off to class. He would usually burst back into the room tired and out of sorts, like he did the day he slammed down his books and said, referring to his students, "Who *are* these guys?"

Nor did he get much sustenance from his colleagues, especially in sociology, whom he rarely saw or mentioned. He took more lightly and humorously his occasional intellectual conflicts with people in other departments and especially enjoyed a little exchange with Lionel Trilling, the distinguished English professor and literary critic. Mills had published an essay in which he jibed at this colleague and other intellectuals for engaging in what Mills called "the American Celebration"—an uncritical and flowery promotion of the United States. Mills received a long letter of reply from this professor—so long that Mills held it up and said, "My God, he could have published this!" The effort seemed wasteful since the professor's office was only one floor below, so Mills wrote him a card suggesting they get together and discuss the matter. Mills got an elaborately worded reply postponing the discussion, but then one day he came into the office in especially high spirits after meeting his correspondent in the elevator. After an awkward silence the professor had looked at Mills, who was wearing some new sort of motorcycle cap, and said, "Why, Wright, what a lovely cap— wherever did you get it?" Mills simply smiled and answered, "Not in this country, Lionel."

Mills longed to spend some time abroad. His only trip to Europe then had been a two-week BMW motorcycle repair course in Munich (he received a certificate, which he proudly had framed). That fall when I worked in his Columbia office, Mills was looking forward to a sabbatical the following year, and had received a Fulbright lectureship at the University of Copenhagen that would enable him at last to live and travel in Europe. My research job with him was to end in January (1956), and in the meantime I had published my first magazine articles in *The Nation* and arranged for a series of assignments that would take me to Israel. Mills was pleased about both our good fortunes, and during the last weeks of my job, when anyone came into the room, he announced with a flourish, "This office is leaving the country!"

We corresponded after I got to Israel, and Mills wrote me in Jerusalem in May of 1956, just before he sailed for Europe. He reported he had been promoted to full professor at Columbia, but most of the letter dealt with the reception of *The Power Elite* (see part 5 of this book). I had hoped to go on to Europe and visit Mills after my Israel assignments, but the closest I got to Copenhagen was a week of waiting for a plane in Rome.

It was not until December of 1957 that I saw Mills again. He had been through difficult times with family misfortunes and was back at Columbia, living alone in an apartment on 114th Street, which he had managed to turn into comfortable living and working space, imposing his own order of books and files and bright decorations on one of those stubbornly dingy flats in Morningside Heights.

Like a great wounded bear he had retreated inside this comfortable cave, and he refused to go out except to meet his classes. If a publisher or editor—or even a friend—wanted to see him, it was necessary to travel uptown to his lair. There one was rewarded for making the trip not only with Mills's good talk and bourbon but also with one of his superbly cooked meals. He was cooking for himself, attacking that art as he previously had attacked (and mastered) motorcycles and photography, and, as with any of his newfound enthusiasms, he looked with mock scorn on anyone who hadn't discovered this new key to the universe. On my first trip there, after he served me a home-cooked meal, Mills asked me incredulously, "My God, man, you mean you don't bake your own bread?" (Just as he would ask in the same tone, "You mean you'd live in a house you didn't build yourself?")

Mills was one of those rare and resourceful people who in times of personal difficulty work harder and longer and more ferociously; instead of talking about his troubles—which he gave a brief, straightforward account of, in the manner of the *New York Times* covering a story—he talked of his plans and ideas and projects. If he hadn't seen you for a while, Mills began pumping you for information—what were you reading, what were you working on, what was happening that he ought to know about and might have missed in his reading of current events and trends? While you talked he jotted down notes, filing ideas that interested him, ordering books that were mentioned. When he finished that quizzing on my first trip to see him on 114th Street, he asked what my plans were for the coming year—and then told me what they *should* be.

"China," he said.

"China?"

"A third of the earth's population," he proclaimed with hushed drama, "and we know nothing about it."

"But I—"

"You'll be the reporter. We'll also have a photographer, an economist—and perhaps a cook, so we don't have to fool with that. I'll be the sociologist and head up the expedition. We'll fit out a Volkswagen bus, or two, and tour Red China, getting real stuff—it has to be done. We'll worry about the State Department nonsense when we get back." (At that time U.S. citizens were not allowed to travel in China.)

I knew nothing about China, and that part of the world held no fascination for me in those days. And yet, by the time Mills finished his spiel I could hear the mysterious tinkle of bells in ancient temples and feel the immense weight and drama of that massive landscape, and when he harked back to the beginning motif—"a third of the world's population and we know nothing about it"—I was ready to pack for Peking. The great project never came off, but like everything Mills got excited about, he could make you believe it was the most important thing in the world. I'm sure he could have worked the same spell with Labrador.

But while Mills dreamed of China he was stuck at 114th Street between Broadway and Amsterdam. I enjoyed making pilgrimages up to his den, and after some months he began to venture out of it. He told me about attending a party of Columbia graduate students in sociology, and his account of it seemed to sum up the impasse he had reached with the academic side of his profession.

"I simply sat in a chair in a corner," he said, "and one by one these guys would come up to me, sort of like approaching the pariah—curiosity stuff. They were guys working on their Ph.D.'s, you see, and after they'd introduced themselves I'd ask, 'What are you working on?' It would always be something like 'The Impact of Work-Play Relationships among Lower Income Families on the South Side of the Block on 112th Street between Amsterdam and Broadway.' And then I would ask—" Mills paused, leaned forward, and his voice boomed, "Why?"

Mills himself was then working on *The Causes of World War Three,* a book about a subject he considered worthy of the attention of "a full-grown man."

In 1959 Mills married Yaroslava Surmach, and they built a new house in Rockland County. Some local people supposedly mistook it for a bomb shelter because it was built with its virtually windowless concrete back to the road, while its marvelous glass-paneled front faced a scenic view.

I visited Mills there shortly after he moved in, and again when he returned from a lecture trip to Mexico. He'd been frequently questioned there about his—and his country's—stand on the new revolutionary government of Fidel Castro in Cuba, and the overriding interest of Latin American intellectuals in the question kindled his desire to go there and write about it. After intensive preparation in the spring and early summer of 1960, he went to Cuba in August, equipped with his latest beloved gadget, a tape recorder;

on his return, working with furious energy, he wrote *Listen, Yankee* in six weeks' time.

After the enormous effort to get out the book, instead of relaxing, Mills shifted himself back into high gear to prepare for a nationwide TV debate with A. A. Berle Jr. on U.S. foreign policy in Latin America.

I saw Mills once while he was immersed in this preparation, and he was terribly worried, alternately unsure of himself and brashly confident. He seemed to take it as some crucial test that he would either pass or flunk with profound results, as if it were a matter of life and death, which in some weird way it turned out to be. One or two nights before the broadcast in December 1960, Mills had his first major heart attack.

Walter Klink drove me out to visit him the next month. It was incredible to see Mills in a sickbed, and yet his old fire and enthusiasm hadn't left him. He was pleased and proud about the sales—if not the U.S. reception—of *Listen, Yankee,* and above his bed was an advertising poster proclaiming there were four hundred thousand copies of the paperback edition in print. Mills delightedly explained that such posters were carried on the sides of news delivery trucks in Philadelphia. He was reaching a greater public now than he ever had—"mass circulation stuff," he proudly called it. He lectured us on publishing, emphasizing that paperbacks were now the important thing. He told us publishing was done much more intelligently in England, and reported that after seeing the English system, he told one of his older, more conservative American publishers, "You gentlemen do not understand what 'publishing' means. You think the verb 'to publish' means 'to print,' but that is not so. It means 'to make public.'"

Flat on his back, he kept us entertained and laughing, joking about his pills, praising his doctor (a fine young man whose excellent qualifications included a familiarity with some of Mills's work), talking of books and of the world—even then, in that condition, "taking it big." There was one thing, though, that frightened me. He had, in a drawer by the bedside table, a pistol. He had received a death threat because of his pro-Castro position.

When Mills was on his feet again he went on a frustrating journey to Russia and Europe, not finding the answers for his heart problem that he hoped a Russian clinic and specialist might offer, and grappling with unfinished projects. He sent me from there a rough copy of *The Marxists,* which he finished in Europe—an anthology with extensive commentary in which he blasted all political orthodoxies from right to left. When he came home exhausted in the spring of 1962 there were many projects awaiting his attention: the book on the intellectuals; a political book he hoped would foster what he called "the New Left"; an imaginary dialogue between a Russian and an American intellectual, called "Contacting the Enemy"; and a giant, or Mills-sized, book on "world sociology."

I picked up the *Times* one rainy morning that March and while sipping coffee in Sheridan Square saw two stark lines on the obit page that numbed me:

C. Wright Mills;
  A Sociologist

It was the first time I cried at the death of a friend—one who had never let me down. He was forty-five years old.

Of anyone I have ever known, Mills was the most individual, the most obstinately unorganizable, the most jealous of his right and need to "go it alone" and to fire at all sides when he felt so moved. I think his deepest, most characteristic outlook—the long-range one that he always returned to after excesses of enthusiasm—was expressed that summer I worked for him. A man who belonged to a small socialist splinter group came to seek Mills's signature on a petition asking that the group be removed from the attorney general's list of "subversive" organizations. Mills obligingly signed, but then in discussing politics he challenged all his visitor's beliefs and arguments until the poor fellow said in frustration, "Just what do you believe in, Mills?" At the moment Mills was tinkering with his motorcycle, and he looked up and said without hesitation, "German motors."

After the man had left, Mills told me: "It's ridiculous to say those guys are a threat to the government. They've only got about 150 guys—how could they overthrow anything? Besides, they're anti-Moscow and anti-Washington, and that's where I stand." His real home was outside any group or government or intellectual clique, and his favorite political heroes were the Wobblies (Industrial Workers of the World), the homegrown American radicals of the early part of the century who opposed nearly everything and everyone and valued most of all their independence. Whenever Mills liked someone, he'd say, "That guy's a real Wobbly."

He wrote once that his aim was to "define and dramatize the essential characteristics of our age," but I would argue that he went beyond that, in an effort to make it a better age and inspire generations to come. In "taking it big" Mills sometimes fell very, very hard, a risk that he understood and was willing to take. He appreciated others who took such risks, as he showed when he wrote a sensitive appraisal of James Agee's *Let Us Now Praise*

Famous Men for Dwight Macdonald's magazine, *politics*. Mills praised Agee for "taking it big" in writing about white southern sharecropper families, and he said the important thing about the book "is the enormity of the self-chosen task; the effort recorded here should not be judged according to its success or failure, or even degree of success; rather we should speak of the appropriateness and rarity of the objective."[8]

In that same spirit, I speak of Mills.

Though I knew Mills personally as a mentor and friend, and professionally as my teacher and a writer whose books I admired, I have come to know him better and on a deeper level, personally and intellectually, from reading this remarkable collection of his letters and autobiographical writings, lovingly collected, selected, edited, and annotated by his daughters, Kate and Pamela. The letters and writings here assembled and arranged chronologically serve as a kind of informal, highly personal autobiography, a journey seen from inside the mind and heart of the pilgrim himself.

This record of a life conveyed through the highly personal and literary form of letter writing is all the more rare and valuable since the form itself is fast becoming obsolete, a cultural artifact like the quill pen or the Smith-Corona typewriter. In our age of instant communication via e-mail, FAX, telephone, cell phone, speakerphone, and beeper, few of us take the time and trouble to sit down and write a letter that conveys to a friend or colleague our thoughts, ideas, feelings, and news, then read it over, make corrections, sign it, put it in an envelope, address it, seal it (the sealing gives a sense of privacy and perhaps encourages the intimate nature of personal letters as opposed to those sent by electronic transmittal), put a stamp on it, and carry it to a mailbox to drop in for delivery several days hence.

A good letter was its own art form, and Mills often told me he used letters as a way of getting unblocked if he was stuck while writing books or articles. The letter was not only a way of expressing and sometimes codifying ideas and projects but was also an important and useful outlet for venting emotion, a private (sealed) message to a trusted friend who would understand and sympathize with one's personal triumphs, disappointments, and frustrations, as well as a means to convey news, thoughts, and intellectual arguments or discussions. Mills used letters for all this, and in so doing left a moving and powerful testimony of a life lived by one whose work affected the lives of others, in his own country and abroad, in his own time and the future.

8. C. Wright Mills, letter to the editor, *politics* 5, no. 2 (spring 1948): 125–26.

Themes emerge from the letters that not only show Mills's personal and intellectual concerns but reveal much about his character. His lifelong dedication to the development of his writing skills and his eagerness for instruction—his humility in asking for it even from his harshest critics—can serve as a model of commitment and integrity for anyone aspiring to creative work.

In his application for a Guggenheim grant in 1944, Mills explained that he had experimented with forms of writing in various journals and "little magazines" because "I wished to rid myself of a crippling academic prose and to develop an intelligible way of communicating modern social science to non-specialized publics." He revealed how deeply and seriously he regarded his writing when he said in a letter to his parents in 1946 that he regarded the book he was working on (*White Collar*) as "my little work of art: it will have to stand for the operations I never will do, not being a surgeon, and for the houses I never built, not being an architect. So, you see, it has to be a thing of craftsmanship and art as well as science. That is why it takes so long. There is no hurry. It will stand a long time, when it is finally done."

Three years later, in a letter to a friend, the historian William Miller, he shared his frustration in getting the book the way he wanted: "I am disillusioned about White Collar again. I can't write it right. I can't get what I want to say about America in it. What I want to say is what you say to intimate friends when you are discouraged about how it all is . . . how lonesome it is, really, how terribly lonesome and rich and vulgar and God I don't know."

When the book was published in 1951, it was not the good reviews he dwelled on but the criticism, for he wanted to learn from it. In a letter to several friends he sent a copy of a highly critical review from his old friend Dwight Macdonald and said, "There's only one kind of question that seems important to me, and I'd be very grateful if you'd answer it: Can I learn anything from this review?" To Macdonald himself he wrote, "You owe me this: think out concretely what I should avoid and how I might learn to do so. . . . Be constructive. Be practical. I'm a very willing learner in this writing stuff."

I know few (if any) writers mature enough and humble enough to respond in such a way to a harsh review. In one of his "letters to Tovarich," his hypothetical Russian intellectual counterpart (these "letters" are really superb autobiographical essays), he said, "I'm a writer without any of the cultural background and without much of the verbal sensibilities of the 'born writer'; accordingly I am someone who has worked for twenty years to try to overcome any deficiencies in the practice of my craft, and yet remain true to whatever I am and how I got that way and to the condition of the world as I see it."

As late as 1960 he was still holding himself to higher standards as a writer, aspiring to express himself more fully and powerfully. In June of that year he wrote to his English writer-scholar friend, Ralph Miliband, that he was thinking of leaving his professorship and trying to live more modestly in order to devote full time to writing, saying, "I've got four, yes four books, bubbling up inside me. . . . The stuff I've written so far, it really is dry-run stuff; I've never let loose; you must know that."

The following month he responded to Miliband with what was obviously an answer to a request for advice: "Of course you are going to Moscow. Be an idiot not to. Go this summer; it will help the book. Make it help: never lose anything." Mills continued with advice on who and what Miliband should see to get the most out of his firsthand study of the Soviet political system.

When in 1961 his friend Harvey Swados got some critical reviews of his new collection of stories, the fine and lyrical *Nights in the Gardens of Brooklyn,* Mills wrote to him and his wife, Bette: "Harvey is not to allow the shit-liberal types of reviews [. . .] to bother him or hurt him. They are inevitable: would be same if book being reviewed were half blank paper or great American novel. It is a good book, especially the title story, so fuck them all."

In perhaps the most eloquent response to a friend's distress—one that any of us can find inspiring in the inevitable low times of life—Mills wrote to Bill Miller:

> You ask for what should one be keyed up? My god, for long weekends in the country, and snow and the feel of an idea and New York streets early in the morning and late at night and the camera eye always working whether you want or not and yes by god how the earth feels when it's been plowed deep and the new chartreuse wall in the study and wine before dinner and if you can afford it Irish whiskey afterwards and sawdust in your pants cuff and sometimes at evening the dusky pink sky to the northwest, and the books to read never touched and all that stuff the Greeks wrote and have you ever read Macaulay's speeches to hear the English language? And to revise your mode of talk and what you talk about and yes by god the world of music which we just now discover and there's still hot jazz and getting a car out of the mud when no one else can. That's what the hell to get keyed up about.

This is vintage Mills, a man who inspires as well as informs, who stood by his friends and sought instruction from his critics.

The lives of many writers seem surprisingly divorced from their work, in a way that is sometimes disillusioning. Reading these letters I am struck by how closely knit Mills's own life was with his writing: what he professed on the page he practiced in his life. Nowhere is this more evident after reading the letters than in the appendix to *The Sociological Imagination,* a concise, practical guide entitled "On Intellectual Craftsmanship" that is also deeply inspiring to any who wish to inform their creative work with personal experience. I have met people who have told me, "I went into sociology because of reading *The Sociological Imagination.*" This book has also influenced (and continues to influence) readers who are not professional sociologists, but who find this advice as stimulating as it is helpful in whatever their own artistic or intellectual pursuits may be, or simply as a model for a life and career of any sort. Mills writes that the most admirable thinkers "do not split their work from their lives. They seem to take both too seriously to allow such dissociation, and they want to use each for the enrichment of the other."

Then, as always, he gets practical: "But how can you do this? One answer is: you must set up a file, which is, I suppose, a sociologist's way of saying: keep a journal. Many creative writers keep journals; the sociologist's need for systematic reflection demands it. . . . In such a file as I am going to describe, there is joined personal experience and professional activities[:] . . . what you are doing intellectually and what you are experiencing as a person. Here you will not be afraid to use your experience and relate it directly to various work in progress."

Finally, Mills advises, "Before you are through with any piece of work . . . orient it to the central and continuing task of understanding the structure and the drift, the shaping and the meanings, of your own period, the terrible and magnificent world of human society."

Work conducted in such a spirit, Mills assures us, "has a chance to make a difference in the quality of human life."[9] That is the high goal to which C. Wright Mills aspired, and to which he inspires us today. His uncanny relevance to our own time is sounded in advice he offered back in the 1950s, in phraseology popular in the 1990s: "By keeping an adequate file and thus developing self-reflective habits, you learn how to keep your inner world awake." His work will continue to speak to those who want to keep their "inner world awake."

9. C. Wright Mills, "On Intellectual Craftsmanship," in *The Sociological Imagination* (New York: Oxford University Press, 1959), 196, 225, 226.

I

GROWING UP IN TEXAS

1916–1939

Just who are the men with guts? They are
the men . . . who have the imagination
and the intelligence to formulate their own
codes; the men who have the courage and
the stamina to live their own lives in spite
of social pressure and isolation.

> Letter "by a Freshman" to the *Battalion*,
> dated May 8, 1935

Charles Wright Mills, born in Waco, Texas, on August 28, 1916, remained in the Lone Star State for the first twenty-three years of his life. His father had moved there from Florida, but his mother and her parents were born in Texas. Although Mills left when he was a young man, a feisty Texan emphasis on individual autonomy remained in him, along with the psychology of the outlander. On the lighter side, Mills had a recreational interest in novels and movies about the Wild West and, as some of his letters show, he seemed to enjoy dramatizing his Texan roots.

Mills's mother, Frances Wright Mills, also liked telling the stories of her Texas ancestors, although her view of them was quite different from her son's. We would like to share a letter she wrote to us and to our half-brother, Nikolas, one year after our father's death. Frances gave us a romanticized version of our ancestry, the Old West, Irish immigration, and pioneer stamina. Her letter also gives some sense of Frances herself, the mother who remained in Texas after her son moved away. She received twenty-one of the letters published in this book.

San Antonio, Texas

May 19, 1963

I am writing to you, my grandchildren, and endeavoring to tell you about my father, Braxton Wright, because your own illustrious father used him and his greatness as a stepping stone to higher achievement. And this son of mine was much like his grandfather. It relates the life in part of a very simple man who lived and died a long time ago. He never achieved greatness nor honors, yet within him were some of the greatest qualities a man could possess. He understood his fellow man, and he had compassion and love for the down-trodden.

He came in the evening of the roaming Indian, and he told many tales of the Indian. He was a cheerful and dramatic man. He knew

Shakespeare and Browning. He studied the Bible because he always contended that it is a masterpiece.

He loved his country. It was made from guts and sweat and the pioneer women he said were very wonderful. He loved the history of America and imbued a magnificent pride within me. He had a great pity for anything wounded or defenseless.

My father left us when your father was a very small child. He used to rock him and tell him and your father's sister about the wild turkey gobblers, and he would call the turkey like the primitive Indians did—much to the children's delight.

Braxton Bragg Wright (father of Frances Wright and grandfather of Charles Wright Mills) was born at Lagarta, Texas. Son of Calvin Wright and Emmeline Cook. The Cooks were Irish, Scotch, and French. She was a French Canadian girl who traveled down the eastern seaboard in a covered wagon with her family to marry Calvin Wright of New York State. He fought in the Battle of Atlanta in the Civil War under his Uncle Braxton Bragg.[1] The family lived in Georgia and Mississippi and finally settled at Lagarta in Texas. Calvin Wright is buried at Lagarta as well as is Emmeline Cook Wright.

Braxton Bragg met a tragic death at his ranch, La Chusa, at Tilden, McMullen County, Texas, in 1920[2] and is buried on a high hill over-looking the mesquite and cactus land of southwest Texas. He was born April 8, 1860. He had a very colorful life. In 1890, '91, '92, '93, he and his father, Calvin Wright, and his brother, Stonewall Jackson, skinned cattle who died from the terrible drought. At that time the land was unfenced. They took these cattle hides by freight cars to Kansas and sold them. Hides were much in demand for saddles and

1. The Battle of Atlanta lasted from July to September 1864, ending when the Union general William Tecumseh Sherman burned Atlanta and proceeded to lead his troops on the March to the Sea across Georgia. Braxton Bragg was a lieutenant colonel in the Mexican War who became a Confederate general during the Civil War, commanding the primary western army for the South—the Army of Tennessee—from June 1862 to November 1863. After leaving that post, he served as military advisor to Jefferson Davis, president of the Confederacy. Grady McWhiney, *Braxton Bragg and Confederate Defeat* (New York: Columbia University Press, 1969), ix, x. We were unable to confirm a nephew-uncle relationship between Calvin Wright and Braxton Bragg, who had nine siblings.

2. His death certificate states the following: date of death: May 3, 1922; birth date: April 8, 1861; cause of death: "was shot by gunshot"; occupation: "ranchman"; business: "stock-raising."

bridles. With this money they bought hundreds of sections of land for twenty-five cents an acre. Their vast ranch lands extended to Corpus Christi Bay and the border of Mexico. Calvin Wright was a frontiersman and he taught his sons the ways of the Indians and the Mexicans.

He, Braxton Bragg Wright, studied law thru a mail correspondence course and possessed a degree by 1880. He was also interested in medicine, which he practiced. However he never finished medical school. He had a brilliant and inquisitive mind and studied and read constantly. He was considered to be an intellectual on matters of law and politics. He was the father of four sons and a daughter by his first marriage.

On October 3, 1891, several years after the death of his first wife, he married Elizabeth Gallagher. From this union one child was born, Frances Ursula Wright.

Now I shall tell you about your delightful, romantic and beautiful great grandmother, Elizabeth Gallagher Wright (Biggy). She was the eighth child born to Bryan and Margaret Gallagher in the year 1870, November 26th, in a small Irish settlement in South Texas. The Gallagher family are well known in Texas. They came to Texas and made homes during days of drought and hardships. She had seven sisters and four brothers, and most of them are buried in the little cemetery at Gussettville.

My mother was a very beautiful and spiritual woman. She married my father, Braxton Bragg Wright, on October 3, 1891, in the old family home. They lived [in Ramarania, Texas] on a large ranch in a high ranch house where I was born, October 4, 1893. My mother bore a son the year before I arrived, but the child died at birth. In 1898 they moved to San Diego, Texas, and later, when I came to San Antonio to boarding school, they built a home here. Elizabeth Gallagher died on October 12, 1949, at the age of seventy-eight and is buried in San Fernando cemetery in San Antonio, Texas.

Her parents, Margaret and Bryan Gallagher, were born in Leitrim County, Ireland, and together with their parents and many relatives and the McGlains, McMurrays, Shurans, and McMarrows, they crossed the ocean in a second-class freighter. They were driven from Ireland in 1840 by persecution from England on account of their religion (Catholic) and because of the potato famine. They were both seventeen years old. Landing in Galveston Bay after a three-months voyage of cold, hunger, storm, and sickness, they drove through the wilderness with their families by oxen team to Gussettville. The next year,

1841, Bryan and Margaret Gallagher were married and started together to build a homestead, which is still standing.

Back of the lives of these heroic, proud people there is much amazing history. Margaret Gallagher, my grandmother, your great great grandmother, died in her home September 19th, 1901. Her maiden name was McGinnis. Grandpa died May 28, 1909. They both sleep in the Gussettville cemetery.

Charles Grover Mills: father of Charles Wright Mills, born at Blue Lake, Swannee County, Florida, on August 4, 1889. He was the son of Mary Jane Hawkins and Bun Mills, who were born [in] and lived around Live Oak, Florida, and who are buried in the town's cemetery. [. . .] The Mills family were English and Dutch. And the Hawkins were English and Irish.

As you children become older your pride and memory of your own wonderful, brilliant father will increase, and it is good that his memory will be forever green.

I know you will all endeavor to live up to his expectations of you. You have within you the blood of good pioneer stock. From the labors of your ancestors comes this our America.

[. . .]

Your grandmother,
Frances Mills

Charles Wright Mills was five and a half years old when his grandfather (Frances's father) Braxton Bragg Wright was killed. In contrast to Braxton Wright and his independent life on the ranch, Mills's father, Charles Grover Mills, was a white-collar representative of an insurance company. Mills was forty-one years old when he wrote the following selection from the unfinished manuscript "Contacting the Enemy: Tovarich, written to an imaginary Soviet colleague."[3]

Fall 1957

GROWING UP: FACTS AND FANCIES

Let me tell you first about my grandfather and why I am not an oil millionaire.

---

3. See also "On Who I Might Be and How I Got That Way," p. 247.

I grew up in Texas, curiously enough on no ranch but in Waco, Wichita Falls, Fort Worth, Sherman, Dallas, Austin, and San Antonio—in that order. My family moved around a bit. The reason I was not stabilized on a ranch is that my grandfather had lost my ranch. He was shot in the back with a .30-30 rifle, always it's in the back, but he really was. I've never got it altogether clear, but Braxton Bragg Wright, I have been told, liked the girls—married and unmarried, Mexican and white. This one was Mexican and married, a bad combination for him.[4] My grandmother, Elizabeth Gallagher Wright, on the other hand, cared less for men than for the big city of San Antonio, and she loathed ranches.[5] So my grandfather was shot and I did not grow up with cowboys on a ranch. For this I shall always be grateful. I do not want it, but still, late one night, sitting in a bar in Munich, and one afternoon in New York, and again one morning in August in the Hotel Angleterre in Copenhagen, I have thought about the cowboys of my native province.

My God, what men they are. Or were. Or must have been. Or ought to have been. There is no movie like a cowboy movie. All the cowboys on the ranch in Texas where I could have grown up looked just like Gary Cooper. They were tall and slim, and they had that same steely eye, those long arms, and of course the great guns hanging. Every one of them, at one time or another, had taken the long walk in the dusty street before the wooden fronts of the stores behind which merchants trembled and villains lurked unseen but well located for obscene aggression. All my cowboys had come through that, and now they were men, quiet, unafraid men. Tested in that way, certain of themselves, they were each a compact being, just like the voice of Marshall Dillon.

4. This refers to one of several different stories surrounding Braxton Wright's death in 1922. An undisputed fact is that the man who shot Braxton Wright was Alex Ewing, one of his hired hands. Some said that Mr. Ewing interrupted Braxton Wright in an amorous moment with Mrs. Ewing, but Mrs. Ewing testified that the violent dispute was caused by Braxton Wright's false accusation that she and her husband had stolen something, and that her husband had defended her honor. Another story features an argument over Mr. Ewing's refusal to join Mr. Wright in making bootleg liquor, and another says that Braxton Wright did not provoke the attack at all. In any case, a jury acquitted Alex Ewing, based on his claim of self-defense. (This information comes from court records and personal interviews by Richard Davis Gillam, "C. Wright Mills, 1916–1948: An Intellectual Biography" [Ph.D. diss., Stanford University, August 1972], 12–14.)

5. In fact, Mills's grandparents were divorced in 1919.

They cared less for women than women cared for them. In their world some women were altogether bad and some were very good indeed, and all their lives my cowboys were looking for a truly good woman, who at first seemed bad.

About men, my grandfather on his ranch in Texas used to say: "Let them stay just a little on the other side of Winchester-rifle range. Lots safer for everybody that way. And then we'll all be good neighbors." Since he did get shot dead a few years later, he may have had a point. Let them stay just the other side of rifle range.

I don't mind climbing a mountain when I come to it, although I'd not go out of my way to do it. I don't mind swimming a little creek or even building a little boat to get across a big one, although I'd rather a bridge were there. But I don't at all like all these silly little men in uniform all over the frontiers of the world stopping me and holding up travel to see who I might be, or to see whether I'm carrying two or five bottles of French cognac, or whether I've a stamp on a piece of paper, put there by some other little men in other uniforms. It's not really any of their damned business. All this national boundary stuff is a kind of highway robbery, isn't it? And a kind of spiritual robbery too. In a situation of human revolt, notice how quickly the boundaries fall to pieces. So let everyone stay just a little outside of Winchester-rifle range, but let each move along the edges of this range.

"Forgive me," you say, "but you really are wandering. I am trying to find out what sort of man you might be and something of how you came to be whatever you are. Won't you please tell me?"

Yes, but you must let me tell you in my own way and you must not interrupt. The facts will come out, so far as I know them, but it is not altogether pleasant or easy to confront some of them. Surely you must understand that. I've got to clothe them just a little, at least in the beginning. What I was leading up to was that I suppose I could make a big thing out of this cowboy stuff, like a certain kind of good Limey novelist who writes about the "real England," saying what it is and is not. Now Tovarich, let us not do that sort of thing.

I have driven trucks in the East Texas oil fields; I've helped dig a ditch between Long View and Talco; and I've driven a tractor hauling a combine in the wheat fields up in the Texas Panhandle. All that is true. But all of it is also a damned lie—like the lies of executives who claim they started at the bottom of a corporation of which their father, uncle, or brother owned the biggest hunk. I did do those things, but it was only in the summers, always knowing that come the fall, I'd be safe back at school.

It is so easy to pose, to fake. How can I tell you? How can I know exactly how it was, how it is? I think it may help if I say: externally I've always had it very easy indeed, and I've often felt vaguely but undeniably guilty about that. Troubles I've usually brought on myself, and the fact that I have is of course related to the guilt arising from easy and unearned circumstance. Other men, I suppose, live for money, women, fun, comradeship. I seem perversely to like trouble better. I seek it out, and if I do not find it, I try to make it up. I am what any decent executive type or aspiring executive type would automatically call a born troublemaker. I am both presumptuous and, as my grandfather used to say, "as good as any damned body anywhere." But that's merely posing again—perhaps even seeking a "background," or trying to invent one or imagine one. In truth, I don't know a single thing my grandfather ever said, and I doubt if anything he might have said is at all memorable. My grandfather to me is a distant biological fact and nothing else whatsoever.

I have often wondered why so many of my political colleagues need to adopt such postures as they do. It *is* possible to find out what one may really be about at any given time and how one got to be that way; it is possible to conduct this inquiry, this finding out, without being overwhelmed by attitudinizing. The trick, I think—although it's less a trick than a means of self-awareness—the trick is explicitly to include in your work the various postures you tend to fall into, report them, and exploit them intellectually.

You say, "Isn't there some kind of theme that runs through your biography—that shapes it in some way?"

Yes, in time I suppose I sought out certain self-images; at least certain kinds of circumstances began very early to accumulate, so that I think there may be a theme.

First, I never really lived in an extended family. There was just my father, who traveled much of the time, my mother, and one sister three years older than I, whom I've not seen in years. (There was also grandmother Biggy, who seems always to have been around.) The social point is this: I didn't really know the experience of "human relations" within a solid, intimate family setup, certainly not continuously.

My parents as a couple had few if any friends. In fact for long periods, when I was in Sherman and Dallas, going to high school, my immediate family was quite fragmentary, as my father was traveling in his work for weeks at a time. So you see, quite apart from any prior inclination, by virtue of occupational and family fact, I was thrown as a very young child with my mother, and at quite an early age this tie was also broken and I was alone. I do not remember exactly when this tie was broken but certainly this was so by the last year of high school, when I first began to read in the upstairs room with the blue-and-white linoleum floor at 3600 Lover's Lane [in Dallas]. Thus I was well prepared for the explicit isolation that occurred at Texas A & M. That was my first year of college.[6]

This isolation of my family was a prototype of my own isolation. In grammar school and high school and college—in fact, until my first marriage[7]—I never had a circle of friends. There was for me no "gang," no parties. I had a single "chum" in Wichita Falls and another in Sherman—the most important boyhood friend, with whom I spent one or two summers on his elder brother's wheat ranch; at A & M, there was no one. What happened there was that the group I began to care about, to seek approval from, shifted to several professors, a librarian, an English professor, the French professor, and an agricultural economist. Even before that—in high school—the shift had been made to a teacher of architecture and an instructor of psychology.

My "background" contained no intellectual or cultural benefits. I grew up in houses that had no books and no music in them. At least the only music I remember ever hearing in the house was a hillbilly version of "How You Gonna Keep 'em Down on the Farm?" and I was in the second year of college when I first heard classical music. It was Tchaikovsky's *Pathetique* used in a demonstration of some equipment in a physics laboratory. The first stage play I ever saw was also that second year of college: *The Cherry Orchard* by Chekhov. (Isn't it curious that they were both Russian in origin?)

The first books I remember ever reading—in the last year of high school, when I suddenly became awake for the first time—were a set of small books, bound in pale blue, and entitled, I think, "The Psychology of Success." They were all about Will-Power-by-God, which my father had or borrowed in connection with his work as

6. After spending one year at Texas A&M, Mills transferred to the University of Texas at Austin.

7. He was married at the age of twenty-one, while he was an undergraduate.

an insurance salesman. These volumes I took very full notes on, in a minute handwriting, in a set of midget notebooks, as if I were trying to hide it all. The other book I remember from that time was Clarence Darrow's autobiography, an eighteenth-century rationalist tract. In my first year of college I came upon a textbook account of C. H. Cooley and G. H. Mead,[8] in terms of which I first came seriously to begin to analyze myself.

Thus intellectually and culturally I am as "self-made" as it is possible to be. As a friend of mine used to say, "a mushroom." The fact that I seized these academic standards and internalized them deeply meant, in turn, a further cutting off of self from my family background and the social setting at large as well. By the time I went to college, I think no one I had previously known, including family members, really counted for me as a point of reference. I was cut off and alone, and I felt it at the time.

All this also meant that my education was quite poor. There was no context, no background to prepare me for it. To become educated—in the sense in which I first became more or less fully aware of what that might be, at Texas A & M—meant to create myself as if in a vacuum, to find sources of approval for it and models for that kind of life where no standards, models, expectations had existed at all on any cultural level.

A friend of mine from the University of Texas had some inkling of all this: my friendship with him was intellectually and morally the closest I had had up to then. (Of course, one never has any friendships so consequential as those of adolescence.) But its major consequence was to sharpen the focus of all my drives towards work, specifically intellectual work, as my very salvation. I remember the moment when he and I exchanged intellectual roles and I became intellectually ascendant, at least in my own mind, in the relationship. We were walking along in front of the YMCA and I was stronger in some argument. Whether it's true or not doesn't matter. I felt it. At the time I didn't know it, but this meant that again I was alone—or at least very much on my own—my own leader.

Out of all this came the search for, the demand for, absolute autonomy. The great energies the search has demanded and created,

8. Charles Horton Cooley was an American sociologist. George Herbert Mead was an American philosopher and psychologist.

the burdens of loneliness that often accompanied it, and the difficulties of achieving any durable and really deep "human relations" have thus arisen out of quite specific social and cultural contexts. Intellectually I saw with Stendhal: "I see but one rule: to be clear. If I am not clear, all my world crumbles." And with Albert Geurard: "The man who thinks creates a little zone of light and order in the cosmic murk." To realize the psychological meaning of such heroic mottoes for intellectuals— well, it takes one beyond loneliness to the very edge of reason itself: "I think," wrote Descartes, "hence I am." So I have other mottoes too. But the theme is clearly isolation. Its net result is the demand, the compulsion if you will, for autonomy. I don't like "alienation" or any such fancy terms. I am not, and never have been, alienated. I mean just plain isolation; but of course the cumulative effect of it is self-sought isolation.

After graduating from Dallas Technical High School, Mills entered a large military school, Texas Agricultural & Mechanical College.[9] Later Mills thought his father had not believed his son was sufficiently masculine; military college was intended to help make a man of him. In any case, Mills was deeply disappointed with his year at Texas A & M.

Mills and his roommate, who shared the post of freshman class president, also shared the task of stirring up trouble on campus by collaborating on the following letter to the college newspaper, concerning the distribution and use of power within the student body at the college.[10] (Many years later Mills reflected on what this early effort meant to him, in a letter to Hans Gerth, dated December 7, 1943, which appears on p. 55.)

To the *Battalion*, published in the issue dated April 3, 1935

STUDENT FORUM

Digressions on College Life

There are some vital questions which are always a point of issue in every place where men live together. Discontent and unrest can be

9. The school has since added graduate programs and changed its name to Texas Agricultural and Mechanical University.

10. This according to interviews conducted by Timothy Chester.

found wherever society is found. No matter how good, how fair, and how just a group of people may be as a whole, there will always be some individuals in it who feel themselves slighted and maltreated by the rest. Usually these people have only themselves and their incapacity for adjustment to blame; but once in a while we come across a society which has sprung up on a false basis and is sustained on false principles of human conduct justified only by ignorance and narrow thinking. It is just this kind of society that exists at A and M College and will continue to exist as long as there are not enough of its members who dare to change it.

Observation and experience have led me to believe that the influence of living social conditions on the campus upon the students is more harmful than beneficial. I do not aim to take the pessimistic point of view and say that these conditions cannot be changed and so we may as well get used to them. Nor am I going to follow the suggestion to get out since the climate here does not suit me. I propose rather to write down my thoughts on what goes on around me in the hope that they may in some way help to bring about the change which is so necessary for the welfare of the student body.

What effect has the overbearing attitude of the upperclassman on the mind of the freshman? Does it make the freshman more of a man? Most assuredly not, for there can be no friendship born out of fear, hatred or contempt; and no one is a better man who submits passively to the slavery of his mind and body by one who is less of a man than he. Since when has it been true that oppression and the suppression of free thinking have become acceptable to the American youth? Can it be that he accepts these because he has grown indifferent to the problems facing him and takes the easiest way out? It would be hard to believe that this should be the case, in fact. I am sure it is not. The freshman submits to the will of the upperclassman only because he has been led to conceive a distorted idea of sportsmanship and true manhood. He is afraid to defy them and stand alone not so much because of what they might do to him but because of what they might think of him. And so we have the freshman living a life of mental unrest and stress, unwilling to do that which he believes is wrong, and yet forced to do it by his fear of public opinion.

College students are supposed to become leaders of thought and action in later life. It is expected they will profit from a college education by developing an open and alert mind to be able to cope boldly with everyday problems in economics and politics. They cannot do this unless they learn to think independently for themselves and to stand fast for their convictions. Is the student at A and M encouraged to do this? Is he permitted to do it? The answer is sadly in the negative. Indeed, it is established law among upperclassmen that freshmen should not be allowed to think. As soon as one shows signs of rebellion against the feudal autocracy at college, he is forced back into the folds of automats from which he tried to escape. His spirit is crushed, his heart embittered, and his mind molded in a standard pattern. Of course not all freshmen are affected in the same way. Some, the privileged few, may go through it all and come out unchanged. Others, weaker than the former, come out as human robots with shattered spirit, no will power, no self-confidence and no self-respect. Still there are others who become cynics losing faith in man and society. Whoever is in either of these three groups could have been in the class of the energetic, the independent, and the optimistic, if conditions affecting his early life in college had been otherwise.

On the student alone rests the responsibility of making A and M free from sham, hypocrisy and feudalistic customs which can bring harm only upon themselves.

By a Freshman

An anonymous upperclassman defended the traditions at A & M in a response that was printed the following week in the Battalion. *The upperclassman wrote that a look at the lives of A & M graduates will "show that a finer bunch of citizens never lived"; the A & M experience taught students to lead and be led and it "turned out smart men who raised hell and had a lot of fun." The letter stated that, like religion, the status quo at A & M was "good enough for our fathers so why should we try to change it." The student went on to say that A & M builds men, indeed cadets, who "used to have a little guts," who were treated with some respect by the authorities. In closing, the upperclassman wrote that in "the ridiculous article" the freshman had claimed that "some freshmen come through it all with crushed spirit, no will power, and other rot. [. . .] If you want the things you advocate, why didn't you go to Texas, or Tarleton instead of trying to help the rest of your crowd finish ruining A and M?"[11] The rejoinder follows.*

11. "Student Forum: College Life," *Battalion*, 10 April 1935.

To the *Battalion,* published in the issue dated May 8, 1935

Another Viewpoint

Recently there appeared in these columns the most delicate and subtle of satires. I have no doubt that it was written in an inspired moment of a great thinker's life. So beautifully subtle was it and so diligently at study (and busy disciplining the men who have been here only seven months or so) are the great majority of our student body that the thought has occurred to me that perhaps this bit of everlasting though subtle truth was read in much too hasty a manner.

And so assuming that some of the more rapid readers took this thing literally in case they did not see the obvious weakness (I am sure it was intended to be obvious) of its arguments, I am going to be a bit more blunt in expressing my opinion of the juvenile techniques in which the majority of our students indulge. (And if you don't care to hear my opinion this Bat has many other interesting things which you may read. So go read them and don't ask me why I came here, or if I don't like A and M, why don't I go to another school. Such questions are obviously insane, for the highest form of patriotism is criticism. I am interested in the potentialities of this institution and I intend to do my small share toward their development.)

In none of these controversies of principle do the writers seem to pierce the root of our problem. The effect of our system is not so detrimental during our first year as it is during the other three. Outside of taking his time from study or creative leisure, the character of the freshman is not to any extent negatively changed (assuming, of course, that he is not influenced by "the men who have guts"—as last week's writer so artistically labeled our rougher element). And then he trades one for three. For three years he shouts and feet hit dormitory floors; for three years his room is cleaned up and his laundry taken and got by other men. For three years he can, if he wishes, use his class distinction to satisfy his individual prejudices; can force his ego and will upon other men. For three years we run his errands, carry his cigarettes.

And the excuse for all this is that it develops leadership.

If this is leadership then my sociology text is very wrong—because this sort of control is based on nothing save force. Any social control which rests on force is wrong. When paddles and muscles rule, ignorance also reigns.

No one with common "horse sense" can stand on the two feet of the genus Homo and distinctly say that three years of being waited on does not affect an individual . . . true one finds it hard to think of any good effect.

And so if it's good enough for ole pappie, it's good enough for us! What wonderful irony . . . nothing could be more obviously leaky. Then why, my old traditionalist, do you not ride in buggies? Your granddad did. The more intelligent students here are not content with our present system. And tomorrow A and M shall also rise slowly from its foolish buggy and enter a streamlined roadster.

Just because a thing has been done by a number of people over a number of years does not make that thing necessarily good. The hand of the past has its functions; it stabilizes; it held conquered territory. But with it alone there can be no progress, no advancement toward sane and more rational techniques. We must criticize and change.

Lots of verbiage has been slung about men with "guts." Before we use a term, let's put Plato on it. Just who are the men with guts? They are the men who have the ability and the brains to see this institution's faults, who are brittle enough not to adapt themselves to its erroneous order—and plastic enough to change if they are already adapted; the men who have the imagination and the intelligence to formulate their own codes; the men who have the courage and the stamina to live their own lives in spite of social pressure and isolation. These my friends, are the men with "guts."

By a Freshman

After his freshman year, Mills transferred to the University of Texas at Austin, where he completed his B.A. in sociology and his M.A. in philosophy. In October 1937, as a twenty-one-year-old student in Austin, Mills married twenty-four-year-old Dorothy Helen Smith from Oklahoma. A friend of Mills's who was studying literature and knew Norse mythology nicknamed Dorothy Helen "Freya," after a Norwegian goddess. Freya was the second of four children born to a banker and his wife, a former teacher. After graduating from Oklahoma College for Women in 1935 with a B.S. in commerce, Freya enrolled in the master's program in sociology at the University of Texas, where she met Mills. When she and Mills married, she stopped studying so that she could work full time to help support the couple. (She worked on the staff of the director of the Women's Residence Hall at the University of Texas.)

During his last year as a student at the University of Texas, Mills submitted an essay entitled "Language, Logic and Culture" to the American Sociological Review. *On February 23, 1939, Read Bain wrote Mills to let him know that the journal would not publish the essay, although they would be willing to consider a condensed version of it. He also jokingly mentioned that Mills had not included postage for the return of the manuscript unless it had been confiscated by Howard P. Becker,[12] who originally received the package. Mills sent the following letter with his revision of the article.*

To Read Bain, from Austin, Texas, dated March 2, 1939

Dear Sir:

Much that was dear to my heart I have unselfishly cast aside! I have cut and cut and cut, and this is as short as I can make it.

Believe me grateful for your specific suggestions for deletion. I have found them good, and in the main I have followed them. Hence, if you decide to publish the article you may affix to the title a footnote to that effect. [. . .]

Thanks for your considerations, and go easy on Becker. He swiped no postal funds. I remain the unashamed culprit.

Cordially,
C. Wright Mills

"Language, Logic and Culture" was published in the October 1939 issue of the American Sociological Review. *This was Mills's first professional publication; when it came out, he promptly sent a copy to Robert K. Merton, asking for comments and initiating a correspondence and professional association that, as the reader will see, extended throughout Mills's career.*

12. Howard Paul Becker, the American sociologist (born in 1899), not to be confused with another, more well-known American sociologist, Howard Saul Becker (born in 1928).

II

GRADUATE STUDIES
Madison, Wisconsin, 1939–1941

There is a certain type of man who spends
his life finding and refinding what is within
him, and I suppose I am of that type.

> C. Wright Mills, letter to his parents,
> November 15, 1939

Mills applied to doctoral programs in the philosophy department at the University of Chicago, and the department of sociology and anthropology at the University of Wisconsin. The University of Chicago was his first choice, but it failed to offer him a fellowship.[1] The University of Wisconsin did offer a fellowship and Mills accepted. Madison had a reputation for academic quality as well as a progressive faculty.

In late August of 1939, Mills and Freya left Texas for Madison, Wisconsin, where Mills entered the doctoral program in sociology. The couple pieced together a subsistence standard of living with the income from the fellowship, part-time jobs, and loans from a credit union. Mills focused his studies on sociological theory and methodology, with a special interest in the sociology of knowledge and pragmatism. While he was in graduate school he gained some recognition for his publications in the American Journal of Sociology, *the* American Sociological Review, *and other journals or bulletins.*

In Madison Mills met and became friends with Hans Gerth, who taught sociology at the university. Although Mills never took a course from Gerth, Gerth had an important influence on Mills. A native of Germany who had studied philosophy and social science at the University of Frankfurt, Gerth provided Mills with a firsthand view of European learning, intellectual life, and sociological theory.[2] Freya remembers that Mills and Gerth "had such rapport that the two of them could talk at the same time and understand each other."[3]

A few months after arriving in Wisconsin, Mills wrote the next two letters to his parents in Texas.

1. Notes from Freya James, undated (1984).

2. Readers of German may want to see Gerth's book entitled *Die sozialgeschichtliche Lage der burgerlichen Intelligenz um die Wende des 18. Jahrhunderts. Ein Beitrag zur Soziologie des deutschen Fruhliberalismus* (The social-historical situation of the bourgeois intelligentsia at the end of the 18th century: A contribution to the sociology of early German liberalism) (Berlin: V.D.I.-Verlag, G.M.B.H., 1935).

3. Letter from Freya James to Richard Gillam, dated September 17, 1966, as quoted in Gillam, "C. Wright Mills," 102.

To Frances and Charles Grover Mills, from Madison, Wisconsin, dated November 15, 1939

Dear C. G. & Fannye:

I have received your letters of the 12th. The box of sweets mentioned will no doubt be here shortly. Know that we appreciate them. [. . .]

I do not need to tell you that academically I am going over with a bang. I have two more articles being considered for publication now by good standard periodicals in my technical field. I will let you know when and if they are accepted.

I am also brushing up "The Academic" and will send it to several short story magazines before I give up hope. Two professors here and their wives are ecstatic about it. I have also completed another short story, unnamed as yet, which deals with David's and my relationship.[4] It is rather moody and I will not send it to him for checking until we know how the mess he is in comes out. It is one of the most genuine things I have ever written.

Freya has finished all the hours she is allowed to do at the university press. She has the *possibility* of a 4-week job at the big department store here during the Christmas holidays.

My father asks, do we need anything. Does a man ever really need anything but what is in him? The things I need no one else can give me: such things as warm sun and lazy afternoons and leisure to think things through. There is a certain type of man who spends his life finding and refinding what is within him, and I suppose I am of that type. No: there is nothing I need that can be given to me by others. In the end a man must go to bat alone.

Mills

ॐ

To Frances and Charles Grover Mills, dated December 21, 1939

Dear C. G. and Fannye:

The lean years of my marriage have been enriched by several felicitous features; but no one of them has been as heartening to

---

4. David Rose, a friend from Mills's days at the University of Texas.

me nor as concretely helpful as your constant attention and aid. We still stand between childhood and independence. There are still lean months ahead. But I can look forward now and catch glimpses of a personal security. I want you both to know that my confidence and work in the past, and now, have drawn no little of their strength from the exemplary pattern that your lives have traced through long, devoted years.

From my mother I have gotten a sense of color and air. She showed me the tang and feel of a room properly appointed, and the drama about flowers. She gave me feel. She also tried to teach me manners, but I fear I have forgotten many of them.

From my father I absorbed the gospel and character of work, determination with both eyes always ahead. That is part of the America he knows, and it is part of him too. There was a time when I thought he did not possess a feeling of craftsmanship. But I was wrong. It is merely that his line of effort is one I did not understand. Looking back, I see he always did a good job, that he never quit until it was finished. So from both of you I have gotten a living craftsmanship.[5]

The physical distances that have separated us since fall have with startling clarity shown me how much I have gained from being your child. And I want to thank you for that.

C. Wright

In the next letter Mills responded to his mother's concern for his welfare, which may have been related to the fact that Freya had separated from him in the summer of 1940.

Mills also mentioned voting for Norman Thomas, the leader of the Socialist Party and its candidate for the U.S. presidency in the elections of 1928, 1932, 1936, 1940, 1944, and 1948. Thomas started out as a pastor doing settlement work in New York City. A pacifist who, like Mills, opposed Stalinism as well as fascism, Thomas advocated evolutionary socialism. He also helped found the American Civil Liberties Union.[6]

5. The concept of craftsmanship remained personally and intellectually important to Mills throughout his adult life. See his discussion of the ideal of craftsmanship in *White Collar* (1951) and his paper entitled "On Intellectual Craftsmanship," which was reprinted as an appendix in *The Sociological Imagination* (1959).

6. *The Columbia Encyclopedia,* 5th ed. (New York: Columbia University Press, 1993; distributed by Houghton Mifflin Company).

To Frances Mills, from Madison, Wisconsin, undated (fall 1940)

Dear Fannie:

I have just now received and read with interest your nice long letter, for which thanks. I must get on with a book review I am doing tonight but will attempt to answer your questions and get this letter right back to you.

1st I do not need pajamas or cover or anything at all. I bought a pair of pajamas in flannel about a week ago. I have plenty of cover.

I do not work at the Bureau anymore because I finished the job for which I was employed. Besides, governmental service does not exclude one from the conscription necessarily. Only in certain lines. I had to leave the Bureau also because of my work here at the University. You know that I am finally teaching 5 classes a week in introductory sociology. And of course I am writing. I shall send you 2 articles that are being published this fall—one in *American Journal of Sociology,* Nov. issue, and the other *American Sociological Review,* December issue.[7] These periodicals will be in the San Antonio public library and you can look at them when they come out. The current issue of the *American Journal of Sociology* has an announcement of my article in the front of it and in the back a statement that I read a paper to the Chicago Society for Social Research on Aug. 17 this last summer.

To get back to the war . . . I see nothing that can be done that I am not doing. I am taking note of your suggestions, and please know that I am and will continue to use them. I am no longer a half wild, argumentative fool. In any event, if I am called, it will be as an officer because of my A & M work and because of my education.

David did not stay too long. We are still the best of friends. I do not know why he has not contacted you. But I suppose he has his own troubles. He does like you both very much I know.

I like Madison better than Austin. I have more friends here.

I do look forward to the cold weather. I like it.

[. . .]

---

7. "Methodological Consequences of the Sociology of Knowledge," 46, no. 3 (November 1940): 316–30; and "Situated Actions and Vocabularies of Motive," 5, no. 6 (December 1940): 904–13.

I am this November voting for Norman Thomas. I know he will not win but that does not mean the vote is lost. You both vote for him too. His is the *only* antiwar party in the running.

[. . .]

[unsigned copy]

Freya had divorced Mills in August 1940, but Mills convinced her to change her mind and the couple remarried in March 1941. The following letter mentions photographs, which were taken after their second wedding, one of which appears in this volume.

To Frances and Charles Grover Mills, from Madison, Wisconsin, dated April 25, 1941

Dear Mother and Dad:

I received your [Mother's] letter today. Your description of the prize-winning chariot is very vivid and artistic. We are looking forward to seeing it in photo, though we shall miss the color aspect, which is very important in such matters. But then, with your description no doubt we shall "see" the colors too. You write a very nice English, you know. I always know my mother is an artist and a gypsy in her heart . . . Do I not feel it in my own heart every day? And who is to say whose heart it really is?

Wisconsin is beautiful now. We spent the afternoon on a wooded hill with the Gerths. There was no formal school this week and Freya and I tried to catch up on stuff that's past due. I have two years' work to perform between now and next January. However, with Freya's invaluable help and C G's capacity for and love of honest work (inherited! damn it!) I'll make it.

Enclosed are three snaps. I believe them to be the best ever made of us. The lake is where I shall sail this summer. We live 1½ blocks from it.

It is now about certain that we shall not be able to come south this summer. The only way I can see to get together is the following: Dave has a new car, a big one, I think. He might be interested in driving it up in August on a share-expense basis. His address is 633

Castell, New B. Contact him and see if you can make it. If you both
came up—C G & Fannye—we could arrange at a nominal cost
in this apartment house for a dwelling unit. Let us know. Try and
arrange a visit *some way*.

Your son,
Charles M. Jr.

III

STARTING OUT
College Park, Maryland, 1941–1945

Radicalism comes out in detailed and
compelling analysis, not in names and
slogans.

> C. Wright Mills, letter to Dwight
> Macdonald, October 10, 1943

I bought all, every single one of Veblen's
works! They *are* fine. They sit here a bequest
and a challenge.

> C. Wright Mills, letter to Hans
> Gerth, undated but probably early
> November 1944

In 1941 Mills completed his preliminary examinations for his Ph.D. at the University of Wisconsin and began work as an associate professor of sociology at the University of Maryland, College Park. Robert K. Merton had helped Mills get the position by putting him in touch with Carl Joslyn, who was then the head of the sociology department and a former colleague of Merton's at Harvard. Mills completed his thesis, entitled "A Sociological Account of Pragmatism: An Essay on the Sociology of Knowledge," and obtained his Ph.D. from the University of Wisconsin the following year.

During his stay at the University of Maryland, which coincided with the United States' participation in World War II, Mills's political awareness grew, and he bought his first subscription to a daily newspaper, the New York Times.[1] During this period Mills became friendly with three historians who would later become well-known: Richard Hofstadter, Frank Freidel, and Ken Stampp. Meeting regularly for lunch and sharing a critical opinion of FDR, capitalism, and the military draft, the four friends joined forces on academic issues on campus and provided an "intellectual oasis for each other."[2]

While living in Maryland, Mills wrote articles and book reviews for a wide variety of periodicals—from the American Journal of Sociology and the American Sociological Review to the New Republic, Partisan Review, and politics. During his three years at the University of Maryland, Mills also collaborated with Gerth on two books: the collection of Max Weber's writings, From Max Weber: Essays in Sociology, translated, edited, and with an introduction by H. H. Gerth and C. Wright Mills, which was published in 1946, the year after Mills left Maryland; and Character and Social Structure (1953).

The next letter is addressed to Gerth's wife, H I.

1. Notes from Freya James, undated (1984).

2. Susan Stout Baker, *Radical Beginnings: Richard Hofstadter and the 1930's* (Westport, Conn.: Greenwood Press, 1985), 177. Based on Baker's personal interview with Kenneth Stampp, April 2, 1981.

To Hildegarde Ide Gerth, from Greenbelt, Maryland, dated December 24, 1941

Dear H I:

It is entirely wonderful of you to frame the picture and gift us with it. It is Christmas eve, afternoon, and we are about to betake ourselves down to the sea, to Annapolis, which is 35 miles away, to the east.

Here the sun is shining and I have been roaming in the woods back of the house all morning in my shirtsleeves, it is so warm. It is very pleasant and smells crisp and Autumnal.

I write you this letter because we won't see you in New York and neither will you see us, which is very bad. You really *should* have gone.

We've just finished *Darkness at Noon*.[3] Jesus, it is penetrative. There is so much in it that I just had to read aloud in a kind of machine-gun inevitable-like voice. Then, in my seminar, I'd been going over "parties" and "bureaucracies" and so I read certain parts of it there. It is one of the few recent books I've read which on literary grounds meets Eliseo's criterion for good prose! Which reminds me, I just got a letter from Eliseo V[ivas].[4] He is to commit Matrimony the 31st, and then he and Dorothy spend a few days in Chicago. But I suppose you know. He was so very kind: sent me a letter of introduction to Sidney Hook.[5] When Gerth and I get together in New York, I'm going to try and work out a triangle luncheon, if I can.

Oh, yes, another book: *Kabloona* by de Poncins, about the Eskimos.[6] I'm using it next term in connection with a course which

3. Novel by Arthur Koestler, trans. Daphne Hardy (New York: Macmillan, 1941).

4. A philosopher Mills had met while studying at the University of Wisconsin.

5. American philosopher who had a particular interest in the theory of pragmatism and who taught at New York University. Hook, who had been a graduate student of John Dewey's at Columbia University, began his career as a Marxist scholar, engaging in research at the Marx-Engels Institute in Moscow in 1929 and working with the American Communist Party before helping to found a new radical organization, the American Workers' Party, in 1933. Later he became a neoconservative intellectual who received the Medal of Freedom from President Ronald Reagan in 1983. Sidney Hook, *Out of Step: An Unquiet Life in the 20th Century* (New York: Harper and Row, 1987).

6. By Gontran de Poncins (New York: Reynal and Hitchcock, 1941; reprint, St. Paul, Minn.: Graywolf Press, 1996).

will consist entirely of novels about primitive peoples! *Kabloona* is *not* excitingly good, but firm and interesting work.

Just got back from Annapolis. It is a lovely village: Narrow streets curving around between old houses with high creaking eaves. Many little inlet bays running up into the town, past the tall old houses and full of fishing craft, rusting and full of oysters. It is the kind of village you'd like to lounge around in for a full day, walking and feeling and seeing and smelling its every nook and cranny. It is the first place in Maryland in connection with which one may use the adjective "quaint" without triteness. It is a place to which one could *commit* oneself; a place, above all, in which to talk of our dilapidated old friend, the cosmos.

Yours truly,
Mills

In late June 1942, Mills wrote to Daniel Bell at the New Leader, *asking to review* Paths of Life *by Charles W. Morris, which had just been published by Harper and Brothers. Mills, who was spending the summer in Madison, explained that he was then immersed in pragmatic literature. In an earlier letter to Bell, dated June 18, 1942, Mills described his doctoral dissertation: "I think I told you that I am finishing up this fall, maybe, a sociology of knowledge of pragmatism: from Pierce thru Dewey and Mead. I'm on page 570 and my wife is yelling to stop it, as she is the only one who can read my handwriting (typing). Anyway in this I trace Dewey's stands (political) down the line and, in conjunction with the position on logic and theory of valuation, impute him socially. Pan-logism is a type of formal left wingism; its formality is what is at issue politically and it is this which must be explained in terms of the whole situation of American 'progressivism.'"*

To Daniel Bell, from Madison, Wisconsin, postcard dated July 19, 1942

The copy of Morris arrived OK several days ago. You'll get the piece within a week under the title "The Crisis of Pragmatism: Politics and Religion." [. . .] The guy has done the wrong thing with something potentially swell and we ought to fight him, and hard.

Yours,
Mills

To Frances and Charles Grover Mills, from Greenbelt, Maryland, dated
June 29, 1943, 2 A.M.

Just a line to let you know how things are before I go to bed.
Yesterday morning I received a new draft classification of 2-A. This
means that I am considered [an] "indispensable civilian" in my present
occupation and am definitely deferred for 6 months, that is, until December 17, 1943. At that time another application for deferment is
made by the university, and I have no reason to feel that they will not
defer me again for 6 months. You will recall that I was not terribly
worried when you were here, Fannye; now you see why.

I have not heard anything from the Navy and am undecided as to
what I would do if they offered to commission me. They would have
to give me just what I want.

Today I mailed you a copy of the article which I wrote while
Fannye was visiting us. It was printed sooner than I thought and looks
pretty good, although several printer's errors were made, as they always
are. Also got another check for $15 today from *New Republic* for a
little 600 word review they printed last week.[7]

I am now reading up a lot on American history in order that I
may teach the Army how it was with the forefathers. I find some of
the forefathers rather tough old guys. And they are old enough to be
very respectable . . . now. So I am learning American history in order
to quote it at the sons of bitches who run American Big Business.
After all, who can deny Patrick Henry or Tommie Jefferson? I'm not
reading the books about American history but the "sources," that is,
the official speeches and public documents. Old Pat Henry jumped up
one day in the house of Burgesses (congress) of Virginia in 1775 and
began a speech: "God Almighty! God Almighty, Gentlemen! You say
that we are not strong enough to fight so formidable a foe etc. But,
sirs, I ask: when will we be stronger? Next week? Next month? Next
year? When then? God Almighty!" and so on. He was a great old
guy coming from the small farmers and artisans and fighting the Big
Holders who ran the government and everybody else. There are a
lot of guys like that, but the books don't tell you about 'em. So I'm
going to the documentary records and [will] teach American history

7. "Prometheus as Democrat," review of *The Hero in History: A Study in Limitation and
Possibility,* by Sidney Hook, *New Republic* (21 June 1943): 834.

from the direct indisputable facts that lie there. When I get through they'll think American history was one big farmer-labor rally. Which in large part it damn well was.

good night,
Mills
Charlie Jr.[8]

[P.S.] Thanks for the pipe cleaners. Wish I could go out on the ranch with you for a couple of months rest.[9]

In the following letter to Dwight Macdonald, the iconoclastic journalist and critic, Mills responded to Macdonald's plans for starting a new magazine, one that would feature lively dissident political thinking within a leftist context—and an opposition to the mass violence of World War II. Mills had been writing for another political journal based in New York City: the social democratic weekly the New Leader, *of which Daniel Bell was managing editor. Bell remembers introducing Mills to Macdonald,[10] and Mills and Macdonald quickly became friends.*

In the early forties Mills was becoming disenchanted with many of the positions taken in the New Leader, *which represented a retreat from the journal's early radicalism.[11] Although Mills continued to contribute book reviews as late as 1944, in 1943 he no longer identified with the journal politically and stopped writing articles for it. In this context Mills was especially supportive of Macdonald's plan to start a new magazine that would provide a forum for independent radicalism with an antiwar orientation.*

To Dwight Macdonald, from Greenbelt, Maryland, dated October 10, 1943

Dear Dwight:

Just got in from Madison this morning and received your letter and prospectus. Also found out that this Army program in which I'm teaching is now blown up to where I have to give formal lectures in

---

8. Mills typed his name as well as signed it on this and many other letters.

9. Mills's parents lived in a modest house in a neighborhood of small lots. Mills's mother spent part of her childhood on a ranch owned by her father—Mills wrote of his grandfather's life and ranch and how the ranch was lost, in a letter included in part 1 of this book.

10. Letter from Daniel Bell to K. Mills, dated August 15, 1996.

11. Gillam, "C. Wright Mills," 182.

American history to 150 guys at a time instead of (as last time) to 30 in a section. More work and time and energy gone, god damned it. But [I] do want to say this:

1. The outline agenda looks damned good, especially the departments and the general slant on art and culture etc. Have one thing about which I get very earnest and want to plead with you:

2. For God's sake don't call it "The Radical Review." Get some more innocuous name. Maybe you do not realize how many people you estrange by such publicity of names. In academic circles many people who you might win over as readers and even writers would be alienated by the title, and so needlessly! Radicalism comes out in detailed and compelling analysis, not in names and slogans. It would cost many men in many institutions their jobs if they were to write for a journal with such a name. It does not compromise or "expediencize" your viewpoint if you get a more innocuous title. "The Left" is much better but suffers from the defect of suggesting "left out" or some such. Babylon is too playful and trivial for the level of stuff and the seriousness which you want to achieve. I'm sorry I can't think of any suggestions but I'll write again after mulling it.

3. You can of course count on me for the first issue. [. . .] I have been working on and off with a sort of general survey of the "dilemmas of the left," which if I have time I'll try and finish and send you. I think you'll find it provocative, although you won't agree with it all. But maybe it is too much of an "Issues Which We Face" stuff and you'll want to do that order of thing in the editorial yourself. If so, or if I can't finish it in time, I'll let you know about a composite set of books for a major review, for I certainly want to be counted in the first issue with you guys. [. . .] I've been thinking of doing a big composite on Soren Kierkegaard, but can't tell yet, for another journal has half offered [that] to me and I can't violate confidence by asking you for [that] until they let me know definitely. But might you be interested in a sociology of knowledge of the guy and the cultural stuff around him?

4. If we could only clear the copyright stuff, we (Gerth and I) could let you have a translation of Max Weber on "Class and Status" which we've done. [. . .] It's a section from Wirtschaft und Gesellschaft (Tubingen 1922), if I recall correctly. [. . .] It has never been published in English and is not included in part one of W und G,

which Parsons of Harvard has translated and is now in English press. The son of a bitch translated it so as to take all the guts, the radical guts, out of it, whereas our translation doesn't do that!

[. . .]

Yours,
Mills

In the following letter, Mills continued to discuss the connotations of various proposed names for the magazine Macdonald was founding.

To Dwight Macdonald, from College Park, Maryland, dated October 25, 1943

Dear Dwight:

At first I thought "Gulliver" was damn good because in this world one's childhood is likely to have been more pleasant than one's adult tribulations and Gulliver is associated with one's childhood. Also Gulliver went among big people and little people and was a stranger among them both. But the only attention you would attract by such a title would be, I am afraid, negative. "Cute" titles are also frivolous, or "literary" in the bad sense. People play with them! ("Gulliver" equals gullible; "Left" equals left-out, left-over; and such playful characteristics stick). They can't do it with a title like "Political Review" or even "Politics." Don't try to advertise with these damn titles. Make the title innocuous. The magazines that last and grow in influence have plain titles.

Enclosed are some notices on Amerasia, etc. I take it that these little summaries are to be unsigned. I would prefer it, at least for those I send you. Also it leaves you free to rewrite or abbreviate as your space requires.

I will let you know by next weekend definitely whether or not I can do the piece on "Withdrawal and Orientation" or some such title.

Sincerely yours,
Mills

P.S. "The Critic" is too negativistic. "Politics" with some subtitle, I think best.[12]

[. . .]

∾

To Frances and Charles Grover Mills, from Greenbelt, Maryland, undated (fall 1943)

Dear Momma and Papa:

When I got back to Maryland, I found I was saddled with a big Army class of 150 men in American history. Last term I had thirty at a time and could bull along; this time I've got to prepare formal lectures, come every Monday, Wednesday, and Friday morning, and at eight o'clock too. It is very rough to lecture to that many before you're really awake. I will be an old man when I'm 35. But at least I'll probably live until I'm that old! So what the hell.

The Madison trip was quite successful. Gerth and I got some good work done and I got a little rest from the summer, although not much. All the time I'm not working on the history now, I spend on a new civilian course called PRINT, FILM, AND RADIO which I give. It's on the sociology of communication: why people listen to radios and what it does to them and why there are movies and what it does and why they are like they are etc. I've been working up stuff on art also, which I'm going to present in the course, for that too is communication. When I'm not at these two general jobs, I'm working on the book Gerth and I are doing on social psychology.[13]

Anyway, with all this I don't have time to sleep or write letters very frequently! I go to the office every day now, from 7:45 in the morning until around 6:10 at night. I go on my days off as well as on those on which I lecture. I've got to, what with the work. Anyway Joslyn [Professor Carl Joslyn] gave me a private secretary, a big red-headed Irish woman who works for me about 4 or 5 hours every day and also writes her M.A. thesis on trade unions under my supervision. I took the coffee percolator to the office and we have

---

12. Macdonald took this suggestion but used a lowercase *p*.

13. Published as Hans Gerth and C. Wright Mills, *Character and Social Structure: The Psychology of Social Institutions* (New York: Harcourt, Brace, and World, 1953).

coffee all the time. She is very efficient, but I am more efficient and run her!

Anyway that is what I'm doing and why I am busy and can't write very often. I wish I could see you both, but it looks like it will be a long time. Good-bye. I've got to go to sleep.

Your son, as ever,
M.
Mills

The day before Mills wrote the following letter, the New York Times *reported that the philosopher Senator Benedetto Croce and another leading Italian antifascist, Count Carlo Sforza, accused Americans of favoring continued fascism in Italy as a barricade against Communism. Croce and Sforza pointed out that the Allies' occupying southern Italy were prohibiting many civil liberties, such as free speech in newspapers and the right to assemble publicly, thus inhibiting the development of representative government.[14] Gaetano Salvemini had made a similar point the previous month when he wrote, "Our 'realists' tell us that they are only interested in winning the war and are not concerned with the issue of fascism or no fascism. The truth of the matter is that they* are *concerned with the issue. They are endeavoring to force the Italian, the American and the British people to choose either a pro-German brand of fascism with Mussolini or a pro-Allied brand of quasi-fascism without Mussolini."[15]*

In the next letter, Mills's reference to Italian boos at Sforza and Croce related to the news that they had been shouted down at a rally at Naples University when they urged the abdication of the king but also called for a transitional role for a regency prior to the establishment of an Italian republic. The crowd dispersed after a number of fistfights.

To Hans Gerth, from Greenbelt, Maryland, dated December 7, 1943

Dear Gerth:

This afternoon I received the Weber translation. Most of the comments are definitely improvements and I am incorporating most of them and tomorrow the ms. will be sent to Macdonald. If he doesn't want to

---

14. "Italian Liberals See Fascist Trend: Britons and Americans Blamed for Badoglio's Rule—Marshall Calls for Arms," *New York Times*, 6 December 1943, sec. 1, p. 6.

15. "What Price Badoglio and the King?" *New Republic* 109, no. 19 (8 November 1943): 641.

print it, don't worry, for I will get the translation rights cleared anyway and it will be published. I think Dwight will grab it, however.[16]
Will let you know.

Yes, I saw the item about the Italian boos at Sforza and Croce.
The first item the *Times* ran said "republicans" did it, then the next day
Matthews came thru and said "Communists" did it.[17] (See the expose
of Matthews by Salvemini in recent *New Republic*.)[18] It is disgusting—
the whole Goddamn European mess and the way it's being handled.
Most of the time I don't think about it, for I cannot do so without great
wells of indignation coming up in me and this interferes with the
economy of emotion which I'm trying to maintain. The other night,
though, I got terribly aggressive at the whole damn political picture
and sat down and wrote 14 double-spaced pages on the typewriter. I
called it "The Politics of Truth" and I think it is really hot stuff! It is
the nearest I have ever come to objectifying the kind of real deep down
feeling that I have on political questions on evenings when you're just
with one or two other guys whom you trust and before whom you are
not ashamed to verbalize political sentimentalities. But there is no one
here with whom I can really do that and so I wouldn't think about having it published. On such stuff one has to be one's own critic and to be a
good critic on such stuff one must let it soak for at least several months.

Carl Joslyn, last week, inherited $50,000. I said fifty thousand.
[. . .] What would you do with $50,000? As soon as the war ends
I'd buy a little place outside New York, about 25 acres for 8 or 9
thousand dollars and I'd start freelancing and . . . oh, what the hell.

Last Friday I was working at the office at night on [the] motives
chapter[19] and sort of collapsed emotionally and "spiritually." For about

16. Dwight Macdonald did publish "Class, Status, and Party," translated and edited by
Gerth and Mills—in the October 1944 issue of *politics*.

17. "Naples Republicans Break Up Rally Voicing First Open Regency Call," *New York
Times,* 29 November 1943, sec. 1, p. 1; Herbert L. Matthews, "Italian Reds Call for King's
Ousting," *New York Times,* 30 November 1943, sec. 1, p. 8.

18. Gaetano Salvemini had discussed Herbert Matthews's years of support of fascism in
Italy and his "rather belated conversion." Salvemini wrote that Matthews's book *The Fruits
of Fascism* would allow the American public "to learn that a large part of what they had read
about Italy in the *New York Times* for twenty years had been the opposite of the truth." ("Herbert Matthews' Italy," *New Republic* 109, no. 21 [22 November 1943]: 723.)

19. *Character and Social Structure* contains a number of chapters on the sociology of mo-
tivation (see part 5 of this volume).

2 hours, I realized later, I just sat and stared at the row of books, with the light on in the office and the rest of the building all dark. It was the oddest feeling and I can't explain it. Like a trance, only all the time I was thinking madly about war and the hopelessness of things. It was as if you were thinking, yes, you have to use that word, with a sequence of moods. The polarity was probably between helplessness and aggressiveness and both were, I think, rather relished! Also, for the first time, except in what was, explicitly at least, in fun, I had a self-image of being very Irish. I did not realize it at first but that came through very clearly. I do not know why because I do not know anything about "the Irish" and I have never, to my knowledge, been stamped as Irish by anyone particularly. Anyway, there I was alone, helpless, aggressive, and Irish! I think maybe it is all because of the inarticulate feelings of indignation which come up when I confront politics in any serious way and because I cannot locate and denounce (with all the energies I've available and eager for the job) such enemies as are available. Living in an atmosphere soaked in lies, the man who thinks, at least, that he knows some of the truth but would lose his job were he to tell it out and is not man enough to do it anyway . . . if such a man has built such [a] life as he has known around finding out the truth and being aggressive with it, then he suffers.

Immediate, though not final, surcease can be found in partially socializing the truth he sees with an intimate other. Then it is more possible to channel the energies in scientific work, although neither the intimate verbalization nor the sublimation into science is satisfying. For the man knows that he is not doing what is required, and that, indeed, there is no "intelligent" way for him to do so. He is enmeshed in his own intelligence and the trained expediencies and calculation of practical matters. He is a hired man and that he remains and will remain.

The above tripe (?) was written last night when I was tired out. Anyway I'll mail it to you; it may be amusing. I wrote a lot more, and even began a short story, or what might turn out to be one: here is a passage from some of the tripe (not yet socialized very fully):

What happened was that the self distance, and the use of self for objective work which was usual with him, had collapsed. It collapsed and he saw another self for a while. And what he saw was a political man. He had not known before that the well of indignation which had become his basic political feeling was masking such strong political

urges. He associated with the image of this new political man. It led,
like many other things, to Texas A and M and to the first thing he'd
ever printed: a letter of protest against military discipline, signed "A
Freshman." He recalled every word of the letter,[20] saw it in the paper,
saw the anger on the senior officers' faces as they read it. And all this
with pleasure. Then guilt edged its way into the background of the
image. It came in the symbol of the editor of that school paper. And
the editor said, "You should have signed the letter with your own
name. You were doomed anyway."

"How doomed?" the man asked. "Haven't I made it?"

"Listen," said the editor. "You were doomed before you wrote
the letter, and you are doomed even afterwards, because you would
never have written it had you not known that you could and would
sign it 'A Freshman.'"

And so on . . . What (fascinating?) tripe.

I guess I am pretty tired out! The "productivity" of which you
speak is due to the simple fact that I've done nothing else but teach
school and work on the ms. I come to the office every day and have
for the last several weeks come back after supper at night and worked
'til around 12.

I found out today that there is to be no vacation whatsoever here.
I've got to teach right thru the Christmas period, even on Christmas
eve. The history lectures are taking more and more time as we get
into the modern period, and next quarter, beginning sometime in
January, they will take much more. They are such a bore to do.

Anyway I got to take it easier for a few weeks and nurse myself
and read some good novels and such, and maybe write some short
reviews to make some money to pay for subscriptions to magazines,
my lifelines, as all of mine are run out.

I hope to get some nice fat fresh chapters in part two from you
to inspire me to further effort!

O, enclosed find a *New Republic* piece, which I think is really a
fine job. I suppose I like it because it satirizes the kind of "English
criticism" which stuffed shirts like Becker always make.[21]

---

20. Reprinted in part 1 of this volume.
21. A reference to Howard P. Becker.

The translation of Weber was mailed to Macdonald today at noon.

Yours, as always,
Mills

[P.S.] Write me a long letter!

Saul Alinsky— the social activist who eventually wrote well-known books on community organizing—was the executive director of the Industrial Areas Foundation in Chicago in December 1943 when he wrote to Mills, saying that he was interested in Mills's article entitled "The Professional Ideology of Social Pathologists."[22] Alinsky asked Mills for comments on a reprint of one of his own articles, which had appeared in the 1937 Proceedings of the American Prison Association, *and which, in Alinsky's words, had resulted in his "being attacked in the field as a 'radical.'"*

Alinsky's article in the field of criminology had sharply criticized individualistic attempts to explain delinquency, charging that such an approach had instead served as a barrier to understanding human behavior.[23] Alinsky faulted psychoanalysis for an overemphasis on sexuality and a lack of true recognition of the importance of culture, saying that Dr. Freud's viewpoint was limited by its origin in the capitalist class—a limitation Alinsky attributed to modern psychoanalysis in general.

To Saul Alinsky, from Greenbelt, Maryland, dated December 18, 1943

Dear Mr. Alinsky:

It was very good of you to send me the reprint. I enclose a copy of the Journal piece. Why didn't you print the article where people could get at it? You know, not so many [. . .] read the American Prison Association! Had I known about it I certainly would have cited

22. *American Journal of Sociology* 49 (September 1943): 165–80.
23. "The Philosophical Implications of the Individualistic Approach in Criminology," in *Proceedings of the Sixty-seventh Annual Congress of the American Prison Association* (New York: American Prison Association, 1937), 156–71.

it and stolen the beautiful quote from Q, B, & H on p. 164.[24] I am ashamed that I missed that. One point of criticism on that point. I would take the "dis" off disorganization in the last sentence of your paragraph below this quote and in the last line of page 170.[25] Second, I wouldn't want to be so rough as you on Freud! (Altho what you say is mostly true, I think.) But the paper is really very fine and penetrating. You know, what we ought to do is broaden these two papers a little, get a political scientist to go over texts in his field, a historian to do likewise, and we'd have a damned nice little book! I already know a historian, who might do it. Well, maybe after the war. Anyway, altho I haven't examined much of the criminological literature, I believe that you are absolutely correct in what you say.

As far as being attacked as a radical . . . well, you are a radical.[26] "To be radical is to grasp a thing by the root. Now the root of man is man himself." K. Marx. Which is what I always say.

Do you know about Dwight Macdonald's new monthly, *politics*? You'll want to be in on it from the first. His address is 45 Astor Place, New York and the first issue is coming out Feb. first. $2.50 yr. And why not think of writing something for *politics?*

Let me know what is going on in the world from time to time.

Yours,

m.

P.S. Am finishing up a "pop" piece, "The Politics of Truth." I'll try and get a carbon of it to you for criticism before I finally send it to some magazine.

---

24. The conclusion of the quote was that "we cannot conclude that [feeblemindedness] is a 'cause' of crime, since there are five times as many normal persons in this group as there are defectives. *To be consistent we would have to say that normality was the cause of crime!*" (emphasis is Alinsky's). From Queen, Bodenhafer, and Harper, *Social Organization and Disorganization,* 510.

25. Mills was referring to the following sentence by Alinsky: "Not to claim normality as a cause of crime, but to carry their thinking to its consistent, logical conclusion that crime is 'normal' from the point of view of an *expected* product of social disorganization." And, referring to criminology based on cultural determinism, "Crime is viewed as a product of general social disorganization."

26. Alinsky's books, *Reveille for Radicals* and *Rules for Radicals,* were first published in 1946 and 1971, respectively.

Saul Alinsky replied that he was indeed interested in the idea of a book project and suggested that they ask Robert Lynd to be a general editor and to write a lengthy introduction or perhaps a conclusion.[27] (Lynd later became an important ally to Mills during his early years at Columbia.) Mills's reply follows.

To Saul Alinsky, from College Park, Maryland, undated (probably late December 1943 or early 1944)

Dear Saul (let's begin to skip all the crap of titles):

I drew up a tentative chapter outline of STUDIES IN THE SOCIOLOGY OF KNOWLEDGE AND COMMUNICATIONS; you see it has title and all. It runs something like this:

Introduction: by me on "Design for Studies" etc., something I've got about 80 pages on and have been working on for two years off and on: you see, I did my doctors on the sociology of pragmatism.

Part One: five papers, three of them already printed, two to be done on order of content analysis of movies, mass fiction, and so on, including Merle Curti on "the dime novel."

Part Two (these parts are not in this order. I'm at home and the outline is at the office): part two: History. I've got some damned good stuff promised here. A thing on "laissez-faire and democracy, its rise and linkage during the Jacksonian era," by Frank Friedel, good man here at Maryland. "The treatment of the Negro in American history texts" by another good Wisconsin man now here at Maryland, Ken Stampp. Then Hesseltine at Wisconsin, the guy who trained both Frank and Ken on "American History, Southern Style." He will do a bang up job. Writes occasionally for the *Progressive* now. Dick Hofstadter here at Maryland, a Merle Curti man, on "American History, New Style"; locating the post-beard bunch in the first two decades of this century, progressivism and all that.

Then part III: your stuff and mine on criminology and pathologists, and an article on mental hygiene and class structure that K. Davis did for *Psychiatry*. There is a part on psychology but that is still thin.

In philosophy I think of culling Dewey's entire work for a statement of "classical philosophy" and have him recheck it or revise, if

27. Robert Lynd, the sociologist who wrote *Middletown* (1929) with Helen Lynd.

he will, or maybe reprint one of his other essays which make social imputations. Reprint Veblen's swell piece on the intellectual preeminence of the Jew, and have Sterling Brown or E. F. Frazier do one on the Negro intellectual. Have Curti do a summary of his "Ideas of American Educators." What we are weak on is political scientists and economists; and they are just the guys that ought to be done up brown as hell.

Understand please, that I have not approached any of these people and have no publisher as yet, although I think Norton would be the key firm or Harcourt Brace, for they did Mannheim's books and made money on them. The thing is all up in the air, or rather, all on paper as yet.

Please let me know if any ideas or possible contributors pop up in your mind. But let's keep it sorta quiet for a while, for there are at least two bright bastards who might like to steal the idea. Such a book as we have in mind would be a little broader than the two pieces we exchanged. It would lay a basis, in empirical research, for new and fascinating disciplines—sociology of knowledge and sociology of communication—and I think would have some appeal for the upper levels of the trade public.

I wish I could say that I would see you in New York, but the truth is I haven't got any money to go. I had to skip the Sociology meeting for the same reason. If I can sell "Politics of Truth" for any decent money, I plan to make the Easter meetings of the Eastern society.[28] I think I'll do a paper on the white collar strata in [the] US for it; although Lynd hasn't asked me to do it yet. Anyway I'll let you know of all developments on this stuff (also "Politics of Truth").

Enclosed is agenda for POLITICS.

goodbye.
Charlie W.

[P.S.] More on the book plans, which I forgot last night, or was rather too worn out to remember:

Will try to get Lynd to do a chapter on "Ideologies of Middle-

28. We were unable to find a manuscript or a published article by Mills with the title "Politics of Truth," but see his article entitled "The Powerless People: The Role of the Intellectual in Society," *politics* 1, no. 3 (April 1944).

town," suggesting that he break it down into strata, etc. and bring together all the wonderful little insights scattered through the two Middletown books. Also may ask him to do preface and have Columbia Press consider publishing it. You understand it is not set in any way yet, and I can't really go at it until about four months, by which time I hope to have the major part of a comparative and historical social psychology book I'm writing with another guy mostly behind me.

As far as we know there was no further correspondence concerning a possible collaboration between Mills and Alinsky. Alinsky's biographer, Sanford Horwitt, commented, "Nothing more came of this discussion. [. . .] Mills must have realized that Alinsky was not particularly good at developing sociological theories or writing abstract formulations, that he was not a scholar."[29]

In the next letter Mills mentioned Katherine Anne Porter's marital history. Mills and Porter were both Texans who sometimes told stories that dramatized their own lives. Enrique Hank Lopez wrote that Porter's conversation revealed her life as she perceived it, which was "not always the life that was led."[30] To a lesser extent this was also true of Mills's conversation; so when he made statements about Porter's life it is difficult to know where one Texan's exaggeration ends and where another Texan's tall tale begins.

In any case, by the time Mills met Porter, she had been married and divorced four times. She eloped with her first husband when she was sixteen years old.[31] When she was forty-eight, she married her fourth husband, a twenty-six-year-old English professor and the managing editor of the Southern Review.[32]

Born on May 15, 1890, Porter was almost fifty-four years old when the following letter was written. Mills was twenty-seven.

29. *Let Them Call Me Rebel: Saul Alinsky—His Life and Legacy* (New York: Alfred A. Knopf, 1989), 132–33.

30. *Conversations with Katherine Anne Porter: Refugee from Indian Creek* (Boston: Little, Brown, and Company, 1981), xii.

31. Joan Givner, *Katherine Anne Porter: A Life* (New York: Simon and Schuster, 1982), 89. Also Lopez, *Conversations with Katherine Anne Porter*, 31–32.

32. Givner, *Katherine Anne Porter*, 311; and Lopez, *Conversations with Katherine Anne Porter*, 227, 231–32.

To Hans Gerth, from Greenbelt, Maryland, undated (probably
February or March 1944)

Saturday Night

Dear Gerth:

Just a note. First a couple of questions: did you receive from Macdonald the copy of *politics* ? It was understood, at least tacitly, that
both of us were to get free subscriptions for the Weber stuff.[33] But
I did some anonymous stuff in addition for the magazine. I'm not
certain that you got [a] copy. Let me know. I will tell you in a few
days the fate of the translation. [The] first issue of *politics* was, incidentally, disappointing, to me at least. But it will get better. I've a
rather long essay under my own name in the next, second issue.[34]
Please tell me your reactions, sometime, if you should ever write.
But this is not what I wanted to write about.

I read a novel by F. Scott Fitzgerald this afternoon, *The Great
Gatsby,* and it saddened me horribly. It is hard to talk about as a book,
out of the context of my personal reaction, something for conversation and not letters, but there are little lines in it that call up so goddamned much. If you've not read it, try it sometime; only two or
three hours.

I met Katherine Anne Porter the other night. She is utterly charming and so full of little sensitivities and innuendoes (or however you
spell it). Chronologically she is fifty; body: 30; face: lovely early forty
with white hair. Full of "life" (four husbands so far, all much younger
than she!) and full of odd little ideas that make sense only as she says
them, things that fade away when you try to remember them. Little
wisps of fancy. Trying to remember them, you only see her saying
them in that low, husky, Margaret Sullivan kind of voice! Had I time,
money (it would not be expensive) and perhaps the talent, I should
attempt to transfer my heavy load of Oedipus to her. Too late, too late!
Ah! It makes one, as the Japanese say, "know the sadness of things."

---

33. Max Weber, "Class, Status, Party," trans. and ed. Gerth and Mills, *politics* 1, no. 9
(October 1944).
34. This must have been "The Powerless People: The Role of the Intellectual in Society." As it turned out, the essay appeared in the third issue.

But before I get too confessional to a guy who has forgotten me and doesn't write ever, and talk about the dim light of the little towns in Wisconsin blurred by the frost on the train windows as you go by them,[35] I'd better close. I've been reading Lecky, Spencer still, and Lester Ward;[36] engrossed in all of them; also have 20, yes 20 girls in my seminar working on the DAB [*Dictionary of American Biography*] entries, mainly businessmen, bankers etc: Business Elite.

goodbye,
Mills

To Hans Gerth, from Greenbelt, Maryland, undated (probably early spring 1944)

Gerth:

[. . .]

I am at work on chapter six [of *Character and Social Structure*], now weeding the two drafts together. I think your suggestion about breaking up the uniformities of action (convention, law, etc.) and scattering them into institutional orders and social structure discussion is good and am attempting to do this. The stuff on where the role expectations is focused: ends and means, ends, means had better be dropped altogether from chapter six and spliced back into a previous chapter in part one under person etc. As for getting all our eggs together, it is better to have scrambled eggs properly seasoned than over neatly fried in their own juice!

I used to have eggs very often in the little tri-cornered room in the dark Victorian house on Murray Street. Remember? Wine was cheap then, I think about 60 cents a bottle, and I would eat eggs with wine and lots of pepper on the eggs. There was no war and there was no tension that couldn't be provided for rather quickly, and I suppose

35. Compare to "When we pulled out into the winter night and the real snow, our snow, began to stretch out beside us and twinkle against the windows and the dim lights of small Wisconsin stations moved by, a sharp wild brace came suddenly into the air." F. Scott Fitzgerald, *The Great Gatsby* (New York: Charles Scribner's Sons, 1925), 177.

36. W. E. H. Lecky, the Irish historian; Herbert Spencer, the British social philosopher who was often considered one of the first sociologists; and Ward, the American sociologist, botanist, and geologist.

my personal model of freedom is historically located in that era. Eggs and wine and a room of your own and no war. But all the time, outside and all over the world, it was building up to catch up and get us. But I didn't know it except on the hurried surfaces. It wasn't felt, the big hand not my own. It wasn't felt and *not feeling* it was the freedom. Like other good things, it was a fragment of ignorance and of illusion. But that did not make it the less real.

I know it was real because remembering it now, it still seems more solid than most other things. I think maybe it was the only time when I saw a lot of things never seen before or since. True, I worked then, very hard and fast and got stuff done too, but there were other things than work, and work itself was somehow different. Before then there had been unawareness, a vast unawareness, and after that there has been the collapse of all things into work, attempting to remove all tensions and to escape by work. But that was a time when work meant increased and very fresh awareness that was growing and wonderful always and that was before work itself . . . enough!

Forgive me, for these little free associations heaped on you who must have ones of your own, enough and more than enough.

As ever,
M.
Mills

ᕦ

To Hans Gerth, from College Park, Maryland, undated (probably March 1944)

Dear Comrade:

I have been drafted.

I wonder how many guys have begun letters like that! It seems that no "appeal" is possible, for the little card said 1-A and was signed by the appeal board by a vote of four to nothing, although I didn't appeal. Which shows that the appeal stuff is now a fake and appeal and local are collapsed into one unit.

I got the filthy thing this morning, so one doesn't know when the ax will fall. Freya and Pam have made no plans as yet,[37] although I

37. Pamela was then about fourteen months old.

shall try and persuade them to go down on the ranch with Fannye and C G (my mother and father). This is the only place I know where they can live on 80 dollars. I may even drive down there with them during the three weeks which I understand is allowed between exam and final induction. Isn't the word *final* an awful thing? [. . .] maybe I will try being absolutely honest with the psychiatrist. But otherwise there is no way out, I am in.

One feels like Stephen Dedalus at the end of *Portrait of the Artist,* with a few modifications:

> I go forth to recreate the old world, and to forge in the smithy of my soul the created bitterness of their race.[38]

Two fears grip slightly, and they are all I feel so far: 1) about Freya and Pam, especially Pam, and 2) that being in the army God knows how long, perhaps 4 or 5 years, I shall so lose touch with things intellectual, in the many ways in which this is possible, as never to be able to get back into all that I have known so far.

In the meantime there are several weeks at least. The typist I've hired is now finishing up two more chapters [of *Character and Social Structure*]: the "Political Order" and the "Symbol Sphere." The "Political Order" is still very rough, but the "Symbol Sphere" now incorporates the first two drafts with your additions of last year on my manuscript and seems to me to be in fairly good shape. These are the last two I shall do for some time. You'll get copies of them in a few days.

I hope to God they don't get you; let me know how things go.

Yours,
M.
Mills

As the next letter shows, Mills did not stay drafted for long; he was disqualified after his medical exam.

After three years on the teaching staff at the University of Maryland, Mills

38. The original version of this quote from *A Portrait of the Artist as a Young Man* by James Joyce is: "Welcome, O life! I go to encounter for the millionth time the reality of experience and to forge in the smithy of my soul the uncreated conscience of my race" (1916; reprint, New York: Viking Press, 1964), 252–53.

was ready to move on. As part of his job search, he wrote the following letter to one of his former professors at the University of Wisconsin; the letter discusses the genesis of much of his work during the 1950s. (It did not result in a new position, though.)

To Dr. Thomas C. McCormick, from Greenbelt, Maryland, dated July 15, 1944

Dear Dr. McCormick:

I was about to write you a personal letter when Mildred's request for a "personal data sheet" arrived. It has been filled in and is enclosed. Perhaps you will hand it to her.

The other day they examined me for the draft: I'm 4-F, or rather 2A-F, which is a sort of double thing. My pulse and blood pressure are too high. They told me I ticked too fast inside. Afterwards I went to an ordinary physician, who said it was OK, only I really shouldn't try to work 14 hours a day! Well, anyway, now I don't have to worry about child, wife, and self, or so I suppose.

1: Enclosed is a copy of an article, "The American Business Elite," concerning which I would very much like your opinion. Since it is rather heavily statistical—or as you would say in this case, has a lot of counting in it!—I'm not too sure about it. Anyway, I don't want to submit it for publication until you let me know I've made no giant blunders, or straightened me out. You may be interested to know that of the 25 seniors who worked on the project with me for three months, six of them have decided to take M.A.'s with me. Apparently, if you "work them" they ask for more. The difficulty in such matters is keeping your own enthusiasm contagious, and in letting them know that this isn't like a physics experiment, where the instructor knows what you're going to get but is just mean and won't tell you! I'm convinced that seniors and even juniors can do just as well as first year graduate students if you expect it from them and give them the opportunity. Will you let me know your criticism of the essay? Part III is, I think, the best: it concerns what should have been done had the data for it been available!

2: I went to New York last weekend and got $300.00 advance from Prentice-Hall for a book I'm doing on THE WHITE COLLAR MAN:

A Social Psychology of the Salaried Employee in the United States.[39] It's to be a "trade book." I suppose Blumer, who is the college editor for Prentice-Hall, gave me a little buildup; he has been awfully generous with me about such matters. I didn't really want to go into a contract for the book yet, as G [Hans Gerth] and I want to finish some projects, but this university has no money for research or for typists even for me and I had to have a little money for both purposes. I've some six or seven seniors going after interviews this summer in the Washington–Baltimore area . . . on various white collar occupations. Some of the material really does look nice. You may have seen the copy on the Macy saleswomen, which I got from an ex-floorwalker – for ten years—who worked at Baltimore night school with me last year.

3: I suppose Gerth mentioned to you that the Weber translations may be published.[40] I had lunch with the trade editor of the Oxford University Press while I was in New York. If the copyright stuff can be cleared, he'll give us [a] $200.00 advance for final editing of the manuscript. This is, however, a sort of secret, until we know for sure, so please don't mention it.

4: As you will see from the above, and from the enclosed agenda and bibliography, I'm shifting somewhat from articles to books. One just can't get going in an article length piece. I've learned a lot about writing as such in doing these nontechnical essays, but now I'm ready for some larger research projects and book length presentations. Which brings me to a statement and a request:

5: The statement is about my present job: It was very nice when I first took it three years ago. But it is not so good now. Carl Joslyn, one of the finest men I've known, resigned over the unhappy administrative situation and because he had a way out: inherited money. Well, now there is no head and probably won't be. The Business Administration dean—of all people—seems to want to gobble up the department as one aspect of business training! Then sociology would be geared to community and business services, and there would be no sociology as a science. The entire administration is quite badly handled; the men that run it are, well, they're just not very intelligent

---

39. Published with the title *White Collar: The American Middle Classes* (New York: Oxford University Press, 1951).

40. *From Max Weber: Essays in Sociology,* trans., ed., and with an introduction by H. H. Gerth and C. Wright Mills (New York: Oxford University Press, 1946).

men. I work my head off recruiting graduate students and expanding sociology here. I get no raise after three years, during which I've held, and in some instances upped, enrollment in the department despite the sharp decline in total enrollment in the university this past year. There is no money for research, not even for a typist! I taught the Army for four semesters without one cent of pay, and teach all summer—last year and now this one—without any compensation, even though the basic contract of $3,000.00 a year does not include summer session, much less a full summer quarter! And now they mutter about sociology being put under Business Administration. Really it's too much.

6: My request is: If you run into any openings in some university, preferably in the Midwest, which offers some possibilities of a small research budget and a graduate school, will you give me a lead? I don't care much about the money; $3,500 is enough. The rank would probably have to be the one I have, associate, or maybe assistant if the school is big, and there would have to be some assurance about the future, at three or four years, as I have life tenure here. Bob Lynd has given me two good leads, but they were filled before my draft status was clarified and so I lost the opportunity. Something will undoubtedly show up pretty soon, but if I could I'd like to make the shift this September. I'd really appreciate any leads you'd throw my way. Wasn't there something happening at Michigan or Iowa?

Well, I guess that's all for now. Please give my regards to everyone. With best personal regards to yourself.

Cordially,
Mills

To Robert K. Merton, from College Park, Maryland, dated July 26, 1944

Dear Bob:

As you may have heard, the University of Maryland is a sinking ship. Since Joslyn left, matters have deteriorated to such an extent that were the war not under way as an excuse, I do not believe the institution could or should be accredited. I will not bore you with the details, for I am sure these things follow regular patterns, and I am sure that you are acquainted with the pettiness, the inequities, [the] personal despotism and humor of such messes. Anyway, if you run into a decent job, I should appreciate your letting me know about it. I am on the market.

What I really wanted to write you about was the possibility of a job somewhere in New York for a young woman who is completing her B.A. with me this summer. I wanted very badly to get her some sort of fellowship here at Maryland, but due to the situation here, including the fact that Miss Lucille Stein, the girl in question, is of Jewish parentage, she has been turned down for an individual who definitely does not measure up to her qualifications. I really feel that she should be given a chance, as she does not have enough money to finance her own way and is of very pleasing personality as well as intellectual promise. Do you know of any openings within or outside of universities in the New York area for a research assistant?

Cordially,
C. Wright Mills
Associate Professor

In Merton's reply to this letter, he wrote, "When Carl left College Park, I began to suspect that all was very far from being well. However, your note is the first inkling I've had that the University of Maryland should be written off the books, at least for the immediate future."[41]

Robert K. Merton and later Paul Lazarsfeld helped to arrange Mills's employment in New York City: they hired Mills to start work at Columbia University's Bureau of Applied Social Research in April 1945, with temporary summer teaching responsibilities that year at Columbia.

In the next letter Mills refers to Edward Shils, a sociologist who had been helpful to Gerth in the past. (Years later, during the Cold War, when Shils was active with the Congress for Cultural Freedom,[42] he became a harsh critic of Mills.)[43]

Mills also mentions Miss Toda, who was typing and helping edit Gerth and Mills's

41. Letter from Robert K. Merton to Wright Mills, dated August 3, 1944.
42. Letter from Norman Birnbaum to K. Mills, dated August 13, 1998.
43. See E. P. Thompson's analysis of Shils's vehement criticism of Mills in E. P. Thompson, "Remembering C. Wright Mills," in *The Heavy Dancers* (London: Merlin Press, 1985), 269–70.

drafts of translations from Max Weber's work; Honey Toda had been in an American internment camp for Japanese people until Mills arranged to have her released and employed on his projects. (We do not know the specific process involved or which other people or organizations may have been instrumental in obtaining her release.) Later she worked on other projects for Mills, doing statistical research and tabulations.

To Hans Gerth, from Greenbelt, Maryland, undated (probably October 1944)

Dear Gerth:

I am about thru the "Science as a Vocation" and want to give you the following reactions by way of "appreciation." It is true that this translation, in being closer to the German, is in English clumsier than is Shils's. But precisely for this reason, I honestly think it is a better job. I notice in comparing them, and remembering the "texture" of other, more closely literal translations from Weber, the little idiosyncrasies which are retained in this draft. I have deliberately tried to retain them within the limits of clarity and grammar. In the last passages, I think you tried to get a sort of biblical flair into it, or rather bring that out, and I have tried to follow this lead even more, here and there (for instance, with the use of sentences beginning with "And"—short sentences like that after a cascade). After all, one could "translate" W into *New Republic* style, or even *New Yorker* style (has not Mr. Lasswell done so?), but we should honor neither Weber nor ourselves by doing it that way. I like it a little clumsy here and there. Maybe W didn't etch so much as block out in charcoal; and in any event it looks better in English if one doesn't use too fine an acid.

I write this because I detected a slight "worry" in your last letter about this piece and the fact that we had a draft of Shils's. Incidentally, I first went thru it without looking at Shils's, and then compared the two. I found in several places I had shifted stuff to where it looked like adaptations from, or the same as, Shils's. These I have changed back more like they were or done them in a third way. I do not think we need have any worry about accusations, simply because they are neither true nor do they appear to be true.

Miss Toda is doing India now. Then she will get on "Science as Vocation." I haven't received all the China stuff yet. The China stuff worries me. The literati sections I've received do repeat things said more generally in the little fragment on the empire (I've already done it and it's typed in penultimate form). But let's wait for all the China and see how they look arranged and typed in sequence.[44]

Yours,
W.
Mills

[P.S.] Later at school: I got your letter. Thanks.

ॳ

To Hans Gerth, from Greenbelt, Maryland, undated (probably the first week of November 1944)

Dear Gerth:

Thursday evening. I have just received the communication about Shils, and his reaction to the piece in *politics*.[45] Forgive me if I am pedantic in this letter, but it is just my "German" way! Now let us review the case.

First, tho', let me say that I stand with you to the end in the matter, because no matter what you have seen of Shils I know that the translations now being typed up and to be published are fresh translations; they could not be otherwise because they have my ugly paw on every line of them so far as stylistic and linguistic stuff goes. Second, there is no need whatsoever to have any guilt feelings about anything that has happened or about anything that can happen because of the simple truth that we are in no way guilty of doing anything dishonorable. Now what does Shils say in this letter; he says two things:

1. He expresses a hurt that anybody else is doing anything with Weber in English. He feels, in this connection, that you are indebted to him; that is why he mentioned his getting the Nazi party articles in shape for publication (you are aware that he went out of his way to tell me what a mess it was in until he fixed it up . . . here in Washington, I think the first year he was here). Now he knows that he has no rational case here. Thus all he feels entitled to ask is that you tell

44. In a letter dated October 2, 1944, Gerth wrote that he had finished the first draft of a translation of a chapter on China that dealt with the literati, and that he was sure Mills would like it.

45. Weber, "Class, Status, and Party."

him what is to be included in our edition "so that we can avoid over-lapping." He does not reproach you for getting out an edition directly. Now what are the consequences possible from this feeling on his part that we've done him dirt? Nothing, except that it will motivate his doing anything which has a seemingly objective basis to discredit or wreck our project. Thus, he did not comment on any resemblance which he says he saw in the mimeograph edition of "Class, Status, and Party" at the time; nor does he accuse us of any such trick with reference to what we have printed. But when we have printed a translation, he then accuses us of copying a draft he made in our mimeographed editions! You may be sure that, had he seen any real grounds for accusing us of cheating in the printed translation, he would have done so, rather than refer back to some mimeographed edition. So, this feeling that he has been done dirt will and can lead to nothing in itself; it can and will operate as a motive for his search for some objective basis for some accusation.

2. I do not know enough of your relations with Shils to judge his sentimental claim that you've done him dirt. (I say "you" here rather than "us," because I don't really know Shils and certainly feel no ties or bonds of any sort with him as a person. And secondly, [neither] he nor any agent of his has ever publicized the fact of his doing a translation. As long as he has not done so, and your letters from his colleagues don't even mention it but even debunk the idea of doing translations . . . why, I am in no way bound, nor are you on any objective basis of professional ethics.) As I said, I don't know enough of your relations with Shils to judge his sentimental claims that you've done him dirt. But I know enough about you and I can (unfortunately) see from your letter to him that you feel guilty. Now, Gerth, that is your affair, and I wish I could talk with you about it, but the step has been taken and now you have to stand up to the consequences. Surely you knew that a lot of guys, Shils and Parsons especially, were not going to wire congratulations upon hearing that we got out an edition of Weber. As long as our work has been honest, as it has, I frankly think your letter to Shils was entirely too "apologetic." You have got to show a little brass. No matter what one might feel in his innermost, we are working under certain conditions in US universities, and there is an intellectual market with competitive features. Your job situation is affected by getting out the Weber and upon that stand certain obligations to wife and child, etc. Therefore, I urge you

to take a stronger stand, with more indignation in it. Not only is that indignation based on appropriate feelings, but it is necessary because of the reactions which one may expect from others if you don't.

Well, what is to be done?

1. We go ahead of course on the Weber and we go ahead fast. Goddamnit, I have been trying to pressure you into speed. Please don't spend so much time with the first two introductory chapters. As they stood when I mailed the drafts to you, they were quite neat. Today I mailed you the "Science as a Profession." Check it again against the Shils, which I also returned. Go ahead and get it typed along with all the rest and then I will travel to New York and deliver the manuscript to Hatcher.[46]

2. I will feel (gently) out what, if anything, Hatcher has heard of slander. I will of course mention nothing, but I will say that this stuff ought to be published NOW because we know it is a competitive situation and if he wants to sell he's got to print, etc. I'll do it gently, but firmly. I have found out by experience that Hatcher only reacts to personal appearances, not to letters. So in spite of the money, I'll have to go and see him and pressure him.

3. In the morning I will write a draft of a letter to Shils. I will enclose it with this letter. You check and send it back airmail, pronto as hell, and I'll get it off to him.

What we do not do:

1. In no way do we act guilty, Goddamnit, nor especially apologetic. We have done nothing wrong. Forget mimeographs: what matters and only what matters is printed materials.

2. We do not show anything to anybody. To do so is only to display guilt. What they see is what's printed and nothing else and not until then. Communicate, by phone if necessary, any new developments which either of us hear.

Now let me read the letters again. Note, additional on Shils letter: for his damn secrecy, he too has to stand the consequences. He had plenty of chances with you, with the public, and even the two or three times he has seen me, to publicize the fact of his translations in detail. He did not do so. I personally have never made any secret to anybody about our doing translations and it has been announced

---

46. H. T. Hatcher, their editor at Oxford University Press.

in *politics* for six months or so and I believe even in *politics* ads in the *New Republic*. All of this Goddamned secrecy and neurosis coldness. OK. Now the consequences. I'm sorry if that hurts anybody. I am mailing the copy of typewritten stuff which you lent me; it has no name on it as to translator. It contains the original copy of "Classes and Status Groups," which we retranslated and then mimeographed. It also contains a fragment of "Class, Status, Party." Frankly, I had not even read that. The thing in *politics* was the first thing we did together and I well remember the hell it was; Freya must have typed 5 drafts of it. This folder contains everything of Shils which I have ever seen with the exception of "Science as a Profession"; and I think, I am not sure, that Becker loaned me for one night "Politics as a Profession" or something which I do not remember reading before he asked for it back.

Concerning the "Status Groups and Classes," the last chapter in part one: Do not under any conditions admit anything. It is not necessary. Send Shils, if he insists, the stuff that is going into the book: the complete redrafting which I did, and which you checked and had typed, of this chapter (you have a carbon copy). Destroy all mimeographs of this anyway.

After rereading your letter to Shils, I take back the comment above. It seems to me quite nice and decent. But you must know that nothing, nothing, nothing you can ever do will make him hate you less. You may as well realize that and get along in the world without his friendship. Too bad, but inevitable. If he writes again and asks for this or that, no matter what it is, the tone of your letter ought to be something like: "Listen, Shils, I wrote you that I was sorry about this tangle and I am, but what's done is done. And your secrecy is as much responsible for it as anything else. I am, frankly, becoming angry at your intimation that I or Mills would copy or lean upon any translation which you have done and cause such things to be printed under our name. If you do not know me better than that, you are less perceptive than I have always thought. If upon reading our translations in print you feel anything underhanded has been done, then you should bring the matter to the attention of the public. I do not fear this in the least because I will print nothing but the work which I have done or my coauthors have done. Again, I am sorry that you feel as you do. Yours truly." Something like that. Shift the discussion always to published materials because that is what matters so far as [the] reputation of Shils or of you or of me is concerned and is the only legitimate grounds for any kick.

Now let us get on with our work.

As ever,
M.
[. . .]

[P.S.] I am very tempted to phone you tonight and let you know I don't feel there is anything to worry about. But I'll airmail this to you. Take it easy. Everything's going to be all right.[47]

Anyway, I'm mad at you. You don't tell me you're glad about my clinching the Columbia job for next summer! But I know this thing has upset you.

O, listen Gerth, forgive the tone of my last letter about the Christmas meeting paper. I realize now that you didn't know the implications of whatever you wrote La Pierre. I can't back out; I've already done that once after my name was on a program. And it will help you at Wisconsin, too. So we'll do it definitely. I will come to Madison as soon as I can before the Christmas meeting and we'll get a few days to polish it, but we've got to write it now. I'll write a first draft if you'll okay my suggestions in last letter and indicate some outline if you want, stuff you think ought to be in it. Let's not make any footnotes at all. Just write out how it is in this matter! We'll fix it up slick in my new style I'm working on (I've been practicing) and read it in a forceful clear way. We'll make a big show at Chicago, Gerth. Honest.

Come on, smoke a pipe, have a drink, get a good night's sleep and think how really bad off we could all be. This is America, so smile. And be happy.[48]

Freya comes home this Saturday. She sent me your letters to her, and I have been thinking. I'm gonna be good. She's a wonderful girl, I know that, always known that. Gonna be good to her.

A fool gave me 25 dollars for working over a draft of a speech (Democratic); local stuff, and I bought all, every single one of Veblen's works! They *are* fine. They sit here a bequest and a challenge. I feel like Whitman said:

---

47. *From Max Weber: Essays in Sociology* is still in print more than fifty years after publication.

48. Gerth, a German of Christian background, had immigrated to the United States in 1938.

Beginning my studies the first step pleased me so much,
The mere fact consciousness, these forms, the power of motion,
The least insect or animal, the sense, eyesight, love,
The first step I say awed me and pleased me so much,
I have hardly gone and hardly wished to go any farther,
But stop and loiter all the time to sing it in ecstatic songs.

After we get thru with these ten tons of work we've got to do, I'm
gonna quit science and all that and write a novel. You don't believe
that H I ? You wait. I sent an outline of the plot to Felice Swados[49]
and she says it'll do. The setting is in San Antonio. But you don't
want to hear about that and I am too drunk now on this Navy stuff
to tell it right.

One more point before I go to bed. Lasswell phoned me up after
our meeting the other night; phoned me two days later and told me
he really meant it about the Guggenheim and to go ahead and apply.
So I sent for an application and have now drafted out a project. Next
Monday I'm to have him look it over and then mail it off. Now, I
do not believe I'll get it. Somebody will bitch me and besides I don't
deserve one yet. But IF I should get it, it will mean this: the project
is under the title of white collar man, cause that project is solely my
own, but practically it will mean this: I'll spend six months with Ernst
Kris and the New York Institute of Psychoanalysis. Then I'll spend
the last six months in and between Madison and New York and we'll
do some more work on something.

I've played up Perlman as my key teacher at Madison, saying,
"He knows what there is to know of my work at the University of
Wisconsin." I hope he doesn't get scared by the psychiatric dimension
of the project, a copy of which they'll send him, and bitch me. Maybe
he won't. I don't believe I can get it, but who knows. Well, we'll
know next April or so. Blumer, Lynd, Lasswell, Perlman, Gentry,
Joslyn, are my recommenders.[50]

goodnight,
M.

---

49. Harvey Swados's sister, who was a novelist married to Richard Hofstadter.
50. The full names and affiliations as listed in the application were: Herbert Blumer (professor of sociology, University of Chicago), Robert S. Lynd (professor of sociology, Colum-

Mills's doubts about Selig Perlman's response were not borne out; in fact Perlman's recommendation was strongly positive and prophetic in its identification of Mills's potential. Perlman wrote, "I consider Mr. Mills one of the most promising young sociologists and students of social movements. He is intellectually venturesome and not likely to be one of the 'herd,' whether of the cultists of 'objective' or 'scientific' sociology or the conversational radical variety. He permits his mind to 'play' over the material, but his native shrewdness will guard him from hatching a whimsy of his own."

In Mills's application for the Guggenheim grant, he responded to a question about his accomplishments and principal teachers with the following discussion of his intellectual development.

To the John Simon Guggenheim Memorial Foundation, from College Park, Maryland, dated November 7, 1944

RESEARCH EXPERIENCE AND TRAINING

My work has been concerned with the social sciences and philosophy. I have not been able to stay in any one social science and have done more reading cross-field than within the subject I happen to teach. Indeed, I have never had occasion to take very seriously much of American sociology as such; in a paper, *American Journal of Sociology,* September 1943, I have systematically criticized what I take to be its central tradition. In sociology my main impulse has been taken from German developments, especially the traditions stemming from Max Weber and, to a lesser degree, Karl Mannheim. Since beginning an independent teaching career I have developed courses and supervised graduate research in the following fields:

orientation in the social sciences
sociology of knowledge
sociology of communication
social stratification
sociology of occupations and professions

bia University), Harold D. Lasswell (consultant, war communications research, Library of Congress; Institute of International Studies, Yale University), Selig Perlman (professor of economics, University of Wisconsin), G. V. Gentry (professor of philosophy, University of Texas at Austin), and Carl S. Joslyn (independent research, Worthington, Massachusetts; formerly professor of sociology, University of Maryland at College Park).

design of investigation in social science
social psychology

In terms of "specialties," such "contributions" as I have made are primarily in the sociology of knowledge, a borderline field of philosophy, psychology, and social science, concerned with the social bases of intellectual and cultural life. Articles documenting this line of reflection have appeared in the *American Sociological Review,* October 1939, and the *American Journal of Sociology,* November 1940 and September 1943.

During the last two years I have experimented with essays for the journals of opinion and various "little magazines." This I have done out of interest in the topics discussed, and even more because I wished to rid myself of a crippling academic prose and to develop an intelligible way of communicating modern social science to nonspecialized publics.

My formal training at the University of Texas was primarily in American philosophy and modern logic. I took an M.A. degree in these fields. The men with whose work I spent my time at Texas were the pragmatists, especially Charles S. Pierce and G. H. Mead. My key teacher was George V. Gentry, a student of Mead's. He was my first real intellectual stimulus, and he knows what there is to know of my work at Texas. The second man who was decisive for me at Texas was Clarence E. Ayres, with whom I studied the work of Thorstein Veblen, as well as general economic theory and history.

The only teacher at the University of Wisconsin who was decisive for me was Selig Perlman, with whom I studied institutional and labor economics. He knows of all my work in Madison. I was examined for the Ph.D. in economics, philosophy, and anthropology, as well as the several fields of sociology, especially theory, social psychology, and the history of social thought. My doctorate thesis was entitled "A Sociological Account of Pragmatism: An Essay on the Sociology of Knowledge."

At Wisconsin I came in contact with Hans Gerth, who had been Karl Mannheim's assistant in Germany. We have become research colleagues and collaborators, and through him I have come into what I think is a live and fruitful contact with German sociology and philosophy.

In one way or another, I have been decisively influenced by the six men whom I have listed as "references." I believe them to be in a position to judge such "promise" as my "accomplishments" to date may suggest, the worth of my project to the social sciences and philosophy, and my ability to realize it.

On April 8, 1945, the Guggenheim Foundation notified Mills that he would receive a grant of $2,500 to fund research during the calendar year of 1946; his manuscript in progress was published as White Collar *in 1951.*

To Frances and Charles Grover Mills, from Greenbelt, Maryland, dated December 22, 1944

Dear Mother and Dad:

First let me thank you very much for the lovely tie. It is really a honey and I've worn it almost every day since I got it. Freya won't open hers [her present] until Christmas! She'll write later. The other day I got you a year's subscription to a magazine called POLITICS. It is quite left-wing and very stimulating. A very good guide to what is going on in the world. I am sorry as hell that we can't give you all something really nice but God everything is so high, I mean living expenses, we just exist.

About the only thing happening to me is still work, work, and more work. I am writing all the time, trying to get these books thru. I believe that I've already told you that I have delivered a book Gerth and I did to Oxford Press, it ought to be manufactured by next Sept. at the latest.[51]

Last week I went up the Hudson River from New York City about 100 miles to see a little school called Bard College. They have offered me a job at $4,000 a year, and they paid for my trip to be interviewed, etc. Despite the increase in pay, I have about decided that I won't take it. You see, the college is like a country club, out in the beautiful woods, but there is no research library there and it takes too long to get to New York; also it is very exclusive (it costs a student about $2,200 a year to go to school there: they only allow 200 students), and I don't like exclusiveness. Why should I waste my time pampering the sons and daughters of plutocrats? To hell with them.

---

51. *From Max Weber: Essays in Sociology* was published in 1946.

I'll wait a while here until I get what I want. What I want is either a big state university in the midwest, or a place in New York City, or the west coast, preferable near San Francisco. If I hang on it'll come in time.

Freya has written you that I am invited to teach two graduate seminars lectures at Columbia University this next summer session for 6 weeks. I get 100 a week for the job and of course a hell of a lot of prestige. I am probably the youngest guy ever to act as associate professor in Columbia.[52] It is of course one of the three biggest schools in the U.S. So I haven't quite gotten over it yet.

I bought a model airplane kit the other day and I am making a little model plane (40 inch wingspread) in order to relax at night. I am also trying to read a little bit of Henry James. All his novels are wonderful.

Pamela and Freya are both well.

My friend, poor Dick Hofstadter's wife [Felice Swados], is dying slowly of cancer. [. . .] Dick is in Buffalo, NY, with her. Poor girl: she had finished one novel and was on another, a very talented and lovely creature.[53]

Please know that even tho I don't write often, I think of you both often, that I am well and fairly content in this lousy damn blood-bath of a world. Take care of yourselves.

Yours as ever, with love,
MILLS

Felice Swados and Richard Hofstadter were born in Buffalo, New York, and married when they were at the University of Buffalo (now State University of New York at Buffalo). Hofstadter took a leave of absence from his post at the University of Maryland and spent the academic year 1944–45 caring for Felice and their one-year-old son, Dan, in Buffalo, at Felice's parents' home.[54] Felice died there on July 21, 1945, at the age of twenty-nine.

52. "It's a hell of a big break for a kid 28 years old. The average age of associate professors is 45," Mills wrote in another letter to his parents (undated).

53. *House of Fury* (New York: Doubleday Doran, 1941), which was reprinted as *Reform School Girl* (New York: Avon Diversity Romance Novel edition, 1948) and made into a movie.

54. Dan Hofstadter is the author of several books, including *Temperaments: Artists Facing Their Work* (New York: Knopf, 1992), *Goldberg's Angel: An Adventure in the Antiquities*

In 1947, the young father married Beatrice Kevitt, and they remained together until his death in 1970.[55] *Richard and Beatrice K. Hofstadter had a daughter named Sarah Katherine.*

To Frances and Charles Grover Mills, from Greenbelt, Maryland, dated January 1945, Sunday evening

Dear Mother and Dad:

Thanks a lot for the can of chile; I ate it with great gusto; and it was mighty fine. Very soon, I shall be somewhere which has genuine Mexican restaurants; we are moving to New York City within four months.

Yes, I have accepted a job in New York, right in the middle of Manhattan Island, at $5,000 a year plus $800 extra for this next year for teaching during the summer session. I am to be a Research Associate at Columbia University. That is, I won't teach but will just *do research all the time!* In the next ten months I will be in complete charge of a research budget of $25,000 for a research job on opinion leaders in a midwestern city, probably Cedar Rapids. I will stay in New York, of course, with only a trip or two out there (expenses paid) to set up the fieldwork and to check on my staff from time to time. This is the offer they made to me yesterday in NY and the chances are that I will take it. However, I am anticipating another offer from Yale, which should pay about the same amount; since I don't know the details of the Yale job yet, I am stalling the decision at Columbia. But I think now it will be Columbia. That is what I've been waiting on and this is it. Within ten days the decision will be made. I shall stay at Md. until the end of this quarter—that would be April first—but would run to New York for one day a week, beginning around February first. I'll have a staff of around 15 interviewers

---

Trade (New York: Farrar, Straus, and Giroux, 1994), and *The Love Affair as a Work of Art* (New York: Farrar, Straus, and Giroux, 1996).

55. Beatrice Kevitt was an editor who worked on several books by Hofstadter, three books by Mills (*New Men of Power, The Puerto Rican Journey,* and *White Collar*), and later four books by Theodore H. White, whom she married in 1974. See also *Great Issues in American History: From Reconstruction to the Present Day, 1864–1981,* ed. Richard Hofstadter and Beatrice K. Hofstadter, rev. ed. (New York: Random House Vintage Books, 1982).

in the field and two M.A.'s for office assistants and one stenographer. Also a Dictaphone, which I've needed for some time.

It was great fun talking to these guys [Robert K. Merton and Paul Lazarsfeld]. I had no idea what they wanted to pay, but they started throwing money around, spent $20 on a dinner for three of us,[56] and all that. After they had laid out the job and said: "Well, that's it; we want you. Will you come?" I said (holding myself in with bursting joy at the whole idea; Christ I'd go for food and shelter) anyway I kept the face immobile and just said, "For how much?" They wouldn't say, but replied, "You know what you're worth, name it." To which little Charlie said very quietly, "I won't charge you that much, but I couldn't think of it in terms less than $4,500." Immediately the guy said, "Then your beginning salary will be $5,000," to which the appropriate reply was: "That is closer to what I'm worth." And everybody laughed and felt good. (My salary at Maryland is still just $3,000.)

After this $20 meal, we broke up and I went up Fifth Avenue and cut across to Times Square and wandered into a restaurant and ate another huge meal! I didn't realize what I was doing until I was half through with it. It cost me three bucks, but it was worth it.

Well, you see the good blood and bones and brash you all put into me began to come through a little. Incidentally, Columbia's research office is doing a lot of war and direct Army research,[57] so it's absolutely as near draft proof as anything in the US today.

Yours in appreciation of good early training and heritage.
Your son,
M.
Charlie M.

[P.S.] The January issue of "politics" has a wonderful cover picture.[58] I met the Italian boy who made it last night.

---

56. In 1945 this was a very expensive meal.

57. The Bureau of Applied Social Research

58. The cover picture was a collage of newspaper clippings in the shape of a Trojan horse, with headlines such as "Britain: Tanks Fire on Greek Leftists," "Spitfires Strafe Leftists in Athens," "Freedom of Speech," "Freedom from Fear," and "Freedom from Want."

When Oxford University Press announced publication of From Max Weber, *the credit in their catalog listed Mills's name before Gerth's. Needless to say, this upset Gerth. Mills wrote to their editor at Oxford, H. T. Hatcher, on February 5, 1945, asking him to correct the order of their names in all future releases concerning the book. Unfortunately, Meyer Schapiro subsequently made the same mistake and listed Mills's name first when—in an essay in* politics—*he responded to the publication of Gerth and Mills's translation of Weber's "Class, Status, and Party" and the accompanying note on Weber. The issue of credit was a sore point, especially since Gerth had wanted to have sole credit for the long introduction in* From Max Weber; *Mills had insisted that the introduction represented the thoughts and efforts of both of them and that his own contribution was more than simply writing and organizing what Gerth had to say. Gerth, whose first language was German, had translated the Weber essays into rough English, and Mills had edited the English versions, consulting Gerth in order to assure continued accuracy.*

In Schapiro's essay for politics *he took issue with the notion that Weber was a prophetic political thinker, stating that Weber feared the left and was drawn to nationalist and strong leaders. Schapiro wrote that if Weber had lived after 1920, "it would have been a cruel dilemma for him whether to accept or reject the man who was re-establishing German power and preparing for a war against the national enemy."[59] In the context of the assassination of Liebknecht, Schapiro stated that "like many others who support the violence of the state against the working-class, Weber laid the responsibility on the victims."[60]*

To Hans Gerth, from Greenbelt, Maryland, dated February 7 (1945), P.M.

Dear Gerth:

Enclosed are advance proof sheets of Schapiro's essay on Weber, which is to be published in *politics,* presumably in the next issue. You will note that Schapiro has, good God, mixed up the order of our names. I have therefore just written a card to Macdonald telling him to correct the matter. This I cannot understand at all, in view of the fact that the translation as printed in *politics* clearly reads, "Gerth and Mills." However, the deadline for the issue is Feb. 15th, so I think we have no need to fear that it will not be corrected. [. . .]

59. "A Note on Max Weber's Politics," *politics* 2 no. 2 (February 1945): 44.
60. Schapiro, "Note on Max Weber's Politics," 47.

I am sorry Gerth, but *I* have nothing to do with this; I have never even seen Schapiro, and the piece in *politics* was, of course, in the correct order. I don't know what I can say beyond that, except that I am very sorry that such an erroneous impression should recur. As you see, I am prompt to correct it.

Now, my suggestion on how to handle the Schapiro essay is this: We need not and must not appear to "champion" Weber, and we cannot write a full length essay for *politics,* as we have the Oxford Press to think of and the success of our book. Therefore the question is: how can we "defend" ourselves from the thing insofar as it is an attack upon WHAT WE HAVE PUBLISHED ABOUT WEBER? The answer, so far as my spot reaction goes, after only two readings of Schapiro's proofs, is: concentrate on just two points and then refer the readers of *politics* to the forthcoming book in which these issues are more fully discussed. Above all, I see *no need* to appear to "fight" with Schapiro. Enclosed therefore please find a rough draft of about one-half or one-third of the "reply." The deadline on the issue is February 15th. We probably can't make that. So, unfortunately, the comeback will have to appear in the issue after the Schapiro piece. Nevertheless, please get back to me as soon as is possible [with] your reaction and emendations and additions to the note I began here.

Finally, Gerth, let me say flatly to you, in view of the recurrence of the mix-up in the order of our names, that I am most sincerely in full and intimate agreement that you are the senior author in all that we have done with Max Weber,[61] that I am not only content, internally and externally, with being the junior author of the book, but am most grateful to have had the chance to learn what I have of Max Weber while acting as the junior author in collaboration with you. There is really nothing else I can say; but you may be sure that I shall jump to the correction in print and in conversation whenever the occasion to do so arises.

Yours as ever,
Mills

   [P.S. . . .]

---

61. They worked on *From Max Weber* over a period of five years.

"Max Weber's Politics—a Rejoinder," by H. H. Gerth, was published in the April issue of politics. *In response to Schapiro's comment that Max Weber may have had difficulty deciding whether to support or oppose Hitler, Gerth's rejoinder said, "If we may playfully venture a retrospective prediction about Schapiro's assumed 'cruel dilemma,' we feel Max Weber in 1933 might rather have become a colleague of Schapiro's than a Hitlerite." The rejoinder discussed Weber's responses to the politics of his time and ended with this conclusion: "Today Weber may well furnish any party of freedom 'with a mass of valuable material,' as the late Nikolai Bukharin has put it. May the reader of our forthcoming volume of translations judge for himself."[62]*

In February of 1945, Mills took on a new project on the topic of small businesses versus big businesses and their respective effects on civic welfare. The Smaller War Plants Corporation was apparently interested in showing the superiority of small businesses in order to fight the trend toward increased economic concentration,[63] and they wanted Mills to do the research.

To Hans Gerth, from Greenbelt, Maryland, undated (probably February 1945)

10 P.M. Good God! The telephone just rang and it was a guy in the Smaller War Plants Corporation, headed by Maury Maverick. He said (I'm so god damned excited I can hardly write!) two or three guys had recommended me and he wanted me to do a special job for a Senate hearing. To do the study and then appear as an "expert" before the committee hearing on setting up a small business agency on a permanent basis. The hearing will be sometime in April. I'm to see him this Saturday, and if I can, to start work next Monday or Tuesday. Here's what they want: a man to integrate and supervise a spot study on four or five small towns: these towns to be selected with the help of the Census boys in various parts of the US, ranked according to whether small businesses with the owners living there predominate or whether "central office groups" of outside corporations dominate the towns, industry and retail trade. The job is to get hold of the differences between communities characterized by those two general types of industry and business. The time is so short that all they want is the basic

62. *politics* 2, no. 4 (April 1945): 119–20.
63. Gillam, "C. Wright Mills," 261.

(census) stuff on the towns, which a staff will gather under the director's direction, and then interview stuff with leading guys of the town,
including the heads of all the government agencies located nearby: in
short a kind of super journalism: *Fortune* article–level stuff. He wanted
a guy who could write and claimed that I could. Harry Elmer Barnes
recommended me, and apparently Maury Maverick (who is from
Texas!) had heard about me, had read some stuff, etc. Well, Maury
Maverick is to call Pres Boyd of Md Univ on the phone, cold like, and
ask that I be given time off to do this special job. Then I work three
weeks or so around Washington, conferring and selecting the towns
and getting the basic stuff together insofar as it is in print; then by
airplane with A-I senatorial priority (good God) rush around the
United States of America writing and talking with guys in these towns.
For this sheer pleasure and learning *they* pay *me*. On a per diem basis:
10 to 15 dollars a day plus all first class expenses, which means an extra
10 a day rake off, or so the guy says. After that I write the stuff up in
30 or 60 pages; it is printed in the hearing stuff, and then I am cross-
examined as an expert on "the sociology of small business," the only
one of his kind: found in a wild onion patch forty miles from sea and
forty miles from land. It is really amusing, when you think of it, or
even more amusing when you don't think of it. You mustn't think of it
very much or very long; you have got to just go ahead and do it. Please
forgive my enthusiasm; but I had to get over it before I go thru the files
at the office on small business. I think I've got some stuff there.

Good night.
As ever,
Mills

PS: After a very careful study I have just discovered that one of
the towns is bound to be in Wisconsin very near Madison. See you
soon. And thanks for helping me make up my mind in this letter!

*Taking a leave of absence from the University of Maryland, Mills moved to New York
City in early 1945, with Freya and Pamela joining him a few weeks later. At the
time, Daniel Bell and Mills were still on friendly terms, and Bell helped the Millses
obtain an apartment on East 11th Street in the same building in which the Bells resided.*

*Soon afterward, Mills went on the research trip he discussed in the previous letter
to Gerth.*

To Frances and Charles Grover Mills, from "Washington Airport,
1:10 A.M., Wed.," undated (probably March 1945)

I flew in from Boston this morning, having spent almost one
week in New England, mostly in New Hampshire (a lovely state).
I'm now waiting for a flight to Atlanta, GA. I'll spend 2 or 3 days
there and in Birmingham, and then fly across to Los Angeles. I'll
probably have a stop over in Dallas. Maybe an hour, maybe two, not
longer, and I won't know how long or on what date. Depends upon
time of success in Atlanta and on connections. On airlines today,
you've got to take your chances, and even tho' I've got a senatorial
priority, generals and admirals outrank me!

From Los Angeles, I fly to Butte, Montana; then to Michigan—
several towns there, and then on in to Washington. I've got to get
back here before March 28th.

I tried to select a town near San Antonio as one of my stops,
but it didn't come out that way. If I get a stop over in Dallas, I'll ring
Ursula,[64] and also will ring you in San Antonio. But I can't say when
it'll be.

My work is fascinating and I'm learning a lot—talking with
police chiefs, sociologists, Chamber of Commerce secretaries, labor
leaders, preachers, etc. I'm all things to all men, but Irish to most.
And I'm getting the information the Senate wants. I eat enormous
meals and sometimes 5 a day, and sleep 4 or 5 hours. I feel well and
all alert and keyed up.

Stopped by to see Freya and Pam in NYC last night (4 A.M.–
5:20 A.M.!). They are doing well. And they had good news: my draft
board has permitted me to accept the Columbia University job, which
begins April 1st. Of course I'd already moved there, but I was worried. I guess this Senate thing impressed them somewhat. Like I told
you 3 years ago. I'll sit this one out. It's a goddamned bloodbath to
no end save misery and *mutual* death to *all* civilized values.

Got to go now.
Good-bye.
Your son,
Charlie M.

64. Mills's only sibling.

IV

TAKING IT BIG
New York, New York, 1945–1956

When you're involved in a job of writing,
to do it well you have to live it: the notes
you take on books you read, the meanings
you are aware of in events, even how the
street scene looks to you.

> C. Wright Mills, letter to
> Dwight Macdonald, dated Saturday,
> November 20, 1948

Almost any advice he gave ended with the
exhortation, "Take it big, boy!"

> Dan Wakefield, "Taking It Big:
> A Memoir of C. Wright Mills,"
> *Atlantic Monthly,* September 1971

Mills had begun to become acquainted with the radical intellectual milieu of New York City through his writing for the New Leader and politics while he was still in Maryland. After his arrival in New York, Mills's projects for Columbia University's Bureau of Applied Social Research helped provide him with some of the research materials and skills needed to work on his trilogy on American society. The Bureau subsidized much of the research for Mills's book on labor leaders, New Men of Power (1948), and backed some of the interviewing needed for White Collar (1951). Also, his affiliation with Columbia provided a good platform from which to address the public. As Jamison and Eyerman point out, "Mills was in the unique position of being an outsider social critic armed with insider skills and information." [1] Mills's third book on American society, The Power Elite (1956), added the title phrase to the American vocabulary.

At Columbia Mills also continued to write articles. Noteworthy examples from the early 1950s include "A Diagnosis of Our Moral Uneasiness" published in the New York Times Magazine (November 23, 1952) and "The Conservative Mood" in Dissent (winter 1954).

He continued to see some of the same friends despite his move to New York. Two close friends whom Mills had met in Maryland—Harvey Swados and Dick Hofstadter—settled in the New York area in 1946. Hofstadter left the University of Maryland to take a job at Columbia University. Swados, returning from a few years with the merchant marines and beginning his career as a writer, got married and settled in nearby Rockland County. Mills also kept in touch with his old friend in Wisconsin, Hans Gerth. They would finish their second collaboration several years after Mills arrived in the big city: Character and Social Structure: The Psychology of Social Institutions was published in 1953.

Judging from a letter Gerth wrote March 10, 1945, he was still smarting from the fact that Oxford University Press and politics had both mistakenly given Mills top

---

1. Andrew Jamison and Ron Eyerman, *Seeds of the Sixties* (Berkeley and Los Angeles: University of California Press, 1994), 37.

billing in credit lines for From Max Weber. *To make matters worse, Gerth's posi-tion at the University of Wisconsin was uncertain. In a letter dated April 25, 1945, Mills had asked Gerth if it was true that Gerth had no job lined up at Wisconsin for the coming year.*

To Hans Gerth, from New York City, dated April 30, 1945

Dear Gerth:

The State Department has asked me to go to Germany. The position involves tracing down possible links in the communications network which the Nazis have set up—in all countries. Due to my heavy com-mitments here in NY I am unable to go, and am writing them to that effect. With the letter, I am making the strongest recommendation which I can that you be given the job.

Last night I talked with Hannah Arendt in detail about the thing, and she thinks it is a wonderful opportunity. She does not feel that at this time the kind of work involved would identify one with any particular political setup or government in such a way as to obviate later connections. . . . What you would really be is a *finger man on the Nazis.*

I do not know whether anything will come of it for you, for there is the matter of citizenship, but they are beginning to relax some of those rules. Apparently the need for people is very great, now that they have pulverized the entire society. At any rate should they get in touch with you, this note will give you a preliminary clue to what's up, and will give you time to think about it.

I am personally mad with grief that I can't go. But it would mean being a real bastard to Columbia, as we are about to go into the field with a rather expensive piece of research involving a continuous admin-istration. It's just impossible.

M.

Gerth was eventually rehired for the coming year at the University of Wisconsin and given tenure.

In the summer of 1945, Mills and Freya separated and Mills moved to an apartment of his own on 14th Street, in Greenwich Village. When Mills was living alone in the mid-1940s, he had two love affairs known to us. The first was with a Polish sociologist named Eva Hoffberg.[2] We believe she is the woman Mills refers to in the following letter. (The second romantic relationship was with Hazel Gaudet.)

The next letter also mentions J. B. S. Hardman, an experienced trade unionist and intellectual who was an important influence on Mills during the time he was studying labor activism. Although Mills and Hardman did not follow through on the book they discussed preparing together, they did collaborate on Hardman's magazine, Labor and Nation; *Mills became one of its contributing editors. Later Mills dedicated his book on labor leaders,* The New Men of Power *(1948), to Hardman. The dedication reads: "for J. B. S. Hardman, Labor Intellectual."*

To Frances Mills, from New York City, dated January 28, 1946, 8:30 A.M.

Just got your letter and before I start the mad rush will drop you a quick answer. My god, how can I tell you in a letter or in a whole flock of them what I am doing and what I am thinking? I am living very fully, I should say, but with many distractions and some uneasiness. Here is my routine: I go to the Bureau office off Columbus Circle every morning and work on statistical study 'til 12:30 or one, then I either go down home (323 W 14th Street) and work the afternoon, or to the Public Library or to Columbia University Library. I stay at down[town] home Tuesday, Thursday and Saturday nites and stay [at] up[town] home (upper east side) with my girl Monday Wednesday and Friday. She is a young professional woman a little older than I and I guess you could say we are sorta crazy in love.

I make lots of speeches unfortunately. Next one at Princeton next Feb. 12, then Cleveland March 1st. I am as you know writing three books:

- a book on influence: statistical study;[3]
- on labor and politics with J B S Hardman . . . a wonderful old man who runs a magazine down in the village;

2. Also known as Eva Rosenfeld, she had a Ph.D. in sociology from Columbia University, and she coauthored *The Road to H: Narcotics, Delinquency, and Social Policy* with Isidor Chein, Donald L. Gerard, and Robert S. Lee (New York: Basic Books, 1964). She was born in Poland in August 1915, almost exactly one year before Mills's birth.

3. A study of influence and public opinion based on interviews conducted in Decatur, Illinois (sponsored by the Bureau of Applied Social Research).

- The White Collar Worker . . . my Guggenheim book (I am now half pay on Guggenheim and half pay from Columbia).

So I am not only busy; I am in transition in all sorts of ways but have things pretty well under control now.

Yes, I remember how we used to roam around in architecture and I still spend a good deal of time thinking about interior decoration and odd things. I wander thru the junk shops occasionally but they are so high here that you just can't buy anything. Little tables 24 inches high with thin legs are 100 dollars; bottles of good type for lamps run to 40 and 50. It's just impossible to buy anything. So you see, if you do get things cheaper, glasses cut from bottles and so on I'd be very grateful if you'd send me them and of course let me know what they cost. I sent you the plan for my apt some time ago, I think.

Got to work now. Good bye.
Mills

&

To Hans Gerth, from New York City, undated (January or February 1946)

Dear Gerth:

The index proof came today [for *From Max Weber*]. They did a fine job on it, retyping the whole thing, simplifying etc. before sending it to the printer. I've checked it and am sending it back. [. . .]

Am editing a little book with J B S Hardman of the Inter-Union Institute on Labor and Politics. Would you write a piece for it? On gy [German] labor. Sturmthal does one but that's not enough. I'll write you about it when it jells a little and send you a list of people. We will combine trade union men and academics, one or two of each writing on the various themes. Have met a lot of trade union research men around here and spend my evenings often with them. Every now and then we have a stenotypist take down the whole evening's discussion and build dialogues from it; last nite, e.g., on role of the professional staff in trade unions. All of this centers around the Inter Union Institute. Hardman is a wonderful old man; Russian socialist about 64. I'm learning lots from association with him. He's a type I've not known too well before. I think it was Perlman who once said in explanation of him, "He is in revolt against boredom in the labor movement."

So you see I'm getting the edges knocked off me in talk, not working too intensely at any one project, but feeling my way among some fine human beings, accumulating the lore of variously located people.

Going to try to get to Cleveland March 1. Maybe I'll see you there?

Mills

ᘇ

To Frances Mills, from New York City, undated (probably April 1946)

Dear Mother:

Just a note to thank you for the lighter. I don't know how you always know just what I want but for two months now I've been trying to get some serviceman to get me one just like that. It really works and I like it enormously. Thanks a whole lot.

I have been appointed as a professor to Columbia University at $4,500 a year.[4] It carries life tenure and I only teach 8 hours a week. I will begin working there Feb. 1947. From Jan. '46 to Feb. '47 I'll be on the Guggenheim and at this Bureau. Well, I made it; as you know that's what I've been working for. I am resigning from Maryland University for good and taking up permanent residence in NY City. I can expect a raise at Columbia in about 18 months after I begin—up to $6,000. In the meantime, despite the terrible expenses of NYC I can get along and keep up two households, as I'm doing, with the $4,500.

Be seeing you. Thanks again for the wonderful lighter.
Mills

In the next letter Mills responded to comments from Miller on a draft in progress; we believe the draft was for Mills's article entitled "What Research Can Do for Labor."[5]

4. Assistant professor. The appointment was filed April 1, 1946.
5. *Labor and Nation* 2 (June-July 1946): 17–20.

To William Miller, from New York City, undated (probably spring 1946)

Dear Bill:

Got your criticism this morning, for which many thanks. It is immensely helpful. On the style points I think you are 100% right. I am, indeed, happy to get that kind of criticism—that it is too loose and talky and etc.—for always I've been fighting being too formal and academic. Anyway I'm going to stiffen up the language and all a good bit altho keeping it simple.

About the large point you raise: You are right that I am not clear about technician vs. intellectual problem. SO: I'm going to move "types of intellectuals" up front and really clarify it; also, I think, add a fuller account of the research possibility.

In general tho, I am going to hold to the word intellectual and insist that to be useful to labor in political and economic fight, the intellectual has to be a technician also. But the technician also has to be an intellectual. What are we fooling around with it for: by intellectual here we mean humanitarian socialist. What the hell else? So I'll say so in some innocent, hard-boiled way.

Thanks. Thanks again and again.
Yours forever,
Mills

❧

To Hans Gerth, from New York City, dated August 1946, Monday

Dear Gerth:

Thank you for the memorandum about the contributions to M. W. [Marianne Weber]. I didn't know she was writing memoirs, but am indeed very glad to hear it. [. . .]

Pamela (and you will forgive my writing about it) is getting to be an uncontained joy: she talks so much and learns so fast that it makes me dizzy when I calculate what would happen if she kept it up for 10 years at this pace![6] She often spends whole afternoons with my paints now (I'm doing some oils!) and gets them all over herself in a terribly

6. She was then three and a half years old.

funny pattern. (Somehow her bottom is always painted blue when she is finished with it all . . . can you please tell me what that might mean?) [. . .]

I still read a lot of history at night and politics; I ran into another nest of very cheap books (20 and 30 cents a piece) in the Marxists revisionist vein and a lot of Trotsky and Victor Serge pamphlets and so on. I'm trying to get a whole view of post 1917 radicalism. Could you loan me for 10 days Trotsky's *Literature and Revolution?* (I'll mail it right back.) Libraries here don't *have* it, and I'm anxious to read it.

I am writing a few little things, and a lot on the New Middle Class (white collar man . . . old title); I've now got really good figures on white collar labor unions from 1900 to 1944; it is surprising how large a total they make. I have worked out the proportions of the total wageworker and the total white collar worker that is unionized for each 5 year point within these 45 years. (By 1944, 14.8% of the white collar workers and 30% plus of the wageworkers were members of unions.) So these tables, with their cross tabulations, make up the backbone of a good 50-page hunk on white collar unions. I'm going back to 1900 with most series and examining party platforms and speeches to pin down the appeals made to them. It is a lengthy job, but I hope it will be definitive in several respects.

I have not seen *any* reviews of the Weber; I gather from your letter that the *Nation* carried a review of it. I have to look that up.

Am glad to hear you are getting down earnestly to the text on social psychology *[Character and Social Structure]*, as you say in your note. My files on it are quite active and I've written during the summer a few sections for chapters still pending. In this connection, I wish you'd sometime answer my last letter about our arrangements.[7] If you don't, and if we don't come to some sort of mutually agreeable understanding, we'll only jam up in the future, so won't you think about it? [. . .] Please believe that I do not wish to "row" in any way about it all, but why don't you give me a full reaction to my letters?

Yours Sincerely,
Mills

∾

7. This refers to agreeing on a plan for dividing the work and settling on a publisher.

To Frances and Charles Grover Mills, from New York, New York,
undated (probably late summer 1946)

Dear Mother and Dad:

Thank you very much for the brush, which just arrived. The old one
was downright unhygienic by now, and I shall throw it away and
replace it by this one. It is very fine, and pretty too, so thanks for it
very much.

Nothing has changed since I last wrote you. I still work at home
a great deal of the time and I am alone most of the time. I rather like
living alone, you know, as it enables me to apportion just the time
I want to various things. I read a lot late into the night: books on
history and politics mostly. I think maybe I am almost secretly "preparing" for something, with all this, but I don't really know what. I
write some on the book about the "new middle class" (white collar
man) and it is coming along.

Dick Hofstadter came back into town a few days ago, for his
term at Columbia this fall, and I'll probably see a lot of him.

Pamela is well and as precocious as usual. That one is coming
along all right; she'll amount to more than any of us. [. . .]

Goodbye, and thanks again for the lovely brush.

Your son,
Mills
Charlie Mills

*The following letter mentions Ruth Harper, who later became Mills's second wife.
Ruth was the only child of immigrants from Scotland and Norway; she was born in
Seattle, Washington, and grew up in New Jersey, where her father was an electrical
engineer for the Bell Telephone Laboratories.*

*Ruth graduated from Mount Holyoke College in 1943 with a B.A. in mathe-
matics (and minors in physics, political science, and economics). She met Mills in October 1946, when he interviewed her for a job. At the age of twenty-four she was executive secretary for the League of Women Voters in New York State, and she had
about a year of prior experience with interviewing and statistical studies. Mills, then
thirty years old, hired Ruth to do research for* White Collar, *using part of his Guggenheim grant.*

To Frances and Charles Grover Mills, from New York City, dated
December 18, 1946

Dear Mother and Dad:

I have just gotten the nuts, which I have now eaten—yes, all of
them—and the lovely rooster, which I intend to take to my new
office! He, the rooster, is just the sort of thing you would never buy
for yourself but would just want like hell. And here he is, all mine.
Thank you very much. I am truly delighted with him. He is so white
and fierce looking, and yet he is only a peaceful little rooster.

Things go all right here, I suppose. I work very hard now getting
my desk cleaned up and the new semester, when I begin regularly to
teach at Columbia, lined up. I have a lot of papers and things to give.
I go to Boston Saturday the 28th and Sunday the 29th to give one;
then back here for Jan. 6th. But it will all get done somehow. Today
I had mailed from the office to you a little paper, or address, I gave
last spring in Cleveland, which is only now being published.

The book on white collar workers is coming along slow but sure.
I'm not wanting to rush it. After all, the translation Gerth and I did
was a book for specialists (incidentally it is selling well; I expect by
next 18 months or so to make a couple of thousand from it) but this
white collar book: ah, there's a book for the people; it is everybody's
book. So I am trying to make it damn good all over. Simple and clean
cut in style, but with a lot of implications and subtleties woven into
it. It is my little work of art: it will have to stand for the operations
I never will do, not being a surgeon, and for the houses I never built,
not being an architect. So, you see, it has to be a thing of craftsmanship and art as well as science. That is why it takes so long. There is
no hurry. It will stand a long time, when it is finally done. It is all
about the new little man in the big world of the 20th century. It is
about that little man and how he lives and what he suffers and what
his chances are going to be; and it is also about the world he lives in,
has to live [in], doesn't want to live in. It is, as I said, going to be everybody's book. For, in truth, who is not a little man?

About January 15th I occupy the new office that has now been
remodeled uptown at Hamilton Hall, Columbia campus. I will still
come to the Bureau about one day a week but my headquarters will
shift. I intend to sink a little money into office furnishings. I've worked
in barns long enough; you both know how the Bureau looks. Well,

I'm going to get a leather couch in dull green and stuff like that. Also a rug on the floor. The University will get my bill. If they won't pay it, I'll kick like hell . . . and pay it myself by the month or something. But the damn thing is going to be right. Drapes too, in grey monks cloth or something like that. I know a man who does interiors and I'll have him fix it up.

Ruth and I are doing very nicely; she is on some interviews now for White Collar. Hazel, as I think you know, is in Reno, completing her divorce and doing some tabulations for me via long distance. She will marry some guy out there and remain there. Eva is teaching in Bard College, a cute little place up the Hudson. I spent the weekend out at Jeannette Green's in a New Jersey suburb. Lots of woods there and I rested quietly and ate a lot of ham and things. Eleanor, whom you don't know, ran off to Europe with some guy to write another novel (see THE BITTER BOX by Eleanor Clark); Thelma Erhlich is doing some analysis for me on labor leaders; Helen Schneider is also working now with me on people who belong to unions as compared with those who do the same kind of work but don't belong to unions. In short, part of my staff runs off, and to some of them I farm out work to do for love, at a distance. Some remain and they are all kept busy as little bees. And some new ones come along from time to time to contribute to the advance of science and the academic profession.

Got to go to sleep now, as am dead tired. Thanks again for the rooster. Every morning in the new office I will say Hello to him, and it will make all four of us feel better: you and you and the rooster and me.

your son,
Wright Mills

To Frances and Charles Grover Mills, from New York City, dated February 15, 1947, Saturday afternoon

Dear Mother and Dad:

Thanks for your long letter. Everything here is getting along OK. I am not yet moved into the new office and there is even some doubt that I will get the beautiful one I had my eye on. I may have to take a room I don't really like, in which case I won't fix it up at all. I am now teaching, for the first time in two years, and I find it takes time. In addition, all the research jobs are going along as usual, so the teaching is just an added burden. I work on three books: the White Collar volume, the book on labor leaders, which should be soon finished, and the book on opinion leadership, materials for which I gathered in Decatur, Ill. two summers ago. I have a total of 15 people who are assisting me on this, but still it takes time to get them at it. In addition, the Navy consultation job is maturing and we may land the $70,000 contract, in which case I'll have to direct the study. I almost hope it does not come thru.

Freya is apparently OK and Pamela, whom I see every Sunday as usual, is wonderful as ever. You can imagine what my life is like from the above paragraph; it is a fourteen hour day and at night I dream of it all. [. . .]

Bye now.

Yours,
Mills

After two years of separation, Mills and Freya finalized their divorce in Reno, Nevada, in 1947.[8] Mills wrote the following two letters while he was spending six weeks in Reno in order to complete the divorce, prior to his marriage to Ruth.

To Ruth Harper, from Reno, Nevada, dated June 2, 1947

Monday morning

Well, things are not going so badly. As you recall, I got here last Tuesday and was settled here on the ranch by Tuesday night. I wrote you then. The next morning the guy that runs the place asked me in the

8. In 1946, Freya had written a book for children, *Susan's Surprise* (New York: Oxford University Press). She later became the director of the Speakers' Bureau at Rutgers University (1953–61). After moving with her husband, Alan James, to Rio de Janeiro, Brazil, she organized and directed the Educational Counselling Service for the Fulbright Commission in Rio (1969–79).

morning didn't I want to take a little ride on a horse and I said how long and he said just an hour or so, and I went. We rode all day long, chasing deer up around the mountains. I wasn't sore at all either in the ass or in the head; because now I've done that, I believe that a horse is an instrument of production in certain lower forms of industrial life.

So Thursday I wrote most all day and likewise with Friday and Saturday and Sunday morning. The typical days—and they will continue without variation—run like this: up at 7. Write an hour. Eat breakfast 8:15. Stay in room and write 'til 1 P.M. at which time lunch. Loaf an hour after that in sun . . . work during afternoon but not pushing, primarily reading and revising manuscript if have done well in morning; otherwise push. Knock off about 5:30 and fool with guitar or nap until 7. Dinner at 7:15. Then play pool and ping pong for around 2 hours. Sleep at 10 o'clock.

The guy that runs the place don't like this schedule so much because this way he doesn't make any extra on me for horses etc. but after that first day he is getting to know that I'm not organizable. The great individualistic West is a lot of crap; it's an organized setup.

Yesterday around 1 o'clock Hazel and Graham, her husband, came out. He is a very nice guy, really very nice. Naturally they brought a picnic, which meant one whole chicken for each of the three of us. And naturally I ate all of mine—the first time I've overindulged since leaving New York. Well we just talked around . . . he's tied in with architecting and contracting for public buildings and stuff in Reno and they seem very happy indeed. Because of the chicken I was uncomfortable all afternoon: too full.

My god, look at the kind of stuff I'm writing . . . like one school girl gossiping to another. The reason is, though, that last night I missed you, was lonely for you and felt all soft about you. Do you know what I mean? Well, there was a word back in the 20s that fits it like a glove; the point is I'm *goofy* over you.

Goddamn it, write.

I was sunburned (that all-day ride) and am now peeling all over the face. Guess it is necessary after so long without any sun. Will do it gradually now, and all over, not just the face and hands.

[unsigned copy]

In the following letter, Mills mentions the quote that he used as the epigraph for The
New Men of Power *(1948):*

> *When that boatload of wobblies come*
> *Up to Everett, the sheriff says*
> *Don't you come no further*
> *Who the hell's yer leader anyhow?*
> Who's yer leader?
> *And them wobblies yelled right back—*
> We ain't got no leader
> We're all leaders
> *And they kept right on comin'.*
>
> From an interview with an
> unknown worker, conducted
> by Mills in Nevada.

To Ruth Harper, from Reno, Nevada, dated June 7, 1947

[. . .]

Thanks for sending the POQ *[Public Opinion Quarterly]*. It came in
handy. I wish you'd bundle up all the *Business Weeks* and *Labor Actions*
that have come—just those two—and send them along sometime. I
could use them. I have not read one paper or listened to one newscast
since I left New York. I have no idea of what is going on and most
of the time really care less. But there is labor stuff happening and it's
stimulating to read about it from those two sources. [. . .]

Later:

I have 124 pages. It is getting to be nite. Outside it is raining.
But inside it is snug. I feel philosophical rather than statistical. I feel
goofie. About you.

Later:

Christ, wasn't that little prose poem by An Unknown Worker
of Nevada I picked up a honey? That'll go right on the title page.
"WE AIN'T GOT NO LEADER. WE'RE ALL LEADERS." That has just the
right irony for a book on labor leaders.

You know, if a guy could wander around this country taking
notes and talking with everybody, he could do a damn good book on
it all. A sort of folklorish thing along different class lines. Pick up just

casual like, 200 longish "interviews," except nothing systematic. We're going to do that someday, you know. Except you're no good for it. You're too good-looking. They wouldn't tell you things like they do an old guy like me. I'm goofie over you. Especially when it rains.

[unsigned copy]

∾

To Frances and Charles Grover Mills, from Reno, Nevada, undated (June or July 1947)

Thank you for your long letter. I swam for a couple hours today in the lake and am about pooped out from it, but I'll answer your questions. To begin with . . .

I am delighted that you two plan to come to NY during the Christmas season. I hope by then to have a larger apt. set up and so there may be plenty of room. We will have to wait until we see when the Christmas meetings of the sociology society are, but I think they will be in NY; so they won't interfere with any timing you decide is convenient with you. Anyway that is all settled now between us except the exact dates.

It is not really possible to *tell* you anything about Ruth Harper. [. . .] She went to Mt. Holyoke College and has worked for me all spring. She is extremely bright and is going to be a professional sociological partner with me. She is a tall slender girl with shoulder length hair and very large brown eyes. She smokes too much, and is a little nervous like a colt at times. Her mother died when she was very young. They lived out in NJ [. . .] where Jeanette Green lives. [. . .]

Got to go to bed now. See you Christmas. The book comes along fine. I have written 240 pages in the 3 weeks plus I have been here! It just rolls out. A book on THE AMERICAN LABOR LEADER: Who He Is and What He Thinks.[9]

bye, love
Mills

∾

9. Published under the title of *The New Men of Power: America's Labor Leaders* by C. Wright Mills, with the assistance of Helen Schneider (New York: Harcourt, Brace and Company,

To Dwight Macdonald, from Sutcliffe, Nevada, undated (probably July 1947)

Sunday Night

Dear Dwight:

Well, I got out here and put in six weeks on the divorce business. During the last week I ran into a lady, a cowboy lady, who gave me a big stone house on a mountain two miles above a lake, Lake Pyramid, for as long as needed. Ruth joined me, we were married, bought a jeep for transport, and plan to spend another month or so here. The thing is forty miles out of Reno, in pretty rugged country; but it is a hell of a lot of fun.

I have finished a fairly good draft on "The Labor Leader: Who He Is and What He Thinks." Wrote it like free association in 5 weeks: 432 double-spaced [pages]. Now I am browsing through it once, and then it will be typed in six or seven carbons. Will you read one for me?

I am anxious about the poll.[10] Ruth tells me that Mickey Sanes is out of town for the summer. The thing is all coded except the very last section. [. . .] Anyway Dwight, I'm very sorry about the delay and I'll do my best to move it from out here. The first thing I do when I get back, if it isn't done, is sit right down and turn it out. I'll make a nice essay out of it on the phenomenon *politics*.[11]

You know, after turning out that labor leader book so fast (I would never have believed I could have done it) I just don't know whether it is worth a damn or not. So close to it, I guess. Dying for criticism. And naturally am dead broke so will try to get some kind of advance. Bill Miller will get a copy to you, after about 3 or 4 weeks, if you let me know you'll read it and let me have comments.[12]

1948; reprint, New York: Augustus M. Kelley Publishers, Reprints of Economic Classics, 1971). In the "Notes and Sources" section of the book, Mills thanked four people for their interviewing, statistical, and editorial work: Helen Schneider, Hazel Gaudet Erskine, Maud Zimmerman, and Ruth Harper Mills (p. 295, Kelley edition).

10. A questionnaire for the readers of *politics*.

11. As it turned out, Ruth wrote the article about the poll results: Ruth Harper Mills, "The Fascinated Readers," *politics* 5, no. 1 (winter 1948): 59–63.

12. Dwight Macdonald was one of the thirteen friends and colleagues Mills credited for making comments about various drafts of the manuscript for *The New Men of Power* (p. 295, Kelley edition).

I am playing the guitar now, about an hour a day in the sun, with the lizards running around on the rocks. This cabin is under a huge cliff, and from behind it you see a big valley going up and down below, [. . .] 30 miles long and about 12 wide. And all the time in the house or out of it there is the smell of sagebrush, and at night of sagebrush fire in the fireplace.

I had to delay paying the lawyer to get the jeep, but he saw the situation and went along with me. You've got to have a car to get up here, and an ordinary [one] couldn't make it and besides, only new car immediately available here was a jeep (green with yellow wheels and six speeds forward!). I climb mountains in it; go anywhere a horse will, they say. Maybe I will hire myself out with it, and pull things about the middle of August. Anyway we'll drive it back to New York and maybe if have to, we'll sell it. In the meantime here we are with it and it's wonderful.

I start on the Influence study in about 4 days . . . the Decatur study.[13] Ruth brought out the files on it. Will try to shove it fast and come back to NY with fewer commitments.

Let me know what is going on in the world.

Yours,
Wright Mills

∾

To Hans Gerth, from New York City, dated Friday, February 13, 1948

Dear Gerth:

It was good to get your letter this morning, but bad to hear that H I and child have been so ill.[14]

To answer your query: yes, [Joseph] Bensman came around two or three days ago and left a copy of his MA thesis with me. Looks interesting, altho haven't read it yet. He thinks of doing something on men in unions etc. and I wanted to ask you about him. I think if he is worth it, I can fix up something with the UAW for him. Let me

---

13. For the Bureau of Applied Social Research.
14. Gerth's wife and one of their daughters had scarlet fever.

know about how independent a field worker you think he'd make. Did you have to supervise his thesis closely or did he carry it pretty well alone?

Glad to hear you'll read the Labor Leader manuscript. To tell you the truth I am very worried about it: it is so very political; and what I'd like is your judgment about how naive, if at all, it is in that way. God knows what the consequences of it will be, but it had to be said anyway. I'll get a copy to you sometime within the next month. Either manuscript, if possible, or galleys. Your advice on it would be greatly valued.

Right now my time is monopolized, all but polishing up labor leader, on the Puerto Rico study. Going into the field with it next Monday here in New York: will get around 1,500 interviews among the migrants, and am trying to test empirically the "Protestant" ethic among these migrants . . . as a factor in their adjustment here, etc. Maybe it will work, maybe not: it's always that way, with me at least, on fieldwork. You gamble. So you cover yourself by at least getting information stuff. I had to drop my new course that was to be given this spring, on the wageworker in modern society, in order to devote more time to Puerto Rico.

There is some chance that I'll be thru Madison this summer. Plan to get hold of a house trailer, the smallest I can find, and hitch it up to the jeep I have and go west. I'll park on top of some mountain in the northwest and work a while for about six weeks or so, then travel slowly down the west coast into Mexico and back up thru the south. You can live almost as cheaply like that [as] at home in NY. And no telephones etc.! You see the kind of escape visions I have. I dream of this thing at night and when I wake up each morning it is the first thing I think of!

Gerth, will you let me know your opinion of my going to the New School? I don't know much about the setup, but they have approached me informally about it (dead secret please). I think there may be trouble about this book on labor here at Columbia, and wonder whether I should jump in rank and tenure before it's out. You know me and you know some of those people at the New School: do you think we'd get along, or not?

Yours,
Mills

In a letter dated March 31, 1948, Gerth replied that he thought Mills would be better off as associate professor at Columbia College than as full professor at the New School. Mills remained at Columbia.

Mills ended his book The New Men of Power *with the following: "It is the task of the labor leaders to allow and to initiate a union of the power and the intellect. They are the only ones who can do it; that is why they are now the strategic elite in American society. Never has so much depended upon men who are so ill-prepared and so little inclined to assume the responsibility."*

To Hans Gerth, from New York City, undated (spring 1948)

Dear Gerth:

Many, many thanks for reading the first batch of galleys [of *The New Men of Power*] and for being so generous with the comments. I think a few of them will be taken care of in later parts of the book, but I am carefully pursuing to see what can be done with the others.

[. . .]

In a few days I go on the first "vacation" I've ever had! Did I tell you the plan? Drive to Los Angeles in the jeep. Buy a small trailer to live in, 7 by 14 feet big; drive up into the mountains and sit down. I'll take my White Collar files and write three or four hours a day only. I have these 128 depth interviews, which are amazingly fun to read and analyze. Ruth has already laid out the analysis and she will carry on with that a few hours a day. Naturally I look forward to this: THIS summer is going to be my TURNING POINT. You of all people will know what that means! As well as what it doesn't mean!

Pamela is well and a great pleasure. In September I come back here and take her to Maine in the trailer for two weeks. As time goes on, Pam gets bigger, I shall spend much more time with her, including all summer. I hope H I and the children are well.

And thanks again.

Yours,
Mills

In 1948 politics was distributing copies of Let Us Now Praise Famous Men *by James Agee and Walker Evans via mail order. That book stimulated the following letter from Mills, which was published in the spring 1948 issue of politics.*

To Dwight Macdonald, from New York City, undated (spring 1948)

Dear Dwight:

I approached Agee's book with very definite expectations and needs in mind: From what you said when you gave it to me, I thought I might get some answers to a problem that has been consciously bothering me for six or seven years:

How can a writer report fully the "data" that social science enables him to turn up and at the same time include in his account the personal meanings that the subject often comes to have for him? Or: How can the writer master the detaching techniques necessary to modern understanding in such a way as to use them to feel again the materials and to express that feeling to the readers?

I put this question in terms of "social science" because every cobbler thinks leather is the only thing, but it is a problem faced by any writer on social and human topics. Social scientists make up a rationale and a ritual for the alienation inherent in most human observation and intellectual work today. They have developed several stereotyped ways of writing which do away with the full experience by keeping them detached throughout their operation. It is as if they are deadly afraid to take the chance of modifying themselves in the process of their work.

This is not a merely technical problem of analysis or of exposition. It is part of a much larger problem of style-as-orientation. And this larger issue, in turn, seems to arise from the bewildering quality and pace of our epoch and the unsureness of the modern intellectual's reaction to its human and inhuman features. We are reaching a point where we cannot even "handle" any considerable part of our experience, much less search for more with special techniques, much less write it within the inherited styles of reflection and communication.

I bring all this up, because on the surface, Agee's text is a report of a field trip to the south during the middle thirties; but underneath, it is an attempt to document his full reactions to the whole experience of trying as a reporter to look at sharecroppers. As a report on the sharecropper south, it is one of the best pieces of "participant observation" I have ever read. As a document of how a man might take such an experience big, it is something of a stylistic pratfall.

We need some word with which to point, however crudely, at what is attempted here and at what I have tried to describe above. Maybe we could call it sociological poetry: It is a style of experience and expression that reports social facts and at the same time reveals their human meanings. As a reading experience, it stands somewhere between the thick facts and thin meanings of the ordinary sociological monograph and those art forms which in their attempts at meaningful reach do away with the facts, which they consider as anyway merely an excuse for imaginative construction. If we tried to make up formal rules for sociological poetry, they would have to do with the ratio of meaning to fact, and maybe success would be a sociological poem which contains the full human meaning in statements of apparent fact.

In certain passages, Agee comes close to success. Observe how he reports in a sentence or two the human significance of authority between landlord and tenant, white and Negro. Observe how he handles associations in descriptions, never letting them get in the way of the eye which they guide to the meanings. I think the best things in the volume are the sections on work (320 ff) and on the summer Sunday in a small southern town (375 ff). In some of these pages imagination and painstaking reporting become one and the same unit of sharp sight and controlled reactivity: they are visions.

But of course the quality about Agee that is best of all is his capacity for great indignation. Printed less than a decade ago, the book in its fine moral tone seems to be a product of some other epoch. For the spirit of our immediate times deadens our will very quickly, and makes moral indignation a rare and perilous thing. The greatest appeal of this book comes from Agee's capacity for indignation.

The motive and the frustration that lift his work above the plain sociological report is his enormous furiosity at the whole arrangement that sent him to the south and his crying terror at being personally estranged from the sharecroppers. This fury is what makes him take it big. He is furious with the magazine people who sent him into the south "to spy," and he is furious at himself for not being able to break through into the human relation he wants with the sharecroppers he is studying, or rather whom he is trying to love.

If I ask myself, why on the whole it just doesn't come off, the only answer I can find is that in taking it all so big, Agee gets in his own way. Instead of easing himself into the experience in order to clarify the communication of how it really is, he jumps into it, obscuring the scene and the actors and keeping the readers from taking it big. And underneath this is the fact that Agee is overwhelmed and self-indulgent; almost any time, he is likely to gush. He lacks, in this book, the self-discipline of the craftsman of experience: When you get through, you have more images of just Agee than of the southern sharecroppers, or even of Agee in the south among the sharecroppers.

This failure is most apparent when we contrast the magnificent Walker Evans photographs with Agee's prose. These photographs are wonderful because the cameraman never intrudes in the slightest way upon the scene he is showing you. The subjects of the photographs— family groups of sharecroppers, individuals among them, children, a house, a bed in a room—are just there, in a completely barefaced manner, in all their dignity of being, and with their very nature shining through. But Agee often gets in the way of what he would show you, and sometimes, romantically enough, there is only Agee and nothing else.

Given the difficulties of sociological poetry, however, I think that what is important about the book is the enormity of the self-chosen task; the effort recorded here should not be judged according to its success or failure, or even degree of success; rather we should speak of the appropriateness and rarity of the objective, remembering that Agee has himself written: "The deadliest blow the enemy of the human soul can strike is to do fury honor."

If you can think of any other examples of sociological poetry, let me know of them.

Yours,
Wright Mills

To Hans Gerth, from outside Los Angeles, California, dated June 16, 1948

Dear Gerth:

Just received your long letter of comments and the Weber bibliography, forwarded to me here, general delivery. The bibliography looks wonderful! I only wish that I had received the letter about the book two days before: I've already sent galleys back.[15] But in about 2 weeks or 3 I should get page proofs and it is still possible to do things with them. All your points are very well worth very serious consideration, and I am now studying them with an eye to how they might be taken into account. I'm afraid only the smaller ones can really be met at this unfortunate stage of affairs; appropriate adjectives and verb changes can do wonders . . . but the two or three major points I'm afraid are endemic in the book pretty much and represent my own shortcomings that can't be taken out by merely verbal changes. But I'll do my best. Anyway, you will know how extremely grateful I am for your generous giving of time and knowledge to the galleys. After I have gone thru the letter with a typewriter making notes to myself, and with the page proofs before me for changes that are possible, I'll write you a "counterstatement"!

We have got a trailer on order, have to wait a few more days to get it delivered, also for check to be deposited in New York bank. In meantime are living in auto court: miserable existence for a week. But what's a week?

Am just getting down seriously to white collar job, and am overwhelmed by notes accumulated over 5 or 10 years! Will I ever make order out of this chaos of bits and pieces and grand notions that won't come off? I brought two big file drawers (stuffed) with me for the summer work and perusal. This designing of a book, making an architecture out of it, is a tricky business, isn't it? On the labor book I learned a lot about that, but after all, that was a simple kind of outline and things fell readily into place; this thing covers the world of modern society, hence to carve out of it a pathway without stumbling all over yourself is hellish. What I am trying to do is straighten out the *themes* . . . when to introduce each of them and how to hook it into given contexts. Then there is the intensive material from the

15. Of *The New Men of Power.*

depth interviews, and finally the Census type stuff. I'm tempted to do splice-ins, something like the USA by Dos Passos. Call one the CLOSEUP: "ALICE ADAMS AND KITTY FOYLE," e.g., or "The Status Strip." Throw those in about 2–3 pages; then *panorama,* e.g., "Society as Salesroom" which tries to generalize a mood or feeling or just plain fancy. Finally a *census,* which will be straight figure talk. I'll try to embed these three types of splice-ins in a good straight text. Sounds very daring when I write it down like this, and I don't think I'm nearly good enough of a writer to get away with it, but why not try? You can always twist it back into orthodox textual presentation.

Thanks again for your criticism, of which more later. Leave to visit Chicago College next spring has been granted!! Be seeing you.

Yours,
CWM

&

To William Miller, from New York City, undated (summer 1948)

Dear Bill:

Got your letter and the review of the Ford book.[16] Thank you for both: I am very glad to see that you are coming around to flamboyance in style, even tho you don't print it (ahem), and even tho you sell out so cheaply to the commies: $1.65 each. Seriously, the Ford book seems wonderful and I look forward to reading it. About flamboyance: don't you love it? God, only way to live: the only personal answer to bureaucratic precision and form which, part of the managerial demiurge, would stultify everything we do and are. (I'm now writing chapter 6, The managerial demiurge—salaried managers level of wc [white collar workers].)

I.

I don't really know how I'm doing, but Jesus God, I'm in there trying hard; don't mean that I work long hours, I don't: say about 5 or 6 a day, and brooding over it rest of day, but sleep 9 or 10 hours, shamefully. Would you like to see the outline?

16. Possibly a book by William Wallace Ford, a friend of Bill Miller's, or a biography of Henry Ford.

Introduction: The new little man (poetically presents cream of book: insight).

Part one: The old middle class

Ch. 1. The world of the small entrepreneur (sets utopian past; other three chapters tell what happened to it and its heroes).

2. The independent farmer

3. The small business man

4. The distribution of independence

Part two: The new society

Part two, once the dull factual part, now becomes different: all facts buried in poetic-sweep stuff about meaning, for people, for society.

5. The white collar world's general panorama and mechanics of how they rose

6. The managerial demiurge (managerial and supervisory)

7. Brains, Inc. (professional) . . . case: Time and Bureau

8. The enormous file (office workers . . . case: Metropolitan Life)

9. The biggest bazaar in the world (salespeople . . . case: Macy's)

Part three: The new middle class

10. Predetermination

11. Aspirations and success

12. The white collar girls

13. Alienation

14. White collar unions

15. Political role of new middle class

End.

No pronouncements, no calls for action: moods, probings, latent meanings make explicit.

You can see how much I've learned about writing a *book* from *New Men of Power* and especially from the talks with you. I see the structure of the whole quite well now, and you know how important such guidelines are in each individual part.

By the way, am delighted by Earl's reaction to labor book: for God's sake, prod him into doing something publicly if possible.

Schlesinger Jr. wrote Davis at Harcourt Brace this for the jacket: "C. Wright Mills' *The New Men of Power* is a brilliant, original and provocative work, genuinely democratic and boldly radical in its character. Prof. Mills will not expect total agreement from all his readers; but I have not read for a long time any book which in its main bearings casts more valuable light on the tensions of American society or which is more stimulating and fruitful in its challenges to the reader." Well! Anyway, it shows we can get away with it among the liberals. [. . .]

II.

Of course we plan, if you want, to carry out our pattern of last summer: going to New York, picking up Pamela, and you and Bucky, and going to the Cape for about 10 days.[17] Would you like that? The three women can sleep in the trailer and you and I can sleep outside. Cooking just like at home, so it should be no trouble for anyone and fun all around. Let us know. The timing should be about the last week in August, or first week in Sept. OK, it's all set. Write again about this. Current address, for next ten days at least:

C. Wright Mills
care: Yosemite Lodge
Yosemite National Park
California

Travelogue department [from Ruth]:

As you can see it is now Yosemite. Yosemite is a place where the insides of the earth got restless and jutted or pushed their way up to the sky about 10,000 feet. On top it's all bare granite rock with snow and no trees; a little lower down, 8,000 ft, there are scraggly trees, rocky twisting roads and blue blue lakes since the only thing they reflect is sky. [. . .] we came from Frisco straight to the high country, taking the trailer over grades so steep that we had to get into four-wheel drive, and roads so curvy that I'd have to get out and see if a car was coming before we could go ahead—three hours to go fifty miles.

17. "Bucky" was a nickname for Virginia Buckner Miller, Bill Miller's wife.

Mills is convinced and so am I that he now can take the trailer anywhere. Anyway we found a pleasant camp at 8,500 feet in sort of a
meadow, a brook and a view of the rocks. When you got out of the
sun it was extremely cold and the next morning we found that we
couldn't breathe. It was like a big weight on our chests which we
could never fight off unless we kept walking like the energetic hikers
around us—walking forces the thin air into the lungs they say. Wanting only to sit on our asses and work, it was no good, so we hitched
the trailer up and started back the slow fifty miles and came into the
valley, which is at 4,000 feet, about seven miles long, one mile wide
and completely enclosed on all sides by rock walls that go up to 8,000
feet extremely quick, and have water falling over their sides at various
places. Like everyone else here I find the waterfalls quite wonderful,
but Wright says "What else do you expect water to do when it comes
to the edge of a cliff?" as he keeps watching them out of the rear view
mirror. There are about five to ten thousand people in the valley but
you never see them because they can park only in designated camps,
which are hidden under high trees. We are in the only camp that has
people a good hundred yards away from each other—the ground is
on a hill and rocky so it's hard to pitch tents and get cars into, which
gives us rocks and woods on all three sides and a view down the hill
to a few camps of people, a modern john, running water, and the high
rocks on the other side of the valley. About a mile away there is all
sorts of equipment, from a drugstore to a hospital—even a movie
which changes its shows every two days so of course we go every
other night. We expect to stay here till about the end of July when
we'll start a slow trip back east, bringing with us many words.

Wright says he forgot to tell you about Chicago. Yes, it is all set.
He got his leave of absence for the spring term, and, at great expense
to Chicago, a good deal of mutual looking over will be done with
no commitments on any sides. Also, something which, no matter
how much I like trailer life, is rather good to hear. The plan had been
according to Wright, that we might live in Chicago in the trailer, but
Dave Riesman has offered us the use of his big house there, which he
won't be using so we'll be able to fence off a few rooms for ourselves
and have hot running water.

What about Cape Cod?

Ruth

∾

To Frances and Charles Grover Mills, from New York City, undated
(probably September 1948)

Dear Mother and Dad:

I just returned from a 20,000 mi. trip, and received your card, for
which many thanks. Here is where we went: from NY to Los Angeles, CA, where we bought a house trailer. Then slowly up the coast
to San Francisco, where we stayed about two weeks. Then Bill Miller
joined us by plane and the three of us traveled up to British Columbia; and then we zigzagged across the continent inside Canada, ending up in Montreal, from which place we came back to New York.
I picked up Pamie and we went on to Cape Cod, Mass. for about
a week by the Atlantic Ocean. All in all quite a trip. I'd promised
myself a real vacation and finally had it . . . after 6 years of hard
work.

But the real climax was this: about 800 mi. from NYC, in Ontario, at a place called Lake Temagami, we bought two small islands.
One is one and three-quarters acres and the other, about 30 feet
of open water away, is one-fourth of an acre. These two together,
bought from the crown for summer residence, cost 175 dollars! Next
summer we'll go up there and build a stone house from the stones on
the beach of the place. To get to these islands you have to leave the
highway and travel by boat about 32 mi. thru beautiful lakes and river
ways. It is cool up there and utterly isolated. However, a freight boat
comes thru and stops every other day with fresh vegetables and stuff.
I'll have to buy next summer a small outboard motorboat. As soon as
we build a little shack for temporary residence or get a big tent you
both must come up and stay a while with us. I'm recruiting labor for
clearing the land a little. It's now dense forest and underbrush and am
offering food and board for 7 hours [work] a day every other day!

The jeep almost fell to pieces after such a long hauling of the
trailer, so yesterday we traded it in as down payment on a new Kaiser
automobile painted sky blue! The payments are only $89 a month, but
I hope to sell the trailer at a small profit and so be able to pay off the
entire thing in about a month.

I've been asked to lecture at Chicago University from Jan. to July
next year, 1949, and have accepted, obtaining a leave of absence from

Columbia. We're trying now to get a place to live out there for those six months.

Yesterday I mailed you a copy of my book, *The New Men of Power*, which everyone thinks is a handsome book.[18] Write me in detail how you like it, especially the first chapter and the last two chapters, which contain a radical program for America today.

I'm sorry I didn't write during the summer but was on the road all that time and didn't write anyone but a letter or so to Pamela. Too busy fixing tires and mending broken springs and all the rest of it.

Your son,
Charlie Wright

In the next letter Mills refers to the presidential election of 1948, in which he voted for Norman Thomas, the Socialist Party's candidate, as he had in the election of 1940.[19] Debates about Norman Thomas and Henry Wallace, the Progressive Party's candidate, have continued throughout the years following the election of 1948.[20]

Mills also mentions Lewis A. Coser, the German émigré he had met through his involvement with politics. Several years later Coser received his Ph.D. in sociology from Columbia.

To Hans Gerth, from New York City, dated Sunday, September 26 (1948)

Dear Gerth:

I am delighted that you've built a house; it must be quite a good feeling, especially after the hell involved in getting it up! I don't quite remember where Sunset Point is; is it where we used to go swimming?

18. In a letter dated September 9, 1948, Mills gave the following assessment of the book to Gerth: "Some people seem to like it, and other people not to. But since the former are more frequently to be in contact with me . . . hell, who knows? I feel it's about a 75% book, which doesn't please me, but doesn't make me cry either. You've got to practice somehow. Maybe the next one will be 80%!"

19. Notes from Ruth Mills, undated (1984). Also see his letter to his parents, undated (fall 1940).

20. For example, see *Norman Thomas: A Biography* by Harry Fleischman, who served as Thomas's campaign manager in 1944 and 1948 (New York: W. W. Norton and Company, 1964); and Norman D. Markowitz, *The Rise and Fall of the People's Century: Henry A. Wallace and American Liberalism, 1941–1948* (New York: Free Press, 1973).

The point of land out from the university going towards where you used to live—I mean in that direction? I hope you will ask me over some weekend next spring.

I don't envy you the Mannheim job if it's more like his later books than his former. But I'm naturally very interested in just what it is. If you like, I'd certainly be glad, and grateful, for the chance to look it over in manuscript.

Thanks for using my book on labor in your course! Reaction to it here in left circles is so far pretty good. As for the department, Merton has gone into it with me at lunch in great detail and is gushy over it, especially its form (integration of tables and text, typologies etc.). I halfway believe him. But no other member of the department has said a word! So who knows. Anyway, it's done and over.

(Incidentally there is a wonderful fellow named Lewis Coser (Clair) who is teaching at Chicago this fall and next spring[21] . . . if you're in Chicago contact him and his wife Rose, daughter of Laub. I know you'll get along and enjoy each other.)

About the "Manifesto":[22]

I have to be honest with you and say I can't make heads or tails out of your reaction, except that you are completely pessimistic (so am I) and that you support Wallace (which I don't can't won't). Most of your comment is fine: detailed points about the situation and the stupidity of US policy. Well, that's more or less agreed. But what do you want to do, even by way of writing?

Do you think that now one should not advance any "programs," not even *articulate* some idea, even if they can't and won't be realized so far as one can see? Of course we should debunk, debunk, debunk. But is that all we should do? What do you say if Sol Barkin of [the] textile union comes to you and says, help me write a speech for a union leader? What do you say if Norman Thomas does likewise for a speech that will get into pretty wide circulation? I mean are we really at the point where we can't say a damn thing so far as "what to do" is concerned? In short: are you saying that one (by which I mean you and me and 500 other people in the United States who are politically alert and have the leisure to write and think about politics),

21. Coser used the pen name "Louis Clair" when he wrote for *politics*.

22. Mills and others were working on a political position paper; as far as we know it was not published.

that we can only 1) give good journalist accounts and analysis of what
the setup is, [and] 2) debunk the official politics of various powers
that be. . . . Isn't it possible at all to state "programs," even when we
don't have any going movement or power which might carry them
out? (Have you seen David Riesman's article in [the] recent issue of
Yale Law Review?)

Your idea that we are oriented too much to Detroit and NY is,
I think, the reverse of the point that you are too oriented to building
trade unions! There is now no doubt that Reuther is coming out this
fall for a new party.[23] There is, moreover, no doubt but that John
Green of shipbuilders and textile workers will string along. It may
be—at least it is not foolish to think—that Reuther and Co. will get
hold of the CIO minus the CPs in the next few years.[24] I cannot but
believe that such an organization will or may well amount to something. And those people are madly looking for ideas. You can't build
a movement on journalist gossip and debunking. The very pull of
Wallace, especially at first, several months ago, indicates the possibility
in such a real labor outfit.

[. . .]

I can't remember whether I sent you a copy of the syllabus on
labor unions? If you don't get it in a few days, please let me know
and I'll get one off to you. Only one meeting so far but the kids seem
enthusiastic about it. I'm using the same outline in an undergraduate
course and in the graduate seminar, so I've about 45 people all told
working on it.

You have some enemies (I suppose via Shils) in Bruce Smith and
his wife. Saw them the other day here (they go to Chicago for some
bibliographic job). I gather you saw them in Berlin or at least Germany. I was amazed at the way they dislike the Krauts . . . yes they
actually use the term . . . of course their talk is full of all sorts of
"culturally determined" explanations, but in all they are just plain
nationalistically anti-German. Dan Bell is here now with *Fortune;* I've

23. Walter Reuther was the president of the United Auto Workers from 1946 until his
death in 1970.
24. "CPs" refers to Communist Party members; Reuther was president of the Congress
of Industrial Organizations (CIO) from 1952 to 1955 and helped to plan the merger with
the American Federation of Labor (AFL) in 1955. He was the first vice president of the AFL–
CIO, and George Meany was its first president.

seen him only once and don't look forward to meeting him again. He's full of gossip about how he met Luce for lunch and what Luce said . . . [. . .].[25]

See you soon.

Best wishes.
cwm

Mills's friendly relationship with Daniel Bell had ended in 1945, after Mills and Freya separated and Mills moved out of the apartment building on 11th Street. Later, in the fifties, Mills and Bell became political opponents as their ideological differences grew in scope and intensity.

In the following letter to Hazel Erskine in Reno, Nevada, Mills refers to reviews of The New Men of Power.

To Hazel Gaudet Erskine, from New York City, dated Saturday, October 23, 1948

Dear Haze:

Thanks for your note; yes the reviews are OK so far, some even enthusiastic. *Labor Action* came thru nicely; we have yet to see [what the] academic boys do, but who the hell cares.

Tell your mother hello hello.

About comics: do it either way you want . . . hunks or all at once. I'd think to wait and see it whole done would be best from your standpoint. I figure we've got to show manuscript in about a month from now. [. . .] I'm reserving Nov.-Dec.-Jan. as the general area of working on it. So the pace seems to be OK. Nothing drastic by way of rush-rush, but only soon as conveniently possible.

Sorry to say I've had a bad fall so far; just hectic-ity and no quiet munching work possible. *White Collar* is on about chapter 8 (out of 15 chapters). Getting first four or five typed soon with carbons. But think of Nevada, California, Temagami: open spaces all [the] time.

---

25. Henry Robinson Luce, who founded *Fortune, Time, Life,* and *Sports Illustrated* and coined the phrase "the American Century."

SEND ME A BIG BUNCH OF SAGE IN CELLOPHANE SO IT WILL
SMELL HERE. MAIL TO: 611 Hamilton, Broadway and 116th, Columbia
Univ., because am there most of time and want to keep it there.

goodbye,
Charlie

ॐ

To Hans Gerth, from New York City, dated Wednesday (probably
November 1948)

Dear Gerth:

I. Weber and Oxford

The sales on Weber have been slow but steady; the Parsons
volume has almost exactly the same performance curve as our volume.[26] Oxford is therefore worried, but feels it necessary to keep it
in print. This is probably their picture, which makes them not want
to take on more Weber, but to keep what they have available. They
can't, I gather, make new plates; they'd like if possible to reprint with
no changes at all. So the chance of including anything on Judaism is
nil; the chance of the bibliography is also low. After I get your textual
corrections, if any, I'll ask explicitly but I think they'll say no. (They
can do as they please given the copyright thing as it is.) You'd be wiser
therefore to go ahead and let Social Research do it, get 200 reprints
made and ship them around, or at least so I think. They don't like, I
gather, to deliberately kill secondhand market, at least not when it's
obvious! I've only seen Vaudrin once, and that time last week mainly
about white collar book.[27] I just told him he could wait and like it;
that I wasn't going to throw it together now in 2 months; he seemed
to understand and it's due now early next summer, which is possible.
About half is in fair draft and the rest well filed and ready for penultimate writing. Please get textual corrections to me soon as possible,
and only those you feel must be made.

26. The "Parsons volume" is Max Weber, *The Theory of Social and Economic Organiza-*
tion, ed. and trans. Talcott Parsons (New York: Oxford University Press, 1947).
27. Philip Vaudrin, then an editor at Oxford University Press, later went to work at Alfred A. Knopf.

II: The text *[Character and Social Structure]*

I had intended to take up the old text we had planned with you this spring, and we must certainly talk about it. Now that you bring it up, let me say that of course I'm still interested; we've both invested a good deal of time on it and it would be [a] shame not to go thru with it. My own schedule is such that by June *White Collar* is done and I am not going to do any more big empirical jobs at the Bureau. I just won't do it. It drives me crazy in terms of money, responsibility, and budgets and all the rest of it; and besides it just isn't the kind of work I feel good doing. This has been an argument going on here for some time (they want me to take on more responsibilities in connection with [the] Bureau, or rather did up to last year when I got firm about it) and [it] has hurt me career-wise, but God I can't go on with such trash. Anyway this means that I will be free to start up a longer piece of writing, and I should personally very much like it to be the text with you.

Two things now. 1) First can you get a written cancellation of the Heath contract? I don't want and I don't think you want to do it with that firm. If so, and if you and I can get together on it, 2) there will be no trouble at all in getting a good contract with either Oxford or Harcourt Brace. I can do that by mail next spring. We ought to get at least $1,000 advance and a full year and a half to do it in for typing at least two drafts of whole [manuscript] and for some library check-ing work for which we'll need some sort of assistant, so as to be sure and include or at least know about a lot of the materials the "experi-mental" people have done (for one thing).

Anyway I will bring my complete file on the book with me to Chicago and we'll have some full talks about how it looks to us. OK?

Confidential: If Chicago makes me an offer in the college there, I don't know what the hell I'll do. Columbia department has put me in for a boost in rank this year but it could easily be killed by budget committee, which under Eisenhower is really rough I'm told. My withdrawing from Bureau work means my income is cut $2,500. So I'm back to $5,000 with two families to support! Which again means that I'm all tied up in ghostwriting! How to get out of this? Well, I'll certainly consider Chicago carefully if it's a good offer and if there is time free for writing.

It is getting so the image of the old fashioned professor is almost impossible to achieve, at least here in New York and especially at Columbia. They expect you to supplement your income with "entrepreneurial activities" of one sort or another and this, in line with my last summer's decision of which I wrote you, is exactly what I am not going to continue after this year.

If we had if I had any guts, what I'd do is quit this and go up to Temagami and build a snug house and go live on [the] $600 a year you could get from writing what you want to. So you see, I envy you greatly your house and dog! Maybe state universities are the best bet and in smaller cities. What do you think the chances are, if any, for me at Wisconsin? Maybe I remember it nostalgically now but it seems from here awfully good stuff. The other day [Richard] Hofstadter figured how much time a week he spent on nonessentials like parking a car, etc., things due to the big city as such, and it came to an unconscionable amount. Then the frustration of it . . .

Well, ignore this free association if you will, but it adds up to this: where I'd like to go is Berkeley, more than anywhere else, but there's no sociology there; "business is good" here, but I think now seriously of a big state university, or maybe Chicago, as being a happier situation.

Happy Thanksgiving!
[unsigned copy]

[P.S.] For front piece to *White Collar:*

"No one could suspect that times were coming . . . when the man who did not gamble would lose all the time, even more surely than he who gambled."

Charles Peguy

Good! For the book, Introduction: The New Little Man.

In the presidential election of 1948, Harry Truman defeated Thomas Dewey in what was probably the most surprising political outcome in American history. Hazel Erskine had written a series of articles about opinion polls on political issues and the election, which were published in Labor and Nation. *Mills was a contributing editor of that periodical; Erskine's columns, under the heading of "What the People Think," carried the following credit: "By Hazel G. Erskine. Edited by Professor C. Wright Mills."*

The next letter was written in the wake of Truman's electoral victory.

To Hazel Gaudet Erskine, from New York City, undated (probably November 1948)

Dear Haze:

Enclosed is syllabus, which has been mimeographed, so you can keep or destroy this copy. So far we've worked out swell index of oligarchy and crossed it with size (very positive) and with CP [Communist Party] control (very positive in CIO!). We've about 23 columns of information and probably I won't punch more as it takes so much of my time.

I think L and N stuff stood up very well; it would have been better had we stuck by the June July piece, which ends saying that Truman has a good chance.[28] Anyway I'm trying to get base figures on Gallop and Roper in order to see if this couldn't be enough to explain the upset:

Analyzing the dk: which was 8% I think in Gallop . . . he threw it out, but probably ¾; of them were lower ses and ed and Roosevelt voters; if the dk is allocated according to that, would it have been OK? If so, the polls are OK, but the pollsters are inept and what with you out of town, messed it all up.[29]

If this doesn't work, then samples were just off, although I can't believe that all the polls would have the same thing. Everyone here I talk with very puzzled. Come on, explain it for me.

NAM has reviewed book [*The New Men of Power*]: elegantly nonsensical . . . says I made it all up on a bench in Morningside Heights![30]

Editorship of *politics* still in doubt. We meet again this Thursday nite.

---

28. "What the People Think: Straws and Bricks in the Political Winds," *Labor and Nation* 4, no. 3 (May–June 1948): 8–12. A subsequent article reported that polls indicated a preference for Dewey over Truman by a wide margin: "What the People Think: November Prospects," *Labor and Nation* 4, no. 5 (September–October 1948): 6–10.

29. "Dk" refers to people who responded to a survey question by saying they didn't know—the "don't knows"; "ses" refers to social-economic status, and "ed" to education.

30. NAM may possibly be a reference to a review by a writer associated with the National Association of Manufacturers.

O how right you are about cities . . . but how wrong that I'll always be frenetic. I've just got to stop or I'll go mad.

I think only of Temagami, and have some swell little huts planned; really little screened squares with aluminum roofs having big overhang. Trouble is, because of snow in winter, the roofs have to slant pretty sharp, which makes them look funny. What can you do about that? I'll use a lot of one-by-fours laid flat or horizontal between widely spaced 2-by-4 studding and tack screen onto that framework.

Mills

∾

To Dwight Macdonald, from New York City, November 20, 1948

Saturday

Dwight:

Was sick all last week; please take that as an excuse for not writing this sooner. The point is I don't think I'd better take on the editorial job we've been discussing. Here's why:

1. As you know, for four years I've been heavily involved in collective research work which has taken up most of not only my worktime but my life. Now, just when I began to crawl out from under it as a semi-free man, it seems foolish to take on more responsibilities which, again, "interfere" with my own book-writing program, which means my very own work.

2. The white collar man, for instance, is two years overdue, and I'm getting slightly ill of it. It has got to be done by mid-spring. But more important than such specific projects is the fact that when you're involved in a job of writing, to do it well you have to live it: the notes you take on books you read, the meanings you are aware of in events, even how the street scene looks to you . . . they have to be involved in what you're engaged in. Selfishly, I want to be free to garner such materials and get them into my own freely chosen line of work, rather than force them into monthly comments.

3. I feel this point all the more keenly because I am not now clear on so many issues. Certainly I have no "line" worked out that prods me to forceful, quick assertion. All last week I tried to formulate about 1,000 words on liberalism and the election (you'll get this if I can finish it). [. . .] Now, first, [one] can't produce that slowly and hold up [one's] end, even by giving one whole week a month. Second, it seems to me to indicate that such a person shouldn't be a miserable editor but a miserable contributor.

4. As I've got to be in Chicago until July, and after that Temagami, I couldn't really take any role in actually editing the magazine until next Oct.

5. If you decide to set up a Contributing Editor group, or something like that, with no definite expectations of monthly work, I would of course be glad to be included. In so far as you personally are involved in the magazine, it has and doubtless will represent the publication closest to my own confusions.

6. Finally, if the magazine is going and you don't ask me again in the middle of next fall, I will undoubtedly ask you for some role in its production. In the meantime I get on my feet.

Write me a note telling me you understand and that you're not mad.

Yours,
Charlie
Charlie Mills

In early 1949 Mills and Ruth went to Chicago, where Mills was a visiting professor for a semester at the University of Chicago. Lewis A. Coser was teaching at the University of Chicago at the time, and the Cosers and the Millses shared David Riesman's house that semester while Riesman was away.

Mills described the setting in the following letter to Leo Lowenthal, a German sociologist Mills had met in 1944, when Lowenthal was working for the U.S. State Department as well as the Bureau of Applied Social Research.

To Leo Lowenthal, from Chicago, Illinois, undated (probably January or February 1949)

Dear Leo:

This winter we are in Chicago in a big house along fraternity row across from the gym and all around us it is grey, drab, grubby: rain on Gothic. Most all universities are the same, except some are more closely administered than others, further along the bureaucratic path. This one is quite far along that path. Yet I am not part of it really; I am visiting. I am a wonderful visitor; I wish I could visit everywhere I am for all time. I've really no feeling of need for anything to the contrary. To be a permanent visitor everywhere.

After getting here, we rested for a week, and have decided to rest this week too. Just live: eat, sleep, fornicate, drive around a little, meet four hours of classes each week and two hours of staff meeting. Next week we'll start on manuscript again. (Which reminds me, for God's sake prod Rose to send me chapter 9; it's the last of Puerto Rico in her hands this go round. Got to have it, holding everything up.) Haven't turned on the radio since leaving NY, haven't read a newspaper. A state of mild shock, holding us in suspended withdrawal, coasting on past drives, not building any up from new bases: do you know what I mean? Guess last fall, all in all, was more tiring than I thought. Exhausted, really. [Everett] Hughes had us to tea: nice and pleasant.[31] [William] Ogburn had me to lunch: nice and pleasant.[32] The Singers had us over one evening: nice and pleasant.[33] I don't talk much: just ask them what they're doing and sit still, listening. They talk and talk and sell and sell. It's easier this way.

Bought two mountain tents and two air mattresses in a big Army store here. Wonderful, light nylon stuff and very comfortable and neat. Am all ready to go, anytime. Also bought a pair of 8" boots, moccasin type to wear around here in all this wet slop and crap I have to wade thru. Gothic in the rain.

Yours as ever,
Charlie
Charlie Wright Mills

31. The sociologist Everett C. Hughes. See Everett C. Hughes, *On Work, Race, and the Sociological Imagination,* ed. and with an introduction by Lewis A. Coser (Chicago: University of Chicago Press, 1994).

32. The sociologist William F. Ogburn.

33. Milton Singer was chairman of the Chicago College social science division, where Mills taught during the spring term.

∾

To Robert K. Merton, from Chicago, Illinois, undated (probably February 1949)

Saturday noon

Dear Bob:

1. In a few days, I'll be sending a letter to James Reid about the book Gerth and I talk of doing;[34] you will receive a copy of it. I hope the project goes thru, because I really think we can produce quite a book if we're given the financial opportunity of being together for a four or six months stretch.

2. Chicago is amazing; I'll tell you all about it when next we meet. I don't think I've learned as much about "the field" as something to work in in the last five years, as I have in the last five weeks here. Well, I guess it takes time to learn what one is about and what one should be about; and I, of course, learn the hardest way. Am writing a memo on the academic man and his career, which is as much for my own edification as anything else; although, in a different form, some of it will get into *White Collar,* in chapter on salaried professions. When it's done, I'll let you see it, if you want.

3. I hear that two of our colleagues landed De Latour a fat job at Illinois, which, from other sources, I hear was the job they were discussing for me. But all that is rumor; I don't know. Anyway.

4. [. . .] The manuscript on Puerto Rico is all done but one chapter and the notes. I'm holding it for two or three weeks before hitting it once more editorially. You'll get a complete draft . . . I'd say in about three or four weeks.

How about parts II (Srole) and III (Rossi) on Decatur?[35] I was supposed to get drafts of these Feb. 1; it would help me a lot and also provide a prod to finish my parts of the thing if you'd get copies of these to me soon. How about it?

34. Reid was an editor at Harcourt Brace.
35. The study of influence.

White Collar, as usual, goes slowly. I think I'm investing too much in it, trying to do too much within a framework that just won't hold it. Then, as always, one always says, finish this and that and then, *then* you'll really get the chance to get on *White Collar.* It's getting to be an institution with me. Yet it does move slowly.

Let me know how it is with you and what is going on in the world.

Yours,
Wright

ᔆ

To William and Virginia Miller, from Chicago, Illinois, undated (probably winter 1949)

Dear Miller and Buckner:

Notes on the bureaucratic situation at Chicago will be forwarded to you sometime during the next three weeks, in the form of "Chicago Memo No. One: Problems of the College Staff." This will cover the situation in detail and is what Chicago has paid for, whether they know it or not or like it or not. My stake here is most slim, so don't care. Thought I would therefore let them have it on the nose. Will want your criticism before submitting it to deans involved.

I suppose everywhere one gets depressed and bored, that is everywhere in academic places. It is hard to work here. Feel like I am in the field studying stuff. No books. No files that amount to anything. So just take notes and don't write so well. I just can't take these people seriously. They have their own problems—generally those of administrators and teachers and graduate student-like people, not those of research people or writers or people trying to find out how to live. I'm afraid my attitude shows thru and so I've ceased to behave. I just yawn when I want to and attack whoever talks foolishness. Well, hell, what do I care. Guess I can go on living on nothing in New York and ghosting and all that and put off the house in the battery another four or five years. Right now plenty money and can pay off all of car and carry summer too, and if trailer sells can do OK next year too. Ever see a check every month after taxes for $875? Seems natural to me, but first time it's come like that. Will try of course to get thru to Hutchins but it seems hard so far. Got to get to him or not much chance. Scare the others as usual.

And try as I will try on the memo, it will come out the same way: harsh and mean and biting and for god's sake why don't you do it this way, no not that way.

You son of a bitch: of course why don't you write on the industrial paper just for two hours for a friend and send it to me quick. Got to get it off. Been waiting for you to send it; you know I can't publish anything 'til you've gone over it and said maybe well OK.

I like the letter all right but you should have sent it to me before the editor, because it suffers with the weight of a big point put into such small space. Should have been elaborated at a couple of points rather than just baldly stated. That's why it has a little tone of griping even tho of course it's solid. Also I have a diary kept by a Washington journalist who was at Harvard on that fellowship thing they have for big journalists who want a year of rest, and I would have made it available to you. He is as intelligent as all hell and gives the lowdown. Anyway you didn't hurt yourself but god damn it why go off like that when I'm out here in the woods and fog and dirty grey dead end of a shit heeling town. Communicate with me.

yours as ever,
Mills
Mills and Mills

[P.S.] Please phone Rose Kohn at the Bureau right away and tell her you and I had to talk long distance on some business and I asked you to call her and ask her, for god's sake, to have Mary Woods, the typist, send the three chapters on Puerto Rico I mailed her for typing,[36] and for her, Rose, to send me the last chapter on aspirations, for god's sake. Lay it on thick and sob some about it (for me out here in the wilderness and depending on her, for god's sake, to send me the stuff).

36. The "three chapters" were from the manuscript in progress about a study for the Bureau: C. Wright Mills, Clarence Senior, and Rose Kohn Goldsen, *The Puerto Rican Journey: New York's Newest Migrants* (New York: Harper and Brothers, 1950).

To William Miller, from Chicago, Illinois, dated April 7, 1949

Dear Bill,

Thanks for your letter, and news. Be glad to go over the stuff you mention, soon as you send it. Sorry about gug and drag on steel[37] but what the hell: you are, like the cowboy and detectives in the movies, an autonomous man. You don't need that stuff.

Here's how it is with me. First workwise:

1. Puerto Rico all done but small fry stuff, being machine checked at bureau and another copy gone over finally by Bodie. Decided not to bother you with it until galley, which should be summer or fall.
2. Have about $\frac{7}{8}$ of opinion leader in rough draft; will be typed enough for you to see in about 10 days or two weeks at most. It runs to 150 or 200 pages. This I really want you to go over, because it is not just another piece of writing but the counter of a fight that ought to be just right in every way before I give it in to them. So you'll be hearing about this.[38]
3. Ruth was on PR [*The Puerto Rican Journey*],[39] now slowly gets into *White Collar* as I do, outlining small areas mainly so far, but middle of next week I start on it hard; the big spurt.
4. Signed contracts with Harcourt Brace, so did Gerth; so that is all settled.[40]

And that is all, as I'm not the sort of person who does too much at one time. So there.

How it is otherwise:

1. Have made out bill for lumber needed on house and mailed it

---

37. Mills typed "gug and drag on steel"; perhaps he meant "tug and drag on steel" as an expression of a difficulty Miller had described, or perhaps he meant "Sturm und Drang."

38. Mills later left this project in a departure he discussed in a letter to Hans Gerth, dated February 15, 1952, included in this volume.

39. In the preface of this book, Mills credited Mrs. Ruth Harper Mills, saying that she "was in charge of the statistical analysis presented in the chapter on adaptation and offered many suggestions on the statistics and the editing of the entire volume."

40. For *Character and Social Structure*. Actually, the matter wasn't completely settled, since Mills and Gerth still needed to obtain an official termination of their contract with D. C. Heath (which had not paid an advance to them).

today for bids. Magnificent. Am reading at night a little more on carpentry etc. to refresh self. It's a cinch. Will be a wonderful house.
2. Next Saturday we shop for fishing outfits (we found out in Temagami just what's needed). Tools: a whole set of clean, well chosen oiled tools.
3. We have sailed once in the folding kayak and it works just fine. It goes along like hell. A little hysterically in gusts but a good deal. Lake Mich. is a big thing so we stay mainly in the lagoon that's nearby.

So our life focuses upon work, commodities involved in work; and now in my fourth decade, slowly nonwork, noncommodities edge into the picture. No movies now. Play the guitar an hour or so at night. Read more and more and more on movies. My god what a thing they are. We must make them: they've got everything that appeal to me in this damn society and moreover the chance to damn everything else in it. Will write one this summer. See you soon. Send stuff. The title of the movie to be written is: "Enthusiasm."

Yours,
Mills

∽

To William Miller, from Chicago, undated (1949)

Dear Bill:

Thank you, as Ruth says, so much for the trouble on the other side of this sheet. But to hell with it. Anybody wanting $20 for adv. is running a racket or buying in wholesale lots, in either case not for us. The damn trailer will sell come spring and if not we'll just set it up on bricks on the island as a sort of expensive fetish to our travelous youth.[41] Thanks anyway.

Well, my friend, as I hang around here I get into it all deeper and who knows [. . . how it] will end. I interviewed the staff and sorta scared them in doing it. Got my memo on career lines of academics in shape tho. You'll get copy in due course. Been in big depression, which blesses us all from time to time I gather, so no real work.

41. The island owned by the Millses in Lake Temagami, Ontario.

First I thought it was this atmosphere, but hell it happens everywhere; it's inside you and you carry it. The perils of the act of thought. Nevertheless there is something awfully bleak and bad and grey about this atmosphere. Maybe it's not having you around to spill my guts to from time to time but anyway—just between us and God damn it tell no one—I am coming back to Columbia on their damn lousy $5,000 and [will] sit it out regardless of what they do here or don't do. Manhattan, it's in my blood. You are happier being unhappy there. And you know you're at the center. Here everyone feels in their bones that they are on the rim.

I am disillusioned about *White Collar* again. I can't write it right. I can't get what I want to say about America in it. What I want to say is what you say to intimate friends when you are discouraged about how it all is. All of it at once: to create a little spotlighted focus where the alienation, and apathy and dry rot and immensity and razzle dazzle and bullshit and wonderfulness and how lonesome it is, really, how terribly lonesome and rich and vulgar and god I don't know. Maybe that mood, which I take now to be reality for me, is merely confusion which of course might be so and still worthwhile if one could only articulate it properly.

I can write an ordered statement of this and that; I can go lyric for a paragraph or two, I can moan well and feel sad sometimes without showing sentiment too cornily; but I cannot get them all into each sentence or even each chapter. I think, I really do, that my medium is not studies of *White Collar* people etc. but that I ought to launch out in some new medium that is not so restricting, but I don't have the guts to do that because my skill, my tested talent, is in handling the facts and contour according to my own brand of "social science." It is all too god damn much to try to do. The problem is the old problem of creation. How many minutes in a lifetime do we ever get that are creative in any sense?

next morning Saturday goodbye,
Mills

In May of 1949 an informant furnished the FBI with its first piece of information on Mills's political activities: a copy of the letterhead of the Kutcher Civil Rights Committee, which listed members of the National Committee, including C. Wright

Mills. At the time, James Kutcher was a thirty-six-year-old veteran who had been awarded the Purple Heart after losing both legs in World War II. After his return from the war, he was fired from his clerical job at the Veterans' Administration because he was a member of the Socialist Workers' Party. The Kutcher Civil Rights Committee was formed to aid in his appeals of his dismissal, which challenged the constitutionality of Truman's Loyalty Program.[42] (Eight years after being fired, Kutcher was reinstated by the U.S. Court of Appeals.)

The FBI file also noted that in 1949 Mills and Lewis A. Coser sponsored a May Day meeting in their home for the Politics Club at the University of Chicago, and the featured speaker was from the Independent Socialist League. Mills was unaware of the FBI report when he wrote the following letter.

To William Miller, from Chicago, Illinois, dated May 30, 1949

Monday Night

Dear Bill:

As it comes to every man, so to me: the shakes. I look over the damn manuscript on *White Collar* and on every page see the judgments and the possibility for ignorance and error and it overwhelms me. You have your little visions and you pile together statistics, a little pile out of a possible mountain; you read a few books and use some of them, and then in your thirties you have the gall to tell anybody who will pick it up off a shelf how it is today with millions of people. It is absolutely silly. But it would be the same in your forties and in your fifties. Only maybe worse because energy as such carries you thru a lot of it and later that will decline. It is like I say of the new entrepreneur: he has no set standards of accomplishment, no models for his life, no tradition to trust: out there alone. Maybe we ought to quit, except it is too late for that. Like Bogart or Garfield says in a movie ("Force of Evil" . . . excellent): "You make a living, you take a risk." Well, *making* a living is more than making a livelihood; and when you try to make it, you take a risk. The only thing is there are so many

<hr>

42. "Ousted Amputee to Test Loyalty Program in Supreme Court If Plea to Board Fails," *New York Times,* 1 April 1949, sec. 1, p. 17.

ways you know to look at it and all of them are forms you picked
up some place and there isn't any content, so you get dependent
upon others' judgments more than you should, you think, but you
don't know anybody to depend on really. So you're back again on
your own.

And write a lot of crap to your friend.

Anyway, got the shakes and am scared. Too much work. Too
much scope to it. Can't stop. Can't go on. And look how I run to
avoid whatever it is I'm talking about. For two summers driving in
automobiles and trailers all over the continent. Now into Canada to
build a house, to fish. Read two books on muskie fishing last week.
Buy equipment that will make you autonomous, or rather dependent
on it for a week at a time. Up your skill in fishing, hunting, building,
metalworking. (I know how to build a sink out of aluminum strips,
how to lay a camp out so bugs won't get into it.) In short, up the
delicate mind, made delicate and kept delicate by ten years of work
sharpening it: to set up an 1850 homestead and operate it comfort-
ably. Madness! Madness!

And then you worry that everything you write about "the new
little man" isn't about anybody at all but your own God damn self:
an elaborate projection draped in semiacceptable models of proof.
And it is precisely what you sometimes think good and unique and
a new perspective that comes under this category, and the rest is dull,
[. . . or] probably so. There really isn't any out. Except a kind of
animal enthusiasm and egotism and willfulness (the infant wiggles on
its own: it is not a mechanical thing but an organism) that keep you
going except when you think about why you do it instead of keeping
your eye on the object—or think you're keeping it there—which
you're probably not.

This damn book is so *rough*. It is a total damnation of everything
in this setup. If it is so, then one has to ask how and why the damn
setup continues at all. It can't be so; and yet it seems to be just so to
me. (This is reconciliation . . . the two feelings, only on the ground
that I have a vision of it and nobody else has just this vision, so penetrating. That is where the egotism and willfulness, which I don't have
so much of as often appears, comes in.) To write it you have to whip
yourself up tight and unwind for four pages; then depression for a
month, then whip yourself up and unwind. Repeat. Repeat. And all

this makes it sound as if it might really be good, but really you know it isn't so good. A lot of it is a lot of crap. Or so I suppose.

Write me a letter. We leave next Sunday.
Mills

The next letter mentions correspondence with D. C. Heath, the publisher whose 1941 contract for Character and Social Structure *Mills and Gerth were seeking to cancel. Heath had paid no advance, and the assigned editor for the book was Howard P. Becker, who had been Mills's thesis advisor at the University of Wisconsin. In 1944, Mills had had this to say about Becker: "You know, Gerth, I've wasted time and emotion over this little man. I don't really hate him. If I could judge sentimentally rather than consequentially I could even pity him. He is not really a threat to anybody anymore. Really he isn't. His kind hang themselves, even before fools, they hang themselves. I can forget him now, and I wish him the kind of luck he wants, whatever foolish thing it may be" (Mills to Gerth, dated October 1944).*

To Hans Gerth, from Goddard's Garage Hotel, Temagami, Ontario, undated (probably June or July 1949)

Dear Gerth:

Ruth and I just came in from a week in the bush, as they say up here, and got your note and the letter from Heath. It has been one of the happiest weeks of our lives. In one sentence, every bit of it exceeds our wildest expectations, and both of us are pretty damn wild expectators. During the week, we got the foundation down solid on the rock backbone of the island and the platform of the whole house up. It commands a magnificent view of 5 miles of open lake and down by the side is a little channel that can be fenced off safely for wading and bathing purposes, between the two islands. Our layout is bigger than we had remembered, for we first saw it after the great western scenery. There is in fact enough layout for complete privacy etc. for at least 3 large cabins if wanted. The way things go now, being dependent only on ourselves, we should have the house all done in about 20 days from now. 2 grad students are due latter part of next week to help raise the roof. I tell you I worked this week: lifting telephone sized poles for the foundation and chopping them while still wet and soaked from the water; setting up the 2 by 8 sill structure and laying in the sub-flooring. Anyway more of it all later when I have a place to write from, my corner of the big room. In meantime, Ruth is positively blooming with enthusiasm and euphoria and has in the week despite hard work gained weight! Photographs in due course, of course, and I'll soon correspond with you about your place across that little channel.

Now about Heath: I've no carbon here, so will compose letter here and make copy of it and mail to them. (See below.) You see I follow your lead and point completely for I think you are right. Here's what I'll write:

Dear Mr. Walden:

I've just come in from a fishing trip in the bush and received your letter, for which thanks. All this talk about a book that is now only an idea in Gerth's and my head seems very foolish to me. You ask for the "circumstances leading up to my request for a cancellation." They are very simple and I had supposed you were fully aware of them. You must be aware that Mr. Becker and I have not spoken to one another until this spring for 5 or 6 years. We are civilized about it but I doubt if there is any mutual intellectual respect between us, and certainly no comradely feeling such as might be expected to exist between academic editor and writer. Anyway I am, as I stated in my last letter to you, not inclined to do a book for the firm with which he is associated. This says nothing about your firm or necessarily about Mr. Becker. It is simply a fact about life. I regret having to write so plainly but you force me to do it.

Second, you must be aware that no member of your firm contacted me in any way during the life of the agreement; no interest was displayed in its maturation and I have no friends among people connected with you. In the meantime I have published two books and I do have some excellent and intellectually helpful contacts with these firms. Whatever I publish, with Hans Gerth or alone, will naturally be given to those who helped me along before I had published anything, giving me advances in three figures for research and advice etc. Surely, as a publisher, and I have no doubt a good one, you must know how such things work.

Third, Mr. Becker has himself, or so I understand, written you requesting a cancellation, last March 26th I believe.

These are the only circumstances of which I am aware which led up to the request, in which Mr. Gerth is in agreement with me, to cancel the old agreement. I repeat what I told you last time I wrote: if you do meet our request, you will gain at least one well wisher in me; if you don't, you will not gain a book, although you might kill off a book for the profession.

Therefore, I again join Mr. Gerth and Mr. Becker in requesting you to cancel the old agreement.

Sincerely,
C. Wright Mills

> [P.S.] Hereafter my address will be:
> C. Wright Mills
> Care of Ontario Northland Boatlines
> Temagami, Ontario, Canada

> I hope, Gerth, that that is OK. It is about all that we can do. [. . .]

Well, going back in [to the bush] in the morning. Will write in about a week or so and let you know how it goes. Hey, why not drive up en famille during August for [a] long weekend and look it all over for next summer? All it would cost you is gasoline and couple nites' cabins on way. Rest is on me for a week or two. Really. How about it?

The D. C. Heath contract was eventually canceled formally in February 1950. The new contract for Character and Social Structure *that Mills had obtained from Harcourt Brace, the publisher of* The New Men of Power, *included an advance, a payment for typing services, and work with an editor that Mills and Gerth found agreeable, James M. Reid.*

To Hans and H I Gerth, from Temagami, Ontario, undated (probably August 1949)

Dear Gerths:

You will pardon my not writing in so long, knowing that the house has been long in the building. Well, now it is virtually done; all that remains is a little more on the roof and some on one wall and painting the outside. We are immensely pleased with it and, looking at it now, wonder how we ever did it. For some weeks we've only worked on it in the afternoons, spending the mornings on dear old *White Collar,* which is as disordered and difficult as ever.

Here is the way we live: get up about 7:30 or 8 and eat, after plunge in lake. Pamela has been here about 5 weeks now and swims with a little cork jacket on. We then go to work at our desks until 12:30 or so. Pamela plays by herself for that time and is apparently very happy doing it. Then after lunch we work around on the house until we go swimming at about 4:30, when Pamela has her swimming lesson. After that we drift. Maybe I go in the kayak with Pamela to pick up lily pads; or maybe we take the motorboat six miles up the lake to Bear Island to get mail . . . about two or three times a week for that. Or we just sit and look at the house and make plans for next year's buildings. (A bridge across the small channel to the other island. A guest house there. Another dock up on the point.) Well that is about how it goes.

My mother and father were here for two weeks and picked up Pamela in NY on their way up. That was early July. Now they are safely home again. Pamela will probably stay the whole summer, although I had not anticipated it for she has no one to play with, but it is working out just fine.

A friend who's finishing up his Ph.D. and who teaches at Howard, in Wash. DC, is here; pitched his tent outside and we all eat together. He is from Germany and gets his degree at California. Fred Blum is his name. Irving Sanes, a young novelist, is coming up for a week later this month and Hofstadter and family probably although they don't know yet.

I set up a bunk for Pamela and she climbs up on top of it every two minutes. I really believe that only the bunk is necessary to amuse her for a summer. Also I'm building her a sailboat about 25' long and next year we'll put together a real sailboat of such construction and size that children can run it in the big bay in front of the islands. I don't fish any but my neighbor of half a mile away, who is very proud of being such a good fisherman, a retired dairyman from Cleveland, brings us fresh fish about once a week, which is plenty.

So it is a pleasant unhurried sort of relaxing way to live, the first we've had.

Now I slowly gain back weight and Ruth does too and this is comforting because I really wouldn't want to go back to New York so muscularly. (My appointment for another three years at Columbia came thru . . . anyway I'm apparently safe 'til then, at present salary of course.)

Well, why don't you write me? What is happening? Have you heard from Heath etc. at all since I wrote? Advise me about it if anything is needed as I'm now out of the daze of work and escape of June and July, ready to face my sins and troubles.

Did I tell you that they've printed another set of *The New Men of Power?* That means that by the end of this year they'll have sold between 5,000 and 6,000; so I guess after all, it has gone pretty well.

Tell me how all your publications are coming: the Weber, the Mannheim. And what have you been doing over the summer?

Bob Merton writes that his wife will have another child in a few months. They finally responded to [the] Puerto Rico report sent several months ago, saying how glad they are to have it for the Bureau series of publications. But no response on the Decatur manuscript as yet; I don't expect any until [we] get back in fall. (We plan to leave here for NY about 5th Sept.) Let me know how it is and what is going on in the world.

Yours,
M.
Mills

Gerth replied with a long letter to Mills, dated August 24, 1949. On the subject of their collaboration, Gerth wrote that Heath knew about their contract with Harcourt Brace for Character and Social Structure *and that Heath was prepared to let the project go.*

To William Miller, from New York City, undated (late March or early April 1950)

Wednesday

Dear Bill,

What's the matter with you? Why don't you write? Are you sick? Is it your stomach?

Rub it with olive oil.

We are sitting around here in New York tonite thinking about station wagons, Leica cameras, eight-foot speedboats, one of which we intend to build this summer (Ruth hates all this commodity stuff— she says). I am reading all sorts of books on painting and aesthetics in general, and photography. We are also both very heavily at work on *White Collar*. This is where we stand:

Part I (after your suggestions, altho perhaps not so drastically) completely rewritten and ready for typing.

Part II completely in draft, and halfway thru drastic first revision, ready for typing in two weeks at most.

Part III on styles of life two-thirds in draft, making one more chapter which is neatly folderized to be written.

Part IV on ways of power a third finished, making two chapters, [. . .] which are half blocked already.

In other words, a good fighting chance to have the whole thing in a fairly good draft by June one, if we continue for the next eight weeks as we've been going. Oxford will get a copy of this, but they are not going to set the book until August, which means I can fool with it and polish in the summer in a kind of desultory way, which I really think is the best way to do that last touch stuff.

I am collecting the $1,250 from Harcourt Brace in a week or two,[43] and will in all likelihood buy a 1947 or '48 Ford station wagon. Since both Ruth and I are extremely tired, we will probably take one long weekend run to the Cape and Boston, or if you would like, to Boston and the Cape. How far is it from Boston to the Cape by auto? Is there a convenient train connection back from the Cape to Boston? Couldn't we pick you all up in Boston and all go to the Cape for a day and a nite, and then drop you on the way back to New York, at a convenient point so that you could go back to Boston by train? I can always cut a Monday class which means we could have Sat Sun Mon and Tues away from NY. We are interested in doing this as soon as we

43. For *Character and Social Structure*.

complete blocking out a draft of the whole book, which I would judge to be from three to five weeks from now. Let us know what you all think about it.

So: we smell summer and travel and, in anticipation, the feeling of work done. Here's hoping we can hold on with the one brief interlude mentioned until June one.

Yours,
Mills

In May of 1950 Mills was promoted from assistant professor to associate professor of sociology, effective in July.

To William Miller, from New York City, dated June 8, 1950

Dear Bill:

Of course I take seriously your comments and criticism of part one of *White Collar;* and of course I am going to send you the other parts of it as they are done. Am waiting for Irv's comments on that part[44] and then will get down to it in a thorough revision. I consider criticism the high act of friendship and take it seriously altho not personally. You know that.

Glad you let Tom read the piece on method,[45] but what did he say? What did you say? I want to get it off this coming week if possible, before all the meeting-papers jam up the journal for years and years. So: do you think I should publish it? I had another 5 pages or so slanted against the Molecular stuff but left it out in reading because wanted a balance for once and besides no time to read more than this. If you will ask me the four or five key questions about the two methods or about the "correct" way as conceived here, I'll try to address myself to them. Let me know soon as you can, as I want to get rid of the thing.

44. Irving Sanes, William Miller, Hans Gerth, Quentin Anderson, Charles Frankel, Richard Hofstadter, Harvey Swados, and Lionel Trilling were credited for giving advice about the manuscript or galleys (in acknowledgments in *White Collar,* 355).

45. Possibly Thomas C. Cochran, Miller's coauthor of *The Age of Enterprise* (1942).

(I don't really believe in papers on method . . . it is a kind
of disease which interferes with work as much as it helps it.)

Yours,
Mills

∾

To Hans Gerth, from New York City, undated (early October 1950)

Tuesday nite

Gerth:

  I. Here are your 1st runs of the pictures. Please:

      1) give Marshall his choice of them of his wife and self

      2) pick a few yourselves

      3) destroy the rest—they are only the 1st runs.

  [. . .] Let me know the one you like, and send it back and I'll do
what you want with it in a more careful print job. More will come to
you. I sent none to H I.

  II. I've asked the council of research at Columbia U. for $2,000 for
a secretary etc. this year. Chances seem good to get it. Will let
you know soon. It is of course for *C & SS [Character and Social
Structure]*.

  III. Tomorrow!! *white collar* goes to press. My God, how we have
worked—until 3 A.M. every day for 2 weeks now, up at 8. We're
exhausted, but now it's done.

Yours,
Mills

When White Collar *was published, it included Mills's acknowledgment of Ruth's
contribution: "Whenever in this book, I have written 'we' I mean my wife, Ruth
Harper, and myself: during the last three years, her assistance in careful research and
creative editing has often amounted to collaboration" (page 355). Similarly, five years
later, when* The Power Elite *was published, Mills credited Ruth in the acknowl-*

edgment pages of that work as "chief researcher and editorial adviser [who] has shaped much of the book" (page 364).

To William and Virginia Miller, from New York City, undated (probably late 1950)

6:30 A.M. Thursday morning: Hamilton Hall [Columbia University]

Bill, Bucky:

I guess I'm still crazy, or anyway given to strangely youthful things. Yesterday at noon I was going to write you and say [I] need a hundred to eat on; now less than 24 hours later, I've bought $345.00 worth of machine tools, worked all night long, from 11 P.M. to 5:30 A.M. on *Character and Social Structure* and the weekend study, and have food money for the month. Answer: a royalty check on the Weber came thru suddenly and decisively yesterday afternoon. God bless that boy.

I got going last night, rewriting, and since I have to push myself anyway on it now, I just stuck with it: eating and drinking coffee all night at home. It feels good, although I nearly wrecked the car driving up here (I'm killing time writing to you!) before going way downtown to shoot some pictures and look at more tools.

About the tools: we have definitely decided to buy anywhere from 15 to 100 acres, not more than 1 and [a] half hours out of New York, preferably with an old wreck of a house, salvageable for materials, or maybe just the land, and build a weekend place on it. Now that is damn near halfway to Boston. Does it suggest anything to you? Tools are going to get scarce as hell, good power tools, so right now I'm putting $500 or so into them. Will store them in Hamilton Hall, making out they are books in crates. What I got yesterday was a wonderful thing called a Shopsmith. It is a lathe, a disk sander, a table saw (8" circular blade), a shaper and center,[46] a vertical and a horizontal drill press. Also a jigsaw. These are attachments which clamp onto two parallel bars. The whole thing is about

46. A tool for centering wood before it is drilled.

5 feet long and 2 feet wide and about 5 feet high when rigged. It is beautiful. With it I have what amounts to a miniature planing mill. Works on 110 volts. All I need to build a house is four-sided wood and sheets of glass, electrical wiring and sheet tin, and plumber's pipe, for I can make windows and doors and everything according to my own design. In fact, if wood isn't available I can cut timber and wait a year and build with that. I'm serious. Now I need a small cement mixer, which I'll make out of an oil drum and a good power hand-saw, which I'll try to get today. The stuff is already scarce if you want the best type. (The royalty check wasn't all that big. I pay a third down!) Pick up rest on March first, when first $1,250 comes from weekend study.

Weekend study: that is what the TV study has become.[47] I'll call the book METROPOLITAN WEEKEND and I've already set up with MC RC for fieldwork.[48] So I've been running around fixing that up and working like mad on a questionnaire. First intensives on trial basis this Sunday by Jeanette Green and Ruth. It's [a] sorta nice study.

Am building a magnificent "space divider" (cabinet: 48" by 16" by 52" high) out of ply (Philippine mahogany with aluminum angle for corner legs and plastic sides. Copied design from Eames via photographs).[49] Will try to get mahogany today. Already got aluminum for 12 bucks yesterday. Whole thing costs by Eames $108. Cost to build, $40. Magnificent thing.

Listen, you ought to come and see [the] apt: you wouldn't know it. Let me know a week ahead and come down for a weekend.

Sleepy tired.

Yours,
Mills

47. The Workshop on the Cartoon Narrative of New York University hired Mills as a research consultant to direct a study of media-related habits. The project was funded by a grant from *Puck: The Comic Weekly*.

48. MC RC probably refers to a research agency.

49. Charles and Ray Eames, prominent American designers of furniture. In 1946 Charles Eames became the first designer to have a one-person show at the Museum of Modern Art in New York City.

To William and Virginia Miller, from New York, New York, undated
(probably February 1951)

Dear Billy and Bucky:

I think we told you the deal on the five acres went thru: $5,500 for
the five acres, old house and barn with dug well and electricity in the
house.[50] Good contract mode of payment in next three years. Needs
about 3,000 dollars in iceboxes, pumping systems, plumbing, new
ceiling, etc. Got big room with beams 27 by 17 feet big; glass porch
25 feet long on one side and bedroom and dressing room and bath on
other and nice big kitchen in rear. Now big woodstove; will install oil
space heater or self contained floor grate. Well, you'll see it soon. Why
not make it weekend after next: hell, it's only a three hour drive from
Boston. Come down Sat. morning and go back Sunday afternoon. If
OK, let us know and Ruth will give you directions and location.

Bill, I want you to do something about Joe Bensman. You know
I don't recommend men lightly, but this boy is good. A real honest-
to-god sociologist. I've hired him for some intensives[51] on the weekend study and he has the touch . . . the all around touch. Now let
me know when you are coming so as to steer him; he wants to know
about Harvard's deal. So do yourself some good and get authority or
something from the boys to talk with him. Let me know so I can let
him know.[52]

Now look: do you have any cots etc.? If so we need to borrow
them, as our foam rubber bed from Macy's hasn't come yet and won't
for three-four weeks. You'll need them when you come for weekend.
(If you want, you can of course drive on in and have [our] New York
apt.) Sissy. But it's warm and so much space. Ruth says to tell you she
is doing the electrical wiring.

50. The purchase agreement, dated February 3, 1951, gave the Millses the right to immediate occupancy and the right to remodel the old farmhouse on Camp Hill Road in
Pomona, N.Y.; the closing was scheduled for January 2, 1952.

51. Intensive, or in depth, interviews.

52. As it turned out, Joseph Bensman received his Ph.D. in sociology from Columbia
University in 1958. He coauthored *Small Town in Mass Society: Class, Power, and Religion in a
Rural Community* with Arthur Vidich (Princeton, N.J.: Princeton University Press, 1958; rev.
ed., 1968) and *Craft and Consciousness: Occupational Technique and the Development of World Images* with Robert Lilienfeld, 2d ed. (Hawthorne, N.Y.: Aldine de Gruyter, 1991), among other
works.

You'll get your dough the first of month.[53]

Let us know YOUR PROGRAM.

Mills as ever

[P.S. . . .] *White Collar* galleys in middle, late Feb., so get ready my friend! Got to sleep now, let us know YOUR PROGRAM.

∾

To William Miller, from New York City, undated (probably early 1951)

Wednesday

Dear Bill:

Got first set of galleys [of *White Collar*] this morning when [I] came up here to office. What you are doing is just what it appears to need and what I can't do unaided. What I worry about is that you will do this for [the] first half of book and then slow down or get lazy or just bored on last half and not carry thru. God knows I can understand that, but for god's sake don't do it. I need your help [with] this kind of thing, badly, so keep plowing. And sooner the better. Drop all else. Devote your life for a week to it! And many thanks.

You ask for a copy of "an analysis" but by the nature of these first drafts, they do not endure. I have no copy of such a thing. All I can do is tell you how I usually set up such work. It always involves data, quantitative or qualitative, but more or less systematic. The prime aim of an assistant's first draft is to exhaust the data—to somehow get all the relevant quotes, for example, worked into it, even if it doesn't fit well yet. Or to get all the relevant figures into it even if they are repetitious and even bad. For the use of this draft is to keep you from going to the materials themselves, to create a bridge between you and the details. Of course you have to lay this on before they can do it. I usually have them 1) make their kind of outline; 2) go over this in big conferences of several hours and revise it, with my eye of course on

53. Mills had borrowed some money from Miller.

the first copy, which thus begins to form slowly, and with another eye on the instrument, the questionnaire or data; 3) they draft it out; and 4) I rework it drastically but not yet in detail; 5) they redo it at least once in accordance with my rework; 6) I get it and write it with scissors and paste and then, usually, fresh on a typewriter. You understand you are wasting their time in order to save yours. When the draft is in your hands, you still use them for getting three paragraphs on this or that, or let me see a table with this in it, etc.

I think also the method serves to get you over inhibitions about the first plow-thru draft; it makes you more a creative editor and of course an outliner and designer.

I don't know what else to tell you except that this sort of thing doesn't always work on all materials. Only on parts of *White Collar,* e.g., could I do this: the chapter on unions, the sections with figures in parts of chapters.

In the end,

you got to

do it yourself.

I believe also that using a wire recorder is much the same thing, at least in some ways. Just to spill your guts with little thought of continuity, with no thought of anything but getting the data into it on paper. Then you edit or you leave gaps and have an assistant fill them in, after the scissors and paste of the wire stuff.

House goes all right but hard work by god and can't think of it with *White Collar* in such shape and I keep thinking it is no damn good, which is probably so.

Yours,
M.

[P.S.] [. . .]

❧

To Frances and Charles Grover Mills, from New York City, undated (probably March 1951)

Dear Mother and Dad:

Forgive my not writing to you sooner but you have no idea how busy it is. I don't like debts, you know, and so I'm doing some extra stuff on top of extra stuff for money so as to clean up the whole country house deal in 18 months.

This morning (it's now 7:00 in the morning when I usually get to office), this morning at 9, a writer from the American magazine is coming here to interview me and write a piece with me on *White Collar,* for which I get $500.00, which will buy more lumber.

The galleys are here on *White Collar.* Galleys are the first mock up of a book; you have to correct them; in short, rewrite little stuff here and there to make it fit the page right. The house is coming along fine. Kitchen should be all done in about 10 days. I'm using power tools so it goes fast during the two days (Saturday and Sunday) we are out there. I put in new windows (steel casement) in kitchen and completed one whole wall over the sink (stainless steel, no less) last week. I use masonite for walls in kitchen, which take paint well, and between the walls all around I pack thick rock wool blankets and tack them snug with a staple machine. Will leave the wide boards on the ceiling with the beams, but may have to paint them white in order to get good light, but white painted boards are nice between light wood beams just rubbed down with linseed oil and a little creosote.[54]

Well I have to prepare for this interview. By the way the big job that is paying for all the house practically is in the field now and out of my hands for about 4 weeks. Then that frenzy starts again.

You ask can we keep [the] New York apt next fall: No. Budget is too tight. But the house will be done for sure and damn good too by midsummer. I haven't developed any pictures yet, but have some which will send you in due course, about [a] month or so.

Got to go now, your son,
M.
Charlie Wright Mills

[P.S.] Bought a small, red concrete mixer—with ½ h.p. electric motor!

∾

To Charles Grover Mills, from Pomona, New York, postmarked July 12, 1951

54. Mills drew a floor plan of the house in the margin of this letter.

Dear Dad:

Thanks for your letter. Glad you like the book jacket [for *White Collar*]: photo by Mills! The book won't be published until Sept. 6th after which date we ought to get some reviews.

You don't seem to understand about the house here: it is no summer place but a year round residence, and now our permanent and only residence. We have put in steam heat thruout with neat slim radiators,[55] and a 570 gal boiler in the basement, a new electrical wiring system thruout, a new wing to the building, which I'm just finishing (27 by 18 feet) as a workshop and photographic darkroom. We've given up the apt in New York. We don't need it. It is about one hour to Columbia from here and next year the new thruway will be finished, which will mean that I can get in there in about 30 minutes. I only have to go in three afternoons a week, as that is all I teach now. The rest of the time I'll work here, writing and building furniture.

Temagami and the boats are up for sale, although I hardly think they will sell fast. Anyway, we'll go up there for [a] week soon in order to pick up a few things.

I've paid for the house and five and half acres completely except for a small mortgage ($5,000 for ten years) but I am flat broke and the car is not very good. So I can't travel very far, or at least am afraid to, but maybe I can get some money somewhere and trade the car, which I'd like to do; then we might be able to meet for a few days in New Mexico sometime late in August. Will let you know.

I aim to farm this place in the next two or three years, and make it pay for itself.[56] Next fall I'll plow it and put in winter rye, then next year clover and timothy. I'm getting an old tractor with a Ford engine in it for 50.00 (fifty) bucks! But it will take all this next academic year to get the inside of the house fixed up with built-in cabinets and furniture I've got to make.

In the early fall, I'll send lots of snapshots of the place entire, but no darkroom facilities yet.

Your son, love to all.
Charlie

55. Actually, hot-water heat. (Notation from Ruth to K. Mills, May 1998.)
56. This did not work out; the Millses farmed for one year and their efforts produced only enough vegetables and poultry for their own use.

Mills wrote the following letter soon after the publication of White Collar *by Oxford University Press. Knopf was interested in the possibility of signing up Mills's next book.*

To Philip Vaudrin, editor at Knopf, from Pomona, New York, received September 17, 1951

Dear Phil:

I: Yours of 12th received. I don't answer letters, or rather haven't been lately, because after my day is over, my fingers and shoulders hurt from plain fatigue. Fact. But anyway, I went out to Reno and Frisco on business during August; apart from that I've been at it here everyday and by now, it is, as we carpenters say, closed in: tight and heatable.

In addition, I've completed a 30 ft. wall of bookshelves, two 12 ft storage walls for clothing, with little cubicles and things made to size for all items, completed the additional wing, 30 by 18, for darkroom and workshop. All heating and plumbing in. Now all that is needed to make it OK until spring is new electrical system, which I'll put in next week (with dozens of plugs everywhere),[57] and a little more cabinet work in kitchen and bath. So the end of next week will see it OK; painting will go on in bits and pieces thru the fall, but Ruth has to do that with spray gun.

II: No, I've seen no reviews [of *White Collar*]! Have been tied here and clipping bureau hasn't sent stuff yet. I did see the good big ad in *Tribune* last Sunday, but why wasn't it in the *Times?* Where was Kallen's stuff? I assume *New Leader?* I'll try to get Brogan's in SRL when next I go into town. Anyway from those names apparently "names" are getting it. But what the hell, Phil, I really don't care. It's the best I can do with that topic at this time in this country; a dozen people I trust tell me it is OK so I don't give a damn what the literary asses say or don't say.

III: About your question of how to get decent writing out of sociologists. It doesn't look good. I think for two reasons: First, there

---

57. Actually Ruth, who had experience with electrical circuitry, installed all the electrical wiring; a licensed electrician approved it and made the connections to the outside power line.

is no real writing tradition in sociology, as there is, for example, in history. It just doesn't exist. Second, the field is now split into statistical stuff and heavy duty theoretical bullshit. In both cases, there's no writing but only turgid pollysyllabic (sp?) slabs of stuff. So, because that is now the field, no men get trained, have models to look up to; there is no aspiration to write well.

So there is only one way to get it: for you and me to edit good stuff; go out and get it and edit it and train some people up. But that takes a five or ten year program, betting on a dozen guys and bringing them along, and that takes the kind of money publishers just won't put out, if indeed, they are financially able to.

P.S. Just made a decision the other day. After I finish *Character and Social Structure,* which Gerth and I have been on since God knows when (Weber, I guess) Harcourt has it; and [after I finish] the Metropolitan Weekend (no contract), I am going to do a book called *The Rich* or *The Upper Class* or something like that.[58] This will complete my trilogy: *The New Men of Power* (lower classes), *White Collar* (middle class), then upper stuff. Before that or after it, I've got to get to Europe for a year, and maybe I'll do something reportorial (with depth) on that. I'm not sure but I think my sabbatical is year after next or two years more of teaching.

I'll contact you when I start going in three times a week, about 24th of Sept., for lunch or drink, or maybe even both.

Yours, as ever,
Wright

Mills had enlisted Hazel to do some statistical work—from her home in Reno, Nevada—on the study of the role of the media (the TV or weekend study as he called it). The client for this study was the client he mentions at the beginning of the following letter.

In this letter Mills also refers to the mid-1940s when, living alone in his apartment on West 14th Street, he had an affair with Hazel. The early summer he refers to was in 1946. At the time he was almost thirty years old and Hazel was thirty-seven.

58. The final title was *The Power Elite;* it was published by Oxford University Press in 1956.

To Hazel Gaudet Erskine, from Pomona, New York, dated September 1951

Tuesday afternoon

Dear Hazel:

The stuff went well with the client. It was a lunch and a couple of hours afterwards, talk. I managed not to give them any manuscript, but only to talk. Your stuff hit the spot right near its center. I re-arranged it about like this:

  I. TV ownership
     A. city size etc.
     B. characteristics of; and

 II. Impact of TV on exposure to other media
     A. what they say
     B. what they do
     C. reconciliation

III. Impact of TV on time spent with other media

IV. Two reasons why Sunday news is largely excerpts from media supplementation
    Timing of exposures over weekend.

So it went well; I'll write later on timing, and they are not exact [as] to the day as yet. Thanks for sending it so hurriedly, and sorry it had to be that you were rushed like hell.

Coming back uptown I had the driver swing over by 14th Street; I had him stop by the curb there for a minute and look[ed] the place over, and I remembered what it had meant to me. I had wanted to tell you that this summer but somehow there was no chance. In a life which had practically no memory in it, I find I have very sharp images of 14th St. and the middle forties: I remember wild rice and French fried onions and all the strawberries you could eat; lacquer on the hair and thousands of bobby pins and the smell of well-kept offices at noon; the quick noon-time and the night times; and all the letters. I remember the ferryboats and the picture shows on the east side, and upper New York State in the early summer. With cinematic detail I remember the unexpectedness of it and the hard work of it, and the growing up in it. So I said to the cabbie, "That's where I grew up. It was sorta hard." And he said, "Yeah, it's always hard." And there is a worry about it. After all, 14th Street in the middle forties produced *White Collar,* along with so many other things, and the way you live sets a sort of pace of how and what you write. And now when all that is either dead or impossible, which amounts to the same thing, I wonder what I'll write and how I'll write it. As I always did, I fear anchorage.

★ ★ ★ ★

Reviews of White Collar are excellent. It doesn't matter that the Times review was snide at the end. It was beautifully placed and on the whole a selling review. The San Francisco Chronicle did well by it. In fact all over, the newspaper stuff is very good. New Republic excellent, and [Irving] Howe will do it for Nation. The reception is all that could possibly be expected and I'm quite happy about it.

Probably you missed the item in *Times* of 14 Sept. about how the Russians censored my article, done for State Dept. magazine, *Amerika,* circulated in Russia.[59] It was the first article they have censored as a whole! Reason: no bourgeois pieties in it but, stated in their kind of language, it hit home. It's too bad some of those guys sitting in the Russian bureaucracy open to doubt (and I know there must be some like that, and seeing no way out, even as we see no way out) couldn't have known that there are people here who feel that way and managed to get it past all the barriers and curtains. But what the hell, too much to expect I guess. Too late to expect it.

Please destroy this note.[60]

Yours as ever,
Charlie

∾

59. "The Sociology of Mass Media and Public Opinion," posthumously published in *Power Politics and People: The Collected Essays of C. Wright Mills,* ed. Irving Louis Horowitz (New York: Oxford University Press, 1963).

60. Many years after Mills's death, Hazel supplied a copy of this letter to Richard Gillam, who was then doing biographical research on Mills for his graduate studies in history.

To William and Virginia Miller, from Pomona, New York, undated
(probably late November 1951)

Saturday after Thanksgiving

Dear Bill and Bucky:

I've yours of 19th Nov. [. . .] Here are the answers to your questions:

The Oxford press finally turned down BF club for good, or at least
for good now. They argue that it would be just like giving it to Harlum
Book Company . . . a straight remainder kind of deal, except by mail.
They anticipate 6,000 sales by Feb. next. Anyway I can do nothing
and have forgotten about it. As least 'til next spring or so, when 6
months statement comes. In meantime they are always out of print
or out of stock and all, but what the hell.

I've seen galleys on Parsons review and got my 40 bucks for it
so I suppose it will be out soon, maybe tomorrow. I understand P has
said to a small group up there [about] my stuff in *White Collar,* "Well,
the man can write some, but it is all impressionistic stuff." Won't he
be surprised! I like my review on final rewrite.[61]

Why not come down and see us next weekend?

I've followed up on the study idea and have fixed little cubbyholes on one wall and shelves on the other and bought a box of
acoustical tile (12' squares with little holes in them) to cover ceiling
and walls. You can mount photos in the tile, with little $1/8$-inch plugs
in the holes. Also made 8 ft slab desk and it is the nuts.

Worked like hell yesterday etc. and finished hearth and mounted
Franklin stove, which now works. It really looks wonderful; finished
the wall behind it on one side also, with moderately low sideboard
effect and big built-in wood box between hearth and boxed-in
radiator.

Darkroom is also all fixed up except for ceiling and is in working
order with low bench for enlarger and excellent wet bench setup. Have
developed 6 or 7 rolls of summer film and printed perfunctorily.

I've not been able to do any work at all intellectually, although

61. Perhaps a review of Talcott Parsons's book *The Social System* (Glencoe, Ill.: Free Press,
1951).

have excellent excuse: TV study coming due and have [been] handling final ms, half of which is now being finally typed. Ruth and Hazel feed me stuff and I edit for final. Maybe two more weeks will see it all done. Big speech for client due early December. Ugh.

But what is really in my mind all the time is the book I will certainly have to write [as] soon as *Character [and Social Structure]* is done next summer. It will be (maybe) called THE HIGH AND MIGHTY: The American Upper Classes. And I already jot down phrases and first paragraphs of this and that. It fills my head in a disjointed sort of way all the time and keeps me from work.

I'm applying for a Guggenheim renewal in order to take all next year off to work on it. Will spend summer here and in Madison on *Character;* then in fall, if Character [is] done (it bores me now), will begin slowly and leisurely on *High and Mighty,* that is if you approve that title. You see it has to have both money and power and status in it. "The rich and powerful" isn't good. It also has not to prejudge the problem of how much power the rich and how much dough the powerful. There'll be chapters on entertainment people at top and executives somewhat and I think Washington top level as well as socialites and . . . laid out something like *White Collar,* with an introductory part and then the shank describing neatly all the types etc. that go to make up "the top" all over the country, and then topical questions which fill it in as Part Three. I can definitely "locate" Veblen's stuff, which is not, I think, "the theory of the leisure class" but "a theory of the late 19th century nouveau riche." Will have chapter on all families G Meyers picked up in progressive era and follow-up: what happened to them and how are they now?

Do you still go to bookstores? Listen if you find a *complete* set of Balzac, by chance, for not more than 25 dollars, buy it for me will you? Make sure it is complete and small volumes and a decent translation. I have only half a set or so of the 1901 Macmillan edition by Glen Marriage. It is the right size and all but I don't have them all and want to read everything he wrote from the beginning of the sequence. In three or four years want to give a course: Balzac as sociologist. Well, if you happen to run into a good-looking buy, go ahead. (I never see bookstores, living out here. If you found a complete set of the edition I mentioned above I'd like it.)

Why not drive down next Friday and go back Sunday afternoon. Sit before fireplace. Get drunk. Moody broody. Be jumped on by dog.

Observe delicious colors of hills and fields and rocks and everything this time of year. The time of death. The era of lead colors.

See you then next Friday.

Yours,
Mills

ᔕ

To Frances and Charles Grover Mills, from Pomona, New York, undated (probably December 1951)

Dear Mother and Dad:

Everything seems to be going ok around here. So as work goes, we have just about finished the study of TV and its impact on the other media of communication, and after two speeches, one here and one in Chicago sometime this month, that will be all done, thank god. Then I go to work on the book Gerth and I do together: a technical book on social psychology. Around next summer however I begin on my next major book. I think I will call it THE HIGH AND MIGHTY and it will be on the upper classes of the US. In the meantime *White Collar* gets good reviews and is altogether a success. Unfortunately it does not make any money because they paid me $2,000 in advance several years ago so it will be a year at least until it earns me more.

The house is a great joy. My darkroom is all fixed now except the new ceiling I'll put in later, and my study is fixed really wonderfully. I used the 12" squares of acoustical tile, with little holes in it, for three walls and the ceiling. So it is soundproofed! I've a built-in flat file with 30 cubbyholes by one end of the 8 foot desk slab of plywood (also built in) and at other end, shelving for all sorts of camera equipment and books. But so much remains: the entire flooring must be plywooded and then tiled. We've decided to do the thing thruout in a good slate grey kentile; unifies the house and is neutral so doesn't bias for any other color schemes. Interior painting of course and exterior painting. And all sorts of cabinets must be made, especially for kitchen. The fact is however that we have no money at all, literally exist from month to month now and can't even buy $25.00 worth of cabinet wood anymore. But it is livable and we'll do it gradually. By the way, Christmas is *out* this year. We just are not doing a thing, please don't embarrass us by sending gifts! Next summer or so, my head will be out from under I hope but in meantime we'll do well to continue to eat.

Living out in the country's fine, especially since I don't have to go into the city except M, W and F. Next spring I'm trying to arrange a schedule for Monday and Friday only! The only trouble with a setup like this is that what with the darkroom and the workshop and the things to be done (all these places heated just like the house and comfortable), I don't know whether I can get anything done by way of intellectual work! Too many temptations. But it has cut down wandering tendencies. God it is all here and why go anyplace? Later, Europe, yes but not right away. Next year as you know, is my sabbatical year. So I get half pay for full year, with no teaching. We'll stay right here. I've applied for another Guggenheim fellowship, which will just make up the half salary. If I don't get that, I'll have to teach during the spring and will [be] off only in winter term. But either way, it is going to be fine. Will really finish the house and get well under way with The High and Mighty.

Let us know how it all goes with you both.

Your son,
M.
Charlie Wright Mills

ↄ

To David Riesman, from Pomona, New York, dated January 8, 1952

Dear Dave:

I. Enclosed is a copy of the article, for which you ask.[62] I don't think it's adequate any more—and I've rewritten it as a chapter in the book Gerth and I now bring to a finish: *Character and Social Structure*. The Warner review—alas, I've no more copies, not even one for myself. I do think it's still adequate.

II. I'm glad you're doing the AJS [*American Journal of Sociology*] piece on *White Collar*, and look forward to seeing it. Would you send me a carbon? The book goes very well indeed, and it's the best I can do on that topic at this time. But to be honest with you, nobody,

---

62. Probably Mills's "Situated Actions and Vocabularies of Motive."

except a few friends, seems to get hold of what I really intended to do with this book. Mr. Hughes, in *Commentary*, I really don't understand, although I don't mind. He seems to feel it's written too well for its potential importance! That with the same facts others might well write a differently oriented book! (But of course.) That I should write poetry and monographs . . . but keep them rigidly segregated. (But why must they be segregated? My aim is to work out something as solid as a monograph—while hiding the workshop rather than cheaply parading it—but at the same time as well implicated as at least second rate poetry.) O well.

III. You ask what I do now. Well, for one thing, plant 3,000 Scotch fir and Norwegian spruce seedlings on my 5 acres. For another, I've begun to write a book, called *The High and Mighty*, about the US upper classes, which I hope will sort of round out a trilogy on US stratification.

Be seeing you.
W.
Wright Mills

In January 1952, the Partisan Review *published Dwight Macdonald's review of* White Collar, *a brutal attack entitled "Abstractio Ad Absurdum." Macdonald denounced Mills's writing style and wrote that, even as propaganda, "the book was no good" because the author was confused and indifferent. Macdonald had written that Mills might have provided a good description along the lines of the Lynds'* Middletown, *or an aesthetic and moral assessment following Veblen's example, or a new historical interpretation, incorporating description and evaluation, as Marx had done in the first volume of* Capital. *In Macdonald's opinion,* White Collar *had failed in all of these areas, revealing Mills's weaknesses as a writer, as a thinker, and as an advocate. Macdonald complained that Mills interrupted himself in the book before he could say anything "or rather before he can give away the fact he hasn't anything to say."[63]*

Mills responded to the review by seeking the advice or support of several friends and colleagues, including Hans Gerth, Dick Hofstadter, Bob Merton, Bill Miller, Harvey Swados, and Lionel Trilling.[64] His letter to Miller follows.

63. *Partisan Review* 19, no. 1 (January–February 1952): 114.
64. Trilling had become well known with the publication of his book *The Liberal Imagination: Essays on Literature and Society* (New York: Viking Press, 1950).

To William Miller, from Pomona, New York, undated (January 1952)

Dear Bill:

Yesterday I read Dwight Macdonald's review of *White Collar* in *Partisan Review*. As you probably have seen, it is a complete thumbs down. Of course I know Dwight is an irresponsible reviewer, but I can't conceal that it hurts, for if he is half right, the best thing for me to do is close up shop. Doubtless I'll get over it, but the thing temporarily incapacitates me. There's only one kind of question that seems important to me, and I'd be very grateful if you'd answer it:

Can I learn anything from this review? What does he say that I ought to take seriously, and what should I do about taking it seriously? I know as my best friend and editor, that you will know I don't seek commiseration but no-punches-pulled assertion.[65]

Yours,
M.
Mills

Bill Miller responded by drafting a heated letter to the editor to defend his friend's book, but he had some doubts about the value of submitting it, and in the end he did not mail it.

Harvey Swados was the friend who publicly defended White Collar *in a letter to the editor of the* Partisan Review; *he pointed out that Macdonald's review was amusing but uninformative concerning Mills's work, and went on to say that "regardless of stylistic barbarisms,"* White Collar *"is worthy of the most thoughtful consideration as a landmark in American social thought."[66]*

Hans Gerth responded to Mills's note by writing him a supportive letter. Dick Hofstadter wrote asking, among other things, why Mills did not show more warmth for white-collar workers. Lionel Trilling responded by meeting with Mills over lunch to talk about the book's writing style, and Bob Merton must have responded in person or over the phone. (We do not have a record of his response.)

After Macdonald's review was published, Macdonald wrote a letter to Mills with

65. In Mills's variation on this sentence in a similar letter to Lionel Trilling, Mills addressed Trilling as "one who has in the past helped me, sometimes without knowing it." In the version of the letter to Bob Merton, Mills addressed Merton as "my friend and colleague." In the version for Hans Gerth, Mills addressed Gerth as "my friend and collaborator."

66. *Partisan Review* 19, no. 4 (July–August 1952): 383–84.

the opening line "Are you very sore at me?" He discussed his decision to review the book, suggested they meet, and signed off as "Your Old Pal." At the time, Mills had this to say about Macdonald: "He is merely irresponsible. He wrote me a note and is coming out for lunch sometime soon. Boyish stuff. He just gets carried away by his own rhetoric and line. You can't stay angry with him."[67]

Mills's reply to Macdonald's note follows.

To Dwight Macdonald, from Columbia University, New York, dated January 17, 1952

Dear Old Pal:

Of course you should have accepted the book for review and did right to review it in strict accordance with your judgment. I know that there's nothing "personal" in it (but only fast, irresponsible reading), and so I'm not "replying" to it publicly. But—I hope somebody does, because naturally I disagree strongly (otherwise I wouldn't have published the book), and I think it's "unfair" in two ways: *First,* a reader who hasn't read the book doesn't know what the effort is all about. In a review that long you should have told them, and perhaps at least acknowledged the many new facts which I spent seven years working like a dog to dig up. And it really hurt me that you don't mention and so I guess don't like my photographic jacket and the "prose poems" because I did them just for you. *Second,* I don't mind criticism if I can learn from it, but I find it hard to learn from your piece. The only thing you left me to do is: close up shop. You have all the relevant points of comparison and block me off from each of them.

To show you how anxious I am to learn, I've written notes to five friends—who happen to like the book—and asked them to help me learn anything I might learn from your piece. Not time yet to hear from them, but I'll let you know. In the meantime, you owe me this: think out concretely what I should avoid and how I might learn to do so. Anyway, do let's get together: I've something I've created to show you.

Be constructive. Be practical. I'm a very willing learner in this writing stuff. And don't tell me whatever the hell you have in mind isn't at least communicable if not teachable.

Do you now have a car? If so, come out for lunch, with family

67. Letter to Hans Gerth, dated "Sat. Nite."

of course, Saturday or Sunday, the 2 or 3 of February. Give me a ring that you're coming one or two days before. It's about 40 miles out; here's how to get here:

Go across George Washington Bridge and then north on 9W to Haverstraw. [. . .][68]

Address: Camp Hill Road
Pomona, New York

Phone (20 cent toll): Spring Valley 6–1247R1

If you've no car now, let me know that and I'll tell you a bus route (about one hour and twenty minutes from midtown) to Spring Valley, and we'll pick you up there.

You'll enjoy the country air, you ignorant, irresponsible bastard, so plan to leave New York about 9:30, returning about 4 or 5 from Camp Hill.

As ever,
Charlie

Macdonald declined the invitation to visit, citing transportation and schedule problems. Mills was more forthcoming when he declined an opportunity to speak in public with Macdonald two months later. Norman Thomas invited them both to a meeting to discuss the possibility of starting a socialist educational association. Mills declined that invitation on the basis that there was no area of understanding between him and Macdonald; Mills wrote that he wanted to discuss social problems in public only with people with whom he shared "at least the possibility of communication."[69] He sent Macdonald a copy of his letter to Thomas with a handwritten note at the top: "Dwight: So to hell with guys like you!—Wright."

Macdonald's biographer, Michael Wreszin, wrote that the falling out with Mills over White Collar *"was part of the stress Macdonald was undergoing" as he distanced himself from his wife, Nancy, and the political past that they had shared. Macdonald was then spending time with a lover and a new, relatively apolitical group of people; he was not seeing or communicating with his old Leftist friends and colleagues.[70]*

68. Mills provided a paragraph of detailed directions.

69. Letter from Mills to Thomas, dated March 18, 1952.

70. *A Rebel in Defense of Tradition: The Life and Politics of Dwight Macdonald* (New York: Basic Books, 1994), 265.

In the next letter, Mills responded to David Riesman's review of White Collar *for the* American Journal of Sociology. *Although Riesman disagreed with many of Mills's pessimistic conclusions, he presented Mills's points carefully and treated the book with respect. In fact, he stated that few writers wrote with as much energy as Mills and that certain aspects of the book were "admirable" or "brilliant." Riesman ended his review with the following sentence: "Mills is grappling resourcefully with the big questions of our day, and even if this reviewer is inclined to give somewhat less portentous answers to some of them, he agrees that the questions are central, the research methods fundamentally sound."*[71]

To David Riesman, from Columbia University, New York, dated January 31, 1952

Dear David Riesman:

Dick Hofstadter has given me the proofs of your review, and I have examined them with great appreciation and benefit. I want to let you know that I am really grateful to you for taking the time to give my work such close and careful attention—and for the generosity of your response to it. The negative points you make seem to me well made, and I appreciate them no less than the positive comment.

Above all, it's just plain good to know that at least one man understands what one is about, especially that you like my photography![72] Next time you're in New York, you must come out and see my house (handmade by me) and darkroom facilities!

Sincerely yours,
Wright Mills

To Hans Gerth, from Pomona, New York, dated "Sat. Nite" (probably early February 1952)

---

71. David Riesman, review of *White Collar* by C. Wright Mills, *American Journal of Sociology* 57, no. 5 (March 1952): 513–15.

72. Riesman's review referred to Mills's "fine dust-jacket photo of a white-collar man dwarfed by a bleak urban edifice" (514).

Dear Gerth:

You'll have to forgive any incoherence you find in this letter, because I'm drunk on cheap sherry because I worked so hard all day burning my five acres in preparation for spring plowing and also put down 400 sq. feet on ⅝-inch plywood on the living room floor in preparation for rubber tile.

This morning I got your utterly charming and perfectly delightful letter about the Macdonald review and the European venture:[73] God, you are a propagandist! [. . .] Well, listen now, I think you play the Frankfurt thing wrong; you are too quick to jump when they whistle. Either they are really interested in you or they want you for a fill in. If the first, they will compromise on the timing; if the second, why should you get excited and go? My idea in a nutshell is this: you bargain around with them if they come thru with [the] proposition and tell them you can come in Sept. and stay thru December. IF YOU FIX IT THAT WAY, RUTH AND I CAN JOIN YOU AND WE WILL HAVE OUR BOOK *[Character and Social Structure]* IN PRESS AND BE REALLY FREE TO ENJOY OURSELVES AND BRANCH OUT. I will have the money to do that. Next year is my sabbatical year you know. [. . .] You and I got to do this:

(I) both work *like hell* between this week and June 1st;

(II) spend at least 6 weeks together in early summer here and in Madison.

Now don't let these guys whistle and then run: let them know you are a busy man, and that it takes time to arrange things. I don't know these particular guys, except of course thru Leo Lowenthal, and I've met Horkheimer. But don't be so damn easy with them. Tell them Sept. first. That way we are really set up all around.

Now Gerth, I know how much you want to go, and so I say really sincerely that if this timing can't be arranged, you go ahead and go, if you can go only in June. Work as hard as you can on our book until then. I will stay here and finish it and get it into the press. Then in Sept. I'll join you, but I will not leave this country until the book is done. I just can't so it wouldn't be any good if I went ahead. That is the kind of compulsive guy I am on contracts.

---

73. Gerth wanted to teach in Frankfurt as a visiting professor. In 1968 he began teaching at the Frankfurt Institute for Social Research.

You see, I make one-half of my income from publishers and on contracts. So I've got to deliver, living the way I do. I'm known as a fellow who delivers! That is why I walked into Oxford the other day and got a contract set up on my next solo book (The American Elite. Or The High and Mighty. On the upper classes). Anyway they gave me without blinking an eye 5,000 dollars advance: three on signing next week, another one whenever I want it, and the final one on delivery of ms. They also gave me three full years to deliver it, and a clause extending that time on request. [. . .] The simple fact is that *White Collar,* now selling, six months after publication, about 1,000 copies a month is doing quite well and they didn't want Knopf to "steal me." Knopf offered $3,000 flat advance but only two years to finish in. Now the three thousand I get next week will finish this house fully: it can then be maintained for about $80 or $90 per month, including mortgage payment and upkeep. So it gives me the second thousand to play around with: Europe I hope in Sept. if you should go and Ruth and I could join you all. Now the reason I can get that kind of money is because I deliver. So: for Harcourt Brace, we (you and I) have got to deliver. Why? To keep up that kind of reputation in American publishing circles. [. . .]

This Frankfurt bunch are not going to let me (and I doubt you) into their inner circle: i.e. give us enough money to do what we want to do: shuttle between here and there and write what we want about both places. Our best bet is to hook-up with publishers. The only way for guys like us to get what we want is to write our way there. At least for me, nobody is going to love me much. But I still believe that with good books, such as we can write, especially if we shuttle between US and Europe, we can make it: you know Gerth, all you need is one hit to insure yourself this kind of life.

But to follow thru on this vision, we've got to be "dependable," "reliable" and always deliver. That is the rationale for my own com-pulsions about finishing Character and turning it in before I leave the US. Once I got over there, I couldn't and wouldn't work on it. So think hard upon this.

[. . .] Lionel Trilling and his wife Diana Trilling are [. . .] coming out next weekend or so. He was very nice about *White Collar* in galley: read it closely and liked it and will now tell me what he thinks I can learn from the reviews for the next job and as a writer in general. After all he is the number two critic in US (after Edmund Wilson) and altho quite precious, a very able fellow, and capable of handling an idea.

A French firm and a Scandinavian one have both asked for translation rights on *White Collar*. Bargaining now with Oxford's London office, which is deciding on an English edition.

Gerth, what is the "Deutche Kommentare" and tell me about a guy named Charles Carle who was at Mannheim's seminar with you. He's now in NY running something called "TransAtlantic Press" . . . tied in with "Illustriere Reportagen" as well as French stuff. Anyway he and his wife went pretty nuts about the book, and he came to see me, to get biography stuff for a review he does for D.K. Charming fellow, but is he a fascist? Something he said put me on my guard, but I may be quite wrong. Anyway, let me know. His wife is an expert guitarist, teaches it, and imports good German instruments; maybe I'll take fifteen lessons from her. Anyway his big question to me was what with all the "conformism," "how had an American written this particular book," which was naturally very gratifying, and to which my answer was that I wasn't really a regular American, but a Texan. He was very puzzled and said that meant cows and oil. And I said, of course, but also outlanders who came late in life to big cities and "discover them." So he was happy and maybe he will do well by me! Listen, if you know of a good German publisher who might be interested in the book, tell me names and drop a note to them, because French edition and Scandinavian edition are fine, but what I would really like is a German translation.

Here is where we stand on *Character and Social Structure:*[74] the total is now 16 chapters. You have copies of 1 thru 6. My typist now is doing chapters 7 thru 13. These are rough still but they contain everything we have talked about and everything in my files at the moment and they do each form a continuity. So I suppose we could say they are decent first drafts of stuff that needs three drafts, the second being yours after you get these. The last three chapters are:

14 A Survey of Social Structures
15 Master Trends of Modern Society
16 US and USSR

74. Gerth and Mills had agreed to write the book in 1941, more than ten years before this letter was written. Other work had intervened, but now it was time for the last push to finish the project.

Chapter 14 may be re-entitled: "The Range of Institutional Orders" because that is the idea of it. I am beginning this week to draft these three chapters, but our notes are scanty on these, especially on Russia and US. Will you interrupt yourself, while waiting the two weeks it will take to get to you 7 thru 13, and write me ideas for these three last chapters, also sending what you find in your own files that might be helpful? Then, when you get 7 thru 13, please don't write me about them, but rewrite them. Of course you don't have to slow yourself down and worry about orderly presentation at this time, but do what you can as fast as you can. I assume in two or three weeks, I'll get from you the first six chapters rewritten like that? If you want, hold them until you get and read 7 thru 13. But if you get to me by April 1 all thirteen rewritten, I can then have all of April and May to go over them in one final draft. And in meantime, I'll have 14 thru 16 in at least first draft and you can go over them April and May. What I am aiming at is to have a draft we've both fooled with in shape before we meet, if we do meet this summer (for the first half of it) so we can then relax with the stuff and really polish and refine and tighten up. And this schedule is all the more important if you must go to Europe June first.

1. So expect from me within two weeks chapters 7 thru 13.
2. I'll expect from you, soon as possible (meaning one week or so) random stuff on 14 thru 16, and by April 1, a rewrite on 1 thru 13.

OK?

Ruth and I wish you all were here. We've finished eating now and have a big log fire going in the living room and it's cold as hell outside with a wind. You can hear it enter the valley at the top of the hill and come across the upper field. You can hear it come around the house. And we are very glad it can't get in.

Yours as ever,
Mills
Wright Mills

When Mills first began to work at the Bureau of Applied Social Research, he had expressed admiration and ambivalence about the empirical methodology represented by the Bureau's founder and director, Paul F. Lazarsfeld. Referring to work on the study of influence and mass communication based on interviews in Decatur, Illinois, Mills wrote: "Lazarsfeld I find a wonderful man to work with; he gives me absolute freedom to do what the hell I want in all respects on the study and gives me ingenious technical advice when I ask for it. The fellow has got me to see the inside of statistical manipulation in such a way that I see the quantity-quality shuttle operation so as to work with it for first time. There are all sorts of disadvantages also which I see now for first time. I wouldn't think of doing only this kind of research. In other words, it is a hell of a fine experience to do one big job statistically, but a guy ought not to go hog wild about it!"[75]

As the years passed Mills's working relationship with Lazarsfeld became increasingly troubled until a fairly public split occurred. As Mills later noted in a letter to Tovarich, his tensions with the prevailing philosophy at the Bureau and his eventual departure represented an important turning point in his career.[76]

Mills's growing preference for critical analysis within a broad vision was at odds with Lazarsfeld's steadfast focus on quantitative thinking and statistics. The two sociologists also had a basic disagreement over the interpretation of their data. Lazarsfeld thought that influence from people of equal status was more important than a top-down flow of influence through social strata.[77] In 1946, Mills submitted a discussion draft consisting of several hundred pages of summary and interpretation of the Decatur data; Mills acknowledged some evidence for the horizontal influence described by Lazarsfeld, but also argued that vertical, or top-down, influence was important, especially in politics. Mills's discussion of the controversial concept of ideology and his rebellion against some of the tenets of Lazarsfeld's empirical approach made the draft heretical, despite its inclusion of vast quantities of empirical information.[78] There may have been other differences of opinion as well. In any case, Lazarsfeld relieved Mills of the job of directing the Decatur study sometime after receiving his discussion draft in 1946. Although Mills was put in charge of the Bureau's study of Puerto Rican immigrants in New York, he remained involved in the Decatur study, preparing a draft of several chapters in 1949 and reviewing drafts prepared by others. This tense situation finally led to the incident Mills described in the following letter.

75. Letter from Wright Mills to Hans Gerth, dated Thursday, June 28, 1945.

76. See "The Stages of Autonomy" within the letter to Tovarich entitled "On Who I Might Be and How I Got That Way," dated fall 1957, p. 249 in this book.

77. See the Decatur study in its published form: Elihu Katz and Paul F. Lazarsfeld, *Personal Influence: The Part Played by People in the Flow of Mass Communications* (Glencoe, Ill.: Free Press, 1955).

78. Gillam, "C. Wright Mills," 303.

To Hans Gerth, from Pomona, New York, dated February 15, 1952

Dear Gerth:

Thanks for your comments on the PR piece;[79] I take your advice somewhat, cutting out the more "personal" stuff. I put it in because they asked their questions that way, but you are probably right.

It's now between classes on Friday. I wanted to tell you about the thing that happened day before yesterday between Paul Lazarsfeld and me. It is just about a complete break. You remember that for six years now I've been writing and rewriting "The Decatur" ms., with him advising and etc. Well he gave me the latest draft again last week and we met Wednesday morning, and he asked me to do a complete rewrite of about 130 pages of it. As nicely as I could I told him no. The time had come either to publish it or if he doesn't like it still, to rewrite it himself. I offered to sit with him for one full day a week and revise together but [said] that I felt utterly unable to listen to him for an hour and then spend six weeks trying to get into it what he had said. He went and got Merton (to act as a kind of "judge and witness" I suppose). Bob was OK but said why didn't I try it again. I stuck to my guns and said I was utterly unable to do it again. Bob had to go to class. Paul and I sat for 6 minutes (that's a long time) and neither said a word. My God how creepy. Then we chatted for 30 minutes very pleasantly and I left with a "See you soon, Paul." Thank God, I feel secure enough to resist this silly domination and manipulation of his. I suppose I'm his first "defeat" in all this kind of madness he wants to pursue. But now we wait and see what happens. I've worked on that crap more than on any other book with which I have been associated and of course he will now take it away, but I do not care. In fact, I'd rather not be associated with it. To hell with professional acclaim I lose. Nothing is worth the continual feeling that you're not your own man.[80]

Will write more and mail later when something important to tell you.

79. Mills's contribution to a symposium, entitled "Our Country and Our Culture: A Symposium (II)," in *Partisan Review* 19, no. 4 (July–August 1952): 446–50.

80. In 1955, when the Decatur study was published, Mills was credited on the acknowledgments page: "The whole organization of field work for the study was in the hands of C. Wright Mills. . . . Through all the varying phases of analysis and writing the advice of C. Wright Mills was extremely valuable, often opening up completely new perspectives on the data" (Katz and Lazarsfeld, *Personal Influence,* xiii).

Friday at office:

Yesterday I made the big speech for my client about TV to all the agency people in the city at the Stork Club. It was a big success, and Bill Hearst himself offered me a job! He'll give me a guarantee of $30,000 per year plus bonus stuff if I'll troubleshoot for him and handle a "few big accounts on space selling." Of course I laughed at him and insulted him, which is what he liked about my speech, but he was apparently serious. Afterwards, I tried to get him to send me a tractor but he wouldn't do it. Kept coming back to "the proposition." Said he hadn't seen a real salesman around since 1925 and didn't I know that it was all horseshit except a salesman: he could write his own ticket, etc. I told him to read my book [White Collar], and buy 1,000 copies for his organization, and he picked up the phone and ordered fifty copies; cheapskate bastard. Anyway it was all a lot of fun and also somehow embarrassing because every time I see such guys perform it's just like I say in White Collar, although sometimes more so, like in the stereotyped movies and novels.

About 5 or 6 of us hung around the Stork Club until 5 P.M. and bulled. I was interviewing of course for the elite book and by god I've now some real contacts for its researching. They got pretty drunk I guess and mainly for the last hour or so we all boasted about raspberry patches and how many acres of land we had [and] lake, etc. all about "our" places. God help us.

Listen, I'm mad at you. Why in god's name don't you send my stuff back? Jimmie Reid was in here a few days ago and I had to promise him faithfully he'd get the whole thing by August 15, and half of it in early July. We have got to do that. After all, they were nice to us and we spent their dough. Now we have to deliver. [. . .]

Come on now: it's the last big push on a worthwhile job, so let's move it.

Yours,
Mills

Mills and Gerth hand delivered the completed manuscript for Character and Social Structure *to Jim Reid at Harcourt Brace on August 4, 1952, and the book was published in September 1953.*

To William Miller, from Pomona, New York, 1952 (probably in the first half of the year)

Congratulations on the job [at Knopf]; I know why you write so sadly about it, and I think I understand your ambivalence, but what the hell it is a good job and you're a big boy and ought to know you and I and people like us are not going to get to run anything of importance. The criteria by which we should judge good or bad on jobs and such is how much of my life energy does it take, and what can I learn from it, if anything . . . and I think this Knopf thing ranks pretty well on those criteria. Certainly I'm glad you didn't go to Washington. I didn't want to say that while it pended but now that this is more or less set, I'll say it. This is better.[81]

But you'll be here soon and contact us and then we'll know more about it all. In meantime, I'll do one thing for you: make one trip to Cambridge in the jeep and help you move stuff. You set it up as to timing; also you can store stuff here for several months if you want. Now don't throw away books and things; I'll store them for you until you get over the idea, but you were probably kidding anyway. But don't throw away stuff.

You ask for what one should be keyed up? My god, for long weekends in the country, and snow and the feel of an idea and New York streets early in the morning and late at night and the camera eye always working whether you want or not and yes by god how the earth feels when it's been plowed deep and the new chartreuse wall in the study and wine before dinner and if you can afford it Irish whiskey afterwards and sawdust in your pants cuff and sometimes at evening the dusky pink sky to the northwest, and the books to read never touched and all that stuff the Greeks wrote and have you ever read Macaulay's speeches to hear the English language? And to revise your mode of talk and what you talk about and yes by god the world of music which we just now discover and there's still hot jazz and getting a car out of the mud when nobody else can.[82] That's what the hell to get keyed up about.

The trouble with you and what used to be the trouble with me

81. About a year later, Miller left Knopf after obtaining a book contract of his own.
82. This passage was probably inspired by "The Camera Eye" sections in John Dos Passos's trilogy, *U.S.A.*, first published in 1938.

is that you don't use your goddamned *senses;* too much society crap and too much mentality and not enough tactile and color and sound stuff going on. So now if you're like I was a year ago, you've got to coax the sight and sound back, carefully tease it to life again and it will fill you up.

It's only an hour out from here, why not think about it; my offer to build with you on that five acres to the north and east of my place still goes. All you need at first is three big cinder block rooms. You think about it.

See you soon and even though you'll be anxious and hurried, plan on a weekend out here. I want to see Bucky anyway. It makes me feel good to see such a fine woman.

Yours,
Mills

Mills was a visiting professor at Brandeis during the spring of 1953.

To Robert K. Merton, from Brandeis University, Waltham, Massachusetts, postcard dated February 16, 1953

Monday

Dear Bob:

This note is just to acknowledge that you seem to have been correct in your prediction about WC. Today I have received word that it is being taken by Book Find Club, is being translated into French and Japanese, and that by next fall some 35,000 copies will have been printed in English. My god.

How did you like the review of Parsons' in current ASR:[83] do tell me. (I thought it a masterful and accurate piece of work, given its source.)

83. Ellsworth Faris's review of *The Social System* by Talcott Parsons, which featured decidedly negative assessments of the writing style and use of obscure jargon. *American Sociological Review* 18, no. 1 (February 1953): 103–6.

Am staying up here secluded in small room for six weeks, getting a good deal written on the elite. Will commute last six weeks.

Yours,
Mills
Brandeis, Waltham, Mass.

[P.S.] Do you write a foreword to Harcourt Brace for *Character and Social Structure?* (Manuscript is in their hands.) If so, do let me see a copy, will you?
CWM

A foreword by Merton was included in Character and Social Structure.

Mills was never glad to give up summer freedom when classes resumed in the fall; but his reaction against returning to academic life was more emphatic than usual in the autumn of 1953.

To Hans Gerth, from Pomona, New York, dated September 1953

Dear Gerth,

1st day of school, for God's sake. Isn't it all horrible? Why don't we just quit and go out to California and get honest jobs in a big factory?

Received copies of C & SS a few days ago. Don't much care for their binding and blurbs, but who the hell cares anyway? At least we can say "Well we've done a text—look at the binding and format."

Do you use it in a course? I do, in small group of 15 or so students. Write me what you think of it all—now it's done, out, finished.

[. . .]

We have a new Dalmatian puppy. Quite an animal.

In general tho', things are flat and all gray with me and I feel exhausted and I'm flat broke and no prospects of extra money this year and no intellectual or emotional or human energy left.

So write me a newsy uplifting letter!

Yours as ever,
Mills

∾

To Hans Gerth, from Pomona, New York, dated November 29, 1953

Dear Gerth:

[...]

3: Ruth and I just went up to Brandeis and they have renewed their offer to me. I have decided that I will *not* go and am writing that this is final to them this next week. I am further recommending fully that you be offered the position. I figure, what the hell, we don't know about Columbia,[84] and besides Cambridge has many advantages and the more the merrier so far as offers go, even if you use them at Wisconsin. But for god's sake think of yourself, regardless of present income, as $9,000 minimum.

4: Happy to hear that you get a jeep wagon. They are a fine little car, very tough and durable.

5: Also happy that you get good comments on *Character and Social Structure*. I have heard nothing whatsoever, except Coser and Rieff[85]— both of whom like both of us as much, I suppose, as anyone—do *not* seem to like it. I do not press them for reasons, thinking it better among friends in this case to let it lie. But no one else has peeped a word. It is as if we had laid a large white egg. . . .

6: I have read the two Mannheim volumes Kecskemeti edited and find both of them excellent, and certainly the conservative thing is very solid.[86] I do not feel that it is very helpful or "transferable" to the kind of thing I tried to write for the new magazine Coser and Howe get out (*Dissent*) on the conservative mood in the US. At least I couldn't seem to make any bridges and so use the stuff he has. Anyway they are both fine books of essays.

7: By the way you are wrong about me and Burckhardt: I continually read his renaissance book and the one translated as *Force*

84. The possibility of Gerth teaching at Columbia was under discussion.

85. Philip Rieff, author of *Freud: The Mind of the Moralist* (New York: Viking Press, 1959) and *The Triumph of the Therapeutic: Uses of Faith after Freud* (New York: Harper and Row, 1966).

86. For example, Karl Mannheim, *Essays on the Sociology of Knowledge,* ed. Paul Kecskemeti (New York: Oxford University Press, 1952); and *Conservatism: A Contribution to the Sociology of Knowledge.* The latter is Mannheim's master's thesis, "Alt Konservatismus" (University at Heidelberg, 1925). We do not know which translation Mills read, but the one available now is translated by David Kettler and Volker Meja from a first draft by Elizabeth R. King (London: Routledge and Kegan Paul, 1986).

and Freedom.[87] It was the Constantine book I didn't take to much.[88] No focus in it that I could find. But the others are the real McCoy. Sorry you didn't like the *Herald Tribune* speech on leisure;[89] your paraphrase of it makes it seem really horrid, which I don't think it is. Well, anyway, you seem to like the Veblen essay so maybe my batting average is still fair to average.[90]

8: Latest disappointment, although not final yet, has to do with going this summer to lecture at the Free University of Berlin. Some kind of exchange stuff which pays all expenses and enough besides to pay for Ruth's trip and living while there. Neumann, Franz . . . in charge more or less. I wrote him a note telling him I'd love it and he said he'd be glad to recommend me, but that another guy in the Dept., Si Goode, who teaches in extension service, had applied so Dept. had to decide. I wrote Merton who said in reply: "You two talk it out." What is there to talk about? So now I don't know what to do. To hell with it.

[. . .]

I am not at all "in a hurry" as you suggest. I am simply relaxed and meeting the demands of the day and reading novels and having a minor crisis once or twice a week meeting some lecture and feeling miserable in general, this being my spiritual menopause of some queer sort. All this is old stuff with me and with damn near everybody I know at one time or another. The difference with me this time is that I have simply stopped trying to write during this period. In short, I am genuinely trying to learn "to relax" and I am halfway at least succeeding.

Of course one tries to pick up a target, the meeting of which would, in one's mind, relieve all burdens. For both Ruth and me that target is unfortunately impossible; we should so love to take a real trip,

87. Jacob Burckhardt, *Force and Freedom: Reflections on History,* ed. James Hastings Nichols (New York: Pantheon Books, 1949).

88. Jacob Burckhardt, *The Age of Constantine the Great* (New York: Pantheon, 1949; reprint, Berkeley and Los Angeles: University of California Press, 1983).

89. C. Wright Mills, "Leisure and the Whole Man" (paper read at the Twenty-second Annual *Herald Tribune* Forum, October 20, 1953, New York); printed in the *New York Herald Tribune,* October 25, 1953.

90. Perhaps Mills's introduction to the Mentor edition of Thorstein Veblen's *The Theory of the Leisure Class* (New York: New American Library, 1953). Or perhaps it was a section from a chapter in the manuscript in progress of *The Power Elite.*

for a year, to Europe without having any project while there other than to experience the damn place. But that just isn't possible on private money, and it doesn't seem like they'll—any of the thousands of fellowships etc.—give me a hand. I don't really blame them. Why should they?

But enough. Thanks again. Write me. See you in a few months.

As ever,
Mills

∽

To David Riesman, from Pomona, New York, undated (probably fall 1953)

Dear David:

Thanks for your kind words about the little Veblen essay. It is a section from a chapter of *The American Elite* book on which I am still at work, and which—to tell you the truth—I find more and more troublesome. First draft is completed—last spring at Brandeis in fact, but somehow I can't command the attention and love needed to complete the blanks still in it and tighten it into shape. O well.

When next you're in town, let me know in advance. I'm generally in Mon. Wed. Fri.

Cordially,
Wright Mills

In the next letter Mills responded to Gerth's queries related to translating White Collar *into German. As it turned out, Gerth's translation of his friend's book was never published; however, an English translation of Gerth's introductory essay for the book was published decades later as "The Development of Social Thought in the United States and Germany: Critical Observations on the Occasion of the Publication of C. Wright Mills'* White Collar.*"[91] (A German translation of* White Collar *was published by Bund-Verlag GMBH in 1955; Bernt Engelmann, who was a translator before becoming a political columnist, provided the translation for that edition.)*

91. In the *International Journal of Politics, Culture, and Society* 7, no. 3 (spring 1994): 525–68.

To Hans Gerth, from Pomona, New York, undated (received December 26, 1953)

Dear Gerth:

"The man who has risen" is not a book or a story by Howells; it is merely a phrase which he used to describe the age of the businessman. Likewise with Whitman's phrase, "Man in the open air," which is quoted by F. O. Matthiessen in his *American Renaissance,* page 626. I stuck the two phrases into one sentence, appearing on page 21 of *White Collar,* in order to catch in brief way the rise of business in contrast with rural frontier stuff. If I may suggest: it might be better merely to put quote marks around the two phrases without capitalizing them. The whole book, *White Collar,* is of course chuck full of such allusive stuff, which I don't see how our German readers will really follow, but it really isn't necessary. I am sorry, my friend, that I do not—like Nietzsche says one should—write with an eye on translations! Please know again that I know how lucky I am in having you for Germany! Think what the poor Japanese will read!

I am of course much less optimistic than you about my chances to get to Berlin, as all looks yellow to the jaundiced eye, and both of mine are canary yellow these days. The other day I wrote you a long sorrowful letter, but you will be glad to know I tore it up without mailing it. The purpose was perhaps served in the mere stupid act of composing it. Let us be brave and stand up like little Indians, straight and tall, and all that hog shit. Anyway I'm very grateful for your letters to friends in Berlin. We just have to wait and see how the little pebbles of chance slip under whose feet, and whether the baleful glare of all our enemies in the paranoid universe penetrates or not.

Very glad to hear that H I and children go on to Germany rather than trying to get settled for so short a time at Brandeis. That would be very foolish and uncomfortable. [. . .]

I am beginning slowly to read a bit now for the elite book, and even at times to believe that somehow, sometime, it will start to get produced again. It has the makings of a good loud blast at the bastards, one they can't ignore maybe. If I was ambivalent here and there about the *White Collar* elements, and the labor leaders, by god I am not at all ambivalent at the elite: they are not my kind of people. As Burckhardt said of great men, we can say of the elite: "they are everything we are not," to which we ought to add, for which, thank god.

Yours,
M.
Mills

∾

To William Miller, from Pomona, New York, dated January 25, 1954

Dear Bill:

Kind of you to ask about the "Explorations." Yes I did get it and many thanks. Looks so so interesting, although not too relevant to Elite because of period.[92]

Slowly I have gotten back to writing and reading on the topic. It seems now that my fall downfall, the old Untergang, well I slowly get up from it and walk away.[93] This spring I hope to do some work. Got a little windfall for March 20th: trip to California via plane to talk before mental health society: all expenses and a little dough.

The big upset right now came three days ago: H I Gerth, Gerth's wife, died. [. . .] Gerth is on his way, driving with 2 children to Camp Hill for one week.[94] Children will be taken for several months to Germany by woman friend of family; H I was scheduled to take them this spring. (Gerth teaches at Brandeis this spring and is sched-uled for summer school at Columbia.)

It's not terribly likely but he may want in the several days that he will stay here to run around and see people, even if he doesn't know them very well; if so we may drop by your place; and if so do not mention your knowledge of his wife's death. If he wants to talk he will. Hard to tell how any man reacts, certainly hard to know how he will: he was so god damned dependent upon her and they appeared to be so very happy. Life, my friend, is very arbitrary. You have to live to around forty to have known enough people to realize just how arbitrary it really is. [. . .]

92. That is, not very relevant to *The Power Elite*.

93. *Untergang* is a German word for decline, going under, or downfall. In the autumn, Mills often suffered a temporary loss of enthusiasm, energy, and optimism.

94. Gerth and his two daughters, Anne and Julie, who were then twelve and eight years old, visited the Millses at their home on Camp Hill Road.

By all means see current issue of *Partisan Review:* Howe's piece, "The Age of Conformity," brings up to date, if I may say so, my old piece on the powerless people[95] and the chapter "Brains" in *White Collar.* It's a very good job and I'm happy he does it now.

Hope to see you and Bucky soon Bill; Ruth sends her love.

As ever,
Mills

The following letter was written after a visit to Mills's parents at their home in San Antonio, Texas. In the summer of 1954, Mills and Ruth were resident fellows at the Huntington Hartford Foundation of Pacific Palisades, California, while working on The Power Elite.

To Frances and Charles Grover Mills, from Pacific Palisades, California, not dated (summer 1954)

Dear Mother and Dad:

Our trip from San Antonio to Los Angeles was easy going, and now after one night at the Foundation we are quite well settled. The people here are rather mixed: there are three composers, several painters, four fiction writers, and ourselves. The little house they have given us is really the nuts; were we to build a house in the California hills, this would be close to what we would build. It has a living room and bedroom and bath and refrigerator and electric stove and sink for odd snacks and coffee making. And a huge studio with a big north sky-light. Also a little sun patio. There is a lovely pool below us and the "mess hall" is one minute away, down a steep little road.

When we arrived I found two invitations to speak this summer and have accepted them both. One for about August 10 is a conference set up by the University of Toronto and the Canadian Broadcasting Corporation. I'll speak there, in Toronto, on a national hook-up for Canada, flying there and back of course: all expenses [paid] and $350, which will buy me a decent suit!

95. "The Powerless People: The Role of the Intellectual in Society" *politics* 1, no. 3 (April 1944).

Then on August 25 the US Air Force will fly me to Mont-
gomery, Alabama, to speak to about 200 colonels at a school they run
there for future generals. I'm to speak on modern military forces and
the organization of the modern state. And I mean to tell them just
how it is. They don't pay anything but fancy expenses, but I want to
look the future generals in the eye. So you see it really isn't likely that
if the FBI were crouched ready to move in on me, the Air Force
would go to the trouble to have me tell off their elite corps.

In the meantime I must get right to work and write a stern
rough mean prophetical book, damning them all and all that they
have made and are making out of this silly lovely horrible delightful
obscene stupid and magnificent world.

See you around.
Little Charlie

*Mills was right in thinking that the FBI was not actively investigating him in 1954.
The FBI's active and prolific investigation of Mills was yet to come.*

*The University of Toronto–Canadian Broadcasting Corporation speech Mills
mentioned in the previous letter was originally entitled "Are We Losing Our Sense
of Belonging?" Mills inserted a copy into the Tovarich notebook, edited in his handwriting—including the new title we have used here—with a note near the title saying, "Excellent! Use in book." The speech follows.*

TO WHAT, THEN, DO WE BELONG?

I

You and I are among those who are asking serious questions and
by that very fact I know that there is something to which you and
I do belong. We belong to that minority that has carried on the big
discourse of the rational mind; to the big discourse that has been
going on—or off and on—since the Western society began some two
thousand years ago in the small communities of Athens and Jerusalem. Maybe you think that is a pretty vague thing to which to belong;
if you do think that, you are mistaken. It is quite a thing to belong
to the big discourse—even if as lesser participants—and, as I hope
presently to make clear, it is the beginning of any "sense of belong-

ing" that is worthwhile. It is the key to the only kind of belonging that free people in our time might have. And I think that to belong to it requires that we try to live up to what it demands of us.

What it demands of us, first of all, is that we maintain our sense of it. And, just now, at this point in human history, that is quite difficult. For we belong not only to the big discourse of the rational mind; we also belong—although we do not always feel that we do—to our own epoch; accordingly, since we are live people and not detached minds, we are trying to live in and with a certain set of feelings: the feelings of political people trying to be rational in an epoch of enormous irrationality.

II

What is the dominant mood of people like us, who try to think up questions and answer them for ourselves? What is the tang and feel of our experience as we examine the world about us today? It is clear that these feelings are shaping the way we ask and the way we answer all the questions of this conference: it is also clear—let us admit it—that our mood is not buoyant, not calm, not steady, and not sure. It is true that we do not panic, but it is also true that we possess the crisis mentality, and none of us can be up to the demands of our time unless we share something of this kind of mind, for it is rooted in an adequate sense of history and of our place in history.

We are often stunned and we are often distracted, and we are bewildered almost all of the time. And the only weapon we have— as individuals and as a scatter of grouplets—is the delicate brain now so perilously balanced in the struggle for public sanity. We feel that common political sense is no longer a sound basis of judgment, for the common sense of the twentieth century is based largely upon an eighteenth- and a nineteenth-century experience, which is outmoded by new facts of public life with which we have had little to do, except as victims. The more we understand what is happening in the world, the more frustrated we often become, for our knowledge leads to feelings of powerlessness.

We feel that we are living in a world in which the citizen has become a mere spectator or a forced actor, and that our personal experience is politically useless and our political will a minor illusion. Very often the fear of total, permanent war paralyzes the kind of

morally oriented politics which might engage our interests and
our passions. We sense the cultural mediocrity around us—and
in us—and we know that ours is a time when, within and between
all the nations of the world, the levels of public sensibility have
sunk below sight; atrocity on a mass scale has become impersonal
and official; moral indignation as a public fact has become extinct
or made trivial.

We feel that distrust has become nearly universal among men
of affairs, and that the spread of public anxiety is poisoning human
relations and drying up the roots of private freedom. We see that the
people at the top often identify rational dissent with political mutiny,
loyalty with blind conformity, and freedom of judgment with treason.

We feel that irresponsibility has become organized in high places
and that clearly those in charge of the historic decisions of our time are
not up to them. But what is more damaging to us is that we feel that
those on the bottom—the forced actors who take the consequences—
are also without leaders, without ideas of opposition, and that they
make no real demands upon those in power.

III

We do not, of course, feel all of this all of the time, but we often
feel some of it, and in the dark of the night, when we are really alone
and really awake, we suspect that this might very well be an honest
articulation of our deepest political feelings. And if we are justified—
even in half of these feelings—then we have at hand a second answer
to the question of whether we are losing our sense of belonging. Our
first answer, you will remember, was a general Yes, except in the sense
that we belong to the big discourse. Our second answer reflects our
feelings about the sort of world we are living in, and may be put in
this way: I don't know whether or not you are losing your political
sense of belonging, but I should certainly hope so.

The point is that we are among those who cannot get their
mouths around all the little Yeses that add up to tacit acceptance of a
world run by crackpot realists and subject to blind drift. And that, you
see, is something to which we do belong; we belong to those who are
still capable of personally rejecting. Our minds are not yet captive. I
believe that, just now, in the kind of political world we are in, rejection is more important than acceptance. For, in such a world, to accept

freely requires, first of all, the personal capacity and the social chance to reject the official myths and the unofficial distractions. [. . .][96]

IV

I hope I have made it clear that the question of losing our sense of political belonging cannot be answered with moral sensibility unless we also ask: To what is it that we ought to belong? Mere loyalty alone is less a virtue than an escape from freely thought-out choices among the many values that now compete for our loyalties.

My own answer to this question, which may well be different from yours, can be put very simply: If we are human, what we ought to belong to first of all is ourselves. We ought to belong to ourselves as individuals. Once upon a time that answer would have seemed clear, for it used to be called "the appeal to conscience," but we now know that this is much too simple an answer, for we now know that there are people whose conscience is perfectly clear and perfectly sincere—and perfectly corrupt in its consequences for themselves and for others.

So we must add to this answer one further point: to the extent that we are truly human, we should try seriously to participate in that rational discourse of which I have spoken. And to the extent that we do so, our sensibilities will have been shaped by the high points of mankind's heritage of conduct and character and thought. Accordingly, we shall belong, and we ought to belong, to mankind, and it is to mankind that we ought most freely to give our loyalties.

All other loyalties, it seems to me, ought to be qualified by these two: loyalty to ourselves and loyalty to the cultural heritage of mankind that we allow to shape us as individuals. This answer is more a beginning than an end; we ought to use it to judge all principles and organizations that demand our loyalties. No corporation, no church, no nation, no labor union, no political party—no organization or creed—is worthy of our loyalties if it does not facilitate the growth of loyalties to ourselves and to the heritage that mankind has produced in its best moments.

Moreover, we ought not to be committed absolutely to any organization. Our loyalty is conditional. Otherwise, it is not loyalty. It is

96. We have deleted a discussion of various kinds of organizations and background for the then current state of affairs.

not the belonging of free people; it is a compelled obedience. Let us not confuse the loyalties of free people with mere obedience to authority. When organizations or nations sell out the values of free people, free people withdraw their loyalties. Not with a "Yes, But" or a "Maybe Yes, Maybe No" but with a big, plain, flat "No."

V

The positive question for us is not so much whether we are losing our sense of belonging as whether we can help build something that is worth belonging to. Perhaps that has always been the major social question for men and women shaped by the big discourse. For just as freedom that has not been fought for is lightly cast off, so belonging that does not require the building and the maintaining of organizations worth belonging to is often merely a yearning for a new bondage.

To really belong, we have got, first, to get it clear with ourselves that we do *not* belong and do not want to belong to an unfree world. As free men and women we have got to reject much of it and to know why we are rejecting it.

We have got, second, to get it clear within ourselves that we can only truly belong to organizations which we have a real part in building and maintaining, directly and openly and all of the time.

And we have got, third, to realize that it is only in the struggle for what we really believe, as individuals and as members of economic, political, and social groups, that the sense of belonging befitting a free person in an unfree world can exist. In such a world, only the comradeship of such a struggle is worth our loyalty; and only to such truly human associations as we might create do we, as rational people, wish to belong.

To William and Virginia Miller, from Palisades, California, undated (July 1954)

Dear Bill and Bucky:

I know I should have written but many things have happened and have not yet added up to much. The trip out was a Porsche trip, which means very fast and very limousinish. You cruise at 85 to 100 mph and it is as if you are going 50 or so: the Krauts have built a car. The place is very good; nothing disturbs you and you are served meals and you are absolutely free to set your own pattern apart from meal hours at 8–9 A.M. and 6 P.M. People here are OK, and one or two really worth knowing. And we are both personally content with the everyday routine and all of that.

The book, the book: it comes slowly I suppose but it does come. Ruth is pretty well sticking to one chapter after the next right thru and I am leaping around a bit but steadying down now to the general sequence. It would do no good for either of us were I to attempt to let you know in [a] letter the shifts and strategies we are coming to, but it may be enough to say that the book will show a much more unified upper class and power elite than even I had at first thought possible. And there is one thing I do want to tell you, although [I] won't try to explain it too fully. In brief it is this: for the very rich and for the executives, the terms entrepreneur and bureaucrat just won't do. Those are middle class words and retain too much middle class imagery and perspective. They are all right for middle class levels of economic life; they make no sense and are misleading when used for the very top guys. I know we have all used them, and coded stuff into them. But you know what made it clear to me that they were no damn good: reading carefully the notes I took on the write up of your data that this Keller girl did.[97] Her analysis is a good careful statistical analysis: no one could do much more with that data from a statistical point of view. But it just isn't so. It just doesn't give you how and why those guys got where they were, and it gives a very false image of what they actually do when they are there. When you wrote those words in several articles you did,[98] which I come to admire more and more, you could get away with those words because they were embedded in knowledge and cases about what the hell went on, but she doesn't know. So in the chapter on the very rich, I am trying

97. This must be Suzanne Infeld Keller, author of *Beyond the Ruling Class: Strategic Elites in Modern Society* (New York: Random House, 1963), as well as other works.

98. Miller had written several articles for the *Reporter,* including "Can Government Be Merchandised?" (27 October 1953); "It May Be Box Office, But Is It the Bible?" (29 September 1953); and "Tyranny of Virtue, the Emptiness of Tolerance" (16 March 1954). Other relevant articles by Miller might be "American Historians and the Business Elite," *Journal of Economic History* (November 1949); and "The Recruitment of the American Business Elite," *Quarterly Journal of Economics* (May 1950).

to destroy the word entrepreneur and in the chapter on the executives I am going to destroy the word bureaucrat. I won't make a big production about it, just two or three pages as to why I won't use them. But, God damn it, I can't get good slogan-like terms yet to replace them. What has been called bureaucratic career for top businessmen I refer to as moving within and between the corporate hierarchy and stuff like that. And entrepreneur: merging smaller firms and promoting and etc. If you think of terms phrases etc., let me know.

Did you see in last Sunday's *Times Book Review* the piece by Ed Saveth? God, how disgusting. You are mentioned OK though.[99]

Read Hofstadter's mimeo chapters, all but front and tail, which he hasn't sent yet. Please don't tell him I said so, for what good is it, but my god it is thin stuff: nothing beyond Walling and Josephson and Griswold on farming and, if I may say so, a good bit of old Mills on status and all, but no acknowledgment but, hell, who cares.

Will try to drop a little A-bomb on them all with Elite but hell they will all ignore it, except maybe five or six hundred people who will love me for it. And that is enough. Who wants to be loved by masses, or by mass-like minds?

Let me know how it goes, Bill.

Yours as ever,

Who else?
[unsigned copy]

When The Power Elite *was published in April 1956, its description of interlocking power relationships between the economic, political, and military elites in the United States was far from accepted knowledge; Dwight D. Eisenhower did not make his famous speech about the dangers of the growing military-industrial complex until he left office in January 1961.*

99. "Exit 'Robber Baron & Co.,'" *New York Times Book Review* (4 July 1954): 6–7, 12. Ed Saveth had discussed the approach to economic history taken by Allan Nevins in his biography of John D. Rockefeller Sr. and his history of the Ford Motor Company: "Thorstein Veblen's predatory captain of industry, all tooth and claw, is almost unrecognizable in the portraits of the industrialist as philanthropist." Saveth wrote that this revision of historical perspective led to greater truth about the role of American business. He also respectfully mentioned a collection, entitled *Men in Business,* edited by William Miller, and *The Age of Enterprise* by Thomas Cochran and William Miller.

To Leo Lowenthal, from Pomona, New York, dated May 20, 1955

Friday nite

Dear Leo:

How in the world can you know anything about promotions and all, and yet you always know the quote interhuman unquote realities of everywhere. But the budget is all in already. And I got a letter saying for your wonderful contribution we give you this little raise and you are still associate professor and it is signed by Kirk. So what the hell goes? Could Leo be wrong? Of course he could be wrong, on this at least. Anyway we don't think or talk about nasty things like money anymore. We are above that, or rather below that.

Today I sent you book rate a dittoed copy of "The Power Elite." I waited at first and worried about sending it to you because you are way out there among so many enemies[100] and I do not want this copy read by *anyone* but friends or talked about because I am still very much changing it, maybe drastically, and I do not want guys who have read it talking bad about the poor little thing to other guys who haven't had a chance to read it and can't yet go down to the book-store and put up their 5 bucks in my defense. This copy is for your eyes only. How can I finish it until you have told me what I must next do? So, tell me.

One thing you must know: on my master copy I have now:

1) begun the book with what is now chapter two.

2) taken what is now chapter one and added to it the first five or six pages of what is now chapter 15. Made this new chapter, called "Of Ideologies and Moods," go between what are now chapters 14 and 15.

The idea is that these silly boys I talk about there in chapter one are too unimportant to start with; neither the elite nor the mass public pays any attention to them, so why should I feature them so?

Another thing: there are 100 pages of footnotes that will go in the back of the book with numbers on the text pages. I didn't print that in *White Collar* and think I should in this one.

As soon as you get the manuscript, lock yourself up in a quiet

---

100. Lowenthal was a fellow at the Center for Advanced Studies in the Behavioral Sciences, Stanford, California, 1955–56.

room and let it flood your mind for 48 hours; then after the first wonder of it, begin to read it slowly for about a week, marking it and tearing it up and writing copious criticisms and compliments and debunkings. Then send it all back to me.

Everything here is as much as it could be without your being here. At night the women cry and in the daylight the men are confused and once a week they all come together and wail and they are sick and full of spleen, here in the East, without Leo.

Yours as ever,
Mills

In the following letter, Mills responded to a reader's report on a draft of the manuscript of The Power Elite. *The reader, who had been commissioned by Oxford University Press, stopped reviewing the manuscript after the second chapter, writing in exasperation that Mills's draft contained "the sort of sterile verbalism that does real harm to the cause of genuine learning."[101]*

To Lee Grove at Oxford University Press, from Pomona, New York, dated June 10, 1955

Friday noon

Dear Mr. Grove:

Thanks for sending me the criticism. Of course, I'll wait until all of it is in, and taken account of, before getting together with you. But I do now want to say that I hope you're no more upset by this sort of carping about the surface than I am. I've never written anything about which, at some stage or another of the draft, someone hasn't said this sort of thing. And I've never turned out a book about which any reviewer said it.

These comments have to do with old chapter One—which, as you know from the three later drafts you've received, is now rewrit-

101. Report attached to Lee E. Grove's letter to C. Wright Mills, dated June 8, 1955.

ten as new chapter 14. None of the particular sentences quoted is, at the present stage of my master copy, in the chapter.

Things go well. I've now three really well marked up copies: one from Harvey Swados (novelist), one from John Blair (FTC economist) and one from William Miller (formerly *Fortune* writer, formerly Knopf editor, now freelance). So I'm at the manuscript hard. Please send along criticism just as soon as you get it. As the manuscript gets stronger I get weaker, so the sooner the better.

Sincerely,
C. Wright Mills

In the summer of 1955, Mills asked Oxford University Press for an advance of $5,000 for a book on American intellectuals; this was equal to the advance he had received from Oxford for The Power Elite. *However, believing that a book on intellectuals would not be as popular as* The Power Elite, *the press offered an advance of only $2,500, just $500 more than Oxford's advance for* White Collar *many years before. According to an internal memo, dated August 9, 1955, Mr. Grove expected a negative reaction from Mills but believed that the project could not sustain an advance higher than what was offered. This is the letter Mills sent via special delivery in response to the offer from Oxford.*

To Lee Grove, editor, Trade Department, Oxford University Press, from Pomona, New York, dated August 18, 1955[102]

Dear Mr. Grove:

Thank you for your letter of 17 August 1955.

The terms which you propose for *The American Intellectual* are disappointing, but acceptable to me. They even make sense from the horrible standpoint of reality.

Please go ahead and draw up the contract *today;* I'll get it back to you by return mail.

Sincerely,
C. Wright Mills

102. "Arrived Special Delivery" was written on this letter.

∾

To Leo Lowenthal, from Columbia University, New York City, dated August 29, 1955

Dear Leo:

Since *The Power Elite* is now in press, I've begun a book on "The Intellectuals." Although it is primarily about the Americans, I hope to make it comparative; so I'm applying for a research Fulbright for England for 1956–57. Would you help me by laying something as thick as you can on the enclosed? They are due by 1 October 1955. (You're the only sociologist I'm giving: my other references are Dean Chamberlain, Clara Thompson and [William] Oman of Oxford Press.)

I fear the images of the American scene I've printed are against me; but don't you think I'd be a good little ambassador? I've applied for England as first choice, but I'll go anywhere that requests me.

Buvez Coca Cola,
C. Wright Mills

Leo Lowenthal, who had known Mills professionally and socially for twelve years, took Mills's request to heart and did indeed "lay it on thick." On the topic of being a good ambassador, he wrote the following about Mills:

> *I feel on particularly safe grounds in answering your question whether he would be an "effective representative of American academic and cultural life." Having served for nearly six years as Director of the Evaluation Staff of the Voice of America with the US Department of State and later with the US Information Agency, I have become thoroughly familiar with the facts as well as the purposes of US public policy in international cultural relations. From the standpoint of my knowledge of this policy, I would not hesitate to recommend Mr. Mills as a representative of the best in this country's cultural and intellectual life. He is both deeply rooted in regional heritage and dedicated to practical and realistic progress and at the same time productively sensitized to the burning issues of the Free World as a whole. His outgoing, buoyant and kind personality cannot help but make many friends for the United States here and abroad.*

The following April, Mills was granted the Fulbright award to lecture at the University of Copenhagen for the 1956–57 academic year.

Mills, who began to ride a motorcycle out of frustration over the difficulty of finding a parking space for a car near Columbia College, soon became interested in motorcycling as a sport. In the spring of 1955 Mills drove his motorcycle from New York to Massachusetts to visit Lewis A. Coser and Irving Howe and their families. He described the trip to Harvey Swados:

> The other day I rode up to the Cosers and Howes, spent the night, then rode around
> the Cape, returning that night to Harvard, where Ken Stampp teaches this year. Then
> back here, about 800 miles plus, very high speed averages, very low gasoline consump-
> tions. It utterly exhausted me. My hands were half numb for several days and my left
> eyeball twitched. But it is the only thing I know that gets away from it all on a go-
> anywhere machine. Concentration is such that it completely empties you for a good
> stretch of all the little stuff, and the roundness of the old earth flows under the wheels.
> It's like a horse; it's like a sports car; it's like controlling motion itself in [a] pure form
> of speed. And if you want, you can walk with it, down to a slow crawl in bottom gear
> for miles and miles and you see everything: more than if you were walking and much
> much more than in any automobile.[103]

To the *Motorcycle* (London, England), from Pomona, New York, dated October 14, 1955

Gentlemen:

Apart from riding itself, whatever I have learned about riding a motorcycle with skill and safety I learned last year from your re-printed pamphlet "The Methods of the Experts." In contrast with other sports, there is so little of this how-to-do-it literature for the motorcyclist. Do you know of any other such writing? (I've read all the books you advertise, including "Cavalcade.") I, for one, would very much like to read a series on the technique of the trials rider, another on scrambling, and most of all—because it is more closely related to my own practice of fast touring—a series on road racing.

In order to encourage you to carry on with "The Methods" series, I herewith submit some questions having to do with cornering. Perhaps you might find it worthwhile to submit them, along with other such questions which you might devise, for other features of riding, to road racers or trial riders:

103. Undated letter to Harvey Swados.

Question: You are on dry, clean concrete or asphalt, entering a flat
90 degree corner, mounted on a 500 twin with dual seat. You've mis-
judged it a little. You're into it too fast. There's no straight-out escape.
You can't straighten up in order to brake. Good visibility and no traffic
permit you to use the full width, but even so you feel that you may skid.
What should you do? (Please don't reply: "It depends on conditions." If
I've failed to mention any relevant conditions, specify them as you like.)
[. . .][104]

Even if you're not interested in doing more advanced articles along
the lines of "The Methods" series, I'd be ever so much obliged . . .
and would feel safer . . . if you'd send me an answer. Maybe there is
a simple obvious one which I, having been riding only about one year
and not being in close contact with other riders, just don't know.

Sincerely yours,
BMW R69[105]

∞

To Lewis A. Coser, from Pomona, New York, undated (probably late
1955 or early 1956)

Dear Lou:

Thanks so much for your letter. I've oiled the machine several times
and prepared it for a long fast run up to Wellesley,[106] but each time
the weather has been impossible. I'm coming up as soon as I can
now and I'll let you know a week ahead if at all possible. Feel very
depressed these days. [Until] April everything is in balance, or so
I foolishly feel.[107] You see, the point is that it doesn't really matter
to me whether the PE is acclaimed or debunked: oh, it matters of

---

104. Here Mills provided a detailed and fairly technical outline of questions related to
his main question. Topics included the machine and the body of the rider, the placement
of the weight of the rider, the posture of the rider, the placement of the hands, and the use
of the throttle.

105. Mills signed his own name to the letter but asked that "BMW R69" be used if the
letter were published. His motorcycle was made by BMW.

106. Lewis and Rose Coser were living at Wellesley College, where Rose taught; Lew
was teaching at Brandeis.

107. Mills was expecting a final answer in April about a Fulbright professorship in Europe, and *The Power Elite* was due to be published March 22.

course but not as much (or perhaps too much) as it ought to. Maybe I mean, and need to say to you, that the success of such a book would in a way be a failure. But that is not to say that failure is not also a trap. If anybody is an expert on this success stuff as social phenomena, surely I am; but being an expert does not enable you to avoid it in your guts even though you are contemptuous of it. Heads I win, tail you lose. Sub specie fuckus.

Anyway, I'm glad you talked with Dennis [Wrong].[108] His reaction as you tell it is part of the Star system (either smash hit or nothing), which I hate so much in American culture. Isn't there room for just plain solid stuff; workmanlike stuff by an artisan stratum? That's my ideal kind of production and reception.

By the way, if Bernie [Rosenberg] likes it, please tell him for me that it makes me very glad.[109] I've come to like his stuff and am very happy he likes mine since he is one of the dozen at most people about whose appraisal I really give a damn.

Do tell me any gossip, good or bad, you come across because as you know I do not see many people and don't know what goes on . . . I mean about the book.

I've not yet rec'd copy from Free Press of your book.[110] I can't ask for it for review from *Times* or *Saturday Review:* they frown on that, at least the two times I've done it, but I shall certainly put in a word. [. . .]

No word on Fulbright. No word on promotion, which after 12 years and three really good offers over the last several years might be due by now.[111] No work under way on intellectuals except busy work. And not much spirit.

Let us know when you're all coming down.

WM
Mills

---

108. The sociologist (who received his Ph.D. from Columbia University in 1956).

109. Bernard Rosenberg, a sociologist who taught at City College as well as at the New School for Social Research, coedited *Sociological Theory* with Lewis Coser (1957) and coedited *Mass Culture: The Popular Arts in America* with David Manning White (1957).

110. *The Functions of Social Conflict* (1956).

111. Mills had turned down offers from the New School for Social Research, Brandeis University, and perhaps the University of Chicago. Brandeis had offered him a position after he was there as a visiting professor in the spring of 1953.

A few years before Mills's first trip to Europe he had tried to arrange a visiting pro-
fessorship in Europe for 1954–55, to no avail. In 1952 he described his reasons for
wanting to live and work in Europe this way: "I have all my life lived in a country
that is only some six or seven generations old, and the longer I work here and the
older I get, the more provincial and limited I feel. I want to live in Europe for a while,
to put it positively, in order to establish points of comparisons."112

To Leo and Marjorie Lowenthal, from Pomona, New York, dated
January 7 (1956)

Dear Leo and Marjorie:

[I.] It's about 3:30 in the morning Sat. Jan. 7. I fell asleep early last
night and now have waked up and eaten. Over the last month or
so I've done this pretty frequently; it's not a bad pattern. You don't
accomplish much by way of thinking or writing but you believe,
for two or three hours, that you are probably putting the world on
a string—or in a bottle, except that just now there is no bourbon in
the house. Maybe it's because on the 21st of this month, by Dutch
airline, Mills enters Europe for the first time. I go, as I quite properly
should, as an amateur mechanic of sports cars and motorcycles. Here's
the deal: the importer for BMW and NSU here in New York is a
good friend of mine, a fine old Austrian gentleman. He is chartering
a plane to take the mechanics of his dealers to the factories for a short
service training course, on the care and feeding of little BMWs. He's
letting me go along. The whole trip, including round trip air, all
meals, all hotels . . . everything . . . will cost me $380. About two
weeks in all. First week in Neckersulm, just above Stuttgart; second
week in Munich. I suppose I'll be pretty busy at the factories because
honest to God I'd rather hear the roar of an R-69 being bench-tested
by a man who knows his motors than see the finest cathedral in the
world. It is very proper, I feel, that no intellectual group or agency
should send me to Europe but that I should smell it for the first time
as an amateur mechanic. Do let me know if anything occurs to you,
that I ought to see or do without fail in Munich.

112. Letter to Professor Max Horkheimer of Frankfurt, Germany, dated December 15,
1952.

II. The other day I got a letter from the Fulbright people. They say that the University of Copenhagen has asked for me to lecture in social psychology. So they shifted me from England in research to Denmark in lecturing. I told them OK. Hell anything is OK, as long as I get there. Of course this is not final, but it does mean that I slipped thru the academic committees and now have only to be cleared by State Dept. Still several sorts of mechanical catches could stall the deal, but it does look very good. [. . .]

III. The family is fine. Ruth is very happy, as am I, with the child. Katie is a monstrous girl, weighing at 5 and half months some 20 pounds, all muscle of course with very alert and knowing blue eyes and full of idiotic chuckles and euphoria.

[Unsigned copy]

To Leo and Marjorie Lowenthal, from Pomona, New York, dated February 16, 1956

Dear Leo and Marj:

If by one's hometown is meant the town to which one wants to return, then Munich is now one of my favorite hometowns, ranking with San Francisco. You will realize that, being there only two weeks, I was of course only on the surface. But how good for once to be on the surface without any of the tensions of thought involved in digging beneath it! I met some magnificent people, mainly technicians and engineers with whom I ran around in the evening and worked on motors during the day. (I now have a factory diploma as a first class mechanic on BMW motors.) I also found out that you do not need much language. They don't know English. I don't know German but we talked all the time and understood enough. The trick is to mispronounce English in a German direction; there must be many cognates between the two languages; and of course to develop a subtlety of gesture. Anyway, seriously, in six weeks there alone I could get the language fine. One night in a wine stubba (phonetically spelled) alone, with no other English speaking person, is better than 15 lessons in German. They help you with it wonderfully. If you just try it, strangers will spend an hour teaching you and buy you wine as well. So: why not migrate over there? Haven't I finished around here?

Now I wait until April to know about Copenhagen and the Fulbright for next year. In the meantime the trip revived me enough to
do a little writing on the intellectual book. Oxford is going to throw
a little party for book reviewers and such on Elite book next month
(but it won't do any good . . . even my best friend won't comment on
galleys of the damn thing). Ruth and Katie are well. What is going on
with you? Hear from Oxford yet? I go to university seminar, at least
for a few times; Paul [Lazarsfeld] runs professional training in social
science, with all the big shots there. I ride [the motorcycle] whenever
the weather permits. I wait for Copenhagen, and for letters from you.

Wright

∾

To William Miller, from Pomona, New York, dated February 25,
1956

Dear Bill:

I have your confused and disgusting letter about Miller in Europe.
I guess everyone finds a different Europe and some keep themselves
insulated and isolated in those little Americanized circles, such as
Salzburg must be,[113] and don't find any Europe. You ask what I mean
by my jaunt to Munich being a "huge" success. Well, seriously, it
was just that. By which I mean above all that I discovered people
again. People worth talking to half the night, people with histories
so different from mine, and as full of individuality as I ever hope to
be. Language is no difficulty. I got a Berlitz phrase book, which is
excellent on phonetically spelled German. And then when I didn't
know a word I used the English word, mispronouncing it in the
German direction. Everyone laughed but I was understood and then
they taught me. Strangers spent hours teaching me words and pro-
nunciation, and also bought me wine.[114] You have got to plunge right
in you know. During the day I was mostly out at the plant, BMW,
and there met technicians and minor managers, with whom at night
I often went around. But I was on my own in Munich for four days

---

113. Salzburg, Austria, where Miller had participated in the Salzburg Seminar.
114. A note from Ruth at the end of this letter said that Mills's visit to Munich had coincided with festival time.

before the bunch arrived. And that was when I learned the most German. Of course all of this was on the surface, but how good for once to be on the surface and not to get into the tension of analysis!

I can't wait to make my big European tour by BMW this summer. No definite word yet on the Fulbright. [. . .] In the meantime, why don't you make Salzburg get me for the summer?[115] Would be very helpful moneywise, as I'm, as usual, in trouble with all that.

By all means try to run over to Munich. It is cheap, at least in Germany, to rent a VW for a couple of days and not much trouble at all.

Bill, do let me know right away your schedule: when do you leave there and when do you get back here? I want to know so as to know whether or not to send you there a copy of my book [*The Power Elite*]. Physical copies any day now. And did you or did you not finish up yours? And what are you actually doing in Salzburg? Give me two typical days time budget. And what the hell are you teaching? Lecturing or seminar stuff? God damn it don't philosophize so much. REPORT. EXPERIENCE. RELAX INTO IT.

M.

ᨆ

To Hans Gerth, from Pomona, New York, undated (probably April 1956)

Dear Gerth:

I was so glad to get your letter. Quite frankly, I was worried when you did not write for so long, worried that for some reason you had become angry with me, or that you thought the book [*The Power Elite*] lousy and did not want to say so. Well, you've got to remember that I too am alone intellectually and the crushing burden of some reviews is hard to take from such hired shit-heels as write them. So although I don't suppose I can be panicked at my advanced age, still they can worry me.[116] I only hope I worry them a little bit too.

The brightest thing anyone has said about the publication of

---

115. The following year Mills did receive an invitation to lecture for two weeks at the Salzburg Seminar.

116. Mills was not quite forty years old.

the book was said the other day by a "World Telegram" journalist who did a personal interview thing on me. He said: "Everyone smart enough to understand it is either for it or against it." I think that is real cute. The fellow likes me, you see.

Anyway to hell with them all and with the book too now. It is done. The idea is to keep thinking of the next one. As long as there is "the next one" you are alive and if you believe in the next one you are really living. That, my dear friend, is what you have got somehow to do: get started on the next one and come to believe in it. There is a lot of work to be done, work that transcends any personal problems. We have to learn to use personal problems for intellectual purposes. That is our sacrilege.[117] It's a sacrilege we must make else our very grief will become within us mere ritual and at the same time our only reality. In the decade and a half we've known one another, that is the most serious and important thing I've ever said to you.

Later:

My promotion came through.[118] I owe it to my dean, not my department, although they did not get in the way. It doesn't mean much to me, except the money. That's the trouble with such an egoist. He's already there, so when he really is there, it's all anticlimax. I'm glad too because it makes it more difficult "to get at me" and makes me feel freer to write with less anxiety than before. This letter is getting too damn psychiatric!

Well, here's some unambiguously good news: On the 29th of May, Ruth, Katie and I fly to Copenhagen for 16 months. Yes the Fulbright came through two days ago. I plan to fly on to Munich and pick up a motorcycle at the factory there. [We're] selling the VW and motorcycle here. Also [we're] selling the house here. It's built up now and so I'm more or less through with it, and so is Ruth. When we come back we'll build again a little closer to New York—a different kind of house since we'll be different people. One lives on the expectation that no matter what goes on now, next year, next week, next decade, everything will be different. Not necessarily better, but surely different.

[. . .] I have to work in Copenhagen; I have a rather heavy

117. "Sacrilege" is the word Mills wrote; it's possible that he intended to use "sacrifice" or "sacrament" instead.

118. Mills was promoted to full professor at Columbia in April 1956, effective July 1.

schedule of lectures, damn it. But maybe it will get me going again. I've not written since last fall, with all these decisions being delayed so. Just no energy and morose.

Do write me once more before we leave, telling me anything that I must not fail to do in Europe. If there is any business of yours over there you want done, let me know.

Yours as ever,
Mills

A portrait of Mills appeared on the cover of The Saturday Review *(April 28, 1956), which included a mixed review of* The Power Elite *with a biographical insert refer-ring to Mills as a sociologist on a motorcycle, a Renaissance man, and a successor to Thorstein Veblen.*

To Hans Gerth, from Pomona, New York, undated (probably May 28, 1956)

Dear Gerth:

It was so good of you to write at once in reply to my notes. It is now Monday nite and we leave in the morning. Linguanti is driving us to Idlewild at 10 in the morning.[119] Everything is packed in Harvey's basement, or freighted to Copenhagen or piled up for plane luggage (exactly 88 lbs of that). I've paid my bills or most of them, sold the house, gave the new owner my dog. So a little epoch which began five years ago with $500 in cash, a crowbar and a typewriter, has come to an end.

Before I leave I want quickly to tell you why I am so disap-pointed by the kind of reviews the *Power Elite* is getting. Put very simply, it is this: NOBODY REALLY TAKES IT SERIOUSLY. I didn't expect many to do so, but nobody does so in public. And the reasons they don't take it seriously are so trivial. Lynd because of semantic silliness, or whatever. I have now before me, just rec'd, a review in the *Re-porter,* 31 May '56 issue. The guy summarized *White Collar* and then

119. Charlie Linguanti was a neighbor and friend who worked in the construction busi-ness and who, in 1959, helped Mills build his second house in Rockland County.

Elite in terms of some of my little portraits and gossip I put in for sauce and IGNORES THE WHOLE THESIS. Then he concludes: but isn't it all merely a caricature? That's all—nothing else. In the very same issue of the *Reporter* there is an article entitled "The Complicated Process of Reaching a Stalemate" which is my major theme on the Congress, etc. They trivialize my stuff horribly, then they don't argue; they just say it's no good. You're right about Lynd of course: I couldn't "answer Him." There is nothing he says that I can debate. There's no discussion. Of course one says to hell with them all, but my God, I worked pretty hard on all this and then it goes into this vacuum. I can only hope that somehow enough people get it into their hands to read it. [. . .] (It does seem to sell: five thousand the first four weeks after publication. 25,000 will be printed in June by the Book Find Club.) So maybe I can say to hell with them but it's just that one would like for twenty minutes or so every three or four years to feel that one were not in this intellectual vacuum. Enough of all that tho.

You ask why Copenhagen? Well, they asked for me; nobody else did. Second, I like the idea of going to this little country. This first summer, I think I told you, I'll tour out of there by motorcycle; then in fall and winter I'll lecture on social psychology at the University. Then the second summer Katie and Ruth and I will spend one month in Austria, one in Spain (the two cheapest places), one in France, one in England. Thanks for the names you sent me. Certainly I'll look them up. Henning Friis (apparently the son of your friend) was very important in getting me over there: he is the social science advisor to the government from the university.

Got to sleep now. Will write after we're settled.
W.

C. Wright Mills's maternal grandparents: Braxton Bragg Wright, a cattle rancher whose family had been in America for several generations, and his wife, Elizabeth Gallagher Wright (Biggy), the daughter of immigrants from Leitrim County, Ireland. Circa 1900. (Photo by Bolton and Mitchell, Laredo, Texas.)

Mills's parents, Charles Grover Mills and Frances Ursula Wright, married in April 1912 when C. G. was twenty-two years old and Frances was eighteen. C. G. worked at a soda fountain before starting his career in the insurance business. Frances was a homemaker. (Mills family photo.)

Mills at age eighteen (with the crooked cap, third from the left in the middle row) with fellow cadets at the Texas Agricultural and Mechanical College, 1934–35, before he transferred to the University of Texas at Austin. (Detail: Texas A & M class photo.)

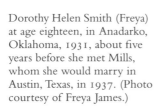

Dorothy Helen Smith (Freya) at age eighteen, in Anadarko, Oklahoma, 1931, about five years before she met Mills, whom she would marry in Austin, Texas, in 1937. (Photo courtesy of Freya James.)

C. G. and Frances Mills
in San Antonio, Texas, on
June 1, 1940, when Mills was
studying at the University of
Wisconsin at Madison. (Mills
family photo.)

Hans Gerth, a German sociologist at the University of Wisconsin who had studied philosophy and social science at the University of Frankfurt. Gerth became Mills's collaborator on *From Max Weber: Essays in Sociology* (1946) and *Character and Social Structure* (1953). (Photo by C. Wright Mills.)

Freya and Mills in Madison, Wisconsin, in March 1941, when they remarried. (Photo courtesy Freya James.)

Mills and Pam in Greenbelt, Maryland, in 1944, when Mills was an associate professor of sociology at the University of Maryland. (Mills family photo.)

Mills at age twenty-eight in a photo he submitted with his application for a Guggenheim Foundation grant in late 1944. (Photo by Brooke Studio, Maryland.)

Ruth Harper at age twenty-four, in a photo she gave Mills several months before their marriage in July 1947. They met when Mills used some of his Guggenheim funding to hire her to do research for *White Collar*. (Photo by Blackstone Studios, New York, New York.)

A gathering at the Millses' apartment in New York City in the late 1940s. From left to right: Dwight Macdonald, Leo Lowenthal, and Mills. (Photo by Ruth Mills.)

Richard Hofstadter at the Millses' apartment in the late 1940s. (Photo by C. Wright Mills.)

Mills and Pam in the summer of 1949 at Lake Temagami, Ontario, Canada. (Photo by Ruth Mills.)

Mills at thirty-three or thirty-four years of age, as shown on the jacket of *White Collar*. (Photo by Ruth Mills.)

Ruth in the old farmhouse in Pomona, New York, that she and Mills were in the process of rebuilding in 1951. (Photo by C. Wright Mills.)

In 1952 Mills tried his hand at growing vegetables, including lettuce and corn. (Photo by Ruth Mills.)

Mills, at the head of the table, teaching a seminar at Columbia College, where he taught from 1947 to 1962. (Only male students attended during that period.)

Harvey and Bette Beller Swados in the 1950s, on the porch of their home in Valley Cottage, Rockland County, New York, where Mills was a frequent visitor. Mills sought editorial advice on nearly all his books from Swados, who was a novelist, short-story writer, and essayist. (Swados family photo.)

William Miller, a writer and historian, in the summer of 1958. Like Swados, Miller was a friend whose editorial help Mills repeatedly acknowledged. (Photo by C. Wright Mills.)

Mills and Katie in Copenhagen, Denmark, where Mills was a visiting professor at the University of Copenhagen. (Photo by Ruth Mills.)

Dan Wakefield in New York City in 1958. Mills took this photo for the jacket of Wakefield's first book, *Island in the City: The World of Spanish Harlem* (1959).

Yaroslava Surmach with her
oil painting of Mills entitled
The Survivor (circa 1958).
(Photo by C. Wright Mills.)

Mills with Yaroslava's wool-and-canvas wall hanging *The Fey Tiger* (1958). In a letter written in 1958, Mills said he wanted to write a play or novel entitled "Unmailed Letters to a Fey Tiger." (Photo by Yaroslava Mills.)

Ralph Miliband, at home in Hampstead, London, 1958 or 1959. In a letter to Miliband, Mills wrote, "I refuse to have any more of those pictures of you made up; I am a semi-professional photographer, not a snap shooter; when next we meet I'll take a roll (36 shots). [. . .] In the meantime you ought not to joke about your graven image." (Photo by C. Wright Mills.)

Mills on the construction site of his home in New York, spring 1959. From left to right: Charlie Linguanti, a construction contractor who was Mills's friend and former neighbor, William (Chappy) Diederich, the architect who carried out the Millses' basic design for the house, and Mills. (Photo by Yaroslava Mills.)

Yaroslava and Mills on their wedding day in June 1959. (Photo courtesy of Yaroslava Mills.)

C. Wright Mills at home, circa fall 1959. (Photo
by Yaroslava Mills.)

Mills commuted to Columbia College on his motorcycle, which he assembled himself in the BMW factory in Germany. (Photo by Yaroslava Mills.)

Mills in his study at home, circa 1959. (Photo by Yaroslava Mills.)

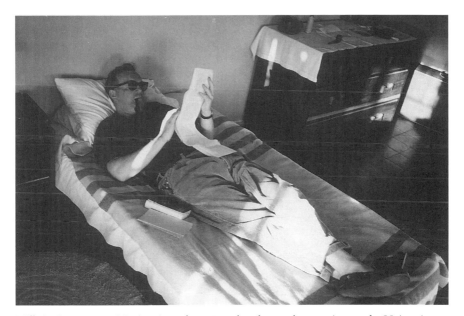

Mills in Cuernavaca, Mexico, in early 1960, when he taught a seminar at the University of Mexico. (Photo by Yaroslava Mills.)

Mills and Katie in Warsaw, Poland, summer of 1961. (Photo by Yaroslava Mills.)

Yaroslava, Niki, Katie, and Mills at Niki's first birthday in June 1961 at a chalet in the Swiss Alps called La Violette. Here Mills worked on an update to *Listen, Yankee* (1960), as well as the manuscript for *The Marxists* (1962). (Photo courtesy of Yaroslava Mills.)

Yaroslava and Wright Mills (in front) with Ralph and Marion Miliband in London, fall 1961. (Time-release photo set up by Yaroslava Mills.)

Mills's children, Kate, Pam, and Nik, in New York, the week of Mills's funeral, late March 1962. (Photo by Yaroslava Mills.)

V

AN AMERICAN ABORIGINAL GOES ABROAD

From New York to Europe and Mexico, 1956–1960

So let them all wait, and pay their two pounds each to follow the wordy little trail of a North American aboriginal.

> C. Wright Mills, letter to Ralph Miliband, dated April 13, 1957

To write is to reason; [. . .] to fight against chaos and murk.

> C. Wright Mills, "What It Means to Be an Intellectual"

Mills wrote the next letters in his temporary homes—in Copenhagen, Denmark; Innsbruck, Austria; New York City; and Cuernavaca, Mexico—and from his new home in Rockland County, New York.

Although we're not sure exactly when Mills began writing his letters to Tovarich, he dated the first letter 1956–57, during his first extended stay in Europe. He probably wrote most of these autobiographical letters to Tovarich during 1957, 1959, and 1960.

While in Europe in 1956–57, Mills completed much of the work on the manuscript for The Sociological Imagination. *In the spring of 1957, he presented early versions of that book at a seminar in Copenhagen.*

Not long after his return to New York City at the end of 1957, Mills embarked on his first mass-market paperback "pamphlet," The Causes of World War Three, *which grew out of articles and lectures on the topic of the Cold War and the urgency of political efforts to foster peace. During the time covered by the next section of letters, Mills also began work on his two other mass-market publications:* The Marxists, *which included Mills's critique of Marxism and selections from classic Marxist writings, and* Listen, Yankee: The Revolution in Cuba. *His writing for periodicals included "A Pagan Sermon to Christian Clergy," in* The Nation *(March 8, 1958); "The Cultural Apparatus," in the* Listener *(March 26, 1959); and "The Intellectuals' Last Chance," in* Esquire *(October 1959). And in 1959 he completed the work of selecting, editing, and introducing a reader of classic works of sociology entitled* Images of Man: The Classic Tradition in Sociological Thinking.

The prospect of living and working abroad was stimulating to Mills for many reasons; he loved to travel and appreciated a continent in which relatively short physical distances brought the traveler in touch with a great variety of cultures, not to mention delicious foods and high-quality liquor. Mills mentioned the possibility of writing a book about his experiences in Europe, and at one point he even wrote a rough draft for an article about motorcycle touring there. Here are two excerpts from what must be what he had in mind in July 1956 when he wrote to Lewis A. Coser and Irving Howe and referred to a European log.

Munich, June 6, 1956

I.

In Europe, it has been said, an American discovers America. But to do that he must first discover himself. It may be an old self long buried, or a new self in the making, but if he is trying to be honest, the first question he must ask is not What Are You but What Am I? Or rather to ask those questions together is the psychological meaning of travel.

In a small Munich hotel one June morning in 1956, after an evening spent in the apartment of a young German technician, I woke up with an unexplained feeling of guilt. I didn't reason about it; it was merely there to feel, but I was glad that I could feel it, for it is through such unexplained tremors in ourselves that we may often discover something about the world and about our own selves as well. If we resist such feelings—as the whole push and shove of how we live tries to get us to do—we will understand neither.

This guilt had to do with money and with work. He—the German technician—worked and had no money or very little. I did not work, not really, but I had money. It was as simple as that, but it ran very deep, this feeling, and I cannot resist exploring it. In fact, it seems necessary that I attempt to explain how this situation, along with the guilt, came about, and what it may mean in the world of nations in which we live.

II.

My favorite restaurant in Europe or America is the third-class one in the Bahnof in Munich. My favorite dish is two glasses (½ liter) of dunkel beer with some "Goulash mit Beilage" and five German rolls (for DM5 or $1.25). You're a little unsteady after that but very full indeed. And you also get a friendly pat on the back by the old woman waitress. You've gotten a bit more too: the faces of some people. My god, they are the human range. There is the bent old farmer with his fat daughter in the city to visit his old crony. The three of them sit there at the scrubbed table as clean as their scrubbed faces, with the daughter trying to keep her old man sober and yet still glowing with geniality.

∾

To Lewis A. Coser and Irving Howe (*Dissent* magazine), from Copenhagen, Denmark, dated July 7, 1956

Dear Lou and Irv:

We are nicely settled; the address until next May is on the envelope. I've just returned from a week's tour of Norway, and am preparing to migrate! Later I'll write you about what goes on, but it is a little hard because I've started to write a sort of European log and it is not yet properly focused and I don't want to see it too clearly as writing until I've seen at least a bit of the south . . . which we'll do later this month and in August.

I write now to query you about the following: I've now seen reviews of PE [*Power Elite*] by Rovere (*Progressive*), Lynd (*Nation*), Rodell (*Sat Review*), *Time, Newsweek,* Berle (*NY Times*), S. Chase (*Herald Trib*), Lee Miller (*Reporter*). At first I did not want to "reply" but now I feel the urge to do so. I'd like to make it a little essay "on reading reviews" and use the occasion to throw light on our wonderful intellectual community and their standards of criticism. It would be as impersonal as I can make it: I do not write in anger. The book sells well, and apart from the reaction of friends, that's all I care about after it is published. Do you think the idea sound? Would you like such a piece? Let me have your ideas on it. If you do like it, or even if you don't, I'd be so grateful if you'd send me clipping of [the] review, if any, when it comes, if it does, from *Partisan Review*. My clipping service might not cover that medium, and it is not available here. The same for *Commentary*. Any one of the reviews I've seen isn't worth replying to, but taken altogether, they might make a little pattern that's interesting enough in itself to stand as a piece.

Ordinarily, I've made it a rule never to reply to reviews, certainly not in "letters to the editor." But these people are really being so arbitrary and silly it might be well for once to crush them verbally. Perhaps I've been wrong and ought to fight back explicitly. If only for the youngsters coming up who are not so firm in their opinion when it is unorthodox, as are we old timers! My God, I'm forty next month already. Translations, by the way, are getting started on PE; an Italian firm is going ahead with it, and [it's] being considered by German, Japanese, Danish.[1] I've the feeling the damn thing will get around despite the reviews. Well, we'll see in a year from now. After all, if all these liberal types had acclaimed it, I'd know that I had failed.

Let me know what is going on the world. I've not seen a newspaper since I left!

Yours as ever,
Wright

Mills's response to reviews, entitled "Comment on Criticism," was published in the winter 1957 issue of Dissent. *The piece was reprinted a decade later, along with essays by Ralph Miliband and G. William Domhoff and reviews of* The Power Elite *by Robert Lynd, Richard Rovere, Dennis Wrong, Talcott Parsons, A. A. Berle Jr., Paul M. Sweezy, Daniel Bell, and others in* C. Wright Mills and The Power Elite, *compiled by G. William Domhoff and Hoyt B. Ballard (Boston: Beacon Press, 1968).*

To Harvey and Bette Swados and William and Virginia Miller, from Copenhagen, Denmark, undated (summer 1956)

Dear Swadoses and Millers:

Well, it's been a great summer and it isn't over yet. One more trip to Munich, to see the Six Day Trial at Garmish in mid Sept. Start teaching 25th Sept. It's the first summer since I can remember when I haven't written anything or at any rate not much. I have just completed a 20 page "answer" to all the reviews of *Power Elite,* which *Dissent* will print in winter. Am letting it sit awhile. I've thought a lot about the idea of doing it, and I think I should, if only for the young men coming up! It's kind of a nice thing, but if any of you think the idea horrible, let me know and I'll send the current draft to you for criticism. OK? I really mean that.

I went to England alone, ferrying across the Ejoserg to Newcastle.

1. *The Power Elite* was eventually translated into fifteen languages.

Ran thru the lakes and down thru Wales, then over to London. Only place in Europe I just don't like at all. Especially London: horrible place from every angle. Blighty has had it.

I've also just done a brief review for NY *Times* of William White's new book, *The Organization Man.*[2] I cut him down to size with some real mean cracks—what a schlemiel. And what [a] thief. But no matter. Let the dogs bark, the caravan passes by anyway.

I've begun to think about my thing on Europe as I ride along: what do you think of the title, *First Impressions?* It is going to be a very strange kind of book, I'm afraid, and maybe I can't get away with it but I've just got to try and see if I can do that sort of thing. You see I am trying—if I may express it so grandiosely—I am trying to make some kind of form out of all that part of my life that has no chance to get into the kind of book I've been writing. Motorcycles and why Swedish women look like they do and why you know as soon as you spend one afternoon in London that Blighty has had it and why I've quit collecting bags and now collect pots and why a krenit bowl on a teak table gets you the way it does and why loden cloth outranks all British woolens and how a woman, any woman, looks best at her prayers but after that in [a] loden cloth cape (you ought to see Ruth in it; of course I've got one too but it don't look the same). Why a Norwegian pack (by Bergan) is one hell of a lot better than Austrian packs. And above all, I guess, why not be truthful . . . above all, how it is, exactly how it is if possible, that an American in Europe, if he got the energy and throws himself altogether into it, how this American discovers what the hell he's all about, or anyway part of it, only in Europe, in Europe where so many things began and where so many things are now ending.

I'm not writing this way for show or even for show-off purposes but to make this point. It isn't merely romantic; it is also a necessity for me just now to get on top of all that bubble, to make it into something more than an enthusiastic letter to some friends.[3] Of course that takes an enormous discipline, I know that, but in doing it I really feel that for the very first time I'll be facing the problems of a writer. I think I have to take that seriously now. Don't you, or is all this merely

2. *The Organization Man* (New York: Simon and Schuster, 1956).

3. Mills corresponded with *Esquire* about writing an article on his experiences while motorcycle touring in Europe, but as far as we know he did not complete the piece.

bullshit? The question is worth your answering as a friend, because it's no temporary mood and I have no cognac left. It's been my mood all summer: Buddha on a motorcycle. My God, what a peninsula. A private race course and a thousand faces I'll never forget. And way up in the Norwegian hills a village with only two big stores: a flower shop and a bookstore.

M.
Mills

ॐ

To Frances and Charles Grover Mills, from Copenhagen, Denmark, dated September 5, 1956

Dear Mother and Dad:

I

You ask whether Katie walks?[4] I really wouldn't say she walks. But she does waddle across the face of the earth, her toes out, her belly out, her back straight up, both arms rigid. If she looks down, the whole apparatus totters and is likely to fall.

She doesn't talk; she does better than that. She squeals. Deliberately and gleefully and often she squeals. I think it is realization of the absurdity of the world. She will look at someone on a streetcar, peer into their face and squeal inquiringly. They all laugh. The Danes, I think, know all about the absurdity of the world and they all laugh.

II

We buy pots and tables, prints and filing cases—all of which are cheap here. Yesterday I bought a Picasso for $5.00: a woman, a man, a child—in rather bright pink and gray, but every line of it somehow indicates how foolish such a grouping really is! I've a worktable for $35.00, with oak legs and teak top: that combination is what we'll stick to. We've a saddle leather armchair. It's quite neat and altogether simple, but the leather on it is $\frac{1}{8}$ inch thick. And all sorts of little

---

4. She was then thirteen months old.

handmade vases and pots—mainly from Sweden—at about a dollar each, which are a joy to look at.

We think seriously now of buying land in Rockland County and building a weekend place—the same foundation size as the final house, 24' x 40', but using the second floor as the roof for several years, and keeping an apartment in NYC. No reason why that wouldn't work until school age. Might even pay for itself in summer rentals.

III

We are very much undecided as to whether we'll remain in Copenhagen next summer or move for 3 months to Austria. I'm afraid the trouble of moving—storing furniture here or freighting it ahead, etc.—will be too much. We're also undecided as to whether we'll get a car or not over here for the summer. Everything is now up in the air.

What are your plans as regards Europe? When do you think you'll come and for how long will you stay? You really must plan it now—especially if you decide to come by boat: reservations ought to be made right now.[5]

I teach from Sept. 25th until Dec. 20th, then begin again Feb. 5th until late May.

Let us know your plans,
Mills

∾

To Harvey Swados, from Copenhagen, Denmark, dated Sunday, September 23, 1956

Dear Harvey:

I. I am so very glad about your job at Iowa. Ten years ago I told you—teach; it's the only half-free way of life in the US because despite everything, it allows you freedom and a physical chance as it were, to write as you like. Do let us know how it goes—and do attend a regional convention or two and meet the silly people: join the racket, boy.

---

5. As it turned out, Mills's parents did not visit him in Europe.

The expansion of higher education during the next two years will give you a chance to make it despite no graduate degree.[6] Or hell, pick up a Ph.D.

II. Just back from Munich, my European hometown, and Garmish-Partenkirchen for the Sechstagefahrt (six-day trial). Marvelous stuff in the Bavarian hills, getting up at 5:30 and going out to a good mud hole or hill shining with mist and knobbled with crankcase busting rocks, to watch the Italians, Russians, Bulgarians, Swedes, Germans, Englishmen take the Gelande Machinen motocross. A real test of men and machines.

Stopped at BMW factory and took old faithful apart again with the Renn-dienst [repair service]. Coming back, made 1,300 km in one day's run, from 6 A.M. to 9 P.M. On the north German plain at dusk the little bugs splattered all over my face and Barbour suit and goggles. Simply filthy with grime and dizzy with speed and the split-second decision at 160 km an hour.

III. Oh well, tomorrow it begins, the teaching again. It's the same everywhere, the same pretense: to talk hundreds of hours and to do it on the assumption that you know that much. To maintain your self-image while doing that, and at the same time admit puzzlement to yourself in order to think you can write a bit. I've no taste for it this year. Want to take a woods machine down through Yugoslavia; next summer I will.

In January Ruth and I go to Munich and the factory takes my BMW, selling it for me at the proper season in March. In January we pick up the Isetta[7] (new US export model) and go to Paris for 10 days.

In June we go to Munich with Katie, pick up my Gelande machine (R26—a lighter model BMW for rough country) and then we tour—Ruth & Katie in the Isetta, me on the motorcycle. I explore ahead and get cheap pensions in Austria, Italy, France. Staying a week to 3 weeks at good spots and touring out of there. Hub-touring the British call it.

Goodbye; got to build lectures.

C. W.

---

6. Swados did teach at Sarah Lawrence College for many years, as well as at the University of Massachusetts at Amherst.

7. A subcompact car that could carry only two passengers.

∾

To Bette and Harvey Swados, from Copenhagen, Denmark, dated
October 10, 1956

Dear Bette and Harvey:

Re your account of highways and slop buckets. Yes, it breaks your
damned heart to think what America could do—or even more,
what Americans—including oneself of course—might be. Of
course, you're right—it's the surplus that makes for the kindness,
etc.—but still it's there. The worst thing about Denmark is the petty
bourgeois tone. I never really knew the meaning of that before. But
my own greatest disappointment was in Italy. You see, from Norway
down through Austria, in all of Germany and Sweden, there are no
road signs (billboards). One day going along in Sweden, I suddenly
realized this was half the charm of the scene. So we came out of
those Austrian Alps into Italy and the first thing we see is the Dolo-
mite peaks. Even with the Alps fresh in the eye, the Dolomites are
impressive. Then you let your eye climb slowly down into the valley,
and you suddenly are brought up with a real jerk. Road signs! My
God. Maybe it's a small thing but it brought back the true horror
of the American desecration of lovely American nature. It really
ruined north Italy for us, that and those unpardonably silly little
frontier guards and soldiers with carbines hung all over them. What
childish idiocy.

Anyway, it should be a ten year prison term in any nation to put
up outdoor advertisements in any shape. When you think of the shit-
heel types who think up that stuff and are allowed to educate the
senses of children for shock, and ruin all possibilities of really *experiencing a roadway*—one of the best things in the whole world of
experience. Fuck them all. But nobody cares, you know. We're just
stray cranks.

So glad to hear of completion of factory stuff—both the stories
and the experiences.[8] Yes, of course I like *The False Coins* better than

---

8. Swados's book *On the Line* (originally published by the Atlantic Monthly Press in
1957) is a collection of fictional portraits inspired by Swados's experiences while working
on an auto assembly line. Dell Publishing brought it out in paperback with an introduction
by Daniel Aaron in 1978, and the University of Illinois reprinted it in 1990 with an introduction by Nelson Lichtenstein.

The Bar of Gold. Much, much better. But you've still not got it. To hell with the quotation. Just make it *False Coin.*[9]

You'll think us mad, but we're sitting over here designing a house. Won't bother you with details now except that it's a radical idea that we think is just the nuts. We're building a little 18" model of it to exact scale next week, fitting in furniture and all. That's really the only way to design stuff. We'll (Linguanti and I) use standard windows and all but fit them into shapes they've never known before.

So that's what we do—this week. We can't get out on the road again until Christmas—from 20th Dec. until 5 Feb., we're free. I think we told you, Ruth and I then go to Munich to pick up BMW Isetta, on to Paris for a week. [. . .]

In the meantime all these goddamned lectures!

Mills

The following letter was written soon after the historic uprising against the Soviet-style regime in Hungary. On October 23 Hungarian soldiers supported a large demonstration of workers and students in Budapest; a prominent statue of Stalin was torn down. Rebels supporting Hungarian socialism and democracy won a temporary end to the one-party system.

To Harvey and Bette Swados, from Copenhagen, Denmark, dated November 3, 1956

Dear Harvey and Bette:

(1) Your good letter of 30 October just arrived, catching me in the proper costume and mood for writing out the tough anti-all-*nations* speech I'm giving later this month to the passive, calm, judicious, smug, civilized and dull student assembly. (Why in God's name am I not in Hungary? Always on the edges when the center doesn't hold.)

---

9. *False Coin,* a novel by Harvey Swados (Boston: Little, Brown, and Company, 1959). One of the book's epigraphs is the following quotation from *Reminiscences of Tolstoy* by Maxim Gorky: "Of science he said: 'Science is a bar of gold made by a charlatan alchemist. You want to simplify it, to make it accessible to all: you find that you have coined a lot of false coins. When the people realize the real value of these coins, they won't thank you.'"

The mood is induced by rereading Huizinga's *The Waning of the Middle Ages*. It's been 15 years since I read it; all the time he must have been a model for me but I'd forgot. Magnificent. By all means read it or reread it. Notice the lead chapter especially. That's the way to do it, boy. O, yes, the costume: I've got on big, thick, tan corduroy bloomy knickerbockers from Munich, medium weight climbing shoes from Innsbruck, green wool hose from Oslo, navy blue zipper turtleneck sailor's sweater from the Hamburg docks! I look magnificent, sitting here at my little slab of Danish teak, with the Swedish pots on it and the Italian flask.

(2) Not a bad lead paragraph?

(3) Your report on the stereotyping of your *On the Line* as "Thirties" is just the nuts. You must know that I've fought that with every book I've done. (See Stuart Chase's *NY Tribune* review of *The Power Elite*.) What happens, of course, is that publishers believe they live by being up-to-date. That means only being up with the gossip of their own circles, as is the way with all fads. The most killing comment on writing that is itself OK, is "old hat"—merely because all the commentator has is a sequence of new hats borrowed from that little gossip circle he identifies as "our times." It worried me with *New Men*—perhaps rightly so, for guys like us were too young for the Thirties and, in my case, in the wrong part of the country. So maybe we've had to get some of the Thirties a little later. But it doesn't worry me anymore. I'm sure it doesn't worry you either—especially with *On the Line,* which was derived from so close up.

(4) It's good to know you've run into some decent people in Iowa. Above all, a duck hunter. A wonderful sport, goes with lots of whiskey and lots of equipment (best source near you: Gokey & Co., Minn.). (Why do I keep playing up to this absurd stereotype of me you've got? Hope you know how merely playful it is.) Yes, I saw [Paul] Sweezy's review as well as [Herbert] Aptheker's in *Mainstream*. Of course they're doctrinaire, but also no less so than all the liberal stuff and much more generous as well. Of course one knows why, but nonetheless, I enjoyed both reviews. When I get back I'm going to write a solid, tight little critique of "Marxism today"—about 80 pages. You see, I've set my stuff always against various forms of liberalism because those are dominant. But it could just as well—in fact easier for me—be set against Marxism. What these jokers—all of them—don't realize is that way down deep and systematically I'm

a goddamned anarchist. I'm really quite serious and over the next few years I'm going to work out the position in a positive and clean-cut way. In the meantime, let's not forget that there's more [that's] still useful in even the Sweezy kind of Marxism than in all the routineers of J. S. Mill put together.

(5) Our travel plans for midterm and summer have been changed—because Ruthie went downtown yesterday and bought herself a VW Bus (8 passengers). It's without the rear seats and we're going to fix up the back end and make bunks. We figure, or rather Ruth does, that it'll be easier to travel with Katie this way than dragging her in and out of pensions for 3 months. As you know, the camping grounds of Europe are marvelous so I don't see why it won't work. We'll tick along and spend a week here, two days there, etc. Eat dinner out, to sample the country, but picnic the other meals. If it works even half time, we'll easily save the difference in cost between a regular VW and the Bus (which costs, with papers and all about $1,700). Besides, when back in NY we'll need a truck if we build again.

(6) Now you really must write us and tell us, on the basis of your own experience here and talk with others, where you'd definitely go in a rig like this. In particular, do you know a good camping ground on the French coast [. . .] where we could stay a couple of weeks? You see, we don't have to worry about a place to sleep, because with the curtains Ruth makes and all, we can park overnight damn near anywhere.

(7) Of course I'm keeping my BMW (18,000 km on it now!—new tires next week) and I'll do side trips from the moving hub of the Bus. Got to do that because many places I can go only by motorcycle due to roads and cost of auto shipping being so high. Also I can't take Katie all day for three months because although I love Katie I dislike children and don't really approve of anything about them at all. Of course I've thought of going to East Europe; damn near left for Budapest the other day when (coming back from Hamburg) I saw a big convoy of Swedish army trucks with Red Crosses on them going down. God I could have joined it; the Swedes are friendly fellows. All the time they sing instead of talk. A pleasure to be with, altho all Danes hate all Swedes. In fact, Danes hate damn near everybody except all Englishmen and some Americans. A peculiar people, the Danes. It is all due, you know, to the glottal stop in their language.

Kill a lot of ducks. And write. You all and Wakefield and *Business Week* are the only sources of information we've got on USA.

Yours as ever,
M.
Mills
cc: to Dan W. [Wakefield]

ᐁ

To Dan Wakefield, from Copenhagen, Denmark, dated November 5, 1956

Dear Dan:

Hope you don't mind the enclosed carbon which gives you the news.

1. Yes, of course I think the Puerto Rican book is good and I think *you* could do it too.[10] [. . .]

2. Yes, I got the egg head clips, for which many thanks. Didn't you get my reply about not ever worrying about somebody else beating you to a book? (mailed c/o Stone to Washington). No, there's no bourbon here—at less than $10 a bottle. Got to smuggle in brandy from Germany. That's $3.75 and almost as good as the French, which costs $9 here! Beer—and weak stuff at that, although tasty with food—is the only cheap drink available, along with Spanish wines which are medium in price.

3. Thanks so much for reference to Auchincloss. Will try to get from here. About your Israeli book: you see, it's like I always said. In serious writing, journalism by itself is being replaced by sociology. In books you've got to get a *little* way back and spread out in time— a span of 2 or 3 years at least. The PR [Puerto Rican] deal will allow that if you can get 5 or 6 good solid themes and carefully generalize topics and events. The knife-edge present isn't for books. You've got to get the trends so set up that readers for several years can fit a lot of knife-edge presents into them. You've got to let the readers do that. The faith that they will is what is meant by "serious" writing of a social and political sort. Isn't that so? And that's why we've got to

---

10. See Dan Wakefield, *Island in the City: The World of Spanish Harlem* (Boston: Houghton Mifflin, 1959).

work out a new form of writing—using some fictional techniques and some reportage tricks and some sociological stuff. Of course all that's nothing without some really big view into which all the little stuff fits and makes sense. That's why this kind of writing I'm talking about can't be done in essays. It takes a book or maybe a sequence of them to create such a world. I guess the rule is that no matter what you are writing about, you're also writing about the whole god-damned world. Huizinga does that—it's easier for the past, less risky. Agee touched it on those sharecroppers. Dos Passos did in *USA*.

The trouble is when you try it, you can fall so very, very hard. It's easier not to try. Go detailed scholarly. Go clean journalist. Disguise it—I use the word advisedly and hope Swados hears—in fiction. No fiction nowadays that I know is "about the world" in this sense. For example, what compares on east Europe with Milosz?[11] Etc.

4. I'm not doing so much intellectually these days. Reading a lot, a mixed lot, but all the European history and geography I can get hold of. But I'm not prodding myself. I figure you've got to fuel up from time to time; turning 40, as I've just done, is a good time for that. And Copenhagen, in its easy, relaxed way, is a good place for it. Of course you can work anywhere, but somehow I don't think of Copie as helping you get down to it. It's not that it's exciting; on the contrary it's very quiet. And not knowing the language—and having no impulse to study it[12]—makes it all the quieter of course.

Take care,
Mills
cc: to Swados

To Mr. Lee E. Grove, editor, Trade Department, Oxford University Press, from Copenhagen, Denmark, dated December 1, 1956

11. Czeslaw Milosz, the Polish writer who authored *The Captive Mind* (essays, 1953) and *The Seizure of Power* (a novel, 1955), as well as many books of poetry known for the interweaving of personal experience with historical events. His literary works earned him the Nobel Prize for literature in 1980.

12. Mills did not have a facility for learning to speak foreign languages. As a result of formal study, he had some reading knowledge of German and French, according to his transcript from the University of Wisconsin.

Dear Lee:

It's so kind of you to ask about addresses for the royalty check of January 1. I think it best if you mail it directly to my American bank with a covering letter indicating that it is to be put in my *checking* account (*not* the savings).

[. . .]

Everything goes well. We've got a VW microbus—fixed up with neat Danish bunks in the back. Leaving December 15 for 50 days in Yugoslavia, Greece, Italy with wife and child. Then back here for spring term, Feb. 4th to June 1. [. . .]

Denmark's a bit dull, but a good base, and [there's] the Ballet every week. All this writing is just a hobby. I'm really a ballet man— with delicate ponderosity I am dancing.

Take care,
Wright
C. *Wright Mills*

Mills took an imaginative leap of another sort in 1956 when he wrote letters to To-varich,[13] *his imaginary friend in the Soviet Union. Eisenhower was reelected presi-dent in 1956, and much of that year's news had been dominated by tensions between the United States and the Soviet Union.*

To Tovarich, from Sarajevo, Yugoslavia, winter 1956–57

TOVARICH, WHY I WRITE TO YOU

I. Our Own Separate Peace

Tovarich, I am continually told that you are my enemy. Well, I am trying to get into contact with the enemy. I am trying to contact you—my opposite number in the Soviet Union. I want to bring you into a conversation so we can make our own separate peace. In doing so I am of course assuming that there are—or that there will be

13. See the preface for more background on the unfinished manuscript "Contacting the Enemy: Tovarich."

soon—zones of real freedom in the Soviet Union. If they do not come soon I will have to wait; but when they come, I want these letters to be waiting for you. Tovarich, it's up to you and your society to identify the scope and quality of your freedom.

These letters should be some kind of combination answer to Lenin's question: "What is to be done?" and Tolstoy's: "How should we live?" Much of what I at least mean by politics and culture is indicated by these two questions, especially when you take them together. I want to write specifically and personally about culture and politics as they affect the ways you and I may be able to live for the rest of our lives—or even for how long.

I'll admit too that I'm using you for ulterior purposes. I feel the need to say a few things about myself and so to straighten out some points that are personal and hazy. Saying them to you is just the thing because—forgive me, but isn't it true?—I don't think you'll readily understand a lot of the things I feel the need to say. I'll have to try very hard to make them plain.

Self scrutiny, of course, is an old American habit. I think it may be an old Russian habit too. Anyway, isn't it the case that neither of us today has the kind of ready-made identity many Europeans seem to have? The worse for them, Tovarich! (In this respect, probably we are more like the Mexicans and Brazilians I happen to know, or more generally, in several curious ways, probably more like the more self-conscious men of any of the underdeveloped worlds.)

Tovarich, please don't take these letters to be some curious kind of American propaganda. Let me say it once and without qualification: I am no spokesman, official or unofficial, for any nation or for any nationalism. In fact, I am against all prevailing nationalism—whether it is found in the United States or the Soviet Union.

The idea of writing to you came to me in the fall when I was here in Europe. Traveling in foreign countries, of course, turns you in upon yourself; you get away from your routines; and you begin to sort yourself out. At the same time, it makes you feel the need to tell the strangers around you what you are all about. You want to look at self and world together before the strangers. Do you understand? But I have to add: all that's when you're young; after a while, when you're a stranger in your own country, you do this both at home and abroad.

Without quite realizing it, all during the first months I spent in Europe I felt the need to write a "Letter to Europeans." I wanted to raise some questions in such a way as to make clear what Europe looks like to one man from America and also to make clear how he has come to see America. I wanted to hand that letter to the old man in the black cloak in one of those Italian hill towns on the road from Bari to Salerno, who on a cold morning in January, arrogantly refused to let the children come into the cafe until I had finished coffee; to the Norwegian businessman who on a road out of Stryn in the Nordfjord helped me fix a flat on a drop-rim motorcycle wheel; to that girl on the scooter who translated for us; and to the unskilled worker in Zagreb [Yugoslavia] who had been one of the Nazis' prisoners of war. One night outside a dismal railway station he said: "Socialism? Maybe that's OK, but around here they don't pay us enough to build it up." I wanted to hand that letter to the young girl—a hotel clerk in South Shields, England—who thought of America as One Big Hollywood where everyone knew everyone else and duly celebrated their all-around triumph; to the worker by the Autobahn near Kassel, Germany, who was a blur to me as I swept by at speed on my main beat between Copenhagen and Munich; to the fishmonger on the southeast coast of Sweden who asked me to phone up his cousin in Minnesota; to the kindly policeman in Paris who so carefully told me to be very cautious in Germany or those barbarians would in some way surely damage me; and to the old woman in the third-class restaurant in the Hauptbahnhof [central station]. She asked me—in that merry confidential way that comes only with Munich beer, "What's it really, really like in America?" And above all, I suppose, I felt the need to write to the young scholars in Copenhagen—and elsewhere—who didn't seem willing to think about anything until they had found out "what the Americans thought about it."

Western Europe—I'm sure you'll agree if you've seen it—is a truly wonderful variety of landscapes and peoples in a human-sized area. On the other hand, I also have come to believe that Europe is all too often a cluster of petty squabbles, of local and nationalist varieties, which dreadfully hamper many Europeans. To maintain their nationalist and regional peculiarities often seems to take up all their moral energies; it's hard for them to think in larger terms about the world. Many Europeans seem unable to gain the self-confidence, the presumption, the wide-ranging curiosity that are so necessary for creative thinking about public affairs and private lives.

At any rate, I never wrote any such Letter to Europeans; I tried to, but each time I began to write to them, I found myself writing to you, Tovarich—at first alongside Europeans and then only to you, although the Europeans were listening. That I feel so strongly the need to write to you is all the more curious because I have not yet been to Russia. Of course I have read something of most of the really big men of your country. For example, once for an entire summer I was up in the Canadian woods on Lake Temagami, reading nothing much but a set of books by Dostoyevsky; it nearly killed me. I think I can say that Dostoyevsky is as much mine as he is yours. Maybe more, if you've never happened to earn him. I do not know what kind of a Russian you are, but I know that Dostoyevsky is no more yours than Melville is mine.

By the way, probably I am going to be writing most of these letters while traveling, while I'm away from my books and files, and from those American friends whose criticisms I value. I do this deliberately in an effort to isolate myself, but also because I can't help it. Every time I travel outside America, I just start writing to you. I suppose it is because I want to find out what I think when I'm without my usual scholarly equipment for thinking.

II. The Difficulties and Importance of Writing

Tovarich, there are so many things I want to tell you and ask you. Some of these feelings are now quite vague; I want to make them less so. Is it any use to cling to vague feelings? Many of them, as you will soon see, are ordinarily thought "utopian" in the sense of futile. I think it is of use. If you feel something, you ought not deny it merely because it is only a feeling; it is also yours.

Feelings, however vague, are the infant beginnings of a political traffic when you start to interchange them. Or they may be. Or I hope they may still be. At any rate, this is the only political traffic you and I might have; maybe we cannot have even that. I am trying to find out. My idea is to ignore the general and to be a bad soldier. The only truly good soldier today is a bad soldier. Or must I be an idiot if my generals are? Maybe you find that necessary, but I don't—not yet at least.

Above all, with all the mythmakers about and many intellectuals among them too—some openly and many more in a kind of unconscious secret way—above all we have got to hang onto the realities of the past and to the realities of the present. I often suppose we always have had standards by which we have recognized what is real and what is illusory, but we never became aware of this until various people in the 20th century—above all, I hope you'll now agree, in your country, Tovarich—started fooling around with the standards themselves and not only with the facts, and yes, sometimes even smashing them. Rulers have rewritten history every other day, including the documents upon which history must be based. So, first of all, we have to hang onto reality itself; and to do so, we must become very much aware of our standards of reality.

Of course, we know the world today largely through communications we receive about it; we are always depending upon what others tell us, and more often than not we don't know who those others are or what their biases and interests might be. As for current events and trends, well, obviously it is becoming more and more difficult to cling to some sense of reality. It is a full-time job and one could easily use a large staff.

I have to tell you that last year I read three or four dozen books by American and British specialists on Russia—and I am going to continue reading such books—but I still didn't get a real answer to the ultimate question I want answered: What kind of a man are you? It occurs to me that you might also be reading books by Russian specialists about America. I shudder to think of them. They are probably as bad as those I've read on Russia.

Let us forget specialists and experts for a while; they have their uses, no doubt, but how relevant are they to *our* doubts and purposes? I don't know. Let us talk to one another "naively"—each telling as honestly as he can, who he might be and how he thinks he got that way; how he lives and what he believes and how he thinks he has come to believe it. And, of course, let us talk politics. I'll begin our conversation, Tovarich, and I hope you will help me turn it into a little drama. Toward that end I'm going to put a great many questions to you but only after I have answered them myself as fully and frankly as I am able.

To Lewis A. Coser from Copenhagen, Denmark, dated January 27, 1957

Dear Lew:

To answer your smaller questions first:

(1) Yes, I enjoy "Europe" enormously; but "Europe" means—can only mean—continuous traveling about and I am a natural-born traveler. As for specific locales inside Europe, I'm arranging my policies, as if I were all to myself a little nation, and I can't go making off-hand comments, even to good friends.

(2) Did I write you that we (Katie, Ruth and I) just got back from a month's trip—in the VW microbus—through Yugoslavia, across to Bari, Italy, and up through the peninsula via Naples and all that? Thousands of images remain. The Yugs are like cowboy movie ruffians wandering up and down their bad-land gulches. You can give Italy to Clare Luce, the Pope and Mary McCarthy,[14] for all I care.

(3) I'll be glad to see the "answer to critics" [of *The Power Elite*] when my copy arrives. I worked on it very hard, and—good or bad—I had to do it. Also glad you're getting out so many publications. Just now I'm not writing anything but I hope to get something done in the spring. I've been asked to give a lecture at the London School of Economics in March, and to go to Salzburg Seminar for two weeks in late May.

As for your major questions:

(1) By all means were I you I'd go to California[15]—on a secure leave of absence from Brandeis. It's perfectly silly to think of it as "far away"—far away from exactly what? As I've told you, it's the one place I'd leave the East for.

(2) As for Columbia College, the situation is more fluid than ever. My impression—from a distance this year—is that the policy will be to hire only young men as assistant professors and gradually raise them. Although a big fight may develop when Casey retires in several years. I just don't know how it will look. You know as well as I how sticky and slow and arbitrary things north of 116th St.

14. McCarthy's book *Venice Observed* had been published in 1956 (New York: Harcourt Brace).
15. The University of California at Berkeley.

seem always to be. At any rate, I won't know how it is going to be until several months after I return in September.

Take care,
Charlie

To William Miller, from Copenhagen, Denmark, dated February 5, 1957

Dear Bill:

1. I'm so glad you think the *Dissent* essay came off all right.[16] I was worried that your (justified) reaction to the earlier version would make it impossible for you to see the effect of your criticism on the final! I worked on it very hard and learned something about writing. I just couldn't let all these silly people say all that and then sulk in my corner. So it was necessary for therapy.

I do not mind telling you (altho I hope you will not mention it to anyone) that "criticisms" of *The Power Elite* hit me very hard indeed. I suppose the whole thing coincided with a lot of self-criticism I've been giving myself and for a while I damn near lost my nerve for writing. It is hard to carry a load as big as Luther's when damn near all the world tells you it's only a bag of peanuts. But enough. I'm over it now. Or almost. Anyway do write Coser you think the piece came off OK; he was naturally worried about your reaction.

2. About your plans to move in '58 to the western NJ area (which I don't know): I want to tell you that when we return to the US we're going to live on Morningside Heights (if Herpers can give us a University apt.), but I do intend to build a sort of weekend place somewhere within an hour or two of NYC. I want a quite small but quite elegant little place and do not need much land. Although there is plenty of time, I hope you will consider our looking around together for a neighborhood. The great point with me—and I suppose with you—is regardless of initial costs, to keep the monthly costs (taxes etc.) very low. Rockland [County] is by no means out of the question. Anyway, keep the possibilities of a joint search in mind as I'm quite serious about it.

3. I've not worked much at anything for some months. Now

16. Mills's response to critics of *The Power Elite*.

suddenly I began to "work at" the little book on "The Sociological Studies," a quite technical book of 150 pages or so.[17] I think it's time I wrote something *about* my own kind of sociology and against the current dominant "schools." I'm not in any hurry about it, but it comes along. I look forward to telling you about it when I return and, I hope, showing you some manuscript—to establish the right tone—and I think you'll enjoy it as much as I.

My other project is this book on The Fourth Epoch,[18] which I find I cannot give up but which I cannot focus. It is, after all, a philosophy of history as well as an explicit taking up and carrying forward of the old sociological tradition of Germany, which was at all times concerned with "the nature of our epoch."

The Intellectuals book I have dropped—temporarily at least— it just doesn't interest me now,[19] although it may become a long essay on "the role of reason in human affairs."[20] At least that's going to be its major theme—rather than being empirically set by the intellectuals. So that one is up in the air for now.

4. Much lecturing ahead: London on March 2, Frankfurt May 2. Salzburg asked me (finally!) for two weeks in late May and June— I wrote them a very superior little note saying it depended on who else was going to be there! To hell with that propaganda outfit. I hope to be asked to Oslo for a lecture and of course I've things set up for around Denmark. As you know, it is very hard to lecture on America in Europe. On every side there are all these stereotypes and try as you may anything you try to say falls into them. I think it is largely having to talk in English, which many Europeans understand much less than they suppose.

5. It isn't true that I am "disgusted" with Europe. I don't know

17. This became *The Sociological Imagination* (1959).

18. Mills did not obtain a publishing contract for this book, and he never completed the manuscript, but see his essay entitled "Culture and Politics: The Fourth Epoch," *Listener* 61, no. 1563 (March 12, 1959).

19. Mills's original contract (dated August 22, 1955) with Oxford University Press for a book on American intellectuals was renegotiated in December 1959; the project was then tentatively entitled *The Cultural Apparatus*. When Mills died in 1962 this work was still unfinished. He did publish an essay entitled "The Cultural Apparatus," *Listener* 61, no. 1565 (26 March 1959).

20. See his lecture entitled "On Reason and Freedom," read to the London School of Economics and Politics and broadcast by the British Broadcasting Corporation, Third Programme (February 1959).

how Hofstadter got that impression. "Europe" can only mean continuous travel, which at all times I love. Only specific parts of Europe can be the object of "disgust." Italy, for example, I do not at all like: give it to the Pope, Clare Booth Luce and Mary McCarthy. Yugoslavia is obviously an altogether fascinating place, and I intend to motorcycle through it again this summer on the way to Athens and Istanbul. (RH [Ruth Harper] will be camped in the VW bus in Austria.) Germany and Austria—as I've told you—are continual sources of pleasure and agreeable puzzlement to me. Of course I don't know much about any of them: these are simply impressions of a fast-moving traveler.

6. All the news of your writing plans—especially the economic history—is quite exciting. I think it's fine you've got the possibilities of such solid endeavors. What else keeps a man on the level? It's only when we don't have such programs that we lose touch with our own center; only when we do that we feel we might be making our own groove (unmix that one if you can).

Keep in touch,
Take care.
As ever,
Mills

[P.S.] A heart doctor told Wright yesterday that he had Angina Pectoris.
R. [*Ruth*]

Mills's case of angina pectoris was mild, and after a few days of bed rest at home, he continued his usual practice of ignoring his high blood pressure.[21]

To William Miller, from Copenhagen, Denmark, dated March 14, 1957

Dear Bill:

One of the amusing features of any exchange of letters is the fact that the answer to one's last letter, if prolonged, reveals so clearly the ups and downs of one's mood. I've just read yours of 11 March, which

21. Notes from Ruth Mills, undated (1984).

was a response, and one I very much appreciate, to a letter of mine some weeks ago. Since then, I must tell you, the world in which I live has again turned upside down: I am about to complete one book, and I am halfway through a second one.

I mean this literally. Never have I written so continuously (yesterday I wrote for 15 hours) and, I do believe, turned out such [a] well-written first draft. These are short books. The first runs to some 220 typed pages, and is a statement of the promise, the tasks, the nature of the social sciences (Ch. 1). It is at once a "defense" (without appearing to be such) of the kind of stuff I've done, and a really detailed criticism of "the methodological inhibition" (Ch. 2) a la Lazarsfeld, and of "the fetishism of the concept" (Ch. 3) a la Parsons. It also contains a complete, and I believe first-rate, rewrite of a never-published essay "On Intellectual Craftsmanship" (Ch. 4)[22] and a brand new version of "The Political Promise" (Ch. 5), which is set within a neat little view of the role of reason in human affairs, in history. Within it I have also finally been able to state the central role of historical studies in the social sciences as a whole. I am very excited about it all, and can't conceive of any sudden shift in my evaluation of it!

I must ask that you *not* mention any of this to our friends, especially those of Morningside Heights. I want it to be just one big, dandy surprise: as from a prophet who comes in from a desert.

The other book I won't write about now, for I am too much inside it still. But it too is to be a short book, and on "The Intellectuals." Here again I think I've found a way to avoid both the moan and the simple denunciation.

You'll be glad to know, I think, that I've shifted my view of London, after being there a week to give a lecture at the London School of Economics. The truth is, I suppose, that I was very glad indeed to find out how well my stuff has been received in those circles, and how much their own work there is in line with it.

In April, Ruth and I go, without Katy, to Paris for 10 days. In late May, with two books out of the way, all three of us close up here, go to Salzburg for two weeks. Then I go alone, by motorcycle, across Czechoslovakia to Poland—if it can be arranged. Then, come back

---

22. Published as an appendix in *The Sociological Imagination*.

to Austria, and drift south and west through Spain. On 3 September we fly from Lisbon.

Yours as ever,
Mills

> [PS] Keep in touch and take care.

❧

To William and Virginia Miller, from Copenhagen, Denmark, dated March 22, 1957

Dear Bill and Bucky:

1: I do want very much to read the new history book, but airmail is prohibitive in cost and sea mail for books is about 6 weeks. (In six weeks, or very shortly thereafter, all the contents of this apartment that won't fit into the VW bus are going into storage.) So your judgment not to mail the book is, alas, correct. Without having seen it, I share your hunch and hope that it will make some real money, and I want to read it not only for history but for writing.

2: Your brief characterization of crime fiction is enticing: "The gambit is the relation of respectable institutions and disrespectable society, not all of it underlying." But you did not complete the cross-tabulation, which is, of course—now don't be upset, study this:

	SOCIETY	
INSTITUTIONS	Respectable	Not Respectable
Respectable	1	2
Not Respectable	3	4

The world as commonly—and erroneously—assumed is confined to 1; the world of most criminal fiction is 3, especially in its relation to 1.

The world of nihilism is 4—there is some crime fiction about this world too, but the fascinating world is 2. That is the world of moral men in immoral society, of the private eye as really the only tough moral center in a universe in which even that center will not hold: see Yeats, but also the best of Dashiel Hammet. No one has done more than fumble with it. What you could do, after you've

[got] the technique of crime fiction really slick and have thought out the world of two, is to give it form and meaning. I do not at all see why crime fiction of such a sort could not become a wonderful instrument with which to think about the world of the USA. Society as a network of rackets does not mean that all individuals are necessarily racketeers. Who is, and who isn't? Why it's the best way to raise the problem of guilt, of original sin, of Kafka's K, and it's why I, for example, sometimes work so hard.

3: That sort of thing (about which by the way I'm quite serious) in my new book I will call "the sociological imagination." In the above, of course, we play with only two "dimensions." We need only a few more, the chief of course being I: the individual. Upon a few of these the crime fictioneer must focus. II: institutions are the more immediate milieu in which these individuals are seen to act. III: society, in most crime fiction, quite vague, but in some, like that wonderful *Tucker's People* by Ira Wolfert, it becomes more of a framework.

The job of crime fiction, apart from making money by entertaining—also important jobs—is the same as the job of all social science worth the name: to make society become as alive and as understandable and as dramatic as the best fiction makes the individual seem. And the job may be done, first, by realizing how individuals must be understood in milieu and how individuals and milieu and society [interrelate]. Second, by a technique of presentation which presents the relations between the three up close and as intrinsic. Such a technique, I believe, is not now available.

But go one more step.

	SOCIETY			
	Good		Bad	
	Institution		Institution	
INDIVIDUALS	Good	Bad	Good	Bad
Good	1	2	3	4
Bad	5	6	7	8

1: the goody goody world

2: the big world is OK but here's a good kid in a bad neighborhood which he transcends

3:

4: the goody good hero: he alone is good in a world altogether bad

5: the goody goody crime story: only the criminal is bad

6: is probably a "null" cell, although I'm not sure

7:

8: nihilism is total

But 3 and 7—there ought to be novels about them,[23] especially 6 and 7. I'll keep a carbon of this to make transaction of ideas easier in case it stimulates you.

I wasn't loafing and merely getting drunk in bed when I spent all that time, months of it, reading paperbacks and Balzac. All the above is obviously part of a theory of fiction which, I just now realize, I've been working on for years.

Yours,
M.
CWM

[P.S.] I have lost 24 lbs in last 5 weeks, and feel better for it.

∽

To Lewis A. Coser, from Copenhagen, Denmark, dated April 4, 1957

Dear Lew:

Thanks for the letter with all the news, good and bad. Yes, I've lost 28 pounds in the last six weeks or so, and will probably be about right— at 185—by midsummer. Everything seems all right, and I work 15 hours a day at my desk.

Congratulations on reviews, promotion and California[24] which is wonderful. Try to stay. Get me there.

My own news is mainly this: I have just about completed a little book of 10 chapters on "The Social Sciences."[25] Here are the chapters:

---

23. Mills left 3 and 7 blank on his list.

24. Coser was a visiting professor at the University of California at Berkeley, 1957–58.

25. The final version of *The Sociological Imagination* has ten chapters, but only a few chapter titles match the ones in the working outline presented here. The phrases within quotes for numbers 4–7 were Mills's handwritten annotations to his typed outline.

You remember, I told you I was going "to return" to the profession. Well, here it is. Next fall I'll of course ask you to look it over. In the meantime, believe me, it is really quite an exciting little thing, about 90,000 words, I'd guess, in print.

I have also begun a 5-chapter little book called "Politics & Culture," which consists of 5 lectures I am to give in late May-early June at Salzburg: it is now in the form of a "Letter to Europeans"—about USA and Europe, and also about many of our little stuffed-shirt friends and colleagues. That's also the subject of another little book half done on "Intellectuals"—again some 5 or 6 chapters.

At the London School of Economics a few weeks ago, I was much enheartened by the way my kind of stuff is taken up there. My God, it is nice to know it makes a difference somewhere. Well, it damned well does there. Naturally, I'm nuts about the place and everyone I met there.

April 15 Ruth and I go to Paris for 10 days, then back; then I fly to Frankfurt for a lecture, then back. About 15 May we close up here and go to Salzburg seminar for 2 weeks. Then I go alone, by motorcycle, to Poland, if I can clear everything, for 3 weeks; come back and join Ruth and Katie in Austria—to loaf slowly toward Lisbon, from where we fly to NYC on 3 September.

It's becoming quite a year. A pivotal year, I think, for me. Sud-

denly, I feel I might become a writer after all. Suddenly there's the
need to make a big sum-up. Suddenly there's a lot of ideas to do it
with. They write themselves. Words aim. Words flow. Ready? You
can see what it's all about, can't you? Fire.

Yours ever,
Mills

*When Robert Lekachman, who was then an economist on the faculty of Barnard
College, reviewed William H. Whyte's* Organization Man *for* Commentary *in
1957, he included a critical discussion of Mills's* New Men of Power *(1948). Responding with the following letter, Mills took the opportunity to set the record straight
concerning his position in relation to Marxism.*

To the editor of *Commentary,* from Copenhagen, Denmark, spring
1957[26]

To the Editor of Commentary:
Little unpleasantries I always try to ignore. . . . But now comes Mr.
Lekachman whose errors of statement in [his] "Organization Men"
bring him into view. He asserts that I have analyzed *Fortune;* that I
have found it to have "a unity of outlook"; that I think it a "consistent and sure-footed organ" of one ideology; that it goes international in order to put down leftward tendencies at home; and he
implies that I believe its editors omniscient conspirators.

   1) I have not read *Fortune* with any regularity for many years—
so superior on economic fact and business opinion do I find *Business
Week.* I have never "analyzed" *Fortune* magazine, nor the strange
varieties of ideology which at any time may have possessed its as-
sorted editors, whoever they may be. I have never assumed that it
is "a consistent, sure-footed organ" of any ideology. In fact, I should
have characterized it as inconsistent and stumbling. With one exception: although seemingly informed by often radical backgrounds,
whoever produced it appeared consistently to lack omniscience.

---

26. Published in *Commentary* 23, no. 6 (June 1957): 580–81.

2) My major use of *Fortune* in the book cited by your writer is based upon explicit quotation. [. . .]

3) In [*New Men of Power*] I also cite *Fortune* as an example of "sophisticated conservatism." This little phrase, so often kidnapped and abused, cannot be properly understood without its twin brother, "practical conservatism." Among other terms of definition, "sophisticated conservatives" seem more aware of the political conditions of money-making and corporation-maintenance, which of course include the international. This I contrasted with an older vision of a more utopian capitalism: the "practical conservative," in his outlook and drive, is immediately economic and less aware of larger political realities.

When I wrote this book, a decade ago, *Fortune* had been for some time a vehicle of the sophisticated rather than the practical variety of business ideology. I do not see how this can reasonably be denied. Mr. Lekachman fails to mention the contrast without which either term loses much of its meaning. He does not name the date of my publication, which, however convenient for him, is surely a disservice to your readers. What he has done, in brief, is mistake my explicit use of one ten-year-old article in *Fortune* for an "analysis" of the magazine's "ideology"—which he presumably takes to be permanent. Having made this up, he then uses it in spurious and invidious contrast with what I suppose must be called his own analysis of "*Fortune*'s view of the world," which turns out to be conveniently and ambiguously expressed by one writer, Mr. William H. Whyte, Jr. I cannot imagine what Mr. Lekachman takes all this to be in aid of.

4) As for the statement, alleged to be mine, that "*Fortune*'s stand in favor of international aid [is] motivated by a desire to stave off" leftward tendencies in America: I do not know the motives of the editors of *Fortune* as of ten years ago: and I think them of small importance. But as for the general idea, so crudely stated by Mr. Lekachman: certainly I have believed, and do now believe, that since World War II any sound business ideology is likely to be relevant to international expenses as well as to domestic politics. The motive indicated above, however, is nowadays not likely to be important, if only because in the United States there are no leftward tendencies to "stave off."

I do not believe that U.S. foreign policy can be adequately explained, as in the current formula, by (a) the numerous and evil actions of the Soviet Union, plus (b) the numerous proclamations of ideals by America. (a) + (b) = the wearisome voice of America. There are perhaps other elements those who would understand the world must consider. The relations of domestic and international problems are most intricate; I do not know of an altogether adequate statement of them. But I have been and I am trying to confront such problems.

5) Rather than doing so himself, Mr. Lekachman adopts a tone and with it covers up the issues—a fashion often displayed in your magazine. It is a way to stop thinking by the use of such easy phrases as Mr. Lekachman's "Marxist and Hobsonite echoes." I am less interested in echoes, Marxist or otherwise, than in explicit statement. It is less important that your writer imputes to me opinions I do not hold than that he obscures serious problems by such fashionable superficiality. Let me say explicitly: I happen never to have been what is called "a Marxist," but I believe Karl Marx one of the most astute students of society modern civilization has produced; his work is now essential equipment of any adequately trained social scientist as well as of any properly educated person. Those who say they hear Marxian echoes in my work are saying that I have trained myself well. That they do not intend this testifies to their own lack of proper education.

6) I need comment only briefly upon Mr. Lekachman's rather ungenerous review of *The Organization Man*—my own view of which was printed in the *New York Times* of December 9, 1956. As readers of *White Collar* (1951) and *The Power Elite* (1956) will have immediately seen, both Mr. Lekachman and Mr. Whyte agree with much of what I have written about bureaucracy and the higher business life. About the general run of the facts and about many of the meanings, that is. The political judgments involved on all sides are divergent. For I have, of course, in my several discussions of these matters, taken a consistently critical and altogether independent view.

C. Wright Mills

Mills was planning a research trip to Poland to conduct interviews for his book-in-progress on intellectuals when he wrote the following letter to Ralph Miliband, whom Mills had met at a London School of Economics seminar that year. Miliband was a

Marxist scholar who became a personal friend and political ally; they remained friends for the rest of Mills's life. Miliband introduced Mills to members of the New Left in Britain and Europe in the late 1950s.

To Ralph Miliband, from Copenhagen, Denmark, dated April 9, 1957

Dear Miliband:

I do not see why you don't come to Poland with me! As I think I told you, I lecture at Salzburg 26 May to 8 June. On the 9th or 10th of June, I plan to leave my wife and child camped out in Austria and by motorcycle (BMW-R-50: international six days trial model) cross Czechoslovakia to Poland. Total time of trip—well, ten days or 2 weeks. I don't know. Why don't you come along?

It should not cost much—your trip to Austria & back from London. We'd stay at the cheapest places and picnic for most of our food.

If it's possible and you're interested, let us know and we'll arrange details.

I've finished 9 of the 10 chapters of the little book on the social sciences. Last night in drunken celebration, it seemed a wondrous book. This morning, very sober, by god it may well be.

From the 17th to about the 25th of April, my wife and I will be in Paris. [Edgar] Morin, I think, is loaning us his apt,[27] but I can't altogether work out his French. Is the fellow a foreigner of some sort? Anyway, if not there, we'll perhaps be at one of the hotels Norman [Birnbaum] gave me the names of.[28]

Sincerely,
Wright Mills

To Ralph Miliband, from Copenhagen, Denmark, dated April 13, 1957

27. Morin, the French sociologist and political commentator.
28. Birnbaum, a sociologist from New York City, was then teaching at the London School of Economics.

Dear Miliband:

1. I am not able to see why the LSE [London School of Economics] cannot this year close up shop earlier in order to suit our convenience. Perhaps it is due to some local peculiarity, some curious inability to reason properly and to act well. But no matter. That it is unreasonable is no reason for us to be. What is the very earliest date that you could be in Salzburg? As I think I've told you, I love Austria, much more than Texas, and if I tarried there I might well write another little book, in some Baroque way, on some mountainous topic.[29]

2. No, I have not been asked to come to London during the summer, and I do not know whether I could go there were I asked this summer. What would delight me no end is to come for a month next January, and, in 10 lectures of one hour each, give the social science manuscript, which just then will be about ready to go to press. About then also, I shall have in hand "The role of reason in human affairs" or "The Intellectuals" (an 8-chapter item). Oh, these days I'm a regular wholesaler of ideas, a department store of cultural wares. And so modestly priced too: for transport and living expenses while there, I'll go anywhere, and there present the unpublished word. But I suppose London next January is mere fantasy, all the more attractive, though, in that I can think of nothing that would better enable me to improve these books. But if they do not ask me, it only goes to show that they do not deserve me. So let them all wait, and pay their two pounds each to follow the wordy little trail of a North American aboriginal.

3. I think a letter to Paris, care of the author's agent, Miss Ellen Wright, 14, Rue Mr-le-Prince, Paris VIe, will reach me, as I want to try to see her. But send a carbon to Copenhagen to make sure. Returning from Paris, I turn right around and go by train to Frankfurt for 2 days, then back here for 2 weeks or so; then to Salzburg.

4. Listen, if you are serious about going, and can go about July 1, please now do this:

(a) figure out a rough plan of where we go via what: Salzburg

---

29. He spent several months in Austria later that year and worked on a manuscript: the letters to Tovarich.

to Salzburg. (Remember I am on a US passport but I suppose I can go across Czechoslovakia.) Maybe Mrs. Birnbaum will give you ideas of the best route. Road conditions don't matter; if a goat can walk it, the machine can scramble it. So choose freely some vast and intricate circular route. By the way, where is Poland anyway?

(b) Go to the Automobile Association (Fanum House, New Coventry Street, London, W.1 Whitehall 1200) and in my name (Membership Number 895851 OD/6) tell them your route and ask them to give you a "strip-map." They'll make it for free; but act right away because my membership expires soon.

(c) But from them or elsewhere [get] the best maps available of the terrain, in some language we can read or learn to read in a day or so. Try *not* to get a great sheet; small, cleverly foldable ones are much better on a motorcycle. I'll reimburse you the cost.

(d) Tell me what if any experience you've had with motorcycles. None is required, but perhaps then I'd best tell you something of this way of life. Also about luggage and about clothing. About luggage: forget it, put it in your pocket. We have more important things to carry: these are far wilder places than we have ever known, and what we do not know is whether we can drink what people there may mistake for wine, whiskey, even water, should we be reduced to that. About clothing I shall write later a little technical exposition for you, which I've been wanting anyway to get done. But in the meantime, please tell me your own expectations about it all. Also your weight, as we are both so gross I fear I must have the factory at Munich heavy up the rear shocks. They like to do that sort of thing anyway as the machine is one of their special little competitive creations. Merely to look upon it is to experience the essence of the only truly human mobility.

Do you like the way I have written this letter? You ought to. I have only been writing as you spoke one Friday night in Surrey. Both of us, I take it, are admiring strangers of the English. Perhaps, if all goes well, other things remaining equal, someday we shall show them how to do it.

Sincerely,
Wright Mills
C. Wright Mills

When Mills and Miliband visited Warsaw, Poland, in July 1957 (traveling by car instead of motorcycle), it was a time of great ferment against the repressive Soviet-style government. Socialist intellectuals were deeply involved in the political upheaval. Stalin had died in 1953, and Khrushchev had publicly attacked Stalinism at the Twentieth Party Congress in 1956. Following Khrushchev's speech, a strike by Polish workers against food shortages and other restrictions had helped pave the way for a degree of liberalization: some enhancement of civil liberties, a halt to the collectivization program, and the return of Wladyslaw Gomulka as First Secretary of the Communist Party in October 1956, after his release from prison.[30]

Mills's meetings with dissenting socialist intellectuals in Poland, including Leszek Kolakowski, Pawel Beylin, and Adam Schaff, made a strong impression on him.[31] A few months later, in a letter to Adam Schaff about the possibility of giving a lecture at the University of Warsaw, Mills wrote: "My visit to Poland—and Yugoslavia before that—although dreadfully brief, has been very stimulating to me. It has deepened my own socialism and hardened my attitude towards the triviality and formalism of much 'social science' in the US. It has also shown me something of the great difficulties now faced in eastern Europe and made me want to confront them. I shall never write seriously again without including in the inner forum to which one writes the kind of intellectual public representatives of which I met in Poland."[32]

To Tovarich, probably from Innsbruck, Austria, 1957

ON GUILT

Over in Munich, West Germany, I visited a friend of mine of whom I am very fond. It was he who introduced me to many features of German life that have, I think, been not only enjoyable but formative as well. What I did that morning in Munich was first to work four hours on a book I am doing, which went very well.

---

30. Later, in 1966, Gomulka was expelled from the Communist Party.

31. Kolakowski, a philosopher and fellow of All Souls, Oxford, wrote *Toward a Marxist Humanism: Essays on the Left Today, Main Currents of Marxism* (3 vols.) and many other works. Pawel Beylin, a Polish sociologist, philosopher, and dissident, inspired—along with Kolakowski and others—political and intellectual ferment. Adam Schaff, a Polish philosopher and theoretician, was a member of the Central Committee of the Polish Communist Party at the time and had served as an intermediary between the dissident Communist intellectuals and the government.

32. Letter to Adam Schaff, dated October 29, 1957.

Afterwards, walking the streets, I had a great realization: I do not want a single one of anything they've got to sell, I thought. But later in the hotel room, I knew it was a lie. I wanted my absolute choice of all of them. Am I talking to you about the fleshpots? Yes of course, but of something else too. What? My bourgeois soul, my philistine self, my unsolid identity of which I know so little.

Here were boxes of dark Brazil-type cigars made in Bremen, piled up carelessly in the back of a window in fifty boxes behind twenty much more expensive ones; they are magnificent after a good meal of hot soup and roasted meat and vegetables full of color and salad and cheese and fruit, and expresso. Six big [coffee bean] grinders, whirring away behind the great stretch of plate glass; and through the open door comes the odor of nine types of bean. You understand all this was only Munich; I've not been to the USA for well over a year. God knows I passed a meat market and looked at the windows. Landwurst from the Tyrol, the lovely pink salami from Denmark; twenty kinds from Italy. To see the leather was to smell it right through the plate glass. Think of the woolen pullovers for sport and cardigans as thin and rich as fine silk. Egyptian cottons for shirting and loden suitings and all the English and Scotch stuffs as well, ready for custom fitting and careful tailoring.

I went into a small Wurststand [sausage store] and immediately counted thirty-eight huge jars of fresh gherkins on the shelves in back of the counter. On the black market in Krakow how long could a family live on the sale of that, and in my own wallet were the solid Deutsch marks to buy all of them—five times all of them.

I came over the mountains from Munich to the Inn Valley by a network of back roads; in some stretches they were mere trails. The BMW motorcycle sings in all gears on all gradients; when it's in the woods it's like a mountain goat, a go-anywhere apparatus—not a tool, not a machine—a true apparatus.

I went to a hotel that was between second and third class, got a room and the key for it, and pushed the button for the automatic elevator. I thought of the elevator that didn't work half the time in the best hotel in Warsaw. This one came at once and in it stood an embarrassed cleaning woman. Evidently the lobby button had electrical priority and evidently she wasn't supposed to be using it anyway. The hall porter told her to walk up. I grabbed her shoulders as if they were salvation and with one arm around them we went up together.

But these little gestures, they're not good enough. In fact, they are not any good at all. I know that.

We've got to get into our bones the need to get into real contact with our colleagues in East Europe. Intellectually and morally and politically we've got to understand and act with reference to the underdeveloped countries as well as the overdeveloped countries of the world.

∾

To Ralph Miliband, from Innsbruck, Austria, postmarked August 1, 1957

Monday

Dear Ralph:

You really can't know how glad I was to get the second issue of Univ and Lef Rev [*Universities and Left Review*]: it made for two evenings of quite good reading, although this issue isn't up to the first. I'm managing to work a good deal on the letter to the Russians thing [Tovarich], but I do have times when I'm not quite up to that but don't want to read trashy private eye stuff, which is all I can get here and not much of that. I'm enclosing a check for 30 American dollars; if you have any trouble cashing it let me know, although I don't see why you should have trouble. If you'll keep a little rekogning [reckoning] (how do you spell it?) of the subscriptions and books . . .

Would you please send me the following:
1. DISPUTED BARRICADE. By Fitzroy Maclean. Cape.
2. THE NEW CLASS. By Milovan Djilas. (The US edition is by some little firm called Fred. Praeger, but surely there's an English edition.)
3. [Isaac] Deutscher's letters. *Russia After Stalin,* isn't it?; but this only if you judge it still worthwhile; better send it. I've not read— or if I have [I've] forgotten—any book of his.

If anything in magazine or book comes along which you think neat and suggestive of the bloc, go ahead and send it. I don't think I want just now very very scholarly stuff but more *good* reportage and speculation I suppose. Thanks a lot.

I'll let the London and Warsaw lectures ride a while, perhaps a month. As for Warsaw anyway I've not even been invited yet: no response to a carbon I sent Gottesman . . . the same as I sent to you.

O by the way if anything is recorded or published on the Rockefeller seminar on Marxism (Bottomore) [that] you mentioned, do send it.[33] I'm right in the middle of that. The sponsorship is amusing, my god.

Katie is doing very well; couldn't be doing better. [. . .] The only thing happening is my own writing, which is rather curious. Here I am writing rather impassioned stand-up-all-you-bastards-and-begin-to-fight stuff on world politics and intellectuals for two or three or even as many as six hours a day, and then collapsing exhausted. I shall remember these days. There ought to be some way to exploit them intellectually.

As Ever,

Mills

ᏇᎦ

To Leo Lowenthal, from Innsbruck, Austria, postmarked August 8, 1957

Dear Leo:

Thank you for your letter and the lovely made-up story about the cabbie. Which reminds me, if you see Eva Hoffberg around, do tell her that last month when I was in Warsaw I thought of her. She hates me now, probably, because once upon a time I was such a bastard, but no matter. I still love her most of the time, so tell her so, and then tell me what she says, really.

I went to Warsaw for 16 days to interview for my book on the intellectuals. They have asked me to fly back there in January and give them three lectures on Marxism and Social Science: imagine! In January also I am supposed to give "The University Lectures" at the London School of Economics. But alas, my year of looking around Europe is not ending so well.

---

33. The seminar was probably at Bellagio, Italy; Tom Bottomore was a sociologist at the London School of Economics.

[. . .]

Innsbruck is very gay now, in full holiday stride. I still manage
to write several hours each day—lectures to the crazy mixed-up kids
in Poland and to the benumbed English. The atmosphere is very
curious for me. It is like one of the German films of the early 1920's
in Innsbruck these days.

Mills

[P.S.] Leo-[34]

Later: Write me a huge, quick letter about the world. Nobody
ever writes me. Tell me the most important thing that has happened
in the USA since 1954, say, or what you really think of, say, Poland.
Tell me gossip. Or as somebody, Gide I think, said to somebody, Cocteau I believe: Astound me! But most of all, tell me gossip, thick and
rich like gravy. Sitting here in this silly, wonderful little town, with
a pillow in the window for the elbows, gazing at the medieval street,
I yearn for gossip. As you must realize, I've plenty of weinbrand.[35]

ᐁ

To Harvey Swados, from Innsbruck, Austria, dated September 9, 1957

Dear Harvey:

The last three evenings I've spent *On the Line*. I've enjoyed it thoroughly; but more than that, I think it has added a new dimension
to my rejection of Amerika. The wageworkers, the factories, as of
now, they are really a new world quite unexplored. Nobody examines
them with any compassion; they don't know them at all but merely
assume them; or more likely they think they know them as of the
images of the thirties, which they all want to forget. But you've
examined them and by doing so have opened up the thing. It's going
to be said, as you well know, that it's overdrawn; it's not real; for in
the unreal world in which books are selected and rejected, criticized
and celebrated, anything real is almost automatically thought unreal.

34. Mills wrote this short note by hand on the outside of the aerogram; the body of
the letter was typed.
    35. Brandy.

Still the thing is so professionally constructed and has such a neat swing about it, if you know what I mean; I think even in the unreal world of Culture, it's got a real chance. Besides, that world's unreal, and so not for keeps.

I've not read American publications for over a year now, except a very few now and then, but isn't it true that there's something of a swing away from the conservative silliness and incapacity for moral discernment that's paralyzed the postwar imagination? Aren't there signs I wouldn't have seen? I've the vague feeling that "we" may be coming into our own in the next five or ten years. And it makes me want to hurry and finish the next one.

[. . .]

Mills

&

To William Miller, from Innsbruck, Austria, dated September 24, 1957

Dear Bill:

I got your letter yesterday. Why are you petulant? [. . .]

As for myself I am getting down to a little work finally and of course I have been writing stuff all along, some of it quite usable in an odd way. As you know, I've a manuscript pretty well done . . . in Copenhagen . . . on The Social Sciences, which I think very hot: a short book of ten chapters, it requires several months with my own library and files and then will be ready.

I have about one half of a book, the size of *White Collar,* I suppose, which I now call *The Cultural Apparatus:* all about artists, scientists and intellectuals, in US, West Europe, and the Soviet bloc. Do you like that title? Anyway, the manuscript has some of the best stuff I've ever written, if that means anything, in it. Or so I think and that is what I am now working on.

[. . .]

The fall is beginning to break now in the Tyrol. My God it is a magnificent place. I climb a bit and ride up in the hills on my motor-cycle, on back roads and paths. At night I drink too much and eat too much, although I weigh only about 99 kgs. That's about 210 [pounds]:[36] down from Copenhagen 238.

[. . .]

Yours as ever,
M
Mills

∾

To Tovarich, from Innsbruck, Austria, fall 1957

ON WHO I MIGHT BE AND HOW I GOT THAT WAY

> Do I contradict myself?
> Very well then I contradict myself,
> (I am large, I contain multitudes.)
>
> from "Song of Myself"
> by Walt Whitman[37]

Tovarich, of course, you realize that these letters to you are also letters to myself. That can't be helped if only because we are so separated; we are so ignorant of each other. That's why I am going to become very personal indeed in this letter and tell you something about who I might be and how I think I got that way. Yesterday afternoon when I was thinking about how I'd write to you about this, I thought: how can I tell him who I am when I'm not yet sure myself what I wish to become? And as for the past, like almost everyone, I've got several different pasts that I find variously useful, and comforting; and all of them are equally convincing. Perhaps the best thing to do is resort first to the conventional dodges? Let us see.

I. Growing Up[38]

Several of your colleagues, Tovarich, last month asked me, "Where did you grow up?" I answered them politely by saying,

---

36. Actually 99 kgs is 217.8 pounds.

37. *Leaves of Grass: The 1892 Edition,* with an introduction by Justin Kaplan (New York: Bantam Books, 1983), 72.

38. See "Growing Up: Facts and Fancies," on p. 24 of this book.

"Texas, Maryland, Wisconsin, and New York." But that is not what
I wanted to reply. I wanted to say that I hope that I have not grown
up. The whole notion of growing up is pernicious, and I am against it.
To grow up means merely to lose the intellectual curiosity so many
children and so few adults seem to have; to lose the strong attachments
and rejections for other people so many adolescents and so few adults
seem to have. "To grow up" is a meaningless formula, unless specific
social content is given to it. The content usually given it in America
involves a normal, which is to say a childlike, marriage, and a forward-
looking, which is to say dull and tension-producing, job. It is to become some kind of brisk, energetic executive intellectually empty
although narrowly informed, and morally smug although quite dependable. To use such "adulthood" as a criteria for the good or bad in man
is to smuggle in lack of individuality as a value behind an apparently
objective chronological fact. W. H. Auden recently put it very well:
"To grow up does not mean to outgrow either childhood or adolescence but to make use of them in an adult way. . . . I can imagine a
person who had 'outgrown' both (childhood and adolescence), though
I have never met one; he would be a completely official being with
no personal identity" (*The Nation*, May 18, 1957).

You say you did not ask for all that; you ask, "Where did you
grow up—meaning come of age?" Don't be so impatient; give me
time to become properly intense. Until I was twenty-three or so I
lived in Texas, if that's all you want to know. The point is, it was less
any twists of childhood than the upheavals of adolescence that shaped
me down deep and for good.

Let me try to summarize it all. The son of a white collar man
who traveled all the time, I grew up under the projections of a Carol
Kennicott of a mother,[39] was accordingly a sissy boy until my first
year of college, and so was sent to a military academy "to make a man
of me." It didn't work; it did work; it was a mistake; it was the best: I
revolted. Because of certain teachers, the revolt took an intellectual
turn. Because of isolation, it made me a kind of spiritual Wobbly.[40]

39. Carol Kennicott is the central character of *Main Street* by Sinclair Lewis. She is a
bright and imaginative person who admires artistic and intellectual pursuits and feels stifled
in a provincial middle-class environment; she transfers her unfulfilled and idealistic aspirations to her children.
40. A Wobbly is a member of the Industrial Workers of the World (IWW). The union
of the IWW, established in Chicago in 1905, sought to organize skilled and unskilled workers

Because of the nature of the epoch, this spiritual condition became political. Because I used to be more or less bright, and because of a high metabolic rate, I've gotten away with it. Also, by chance, circumstance, and instinct, Irishly drunk on words, I've liked it—most of it, so far—immensely.

What are the liabilities of such a biography? That you're very restless, and you tend to make a fetish of energy—in order to exploit the restlessness intellectually you need great energy—and you do grow older. To exploit it morally, you're thrown back upon yourself; that does get tiresome, and you have the need to escape. The asset of such a biography is that you have a real chance to get on top of it, to transcend it and to be self-making. In brief, it's possible, most of the time, to act as a free man.

II. Stages of Autonomy

There is this curious fact I have never quite understood: a withdrawal as it were from chronological time. I was an adolescent during the thirties: at the midpoint of that decade, I was 19. I don't know how typical I am of that generation in one very important respect: I did not personally experience "the thirties." At that time, I just didn't get its mood. I've got that only later and indirectly. Only with the onset of World War II did I become radically aware of public affairs, or aware in any way. I was, I suppose, too young; I was in an outlying region—Texas. I was not really alert to any sort of politics, studying philosophy, especially logic, at the time. And, above all, it happened that during the thirties I was reading the literature of the twenties.

I sometimes think that during the thirties I was living in the twenties, and that during the early forties, I was living in the thirties. Maybe now I have caught up with "my own time"—although I'm

---

into one union dedicated to building a new society according to general socialist principles. Wobblies refused to endorse any socialist party, or any other type of political party; they preferred using direct action such as strikes, boycotts, and passive resistance. They were able to organize certain groups of unskilled workers who had been ignored by the established labor unions: lumber and textile workers, copper and coal miners, farmers, and dockworkers, including blacks and newly arrived immigrants. When Wobbly speakers were being arrested in a number of American cities in 1909, Wobblies organized a series of fights for free speech. They sent replacement speakers until Wobblies filled the jails; the authorities were forced to stop the arrests and allow Wobblies to give speeches in public. Bill Haywood, Mary "Mother" Jones, and Joe Hill were well-known Wobbly leaders and organizers.

not sure I know exactly what that means. Certainly it does not mean that I feel myself to be part of any compact and recognizable intellectual community; I never have. I've always felt myself to be a sort of outlander in the East, and particularly in New York City, where I've lived since the mid-forties. Being out of joint with most other people who were reading and writing has often seemed to me one reason I've been aware of and a little upset by the fact of intellectual fads and fashions, and all the silly little postures assumed.

Ever since I can remember, I have had a constitutional inability to sympathize with the upper dogs, and a temperamental distrust of all of them. At the same time I do not, as a matter of intellectual conviction, or of moral feeling, always admire the underdogs, much less those who speak for them. And as for the middle class, let us be honest: what American boy out of middle-class circles who has reached the level of self-consciousness we call intellectual has not spent half his life—and some of the best of it too—rooting out the inhibiting pretensions and the convenient prejudices that seeped into him before he was under his own control?

What this means, again, is that I have been intellectually, politically, morally alone. I have never known what others call "fraternity" with any group, however small, neither academic nor political. With a few individuals, yes, I have known it, but with groups however small, no. The Old Fighters of American radicalism have known that fraternal feeling. Communists in Europe and America have known it. The New York boys who were in the YPSL [Young People's Socialist League] knew it then and sometimes now they cry for it. It must be quite a thing; they all cry for it after they've had it. But I have never had it; I've never joined any groups much less identified fraternally with any. And the plain truth, so far as I know, is that I do not cry for it.

Now the point I want to make about this is that there have been four stages of my "independence."

1. At first, as an undergraduate student, it was just something that happened to me: of course, it had roots in a personal situation of home life, in a very sensitive mother who imparted to me, thank God, many "feminine" sensitivities in the middle of Texas, which insulated me, made me repelled by the rural and military crudities of Texas A & M. There was a genuinely moral choice for me at Texas A & M when I turned my back on The Company (maybe you'd call

it "The Collective"?) with which I lived and completely isolated myself. If one thing can be said to have made me into an intellectual, that was it.

2. Then for a time, it became a conscious set of gestures, until Professor Clarence E. Ayres told me that if I felt that way, good, but by all means to "keep my pants pressed," a bit of advice for which I am very grateful.

3. But then a third stage of the pose began. For after my pants were pressed, I became in due course—what else?—an academic man. As I skirted the edges of the world of learning, looking in now and then, I was fascinated and frightened by what I saw. In some ways it looked like a trap, but in some ways, like a wide-open space. I know now that I was afraid of getting "inside the whale." Not consciously, because of course I didn't yet have a clear view of the sort of man I was becoming. So for four or five years I must have been pretty damned hard to deal with academically. For all I had to lean on, against the trap aspects of the academic world, was that old—and I distort it when I use the words because I didn't have the words then—that old Wobbly feeling.

So in the early part of that third stage, it was all poured into a furor of work, quite technical work in philosophy and a branch of sociology called "the sociology of knowledge."[41] And then the war came. What did World War II mean to me? In threatening personal terms, it meant the rural idiocy and militarism of Texas A & M. In intellectual terms, it meant a greatly increased interest in politics. In one sentence: following it closely and thinking about it made a radical of me. Personally, however, I did not take a moral stand; I drifted. So it happened that I woke up early one morning to be rejected by the Army for the physical reason of "hypertension." That afternoon I almost came to believe in divine intervention.

4. Then I was invited to New York City and began to direct a research staff [at the Bureau of Applied Social Research]. This kind of adjustment is becoming a major academic pattern of success in the profession for which I was trained. The old-fashioned professor who

41. Mills included the following footnote at this point in the text: "For examples see, 'Language, Logic and Culture' and 'The Methodological Consequences of the Society of Knowledge'" [in *Power Politics and People: The Collected Essays of C. Wright Mills,* ed. I. L. Horo-witz (New York: Oxford University Press, 1963)].

quietly writes his books and teaches is passing from the academic hierarchy in social science as well as other fields, but that old role was one of the important roles I had in mind. In due course, when the opportunity came to move up in the manner of the new career, I promptly turned my back. It is inconceivable that I should not have. For this—and I knew it at the time—was another moral pivot of my biography. I turned my back on the opportunity offered me to become an administrator and an entrepreneur of large-scale research; and that clinched the main line of my direction, the direction of the independent craftsman.

You think it must be lonely in America? No doubt. But no need to cry about it. There is also freedom in it. Maybe only in it. I think that after you've been through loneliness and have become aware of it, you feel both audacious and free.

Over the last several years I have become quite aware of a certain mixture of personal and political and professional factors which have come together to determine such intellectual roles as I play, and even such intellectual and moral work as I have done and am doing. All these factors, to put it briefly, have constructed in me the ethos of the Wobbly. You've asked me, "What might you be?" Now I answer you: "I am a Wobbly." I mean this spiritually and politically. In saying this I refer less to political orientation than to political ethos, and I take Wobbly to mean one thing: the opposite of bureaucrat.

(I want to tell you this in order that you may understand my own values as fully as possible and hence be able to better control your understanding of my letters to you.) I am a Wobbly, personally, down deep, and for good. I am outside the whale, and I got that way through social isolation and self-help. But do you know what a Wobbly is? It's a kind of spiritual condition. Don't be afraid of the word, Tovarich. A Wobbly is not only a man who takes orders from himself. He's also a man who's often in the situation where there are no regulations to fall back upon that he hasn't made up himself. He doesn't like bosses—capitalistic or communistic—they are all the same to him. He wants to be, and he wants everyone else to be, his own boss at all times under all conditions and for any purposes they may want to follow up. This kind of spiritual condition, and only this, is Wobbly freedom.

☙

To Tovarich, from Innsbruck, Austria, fall 1957

ON INJUSTICE AND PERSONAL TROUBLE

> Every man who is faced with the possibility of a calamity in-
> evitably plants himself upon the bedrock of his individual charac-
> ter. For one man this may be an idea; for another, his faith; for a
> third it may be love of family. Some there are who have no such
> bedrock, who find themselves standing on quicksand. The whole
> outer life, with all its terrors, may avalanche upon them, burying
> them inexorably.
>
> Anna Seghers, *The Seventh Cross*[42]

I. Fate as Injustice

Tovarich, suppose you encounter something that seems to you
like fate as injustice. Say there is a man, better than you in every
way, who is impoverished while you are rich and mainly because he
happened to be born in a different country than you were. That's fate
as injustice. What to do? Well, there are four possibilities:

1. You can go blasé and call your feeling romantic, and forget
about it. This just doesn't seem possible for me.

2. You can go saintly. Give up all your worldly possessions and
aims; sacrifice yourself for others, anybody, in order to realize yourself. This does seem rather ineffective, and moreover probably selfish.
Anyway my guilt is not the sort to be relieved that way. Tolstoyism is
out for me.

3. You can rationalize unjust fate and see it as after all not unjust
fate, but in some higher and perhaps unknown sense, justice itself.
Then you can bow down to it. I've never gotten satisfaction or relief
from such sacrifice of the intellect. What to do, then?

4. You can go radical politically and personally; you can use your
mind and your sensibilities to try to *make* fate less unjust. Of course,
this is the choice I have made. Isn't it the moral root of socialism?
Isn't this a good definition of a "radical": one who refuses to accept

---

42. Mills provided this epigram and the following citation for it: "(Boston: Little, Brown,
and Company, 1942), 72."

injustice as fate and whose refusal takes active political and cultural forms? For the sociological meaning of fate has to do with the types of biography that arise from the very structure of a society. And politics and culture of a radical kind have to do with modifications of a society and so with the control of fate, as history and as biography.

Those to whom fate has been kind—as it has been to me, generally speaking—have the chance to treat their own characters radically, just as politically they would treat the structure of a society radically. Well, I am not just writing or whistling in the dark. I believe this, and I've gotten hold of some skills that make it quite possible to survive almost anything. These skills I can use and am using wherever I am, and for long periods I can use them just as well alone as with friends, no matter how pleasant being with friends might be. This brings me, Tovarich, to something about being in personal trouble.

II. Personal Trouble

Listen Tovarich, I know in these letters I've been cheating you; I've not told you all about my private life, my women and all of that. But I can't tell you about all that . . . after all, this is probably going to be—I hope it's going to be—a very public letter indeed. Anyway, it's just a tale of monstrous tragedies, Tovarich. (I'll tell you what, if you answer my public letters, maybe we'll write some private ones too. I'll release the stuff on women and children to you privately; or better still, when we meet—in Peking?—I'll tell you all about women and such. But we mustn't lie, Tovarich, no more than we can help.) What's important anyway is not the details of one's past—although one should become aware of them—but how one interprets them, what rules for the present and the future one draws from them. I can't resist telling you one such set of rules: what to do when you're in personal trouble.

When you're in trouble, it's as if you're sitting at a huge table with many little piles of notes on it, as if for the chapters of a book. Every day or so the major themes of the book mysteriously shift so that you've got to sort everything out in a different way. Too many decisions all at once, with too many elements you've got no control over; that's what being in trouble is. The decisions and the re-decisions, the tentativeness of anything you do, of all action, gradually wears you down. Questions no longer prod thought; thronging up on you, they clog reason itself.

The process wouldn't be so bad if you were getting somewhere—if it really was a book, for instance. For that's what writing a book is; no matter how complicated all the questions are, no matter how many times you have to decide again, still you come to have more and more control over more and more aspects of it. That's why to write is to get out of trouble, for the trick is to sort it all out in such a way as to be able to work on one part of it at a time, with the whole merely a vague and helpful outline.

To write is to get on top of it all. Writing, at least the thing about writing I'm talking about now, is another name for the creating and the maintaining of a more or less orderly mind of your own, and so a sense of your own identity. When you're writing, you've got a plan, and the changing of it is more or less in your own hands; but when you're in trouble, you are overwhelmed by events and issues you have no control over. To be in trouble is to be in the grip of fate but not to be able to get any melodramatic pleasure out if it. To be in trouble is not to be able to plan.

To cope with trouble, you've just got to keep on trying "to write"—trying all the time to find an outline of the whole that's stable enough, that's comprehensive enough to permit you to reason about one part of it at a time.

I've only been in personal trouble three or four times, but I'm an old pro at trouble. In trouble I feel like an old man—not a tough old man, but still a survivor. As they say in Austria: "Bend but don't break." Or as I say: "Set up a new file." Plan 9 has collapsed; set up Plan 10. I used to think old George Mead's slogan, "We don't know where we're going, but we're on our way," pretty weak stuff, but it's not. It's the theme song of being in trouble but not being dead.

That's how it has been with me, or how it seems, but how about you? Tovarich, I know it's hard to tell the truth about yourself and your ideas. Look how in these letters I disguise so much of what I think and feel; how elaborately and awkwardly I go about it. But I'm going to try to help you. Let us proceed as if Bertolt Brecht's little maxim were true, that truth is concrete.

In the fall of 1957, when Mills was still on leave from Columbia University, he wanted to dispel some false rumors circulating there concerning his professional plans. As the next letters show, there were also other, more philosophical issues at stake.

To Lewis and Rose Coser, from Innsbruck, Austria, dated October 29, 1957

Dear Lew and Rose:

Thanks for your letter and the information in it. I think you are mistaken about Columbia, but no matter. Anyway, you mustn't think I'm sitting around here in the mountains building little paranoid castles. The world's too big for that, and I am at work. "The Social Sciences: a Cultural Critique" is now in draft, with only a few gaps to check when I get back. Early in the spring I'll mimeograph it for criticism. Quite frankly, I've high hopes for it; it's the first thing I've ever written "about" the social sciences of any length; and since I keep it quite close to practice in the craft, it has, I think a certain freshness and lack of pretension. The Politics and Culture book is about half done,[43] although it won't yet focus just right. There are just too damned many themes written into it too closely, and I've not got the guts ruthlessly to cut it.

The autumn *Dissent* came the other day. It's really excellent— broader and more assured in tone somehow. You and Irv [Irving Howe] ought to be quite proud of how it's grown, and I don't mean only circulation. I particularly like to see books handled critically but also without any smart-aleck bullshit. I think books is what you ought to strengthen, and you ought to include a lot of English stuff coming out. A hell of a lot of people will read a magazine just for the book section if it's really good. Like in the old *New Republic,* and the *New Statesman* today.

Don't you see Bendix—or is he away? You don't mention his name. I've always thought he was a pretty good man; don't you think so? Tell Leo [Lowenthal] I'm mad at him; he didn't answer my letter of last Aug. sent via Paul Massing . . . or didn't he get it?
[. . .]

Take care,
Wright

ↄ

---

43. An unpublished manuscript.

To Ralph Miliband and Norman Birnbaum, from Innsbruck, Austria (c/o American Express), dated November 22, 1957

[ONE:] Forgive my delay in writing and also the rude fact that I write you both at once; the carbon goes to toss up. My excuse is that for 10 days now I've been doing nothing but write long, two page, single spaced letters with carbons to various people about the Columbia situation. I've had to "save" two instructors, Litwak and Siegel, and ward off other predatory silliness [. . .] mounted by Lazarsfeld.

By no means is this sociological brawl at Columbia finished; by no means should it be assumed, as Norman apparently does, that I will lose. On the contrary, this round I think I have won; at least I've strengthened my position considerably and more importantly have broadened to confrontation: administratively by getting it squarely before Dean Barzun and Dean Chamberlain (my college dean); and intellectually by making it turn on something worth fighting about— the cultural crisis of the social studies and the problem of a proper liberal arts education. Until now I have not really fought these people in American sociology; I've ignored them and done my own work; but they've been fooling around behind the scenes and now I declare war: I am going to expose their essential bankruptcy; perhaps with a little circuit of the Ivy League schools; certainly with my book on the social studies, mimeographed drafts of which I shall, if I may, get to you by March.

"I don't hate nobody," he said. "I'm just tired of the bullshit." He said it slowly so they'd all hear it good. Then he swung a couple of chairs into the bar, one following the other like one smash; knocking the bottom off a whiskey bottle, . . . [he] moved in close.

TWO: Seriously, all that is easy—and can readily be taken, as I do, as a sort of relaxation from serious work. [. . .] I've booked a flight and will fly to NYC on Dec. 27th. Who will be on it with me is not yet certain.

THREE: For a long time now I've been designing The House. Probably it's my favorite occupation. Although I haven't got my drafting tools here, I picked it up again the other day, using squared paper. That's just as good, of course. I am working on a module basis: four foot square, with the total layout on the classic Leica size negative 2 by 3. The model I've got just right now is 16 by 24 and two story;

and I am going to build it next spring in Rockland County. It is set up in such a way [that] all partitions are easily moved except one downstairs: you can make out of it a four bedroom house, two in each room with privacy if you want. My model is a two bedroom with shop instead of other two bedrooms. The trick I picked up last spring on a Danish ferry: how to get two people, with privacy, into an 8 by 8 bedroom, also storage and washbasin. I want to build a set of these little houses around the world, four or five of them. The cost in NY state, prices as of when I left, comes to about $4,000 plus land. But it could be done much cheaper: that's with complete hot and cold automatic air conditioning. With a planing mill, any village, say in Poland, of 200 men could set up housing for the whole damn population in 6 weeks after perhaps 3 lectures of two hours each and one supervisor on the job. They could do it in individual houses or multiples of any size wanted and with endless individual variations, and not just phony ones either. An underdeveloped country [. . .] could make five or six standard components by way of utilities; the population could do the rest given wood or stone or cement or even clay of good quality, on a local basis. Best of all the design cuts thru all the bullshit of housing and is set up for several variations—basic ones I think—of styles of life. But enough of that. It's probably boring to anyone else.

Why don't you all come and spend Christmas in Tyrol?

W. M.

Mills returned to New York and Columbia in late December.

To Ralph Miliband, from New York City, dated December 23, 1957

Dear Ralph:

[. . .]

Terrible hard schedule this spring: Feb. 27 Toronto; March . . . last week of Hillman lectures; three lectures in April, Chicago, U. of Ill., Colgate; and two in May. Plus book deadlines and regular teaching load. But what the hell, I accepted them, and what with the mail waiting here, I see I ought to push a few ideas about. Mail really is amazing: the most unlikely people write about this silly little *Nation* piece.[44] One woman bought 5,000 reprints for her own personal distribution. Crazy I guess. And a millionaire toy manufacturer wants me to design toys that will realize craftsmanship as laid out in *White Collar.* What a country What an epoch.

It's not a buzz saw, boy, it's a bowl. Put both hands in.

as ever,

M

ole mills

∾

To Hans Gerth, from New York City, dated December 27, 1957

Dear Gerth,

Forgive me this short note, but I only want to let you know that I have finally arrived in New York City—alone—and that I am well established at [. . .] W. 114th Street; the University kindly held this charming little apartment for me, right back of the University library.

Ruth is [. . .] in Innsbruck. [. . .] We shall probably be separated at her wish upon her return. [. . .][45]

The future is extremely uncertain, but as of now I have so much work to do I can't think about it.

In late March I am to deliver the Sidney Hillman lectures, "On War and Peace."[46] Because of this if you happen to see my piece in the *Nation* of 7 December[47] I'd be very grateful for your comments pointing out any arrogant foolishness that may well be in it. I wrote it before leaving and it may well be an expression of hysteria on my

44. The cover story of *The Nation* had been Mills's "Program for Peace," which presented a fourteen-point proposal including the abandonment of the production of nuclear weapons, the recognition of China and all other "Communist-type states," and the development of worldwide educational and cultural-exchange programs. *The Nation* 185, no. 19 (7 December 1957): 419–24.

45. Ruth obtained a divorce from Mills in May of 1959 after living apart from him for almost two years.

46. Mills presented the basic outline of his book *The Causes of World War Three* in his Sidney Hillman Award Lectures at Howard University, Washington, D.C., in March 1958.

47. "Program for Peace."

part rather than a sound analysis. Let me know what you think of it. Will you?

As ever,
Mills

After Mills's return to the States in December 1957, he had lunch with Irving Howe, who had been a political friend for almost ten years. Howe remembers discussing the political situation in eastern Europe—listening to Mills's emphatic opinions about the changes he expected—and feeling a personal and political alienation from Mills.[48]
Meanwhile, Mills was corresponding frequently with Ralph Miliband.

To Ralph Miliband, from New York City, dated New Year's Eve
(December 31, 1957)

Dear Ralph:

new year's eve 10:30. Enclosed is a print of the *Nation* piece for which you ask.[49] In view of the Hillman lectures being on war and peace, I'd be grateful for as full a reaction as your time and patience allows. Perhaps this, straightened up a bit and filled out, might do as tail chapter of the book to be made out of the lectures . . . a little book of perhaps 5 chapters.[50] I give only three lectures and shall of course not use this again. I think I told you of the Toronto speech 27 Feb: to the evangelical board of the United Churches of Canada. On Religion and War, or Moral Insensibility. I've been drafting it and it's going to be real cute. I turn the whole thing against them and speak to them as a Heathen, calling them You Christians and throwing all the old righteousness of the Hebrew prophets at them mixed up with my angle towards war and peace.[51] This will also be a fill-out chapter in the little book. Got to get down to the Hillman lectures as such soon.

48. Irving Howe, *A Margin of Hope: An Intellectual Autobiography* (San Diego: Harcourt Brace Jovanovich, 1982), 244–45.

49. This must have been "Program for Peace."

50. The finished book had four parts and twenty-five chapters: *The Causes of World War Three* (New York: Simon and Schuster and Ballantine Books, 1958, 1960). In 1985 M. E. Sharpe reprinted the 1960 edition.

51. See "A Pagan Sermon to the Christian Clergy," *The Nation* 186, no. 10 (8 March 1958): 199–202.

Yes, of course I know Lukacs' *Studies in European Realism*. He is great on Balzac, who is indeed himself great. He can be read over and over again, at different stages in one's own life. A real classic that is. But I am not going to buy the big set we looked at. Just too much money and I've no time to read him well for the next year. Got to get educated on a lot of stuff I've not yet looked into.

A word of advice, if I may, about the fascism piece.[52] Bill Miller who is, technically speaking, the most skilled writer I know, says, "Anything but anything can be put into two volumes or into one paragraph." It is always best to begin with an idea in 12 or so pages: numbered points by paragraph, a sort of propositional framing of the thing: lead sentence in each paragraph—a numbered proposition. Split the proposition into two parts. Part One: assertions, descriptions, narrative, the what-is-to-be-explained. Part Two: the explanation. Then if needed, Part Three: the meaning or implications for this and for that. I know that is a very unEnglish kind of writing, but no matter; it is the way to get ideas down in an open form, permitting their shaping in any number of ways. So don't take the fascism notion too big at first; get it down clean. Taking it too big is too easy a way not to do it at all. Nowadays men with ideas are too badly needed to have to work them all out in detail. Let others do that. State the damned ideas.

[. . .]

As ever,
M

∾

To Ralph Miliband, from New York City, dated January 26, 1958

Dear Ralph:

Of course you do not write flippantly. I told you how it was: you decide to live or you decide to die, and I've decided to live. The only questions are: Can you? And how do you want to?

[. . .]

52. Perhaps this article was Miliband's "The Politics of Contemporary Capitalism" in *New Reasoner* 5 (summer 1958): 39–52. Its first section is entitled "Fascism and Liberal Democracy."

I've gotten a small grant from Columbia and have hired a typist and another woman who is copyediting *The Social Sciences* for mimeographing and forcing me to rewrite. She is Mrs. Jarrico, the wife of a blacklisted Hollywood scriptwriter. She's a swell old gal and happens to be a fan of mine, in fact her whole circle is. I expect to get some really professional advice on style and such matters. (In fact, I am blocking out rather loosely now a play-novel-movie script called "Unmailed Letters to a Fey Tiger" which isn't so damn bad.)

I am getting work done—no new writing yet and no reading but periodicals.

[. . .] Slowly I get on top of it all. In some crazy, unknown way that can be neither explained nor denied, I am going to win out. Questions for you: 1. Where is Polish stuff? 2. Please let me know at once when the *Br J of S* [*British Journal of Sociology*] is actually going to be out with my piece in it. (It would be very much O.K. with me if they killed it!) . . . The point is I want to use it in a few speeches around and can't do so after it's published. Inquire discreetly and as *not* from me please. The speeches are scheduled for a month or so away and I'll have to find something else if they print before that.

I share your indignation about the quiet and the noisy Americans you describe, but I don't think it worthwhile to waste energy about it in small ways: analyze the world and locate them as a piece of shit within it. I am glad and skeptical about your apartment. The limeys are thru boy. No style of daily life left in them; they're all knotted up in the soft coils of useless tradition. In the end you'll have to come to America or go to Russia (joke).

Write soon.

yours,
M.

The following letter mentions two essays on peace published in The Nation: *Mills's "Program for Peace"[53] and his fiery piece entitled "A Pagan Sermon to the Christian Clergy." In his pagan sermon Mills railed against moral insensibility to human destruction and the preparation for it, saying, "The brotherhood of man is now less*

53. See letters written in December 1957.

*a goal than an obvious condition of biological survival. Before the world is made safe
again for American capitalism or Soviet Communism or anything else, it had better
be made safe for human life." Mills took Christian leaders to task for generally fail-
ing to create an effective opposition to the arms race: "Nowadays we pagans see that
Christian morals are more often used as moral cloaks of expedient interests than ways
of morally uncloaking such interests." In closing, Mills addressed the Christian clergy
directly when he wrote, "I hope you do not demand of me gospels and answers and
doctrines and programs. According to your belief, my kind of man—secular, pride-
ful, agnostic and all the rest of it—is among the damned. I'm on my own; you've
got your God. It is up to you to proclaim gospel, to declare justice, to apply your love
of man [. . .] meaningfully, each and every day, to the affairs and troubles of men.
[. . .] I hope you do not speak from the moral center of yourself, because if you
do, then in the dark nights of your soul, in fear and in trembling, you must be cru-
elly aware of your moral peril in this time of total war, and—given what you, a
Christian, say and believe—I, a pagan, pity you."[54] The article provoked "a flood"
of letters—most of which were positive, judging by the sampling printed in the
magazine—and so many requests for copies that* The Nation *found it necessary to
order reprints.*[55]

To Mr. Lee Grove, editor, Trade Department, Oxford University
Press, from New York City, dated March 16, 1958

Dear Lee:

As you know, I've been fooling with three lectures on war which
I must deliver at Howard University the last week in March. I have
also done two essays for *The Nation,* 7 December '57 and 8 March
'58, on the subject. Ian Ballantine, who is a longtime friend of mine,
read these essays and has suggested that a softcover book—I'd call it a
pamphlet—be put together from it all. It would be about 40,000 words
in total; he could get galleys to reviewers ten days after manuscript
was received (on or about April 20th, perhaps a bit later, depending on
my personal situation); and publish it sixty days after manuscript. He
would run a 100,000 [copy] first printing.

Oxford, as far as I know, is not set up to do this quickie sort of
thing, which is rather like the old "Penguin specials," with which Ian

---

54. *The Nation* 186, no. 10 (8 March 1958): 199–202.
55. *The Nation* 186, no. 12 (22 March 1958): 247.

has had experience. He has got the kind of distribution apparatus that makes it feasible, and he is interested in it.

The money involved does not amount to anything. However, it's not money but readers that interest me on this topic. The thing would be a blast, a sermon, a warning, a demand, a squeal. I'd like to go ahead with it, so I would like an exception to be made in Oxford's option on my books in this one case.

I want you to know that this has nothing to do with my overall and long-term relations with Oxford. Long ago Ian and I had that settled. He knows he cannot pry me from Oxford, and as my friend he does not want to do so. He knows and I know that Oxford and I are good for each other. This item, however, obviously isn't for Oxford. The fun of it is to get it out fast, to distribute the hell out of it all at once, and so maybe raise a little impolite hell.

Yours for peace and freedom,
Wright
C. Wright Mills

Oxford University Press agreed to Mills's request, and Ballantine Books published The Causes of World War Three *in mass-market paperback in 1958;[56] it was a commercial success. The "pamphlet," as Mills called it, was featured in a display arranged by SANE, a nuclear disarmament advocacy group, at the Pacific International Exposition in August–September 1961, Vancouver, B.C., Canada; it was the only book sold there.*

The fact that The Causes of World War Three *(and* Listen, Yankee, *1960) sold in great numbers to a general audience increased Mills's popularity; and his popularity tended to increase his isolation from colleagues and some friends or former friends, who thought he should be writing for a more intellectual audience. Among his defenders, Jamison and Eyerman point out that Mills's isolation from his professional colleagues and his refusal to be drawn into mainstream work preserved his critical voice and allowed him "to become a spokesman for the next generation, seeking a way out of the wasteland and keeping alive the task set out in* The Sociological Imagination.*"[57]*

This next letter mentions Yaroslava Surmach, who later became Mills's wife. The eldest child of Ukrainian immigrants who founded a Ukrainian book and music store,

---

56. Simon and Schuster published it in hardcover and trade softcover the same year.
57. Jamison and Eyerman, *Seeds of the Sixties,* 46.

Yaroslava grew up in New York City, graduated from Cooper Union Art School, taught art at Manhattanville College, and served as the art editor of the children's magazine Humpty Dumpty. *Before Yaroslava met Mills she had traveled extensively throughout western and eastern Europe, researching various folk arts and folk tales.[58]*

Mills wrote to his parents about Yaroslava, "I am building up a new life and I think I may well have found the woman with whom to build it: an artist, professionally and as well down to her fingertips." He wrote that he loved her thoroughly and had "never been old enough to value love of this sort so well."[59]

She was almost thirty-three years old and Mills was almost forty-two when he wrote the next letter.

To Ralph Miliband, from New York City, dated May 1, 1958

Dear Ralph:

You may very well be right that the first three chapters ought to go in the back of the book [*The Sociological Imagination*]. At any rate it is one of those ideas that deserves a hard try; I'll spend a week playing with a draft that way. I want you to know that I am aware that much hard work is still to be done on this manuscript. Such a reordering may be just the thing to make the doing of it more pleasant and more profitable. I am most grateful to you. By the way I agree that 1 and 2 are the weakest chapters. Know also that the more detailed comment you give me I shall use fully.

Since returning to the US I have also written a little book which goes to the publisher next week. It is only 50,000 words or so and will be a softcover original at 50 cents, published by Ian Ballantine, called REFLECTIONS ON WAR;[60] it incorporates the Washington lectures, [the] Sidney Hillman series, I mean, and the *Nation* articles . . . all redone and fitted together. I'll send you a copy of course; should be out in about 2 months.

    [. . .]

58 Yaroslava later illustrated twenty-five books, including *The Mitten: An Old Ukrainian Folktale,* retold by Alvin Tresselt, adapted from the version by E. Rachev (New York: Lothrop, Lee, and Shepard, 1964); Helen Kay, *An Egg Is for Wishing* (New York: Abelard–Schuman, 1966); and *Tusya and the Pot of Gold: From an Old Ukrainian Folktale,* retold and illustrated by Yaroslava (New York: Atheneum, 1973).

59. Letter to Mills's parents, dated February 1, 1958.

60. *The Causes of World War Three.*

I have been a little ill, with heart nonsense; and I am very tired. This summer I shall try to take it easy and just redo the social science book. I wish I had a good title for it. The present one is no good. It is after all sociology not social science and it is not exactly an autopsy. I want the whole thing to be more positive.

Yaroslava and I have ups and downs, but on the whole it goes very well. She is one damned good craftswoman in wool, oil-paint, silver, wood, paper (paper sculpture) and she has just made me a great mobile of a school of fish, which really is delightful.

The lectures in London are all set now, for the week of 12 to 18th Jan. next, I think.[61] Then on to Moscow for a week. Do you happen to know anything about a hotel there called, I think it is, the Bristol?

I got my motorcycle today, and this evening Y and I prowled the Wall Street district, in fact all the docks and the lower East Side. She knows where all the districts are: here is a whole street full of leather, here is one for yarn, another for buttons and equipment for making, mending, destroying buttons. Fabulous, really.

In general, since I last wrote to you, I've been in pretty good shape but with bad spells and missing a lot of classes, what with the heart and out of town lectures. But it doesn't matter really. Slowly, very slowly I am afraid, I get on top of it all. Two years from now (who knows?) maybe it will all be a vague memory, or even half forgotten.

Take care, as ever, and many, many thanks!

W

Wright

To Richard Hofstadter, from New York City, dated July 10, 1958

Dear Dick:

I am immensely grateful to you for your careful reading of the manuscript and your forthright comment. I have now taken into account all of your detailed criticism and corrections.[62] As I read

---

61. "On Reason and Freedom." Read to the London School of Economics and Politics and broadcast by the British Broadcasting Corporation, February 1959.

62. In the acknowledgments of *The Sociological Imagination,* Mills thanked Hofstadter and thirty-one other colleagues and friends for criticizing the manuscript in whole or in part.

the stuff (I mean my own) now in July, I wonder how in God's name I could have let it stand for ditto last January. On the other hand, quite frankly, I also wonder at how I got anything together then. But no matter. Here is the way it now looks: I am really quite excited about it for the first time.

Chapter one is almost new: it defines in a good euphoric way the sociological imagination (which will be the title for the book) and the milieu vs. structural distinction; then a brief note on peculiarities of sociological tradition. Chapter two is liberal practicality with a new lead section, which is a kind of little sociology of knowledge of the social sciences but not called that. Then come *illib practicali,* grand theory and abstract empiricism and bureaucratic ethos: edited in detail and with more positive stuff thrown in as contrast. This is 7 chapters, but I think none of them more than 30 pages. I'll try to shorten them more still. Chapter 8 is more or less new: it is a summing up and a new beginning. Remember the list of for and against at the tail of the old manuscript that you liked, a sort of balance sheet. Well I elaborate that into a chapter and do so in terms of a sort of definition of "the classic social science tradition" or what have the sociological greats got? [Chapter] 9 is called Biography and History and consists of the old chapter two but pointed up to the two big problems of history making (the fourth epoch) and individuality (the cheerful robot); again this is positive for social science. [Chapter] 9 is the politics (pretty much like the old chapter 10 but shorter); and 10 is the craft . . . the letter thing but God help me again rewritten.

Either in 7 or in 10 or perhaps in a little appendix, I am running an annotated bibliography of great books, past and present: these are the core of the real thing, or so I claim. When I get that in shape I'll send it to you; maybe also the new chapter one.

You've worked hard enough to have the right to see that your reading has made a difference, and to read some decently put stuff! About the chapter you didn't like at all, industrial relations, I won't talk of that now as I am still thinking about it and working on it hard. You may be right. Although I read that to the boys themselves when I was VP of the industrial relations association and they gave it a big hand indeed. True it was in another version then. But we'll see. Anyway can't I save much by just saying up front and again in the back of the chapter that I am not concerned with their consultantship but only with their theory?

[. . .] I would very much like to ride up to the Cape for a weekend with you sometime but I don't know whether I can make it before August sometime. I think of swinging through Vt. to see Dave Riesman, with whom I've been having an enormous sort of correspondence.[63] I've always liked Dave personally. . . . [. . .] Katie does marvelously.

I was in Aspen, Colorado, for the International Design Conference a week or so ago and had a fine time with designers, architects, city planners, artists and other disgruntled types.[64] I still think I ought to have been an architect. But since it's too late I am going to theorize for them! God they are a confused but good willing lot. They now confront all the problems the political intellectual grappled with in the thirties; amazing really.

But again thanks very much indeed for your time and effort on the manuscript; it has helped immensely.

yours,
M

∾

To Hans Gerth, from New York City, dated December 2, 1958

Dear Gerth:

I have read your fine paper, given in Seattle, which you sent me, and I am very moved and encouraged by your generous remarks on WC and PE. They are not that good, my friend. Anyway, we are quite alone among American sociologists in thinking them perhaps worth reading. See for example Mr. Bell's debater's points in current J S [*American Journal of Sociology*], which of course I shall not answer.[65]

---

63. Concerning Riesman's comments and criticisms of the manuscript of *The Sociological Imagination*.

64. Mills's speech at this conference was published as "The Man in the Middle" in *Industrial Design* (November 1958): 70–75.

65. Daniel Bell's negative review of *The Power Elite* appeared in the November 1958 issue of the *American Journal of Sociology*. Bell later reprinted the review in his book, *The End of Ideology* (New York: Free Press, 1960).

Oxford has just gone to press with *The Sociological Imagination* (an earlier version of which in mimeo I think I sent you last spring or summer). Now I work hard on the lectures for Warsaw and London. I really am up a creek in Warsaw: I don't really know these people and don't want to get them into trouble, but of course I must state things as I see them. So I am trying to treat them as if they were in Chicago or an audience in LA and yet *reach* them.

   [. . .]

Yours as ever,
CWM

In Gerth's answer to this letter, he invited Mills to take a vacation in Wisconsin and to plan on writing a book together with him at that time. Gerth wrote that after reading one chapter of The Causes of World War Three *he thought it wasn't as informative as* White Collar *or* The Power Elite, *and that he didn't like the title.*

To Tom Bottomore, from New York City, dated December 9, 1958

Dear Tom Bottomore:

Believe me, I'd love to give another paper while in London, but I just can't. In the six days I'm to be there, I must deliver 4 formal papers (on which I now work) and cooperate with Secker and Warburg's nonsense; they publish upon my arrival *The Causes of World War Three.* Then I go thru the same thing in Warsaw the very next week. On top of that, I am already bone-tired from lecture touring this fall to raise some money.

   I do hope that you understand, that you know I really would like to if I could, and so forgive me.

   Please also try to arrange time that you and I can have a good talk over a bottle of wine some evening.

Yours sincerely,
Wright

To Mr. Russell Johnson, Peace Secretary, American Friends Service Committee, from New York City, December 15, 1958

Dear Mr. Johnson:

I'd like very much to be with you in Boston in April but I cannot. My job is writing books: that is my action. (Sometimes I lecture publicly because I *must* for the money in it—my minimum fee as of now is $500 and expenses.) If I go out speaking as I am asked to do I could not do my proper, and I believe—for me—more important work. Meetings and speeches: that is your job. If I can help you in this by my books I am very glad indeed, for that is a major reason why I wrote the last one[66] and the ones before that. But I have now to complete the next book and the one after that.

I'd like to do everything, but I can't. Accordingly I hope you will understand and, should my position inconvenience you, forgive me.

With very best wishes,
C. Wright Mills
Professor of Sociology

In the spring of 1959, Dissent *published two opposing reviews of* The Causes of World War Three. *The first, by the pacifist A. J. Muste, stated that "Mills has written a sound, brilliant and most timely political tract. In using the latter term I do not mean to put it into a minor category but to praise it as being in a great tradition of books which are of high intellectual quality but which also propose a program and sound a call for action. That an American sociologist of Mills's standing who is also an unusually well informed and sophisticated analyst of political events should publish such a book is an event in the world struggle against war."*

The opposing review was written by Irving Howe, who wrote that he believed Mills's sense of urgency "has led to the analytic carelessness and moral disequilibrium of Mills' pamphlet. Many of his specific proposals are fine, many of his specific observations valid; but the mode or style of thought to which he has recently turned seems to me unacceptable for the democratic left."[67]

Mills replied by writing a pointed "Dear Irving" letter, which Dissent *published along with Howe's tense reply. Mills asked exactly how Irving Howe's position to-*

66. *The Causes of World War Three.*
67. "C. Wright Mills' Program: Two Views," *Dissent* 6, no. 2 (spring 1959): 189 and 191.

ward the Cold War differed from that of the U.S. government, and Howe complained about Mills's emphasis on the similarities between some of the political trends in the USSR and the United States, concluding that Mills was being too soft on the USSR. Each man seemed to feel misunderstood by the other in their argument over emphasis and the merits of Mills's contribution to the pitched battle against the nuclear arms race. According to Howe, after Dissent *published their exchange, they never saw each other again.*[68]

In the spring of 1959 Mills was occupied by other major events aside from arguments about his latest book. That spring he began building a new home in Rockland County, New York—with Yaroslava Surmach, helping to design the house and acting as the general contractor as well as contributing his manual labor. Mills married Yaroslava in June, and soon after the wedding Mills, Yara, and Katie moved into the new house. They had been living there three months when Mills wrote the next letter.

To Ralph Miliband, from West Nyack, New York, dated "late Sept '59"

Dear Ralph:

I'm very sorry that I missed you when I went thru London last week. We got there earlier than expected and I looked forward to several long talks with you on radical matters. I know you must be very busy with the election and all, so if the questions I raise in this letter are too much bother to answer, please forget them. First, a bit of news: I've just rec'd a very *depressed* letter from Julian Hochfeld.[69] Apparently the Poles are trying to suppress the Polish edition of PE; I'm not sure of that, but that's what the letter seems to say. Also Hochfeld's longish introduction to it, which he worked on very hard;[70] also his study of the Polish parliament. He even speaks of "leaving" the institute. Don't let on that I wrote you, but why not write him a friendly, encouraging note? I've just done it. He plans to come to [the] US in January, and of course I shall treat him royally.

---

68. Irving Howe, *A Margin of Hope*, 244–45.

69. Political sociologist and socialist activist who was the director of the Institute of International Relations, associated with the Polish Ministry of Foreign Affairs, from 1957 to 1960, and who later became deputy director of the Social Science Department of UNESCO.

70. A Polish translation of *The Power Elite* was published by Ksiazka i Wiedza, Warsaw, with an introduction by Mieczyslaw Manelli, in 1961.

I saw P. Worsley at Stresa [Italy][71] and tried to help him outline a little study; I think now in my damned enthusiasm I might have been rude or something, but I like him, what I saw of him.

In about a week, I am told, I'll know whether or not the Russians are going to invite me to their fair land. Wish they'd make up their minds . . . It would be in the spring, and I've got to say yes or no to dates in the US, lectures and all. Also there's a chance (also not yet jelled) to go to Mexico; and I think I go for a week to Rio de Janeiro in late Oct, but they only hint around and don't send tickets. God damn it, I want to travel, beginning in Feb or so, with Yaro and Katie. Tired of being a hick.

I don't know what questions, if any, you wanted to raise with me . . . about work I mean, but if you'll write I'll respond of course. So forgive me now for raising my own.

I. I've decided to do a short book on Marx. [. . .] I'm very excited about it but can't get on it just yet; probably start seriously in about 2 months. Questions to you:

A) What do you think are the best two or three summaries of what Marx said? Preferably some kind of precis or propositional outline.

B) What are the best two or three criticisms of Marxism: critiques as it were that one really must take into account? I don't mention those I have at hand for both A and B because I want it off the top of your head.

C) I must now tell you that I've never really read Laski: what of his about Marxism, about socialism in general and about USSR, should I by all means get into?

II. My final question is also open-ended. I've got to edit a Reader of classical sociological, or social (perhaps including political) thinkers. I don't like this sort of thing but I've got to do it to pay a few debts remaining on this house, and I may as well try to do something useful. [. . .][72] Do you think that would be useful to put

71. The anthropologist Peter Worsley, author of *The Trumpet Shall Sound: A Study of "Cargo" Cults in Melanesia* (London: MacGibbon and Kee, 1957), among other titles. Stresa was the site of an international sociological conference where Mills also met Russian sociologists.

72. Mills included a rough outline that closely corresponds with the sources in the final book, including Karl Mannheim, Herbert Spencer, Thorstein Veblen, Max Weber, Karl Marx and Friedrich Engels, Emile Durkheim, and Gaetano Mosca, among others. *Images of Man:*

together? Of course with brief notes introducing each and words defined in footnotes if need be. Who have I missed? Any of these you think to hell with?

Think of this: suppose you had to go off on a mountain without communication for 10 years and could take only 10 books with you. What would they be? Do answer that . . I mean of course only books in social science.

Again forgive my imposing these questions on you, but the truth is I need advice and discussion and there is no one around here to talk with anymore.

I've seen some reviews of *Sociological Imagination* that appeared in England: on the whole rather good, but sort of stale. I'm sick of writing *about* academic stuff, and want badly to get back to writing about realities. The Marx book, however, I realize I really must do, as I've always addressed my stuff to liberal doctrine, since that is so dominant in the audience.

Send me your news.
As ever,
Wright
Mills

ॐ

To Hallock Hoffman, the Fund for the Republic, Inc., Center for the Study of Democratic Institutions, from West Nyack, New York, dated October 7, 1959

Dear Hallock Hoffman:

Your query of 23 Sept, just rec'd, gives me a good chance to talk to myself as well as to you. If you don't mind my rambling, I'm going to write for my own carbon. First, for the externals: I am and have been at the address posted above; this is my Sabbatical year. Have just returned from ten days at the Fourth World Congress of Sociology. Will go to conference in Rio from 18th to 29th Oct. Otherwise— apart from a few speeches about the country—will be at this address

---

The Classic Tradition in Sociological Thinking, selected and edited and with an introduction by C. Wright Mills (New York: George Braziller, 1960).

for the fall. I don't know about the spring yet. The Russians have half-invited me to visit them but nothing final yet.

Second, the state of my comparative project, for which the Fund gave me money last spring:[73] the money is spent and here is where I am on the project. I've got a good file set up, and with the assistant I had spring and summer, we've coded in three big notebooks about half of the information readily available on 110 national structures. Until I am over the rest of that first big empirical hump I'm rather stuck. I'd judge about four or five months with Guterman, the assistant, would see me to a set of cards. It just takes a lot of plain drudgery with apparently simple facts before I am freed, as it were, to make with the theory etc.

Third, as to my immediate situation: I'm on half pay, this being the Sabbatical ($366 per month take home), and without even a typist. I've told Jacques Barzun my problem and he is trying to do something about it; I think probably he will. I should know in about ten days or so. You remember I applied to various foundations for $25,000 . . . enough to do the job elegantly and also avoid my having to scruge (sp?) [scrounge] around for personal income. Well every damned one of them turned it down flat. Some promptly, some with aggravating delay. So I now face up to the fact that I'm not going to get any adequate research money. I'm just off the list. So to hell with them. In the meantime, for the personal income in it, I am editing a Reader [. . .] of GREAT SOCIOLOGISTS for George Braziller:[74] it should be done in about 2 more weeks. I am also in touch with an interesting guy, Ivan Nagy, who turns out to be a former student of mine and who runs a thing called Deadline Data. He's got a file of nation-states and internal affairs he sells as a service, and he likes my stuff. I may make some kind of deal with him . . . to work out indices for him to use and in turn I use his stuff to further my own file and later the cards I need to set up. I see him again next Tuesday Oct 13th.

So much for externals. What I wanted to say is that two things now preoccupy me. This comparative file, first. I've known of course that it was a longtime thing, but I grow more sure that I have got to do it even if in the end I do the clerical work myself. It is the sort

73. The project was a comparative sociological study of 124 countries.
74. *Images of Man.*

of thing into which everything one does seems to fit. A sort of big framework that serves to orient and give point to smaller projects. I know now that it will be at center for me for the next six or seven years at least.

The second thing I must do, and which I have begun, is a real confrontation of "Marxism." You see, I have always written with reference to liberalism, because that is a kind of common denominator of the public for which I write. I've not felt the need to confront Marxism because the audience wasn't preoccupied with it, indeed didn't even know it. So I've just used what I wanted from the body of Marxist stuff but never defined my relation with it. This is getting a little messy now, especially as I get more into the comparative stuff and more into what I suppose is explicitly political philosophy. So I have outlined and begun to draft a little book of about 30,000 to 50,000 words (certainly not more than 50,000) which might run like this:

ONE: liberalism and socialism.

TWO: propositional inventory . . . of Marxism-Leninism . . . reducing the whole thing to 30 or 40 pivotal propositions, and none of these damned boring long quotes. What is being said?

THREE: theses on Marxism, in this take a stand on TWO, point by point, of course taking into account the three "revisions," the turn of the century stuff, the sociologists, such as Weber and Veblen, and the Soviets.

FOUR: Soviet Marxism . . . along the lines of Marcuse's new book.[75]

FIVE: A NEW LEFT? . . . here an attempt, for both East and West, to work out a political orientation.

ONE I've got well in hand: a sort of model suggesting the four major questions that one must confront in any political philosophy.

Well, that is crude, but you see the general idea? Do you like it? Think I ought to carry it thru or just leave it in the kitchen, in the back room of the shop? It seems to me that I'm a pretty good person to do this kind of summing up and orientation because I've never been emotionally involved with Marxism or Communism, never belonged in any sense to it. And yet I know the stuff pretty well.

75. Herbert Marcuse, *Soviet Marxism: A Critical Analysis* (New York: Columbia University Press, 1958).

Despite that I find that I become curiously agitated when I work at it . . . which for me at least means that whether or not I publish it I am going to finish it. By the way did you happen to read the appendix to *The Sociological Imagination*, the thing on intellectual craftsmanship? I'm tempted to send a copy of it along with a reapplication for support to all the bastards that turned me down. But it wouldn't do any good I suppose, and besides I'm not going to ask any more.

Let me know what you think of the Thesis on Marxism; I'll keep in touch about developments in the comparative study.

Yours,
Wright Mills

In Rio in October 1959, Mills read his "Remarks on the Problem of Industrial Development" at the International Seminar on Resistances to Social Development, sponsored by the Latin American Center of Investigation in the Social Sciences.

To Tovarich, from Rio de Janeiro, Brazil, fall 1959

WHAT DOES IT MEAN TO BE AN INTELLECTUAL?
To transcend by their understanding a variety of everyday milieux, but not to be able to modify, to change the structural forces that are at work within and upon these milieux; to sit in judgment, but not to have power to enforce judgment; to demand but not to be able to back up their demands—that is the general position of most political intellectuals, at least of the Western societies today. Finding themselves in this position, many intellectuals have ceased to judge, have withdrawn their demands, have swallowed their presumption, have sunk back into the political and moral routines of their professional and residential milieux. There are many ways, social and personal, of doing this, and all these ways are now busily being followed. Despite all this, there is something about intellectuals and the intellectual life that exerts a strong pressure to take up this political role of transcendence and judgment. There are, in fact, many things, but the first of them is that it is simply true that to think in a really free and wide-ranging way is, as they say, "to stir up trouble," to question and in due course to demand and to judge.

Although for a variety of motives, he may play at being otherwise, the scholar must not only be diligent; he must be obsessed in his devotion and moreover, at least at times, he must possess a supreme confidence in his own mind and judgment, or rather he must feel that he is his own most severe critic—no one else could know so well his own errors.

I don't think it is too much to say that a political intellectual is a person who demands of himself clear statements of policy. He can't go off half-cocked; when he has to do so, he is uneasy about it. What he experiences—in the language of Hollywood—he takes big, and what he says about it, he takes seriously. If his task is to formulate policies, it is also to fight for an orderly comprehension of reality, for such comprehension must be gained if the quality of his policies are up to his self-imposed standards.

In the country you live in, is there room for a free-ranging use of reason—reason beyond mere technical rationality in the service of authority? In the country I live in we can write whatever we want; nobody locks us up. Nobody has to. Many of us lock ourselves up. Many intellectuals of the USA are voluntarily abdicating the carrying out of protest and the debating of alternatives to the stupid policies and lack of policies of the power elite in the United States. They are abdicating the role of reason in human affairs. They are abdicating the making of history.

Tovarich, I want you to know that intellectuals of my sort, living in America or in Britain, face some disheartening problems. As socialists of one sort or another, we are a very small minority in an intellectual community that is itself a minority. The most immediate problem we face is the nationalist smugness and political complacency among the dominant intellectual circles of our own countries. We confront a truly deep apathy about politics in general and about the larger problems of the world today.

I. Uses of Alienation

To be an intellectual human being involves certain choices between grand, although I hope not grandiose, alternatives. The first alternative has to do with everyday life and may be put as follows. Most people relax into the private and everyday life of their milieu. Generally accepting it and their place within it, they take its values as after all the most enjoyable. In the end, the round of family life and the faces of their children, a steady and pleasant job, let us say as a college professor, and later a nice home, an article published every three years and maybe a textbook to quilt together—isn't that about all there is in it? And after all, isn't that a pretty good life? Perhaps most people today would say at once, yes, it must be.

Here is the second alternative, which can be put in the form of questions: Shall I build my life around projects that transcend the everyday and private life? Generally rejecting as paramount the values of that life and my place within it, shall I come into tension with it whenever necessary? Shall I come to see myself as not only an ordinary man but also as in some way representative of the discourse of reason?

One key word here is "project," which I take from Simone de Beauvoir, an admirable woman who has chosen the second alternative, and whom you ought to read, especially if you are a woman or know any women. Another key is "standard," by which I mean the demands that you formulate and accept and make upon yourself. It is not so much that you live for ideas, it is that you really cannot live without them—although of course you can exist. But you are not in involuntary servitude to the powers of the commonplace and the terrible domination of the everyday.

Most people do not go after things which are out of their reach, but the intellectual, the artist, and the scientist do just that. To do so is a normal feature of their working lives. They look at their paintings, they think of their books, they examine again the formula, and they know that it is not good enough and perhaps never will be.

To be disgruntled with the way the world is going is not necessarily to be a disgruntled person. To be uneasy about the world is not necessarily to be uneasy with yourself. Although a good deal of your experience is perhaps necessarily estranged, the capacity for life experience need not be expropriated. It is quite possible to be suitably isolated and therefore not alienated; it is possible to live in an overdeveloped society but not be an underdeveloped person. In part it depends upon the ways in which one escapes from unpleasant features of oneself and one's condition. Everyone with any liveliness does a great deal of escaping, and is continually planning future escapes from which he hopes to learn something more about himself and about the world. For what is important about escapes is not avoiding them (or you would always remain one of your old selves) but choosing them carefully and using them well.

II. The International Character of Intellectual Life

You and I, Tovarich, we are students, writers, and readers; we belong to something that's bigger than any government; we owe loyalty, if you want, to something higher than any one state. Political loyalties are conditional upon our reasoning, and such loyalties are not circumscribed by national boundaries. This is a very important point for our attempt to communicate. Intellectual life, and so the working life of any intellectual, is not confined to any one nation. The minds of intellectuals have been formed by an essentially international process, and their work is essentially an international traffic.

The internationalism of the mind and sensibilities is not an abstract internationalism. Nor is it inaccessible. It is available in the bookstore on the corner, and the library downtown; it is as solid as the feeling set up by the look of a steel beam, as specific as the grace of a bamboo shoot, as general as the idea of nature or humanity. The internationalism of the mind and sensibilities is inherent in the intellectual's principle that all belief ought to be conditional upon the individual's reasoning, and that all his or her sensibilities and preferences of moral and aesthetic value ought to be products of conscious self-cultivation. There is no other meaning of the free use of the human mind, of the genuine liberation of the self.

III. What Writing Means

As a writer, I have always tried, although in different ways, to do just one thing: to define and dramatize the essential characteristics of our time. Whether I have written of labor leaders or farmers, of business executives or Puerto Rican migrants, of office workers, housewives or workingmen, I have tried to see them as actors in the drama of the 20th century. I have often failed in this, and no doubt will again, but that is what I am trying to do.[76]

---

76. This paragraph is from Mills's autobiographical statement for *Twentieth Century Authors, First Supplement: A Biographical Dictionary of Modern Literature,* ed. Stanley J. Kunitz (New York: H. W. Wilson Company, 1955), 674.

The good writer tries to unite a variety of private lives with public affairs. He tries to enrich the private life by making it publicly relevant. At the same time, he tries to put human meaning into what is now called public affairs, reshaping them to allow and to invite a more decent variety of private lives. We ought to refuse to separate the two, for although the proper measure of public affairs should always be the character of the private lives they permit, it is the nature of one of our many traps that we can't expect to solve the problems of private nor of public life separately. What we must do as writers is to begin to turn all of our traps into a series of tasks. For we have often gotten into the habit of the trapped animal; we have often forgotten that we are not merely animals, and that we are not merely trapped.

One other thing we ought to remember, which I always tend to forget, is that we must not underestimate what even a small circulation of ideas can do, especially—if I may say so—comical and inane ideas. Men of power are grim, and our chief weapons in times like these are audacity and laughter. I wish I had more laughter, Tovarich, but I just can't seem to get that, personally, or into the stuff I write.

Writing, if you are at it long enough, is of course a set of habits and of sensibilities that shape almost all your experience. Writing is, among other things, *always* a way of trying to understand yourself. You understand your own feelings and your own ideas only by writing them out.

I don't pretend, Tovarich, to know all the reasons, deep or on the surface, why a variety of people write, but one motive, for me at least, has to do with the feeling of getting some further part of the world into orderly shape while engaged in a real bout of writing. To write is to reason; it is to fight against chaos and murk. There's an enthusiasm that "takes you over" when you feel—it doesn't matter now whether it is so or not—when you feel you're conquering a little more of it for and by understanding. Of course it is also a fight against other ideas and arrangements of ideas and images that you are against, morally, logically, or factually.

Over and above all this, there's an aesthetic element in writing that is probably involved in any craft, in any attempt to impose form upon matter. It's probably similar in stone, wood, or sound, but of course it's most intricate and most gratifying to me in the medium of language.

In the end, I suppose, the main reason I am not "alienated" is because I write. After a long time at it you come to know how altogether alive you can be when you're in the middle of the big flow. After four or five weeks of steady work, you pause some morning to look it all over. Even after twenty years at it, it is always amazing, this hundred pages or so where before there was nothing. They embody the most alert minutes and hours and days you have ever had.

In the next letter Mills refers to Miliband's "sermon" in the New Statesman; *it was a satirical piece that argued, "Christ, whatever attraction he may have had in the past, is now a definite hindrance to Christianity."[77] This was a spoof on the debate within the Labour Party about dropping the commitment to nationalization from the Labour Party's constitution. Decades later, in 1994, the clause about nationalization was dropped by Tony Blair.*

To Ralph Miliband, from West Nyack, New York, dated November 9, 1959

Dear Ralph,

I've just read your sermon in NS. It's great, really great. You've the gift for it. You must do more, not about religion but about all sorts of things—labor party policy and conservative too. That's what's needed: less long-winded analysis than short funny stuff. Do 20 or so—then interleave them with chapters of a serious book—calling them "Words to the Wise, I," "Words to the Wise, II" etc.[78] [. . .]

In a few days am sending off the Classic Sociology writings[79]— a kind of supplement or companion, I guess, to *The Sociological Imagination.* I am not ashamed of it. But it's just a job. Am in the middle of "Theses on Marxism"—have about 25,000 words I guess. Looks promising. In mid-January, we go to Mexico City to give 3 months "seminar on Marxism" at university there. It looks like a paperback for 75 cents—200,000 [copy] edition, a kind of "primer" in book trade jargon, but an advance for me, intellectually I mean. From young Marx to Mao—the whole range. I'm up to my ears in all this

77. "A Re-Thinking Sermon," *New Statesman* (7 November 1959): 618.
78. Miliband did write another piece of satire: "Bold but Sound" proposed abolishing the House of Commons and allowing public relations firms to run the British government.
79. *Images of Man: The Classic Tradition in Sociological Thinking.*

argot. I should call it, after Trotsky: "In defense of me, against the petty-bourgeois oppositionists."

Salut,
CWM

ᴄᴩ

To Hans Gerth, from West Nyack, New York, dated December 22, 1959

Dear Gerth,

Congratulations on the child![80]

Enclosed is a copy of a review (on Bendix's Weber book) just mailed to *NY Times Sunday Books*. Although they asked for it, I've no idea [if] they will run it or not; often they don't run negative reviews.[81] Anyway, I thought you'd be interested in seeing it. But my main reason for writing is to make a suggestion to you—one I've been wanting to make for some time: Why don't *you* do the definitive intellectual biography of Weber? Why in God's name don't you get onto it? You're the obvious man to do it. It would be the way, the royal way, to consolidate all your work in translation. If you did decide to do it, please know that as far as the English is concerned, I should be glad to edit the manuscript with no mention of my name in any way. I mean that. Do think upon it. So far as the publisher is concerned, just now that would be no problem. Thru my agent (who would become yours for 10% and worth every penny of it) I believe you could get between $2,000 or $3,000 advance—half payable now, the rest when there's a couple of hundred pages available. That should be enough for a typist and a summer's trip to Germany if you needed to get at stuff there.

Things with me are more or less straightened out now. Yaro expects a baby this coming June and we are both very glad about that. Katie is in magnificent shape, but I have to face her being taken from me this coming fall.[82]

---

80. Gerth and his second wife, Nobuko, had just had a son.

81. Mills's review of Reinhard Bendix's *Max Weber: An Intellectual Portrait* was published in the January 7, 1960, issue of the *New York Times Book Review*.

82. Katie was supposed to start spending school years with her mother in Indiana in the fall of 1960; instead the move was postponed, first to 1961, then to the summer of 1962.

I am working on a short book, a kind of primer on Marxism, which is going very well. This is my Sabbatical, and apart from short trips to here and there, I stay home and write, refusing all this speaking. It's the only way.

In January we may go to Mexico for a month or—if I should give a seminar on Marxism there—for three months.

Yours,
Wright Mills

Gerth took Mills's suggestion and proposed writing a biography of Weber for publication by Oxford University Press, but the press wanted to see manuscript samples; Gerth did not follow up since he had to teach summer school and feared the risk of investing substantial time in the project before a publishing contract had been obtained.

To Elizabeth Cameron, editor, Trade Department, Oxford University Press, from West Nyack, New York, dated December 31, 1959

Dear Miss Cameron:

Thanks for the information about sales and coming royalties; hope check comes before I leave on 15th Jan.

About the possible updating of WC. It is a very big job, because the basic stuff in that book is recoded occupations from the census. Would take at least two months of hard work. So I am not inclined to do it for an Italian edition, especially since the ideas and the trends stated are still dead right. Cf chapter on "status panic" with "status seekers" etc.!

Perhaps in several years the thing to do is to combine WC and PE and the Harcourt Brace book on *The New Men of Power* (which never did very well after the first year): to use these three as a crude draft, cut them drastically, then build up a really big book on USA. But you can see I can't undertake that the way it should be done, to make it a new book, until I have finished my next really big project: the comparative sociology, the "States of the World" (coding all UN data on 124 nations and territories) and that is going to be slow going. I have an assistant working on it now part-time, out of money the Fund for the Republic gave me . . . a couple of thousand, but in the end some foundation is going to have to come thru with $25,000 to $50,000 to do it right. Anyway, on the Italian edition of WC, let us answer No. It is not a "book of fact" but of ideas and the author feels the ideas are right up to date, etc.

Forgive this letter's form,[83] but I am full of fever from some kind of lethal virus. To hell with the new year.

Yours,
M
Mills

∾

To Ralph Miliband, from West Nyack, New York, dated January 2, 1960

Dear Ralph:

Have yours of Dec. 24, 1959. Glad to hear about the book but hope you've not signed yet. You're very foolish if you sign at all without seeing an agent, even if you sign with Furth. Here's a good one: Innes Rose, J. Farquharson Ltd., 15 Red Lion Sq WC1 Chancery 4843/5. For God's sake use him; he's worth every penny of his percentage. Watch foreign rights especially and try to get it out in cheap edition right away. I know about this because of trouble in England particularly, where I am not at all distributed as you know: cost is ridiculous. It would seem to me your agent and you should retain all foreign rights, specifically American; and that Secker and Warburg would do better by you than a stodgy outfit like Allen. But it's a very complicated and tricky business, getting distribution, so why not use a pro? (I'm breaking in part with Oxford over the silly pricing of the last book . . . see below.) And by the way NO options on next book.

Well anyway here's my news. Just up from week of 104 fever—some damned virus we all had. Leave for Mexico to give seminar on socialism etc. Marxism about the 15th. No address there yet, but mail to here will be forwarded in due course. Seminar to last 2 months; after that no plan except: come back here and work more. Russians just don't peep. So guess it's off. To hell with them anyway. I've now

83. Typed but with some text added in handwriting.

contracted with Dell (softcover at 75 cents) for an edition of 150,000 [copies] of the Marxian book: 75,000 words by me and the same of selections, from Marx thru Mao.[84] This 75,000 words is the middle part of a hardcover book, to be published one year after Dell publishes, on "Liberalism, Socialism, and Communism," which probably Simon and Schuster will publish.[85] Whether it bores anybody or not, I've got first to straighten out my view of Marx & Co. before I can lay it on the line about socialism, etc. In this publishing program I can do that, without many pretenses, you see, because it is a useful job of work to put these selections together: no one has done that in just the way, the scope, I'll do it. Besides in this country people do not know Marx, much less Mao and Tito and Stalin for that matter.

In addition I work very hard now, with one clerk as an assistant (the Fund for the Republic gave me) on the comparative sociology; we are coding some 100 pieces of information about each of 124 nation-states and territories. All states and dependencies in the world above 500,000 pop. This is forcing me to think thru the dimensions of "the big words" Democracy etc. in a way that is quite new to me, for I've never thought in terms of "isms" before at all. Political science, if you don't mind my saying so, is much fuller of richer shit than even sociology. This comparative thing is now all mixed up in my mind and in my files with the Marxian job . . . which is all to the good because today any job has to be comparative and I've neglected that badly, up to now. That's what's been blocking me from writing neat little essays, etc. Got to hold off that until I get it all straightened out.

Of course I'll do something for the *New Left Review* just as soon as I can do it in a worthwhile way; no I haven't gotten copy of one yet, but of course I've subscribed so it's probably on the way. The election does make it a different kind of venture, seen from over here at least.[86]

So all in all, I've worked like hell since returning from Rio— late Oct. I think it was. "Theses on Marxism" is now a 12 chapter draft, about ¾ roughed out, and about half of which will go into

---

84. The following year, when Mills sent out his complete preliminary manuscript for comments, it had about 50,000 words by Mills and about 150,000 words from the classics of Marxism. The plan at that time was to sell the book for $.50 or $.75 in an initial printing of 200,000 copies ("Dear Colleague" letter, dated April 28, 1961).

85. This project was not pursued.

86. The U.S. presidential election of November 1960. John F. Kennedy won against Richard M. Nixon, with a very slim margin of the popular vote.

the softcover job. I should finish that in Mexico, but Dell takes 10 months to publish! Ridiculous; they are all mad. Getting feverish again so better lie down awhile. Let me know what goes on, and again I am awfully glad the book comes along so well. Fuck 1960.

Mills

ॐ

To Harvey Swados, from Cuernavaca, Mexico, dated February 15, 1960

Dear Harvey,

Thanks much for the clipping of the book review—I missed it: I always like to see what they cut, the bastards.

Tomorrow I begin lectures—on the other side of the hill[87]— & will do so each Tuesday for 6 weeks. [. . .] The book on Marxism (including, of course, The Cuernavaca Themes) is coming along slowly—in part because no tape service as yet, & no typewriter even. But no matter.

Harold Rosenberg (head of something called Longview Foundation) sent me a check for $300, to pay me for printing "Decline of Left" essay in "little magazine" (*Contact 3*). [. . .] Am glad of the $300 because university here pays practically nothing.

CWM

Here is Yaro:

Planned a trip to Puebla yesterday but were "snowed out." Heard that roads were blocked by snow and Mexicans curious to see the stuff! [. . .] My [Spanish] vocabulary is growing—must be 20 words by now & I think I said my first grammatically correct long sentence yesterday! Will go into Mexico [City] with W. tomorrow and have a solo look around. We've not socialized here at all, but will look up your friends eventually.

Muchos kisses to all.
Yara

87. In Mexico City at the University of Mexico.

On the back of the aerogram to Harvey, Mills wrote:

address: care of Edith Hart/Casita Azul. [. . .] Good for 8 weeks or so. Have house in backyard of head of English school here—an old lady who's been here forever. In fact, 3 little houses, two baths & swimming pool, all walled in; of Mexico only this: "Mas cornodas da el hambre que los toros." (Hunger wounds worse than the bulls.)

Katie "matures" rapidly; now eats almost everything because we are people with strong stomachs who need much food to climb mountains well. Yaro "matures" rapidly, but in a curiously localized way.[88] Mills doesn't mature, but diets on hard-boiled eggs & beer.

[Yara filled the remaining space.]

Trip a huge success despite hectic start Actually had much fun driving. Katie [. . .] is enchanted now with our little garden filled with birds and flowers. Starts nursery school Monday. [. . .] We had 3 miserable days in Mexico City before deciding to explore Cuernavaca (our VW top slashed). Looked up "Trini" (nice stuff) and Palm mentioned school for Katie. Following his lead we found Mrs. Hart (ancient school teacher) who had this place—and we rented on the spot. Moved in yesterday. A million thanks for your excellent advice! [. . .]

Much love to all,
Yara

When Mills wrote the following letter to Ruth she was working as a statistician for the U.S. Census Bureau in Jeffersonville, Indiana; she had been working there since September 1958.[89]

88. Yara, who was pregnant with Nik at the time, added a footnote in the margin: "The tamales have awakened my little one!"

89. Ruth continued to work for the Census Bureau until she retired in 1978. The U.S. Department of Commerce awarded her the Silver Medal "For Meritorious Federal Service" for her work in the 1970 Census, and the Gold Medal "For Distinguished Achievement in the Federal Service" for her work related to the 1980 Census.

To Ruth Mills, from Universidad Nacional Autonoma de Mexico, dated March 13, 1960

Dear Ruth:

We've just returned from a several days trip to Oaxaca, and I have your letter of the 8th. You are correct in assuming that my last lecture is the 22nd of this month. The day after we shall begin driving back to New York. I am sorry the schedule was vague at 1st but my seminar was wedged between two semesters at the university and I could not know it exactly until I wrote to you.

[. . .] We have to stop in San Antonio for possibly two nights— as my father is quite weak, as you know, and it may be the last time I'll see him alive.[90] As soon as we arrive in NY, I'll of course let you know.

Katie is physically in great shape—brown from the sun and visibly growing. Morally she has come up against the fact of Mexico—which is poverty—and it has been a great experience for her. Her best friend is now Rosita, a housekeeper's daughter, with whom she plays all the time when not in school and loves dearly.

Mills

[P.S.] Enclosed is best picture K has done.

When Mills returned from Mexico and opened his mail he found a copy of The Power Elite *translated into Russian, along with an invitation to visit the USSR for twenty days. The Russian publisher offered to pay his expenses in Russia, as a form of compensation, but Mills had to pay his own fare to and from Moscow. He accepted the invitation and visited the Soviet Union for the first time, leaving in mid-April 1960[91] and traveling with Igor Alexandrov as his guide and translator in the USSR.*

To Tovarich, from Moscow, spring 1960

Up Closer

90. That was the last time Mills saw his father, but, as it turned out, the senior Mills outlived his son by more than a decade.

91. Letter to Gerth, dated April 3, 1960, and letter to Mr. Cameron at Knopf, dated April 5, 1960.

As you see from my dateline, Tovarich, now I am in your country—
and already I have a complaint: I haven't been able to find you—
or if we have met, I didn't know it. In Moscow, Tashkent, Leningrad,
Tbilisi, I have been talking with dozens of your colleagues, always
trying to find you, and often talking with them about you, although
none of them knew that.

Tonight, in my hotel, I have been going over the notes I have
made during all those talks, and every night too, often until early in
the morning. My trip began, I suppose, when I received a cable from
Lydia Kislova, Chief, American section of "The Soviet Society for
Friendship and Cultural Relations." Of course I came as soon as I
could.

Now, after three weeks here, I have at hand a mass of material:
I guess the interviews alone will run to over 300 pages of double-
spaced type. The question is: what am I going to do with all this?
Much of it, of course, is for special purposes: mainly for the book
I am doing on *The Marxians*—a sort of historical profile and critique;
from the young Marx to the present; and for a long-run comparative
study of the intelligentsia of a dozen or so different countries. Some
of it is "merely informational" and just now, at least, I don't have the
time to check it and write a "little book on Russia." This I wouldn't
want to do anyway. I have a great repulsion for all those books on
"My Soviet Trip" by twenty-one-day experts; I could never do such
a book.

∾

To Ralph Miliband, from West Nyack, dated June 22, 1960

Dear Ralph:

This is confidential and makes no requests of you, so relax please.
Chaos still prevails here, and each night I fall into exhaustion about
6 P.M. The *Nation* piece has indeed started on its little way.[92] They tell
me the volume of mail is very heavy at the magazine; and that just
now the *London Tribune* has cabled asking if they can run the piece. I
told them the *Tribune* would have to get it out of [Stuart] Hall; the

92. C. Wright Mills, "The Balance of Blame: Further Notes on the Strategic Causes of
World War Three," *The Nation* 190, no. 25 (18 June 1960): 523–31.

piece is already committed to NLR [*New Left Review*]. If Hall does
turn it over, as a kind of political act, of course, I'll try like hell to get
the Apathy piece fixed up as soon as I possibly can.[93] Anyway by the
time you get this, we'll probably know. I don't really care. And I don't
think the piece is very important for Britain; here I think it is, if I
may say so. The *NY Times* just phoned for an interview about the trip.
I refused to talk on the phone; let them come out if they want to talk
properly. But you see what I mean about the *Nation* piece over here.

Sunday Yaroslava gave birth to an 8 and a half pound man child,
who shall be named Nikolas. [. . .] We are both delighted, as is Katie.
[. . .] I've got to go now and do some errands on the way to the
hospital. But I'll continue this. I've a very important "career decision"
to make, about which I need your advice.

Back from hospital now. In the morning, after 3 days there, Y
and N come home. [. . .] Yaro is magnificently in love with him;
a real joy to see how radiant she is about Him. But [. . .] once and
for all: all, repeat, all infants if they are normal look very much alike.
[. . .] Yet it is true that the hands develop very fast; Nikolai, sorry
Nikolas, has hands exactly like my father's (and mine) and almost as
big! Real mitts he has. I hope he turns out to be an honest carpenter
or racing mechanic, if there are any decent cars left by the time he's
ten or twelve and can get next to a motor.

What I wanted to talk with you about, that is—please at this
point—just between you and me, is this: I'm thinking seriously
of resigning from all teaching, from Columbia. The decision involves
a lot of things, but above all it involves my need to write. To have
time to do nothing else. The money side of it I can now handle, not
lavishly certainly but I can meet all my obligations and live in a decent
way by writing. Besides I don't want to make a lot of money; it is
only a damned worry, with taxes and all. What I want to do is write.
If it were possible to give one big seminar a year, or perhaps every
other year at Columbia, then OK. I'm going to try—if I do anything—to set that up: a sort of half or third time load. We'll see.

Now there is no hurry, except I am in a hurry! [. . .] I've got
four, yes four books bubbling up inside me:

93. Perhaps a reference to *Out of Apathy,* ed. E. P. Thompson (London: Stevens and Sons,
1960). As it turned out, that anthology did not include an essay by Mills.

The Marxians, first: it is turning out fine, a neat little thing of 90,000 words or so; it'll be done by August or so.

Then a terrific idea, about which I may have talked with you, called now *Contacting the Enemy.* It is 10 fat letters—I'd estimate about 90,000 words, again, in all—to a Russian intellectual. Into this I weave the Russian and Polish diaries, but that is only about one-fifth of it; mostly it is about you and me, Tovarich, with an up-close tone and not a line of bullshit in it.

Then there's *The Cultural Apparatus,* waiting there in draft. Now it is a crude thing from which I steal for everything else; but Ralph there is a good book in that stuff, a good, heavy-duty, full-of-awe, but what's-it-all-about book.

Then there's *The Comparative Study:* a long-term thing, to be sure, but if I am to do any magnum opus, that must be it. (In fact, honestly, the stuff I've written so far, it really is dry-run stuff; I've never let loose; you must know that.)

Now I've got to have a drink; it's five thirty and I'm a creature of habit. Be back.

So why shouldn't I quit the philistine nonsense and write my guts out? Please assume I can make the money to live. Then, what do you see against just being Mills of Strawtown Road? Tell me, friend. And nose around on one more point: do you think I could get a year's pay out of some outfit in Britain? If I quit, I'd be free to live anywhere; royalties know no boundaries. [. . .] And don't think I'm drunk; I'm not, and even if I am I began this letter with the intention of writing this to you and I was stone sober. So now I'll go out across my little acre and put this in the mailbox for the mailman and not read it again. As Gide or somebody said to Cocteau or somebody: astound me! But I say: advise me, friend.

As ever,
Your Polish traveling companion,
Mills

He later decided not to resign from Columbia.

Mills's comments about his newborn son, Nikolas—and Nik's remarkable hands—were borne out in more ways than one. When Nik was about twelve years old (many years after his father's death), he began tinkering with motors, by his early twenties becoming proficient enough to completely rebuild several car engines. Trained in art and design, Nik Mills is a sculptor who works mainly in steel, specializing in furniture and outdoor sculpture. Nik's work is in the Permanent Collections of the Metropolitan Museum of Art and the Brooklyn Museum in New York and has been exhibited abroad in galleries and the Musée de Art Moderne in Paris.

To Tovarich, from West Nyack, New York, summer 1960

Specimen Days of My Life

Tovarich, I want to give you, as Walt Whitman once said, "some authentic glints, specimen-days of my life."[94] (But I can't, of course, do it as he did; I haven't the guts, much less the skill.) Anyway that's why I'm writing such personal letters to you; and that's why I hope you'll answer me in just the same way.

I. In My Study

My daily routines happen to be work routines—and I seem to have three of them, according to where I am: in my study, on the road, or at the university. In this letter I'll cover only the first; the others later, perhaps.

Nowadays I'm on sabbatical and so working at home in my study. Each morning I get up sometime between 5:00 and 6:30. After washing and dressing, I go down to make my own breakfast: a large glass of defrosted orange juice and two raw eggs, splashed into a Waring Blender and well mixed; and a quart-sized pot of expresso coffee, taken black. While the coffee is making, I go out to the road and get the *New York Times*. Then, with the paper and the coffee, I go up to my study. No one else in the house is up yet; the house, which I built last summer, is twenty-five miles from New York City, in Rockland County, on two acres beside a lake.

Usually it takes between twenty and forty minutes to read the paper, lying on the couch, marking it for clipping later. Sometimes I begin to write on the margins of the paper, spilling over onto one of the variously sized pads lying around. But at any rate, usually by 6:30 or at the latest 7:30 A.M. I am at my desk. These early morning hours

94. Whitman's *Specimen Days* was published in 1882.

are my best hours for writing, and I normally write until at least 1300 [1 P.M.], quite often until 1500 [3 P.M.].

My daughter [Katie], who is just now five years old, comes into the study around 8:30 or 9:00 A.M. to show me a picture she has drawn, and to show me her own beautiful self. This I do greatly enjoy seeing, and we talk for a few minutes about her day.

During the morning I do not take any phone calls (or at any other time if I can possibly avoid it). I don't like the telephone, and I consider it rude of people to phone without warning; it is much better to write.

Usually I don't take lunch, although sometimes I have a sandwich or a salad. By 1500 [3 P.M.] I am lying down reading the mail and current magazines; also, now I clip and file the *Times* I read early in the morning. I try to answer the mail at this time too—if possible, by jotting the answer on the letter received and mailing it back. For mail that requires a lengthier reply, I do a draft in pencil and try to dictate it, on my tape recorder, toward the end of the next morning. Apart from magazines and books, the mail consists of: *bills* (I give these to my wife); *requests* for articles or lectures (I try very hard to avoid these, managing to turn down most of them except during low financial periods); *comments* people are kind enough to send me about books or articles I have written (I try to respond to as many of these as I can); and *manuscripts* sent from New York City by the woman there who transcribes the tapes I mail her. (These I seize upon, proofreading fully and beginning to rewrite.)

Often though, I begin to write again in the afternoons, usually about 1630 [4:30 P.M.]. This is more likely to happen after I've had a drink—that comes between 1650 and 1750 [4:50 and 5:50 P.M.]. This writing usually consists of scribbles made while lying on the couch reading. Often it is a little wild, but sometimes the beginnings of a very good idea come about just then: often they come as an outline of a new essay, chapter, or book, or a new outline for a project under way. Often too, these "new outlines" turn out to be exactly like the old ones I am too lazy to get up and look for. But anyway, I let myself go, trying not to inhibit in any way the flow, if it should come. The several times I've thought of doing a novel have occurred to me at this perilous time of day. These late afternoon scribbles are the first thing I see at the desk the next morning, after finishing with the *Times*. About one half of them are then thrown in the wastebasket.

We have dinner about 1800 [6 P.M.]; then I read for a while to my daughter [Katie]; I read to her from books she cannot understand, for she hasn't the vocabulary. As I read, I must translate and explain in simpler language; it is a rewriting on sight I do for her. Most children's books I've been able to get are such infantile trash—usually about little animals. Some of that is all right, but I've found that children *like* more of the real thing, if they are only given it in some intelligent manner. Just now I am reading P. Yershov's *The Little Hump-backed Horse* [Moscow: Foreign Languages Publishing House] and Vera Panova's *Time Walked* [English translation of the Russian novel *Serioja*].[95] I tried Dickens recently but it was too hard to explain, so I'll wait a year or so. I exert myself to read to her as well as I can because she has quite a dramatic flair and I want to nourish it. She enjoys this period, I think, and I know that I do, even though I am usually quite tired. After she is asleep, I read books or periodicals in bed for an hour or so, usually falling asleep myself about 2100 [9 P.M.].

So that's my usual daily routine—when I am not at the university and not traveling. To keep the day just about as I've described it, that is my continual goal and my continual struggle. I do not want anything about it to be changed; if it is seriously interrupted, I am afraid I do become most irritable and unpleasant; I do not want anything to tear up its structure or the rhythm of work from day to day that it allows and encourages. Almost anything that upsets long stretches of such days I regard as unlawful interference into what I ought to be doing and what I most want to be doing. (Sometimes of course it just all goes to hell; the routine collapses, and lying on the couch all day I just read. Those are good days too. They usually happen only a few days out of every month.)

But, you may ask, isn't such a day, multiplied by 14,600 (that's forty years) a retreat from the world? Isn't it a defaulting of the political obligations of every man today to act? My answer, Tovarich, is flat no. It *is* political action. It is the most important action of which I am capable and which, just now, I can possibly imagine.

On many fronts, all at once, the world is now going to hell: true. But also it's now rising to human magnificence. Which is which? The

---

95. *Serioja*—the title cited in the English edition— is more commonly transliterated to English as *Seryozha*. This novel was written for adults; its main character is a child living with one biological parent, one stepparent, and one half-sibling, just as Katie was.

most important single nonroutine task in the world today is to try to define the realities of what may be going on, in terms of the ideals of Western civilization. We must confront the new facts of history making in our time, and we must seek their meanings for the problem of political responsibility. Last year, a friend of mine in Warsaw repeated to me what Marx said about philosophers not just interpreting the world but changing it. Then he added, "We must, just now, reverse that: the point is to interpret it." I understand why my Polish friend should say that just then, but I think it's true beyond those reasons. At any rate, even if I don't like it, it's true for me. If this— the politics of truth—is merely a holding action, so be it. If it is also a politics of desperation, so be it. To me it is the act of a free man who rejects "fate"; it is an affirmation of one's self as a moral and intellectual center of responsible decision.[96]

But maybe you have some much better ideas of what we— people like you and me—ought to do? We really ought to begin to carry on, as we say in America, the God-damnedest interchange that's ever been. Let's talk among ourselves about ourselves first, and then about the world. Tell me just how you live. Tell me all that you did yesterday. Come on, Tovarich, set up a new file.

II. At the University

Now that I've seen something of your universities, I feel it's even more important to tell you about my work routine at the university than I had thought it might be before I visited Russia.[97] I've been thinking about what universities mean to me, and perhaps to a nation as well. I'll first quickly run through my own work routines at the university. Then I'll tell you about how universities as a locale of freedom are used and abused.

When I am "in residence" at Columbia University, I usually drive into Manhattan on Mondays, Wednesdays, and Fridays. (It's 25 miles from my home.) Although I lecture only in the afternoons, I find that I cannot get down to work at home in the mornings on

96. The last three sentences of this paragraph and the last sentence of the preceding paragraph were excerpted or adapted from Mills's essay entitled "The Decline of the Left," *Listener* 61, no. 1566 (2 April 1959).

97. Mills visited the USSR for the first time in the spring of 1960. His second and last trip there was in the summer of 1961.

these days, knowing that I'm going to be interrupted by the trip, so I go into my office early, about 8:00 usually, to work there. I try to do everything connected with lectures and seminars on these mornings, and generally I manage that.

What do I teach? The truth is that, in one way or another, I teach about whatever I am writing at the time. Since that is usually two or three different topics, I have no trouble. I don't think I've ever given the same course more than once.

I no longer teach in the graduate school;[98] I had a little disagreement with some of the people over there several years ago, the result of which was that I withdrew into the college. Since then I've published a book, a few chapters of which are a kind of "Anti-Duhring" against one or two of the less fortunate views and habits of some of my colleagues, so I guess the split is more or less permanent. That's too bad, really, because more and more, for a number of intellectual reasons, I feel the need to be in touch with more advanced students, and some of them, I understand, wouldn't mind it.

The disagreement, by the way, had nothing directly to do with political questions, although I'm sure you'll agree that almost all academic quarrels have political implications and undertones, and of course personal ones as well. But directly, at least, it had to do with more technical matters—the scope and methods of social study, the whole question of what the social sciences are all about—and what we ought properly to make them be about. But I won't bore you with all of that. Along with this letter, if I ever find your address, I'm mailing you a copy of the book mentioned: *The Sociological Imagination.*[99]

I don't know how much this minor quarrel—and its results upon where I teach—is responsible for the fact that of late I don't enjoy teaching as much as I once did. What I'd really like to do is to be able to go on half-time at the university in order to spend more time on research and writing. I'd like to give one medium-sized seminar, say 15 students at most, each year or so, and possibly supervise three or four dissertations, and that's all. The main reason for this desire is that I become more and more overwhelmed by the materials and ideas

98. During most of Mills's time at Columbia, he did not teach in the graduate school.
99. This was eventually translated into seventeen languages.

that have accumulated over the years, and increasingly frustrated because I can't find the time to make the most of them.

You see, I work alone without any real assistants—capable assistants I could train and then count on for a year or two at a time. The university does not provide for such assistants—or even a secretary—in its regular budget. And the foundations have turned down my several requests for small research grants,[100] all except one: The Fund for the Republic, which doesn't have much money but generously gave me a little of it.

To a considerable extent, the U.S. university does provide a basis for a life that is pretty much outside the U.S. money trap. Of course, it is not really outside; the trap is merely less noticeable. Still it is an important fact that a college professor who is well located in a good school is a sort of salaried rentier. Although compared with other professions involving the same length of formal preparation, his income is often ridiculously low, it is also true that in many ways indeed he is freer than the men of those other professions. If he is an able man, he is very free to do something that very few men are free to do: he can work on what he wants to work on, and yet be secure financially, even if a little threadbare. He suffers during inflationary periods, comes out only slightly better during slumps, but in the leading institutions he definitely has security of tenure; he cannot be dismissed except under personal moral conditions that only a fool would open himself up to. The successful American college professor, make no mistakes about it, is a member of a privileged class.

I have written rather harshly at times about the academic life and the college professor. I have done so because I have loved that life, and because I do esteem many of my colleagues. Yet I do grow angry that some of them do not avail themselves of their marvelous intellectual opportunities. I do not speak here merely of doing a bad job of teaching, or just teaching and doing nothing else with the time left over from that. I refer to the lack of exercise of the freedom that is theirs. For freedom of thought, if it does not go on under such after-all ideal circumstances of leading American institutions of

100. Earlier in his career, Mills was not so frustrated in his requests for research grants. He received funds from the Social Science Research Council of Columbia University as well as the Guggenheim and Huntington Hartford Foundations for work on *White Collar* and *The Power Elite*.

higher learning, is a mere phrase. To be real it must be exercised, and to be of social importance to a nation, it must be exercised real hard and all the time. It won't wear out, you know, from too much use; but if it isn't used, it will dry up and blow away.

What I dislike most about some of my academic colleagues is how readily they seem to intimidate themselves; they coordinate themselves instead of acting and speaking as they really think and as they would like to do. Take the attacks on freedom of the early fifties—the McCarthy business which I'm sure you've heard about.[101] What should the universities have done when they first heard about that sort of thing? Or more specifically, what should the presidents of the 25 leading universities have done immediately upon hearing that the McCarthyites were going to look into their shops? (I write now from notes made at the time, which nobody would pay any attention to.)

In each of these universities, the president and the leading seven or eight professors should have come together to form a common front, a common policy, a coordinated plan, not a plan of defense but a plan of attack. Perhaps it might well have taken some such form as this: these universities should have relieved of teaching duties for a period of a month or so a dozen of their best sociological, legal, journalistic and—in this case—psychiatric people. An all-American team, these scholars should have quickly researched in great detail the McCarthyites involved, down to the days of their infanthood. As a committee they should have been given the funds to employ two or three ex-FBI men—and they are quite available here—in order to aid them in their investigations. From this research and detection work they should have drawn up a complete report on the men and their activities, a full dossier of character and career. They should have then prepared a series of press releases to be let out over a period of two weeks and focused upon 1) McCarthy's impeachment, if the evidence warranted that, and if it did not 2) the challenging of the man to a full-scale debate on a national hookup one hour each evening for four or five successive evenings. The presidents of the leading universities acting in unison along with leading staff members had

---

101. Mills was not asked to testify at the McCarthy hearings, but when a colleague, the historian William Appleman Williams, was subpoenaed, Mills worried that he would also be summoned (personal communication from Yaroslava Mills, 1997).

prestige and the power to do such things with very little trouble and very little expense. They could have placed their material in the key newspapers, on the national hookups, and in these ways practically have forced local news editors to pay attention to their copy. And if they hadn't, given radio, they would have still commanded an effective audience.

On McCarthy our reports should have been as firm and factual as we were capable of making them; if we of the universities are not capable of knowing what a fact is, who in the world is? The facts we should lay alongside the policies of the universities as centers of free inquiry and free speech. They should be presented, at first, in a straightforward and solemn way. Then after three or four days of that we should start getting downright comic. What should we have done about McCarthy? In one word we should have laughed at him. I know he wasn't very funny, not funny at all, but a deadly serious phenomenon. Still I say laugh at him. But laugh in a certain way and in certain places and for certain purposes. Laugh to reveal what he truly was: a ridiculous and silly little man, an opportunist without principles or brains. We should have dramatized the facts as revealing the most ridiculous and silly situations imaginable. We should have done this with intelligence and taste and discernment but we should have done it. In short, we should have stopped merely defending our civil liberties; we should have used them.

III. On the Road

The one unambiguous exception to the kind of working routines I've described comes when I am on the road. Over the past decade, I've found that for me at least it is best not to travel in a foreign country for more than about one month. (Of course I don't mean living there. That is something else; one then takes some work in progress.) After a month I've reached a saturation point; I've become too tired and the truth is that I get anxious about my work. I know that newspapers and magazines and books are piling up in my study and have to be gone through, marked and clipped. Of course I am working while traveling, keeping very detailed notes and interviews, but somehow that is different.

On occasion I do like to tour, by motorcycle if possible; otherwise by open automobile, but that is a form of sport; also I have done photographic tours, which are a very special kind of working travel; and at times, of course, travel can be a way of escape, a period of self-isolation and quiet reflection.

I detest the more formal greetings, dinners, and farewells in which one sometimes gets involved when abroad. I do not contact the US embassy, nor usually accept embassy invitations, if any. I don't travel in, say, Poland, to see Americans; I want to see Poles. In a short account of a journey to Poland and Yugoslavia which one eminent economist recently published, I had my elder daughter [Pamela] count the Americans and the Poles and the Yugoslavs with whom he talked; a large percentage of the people he visited for any length of time were Americans! How incurious he must be.

In a foreign country, or even in the United States, what I like best is to have a real job to do and to be doing it. A few lectures, perhaps—if necessary to help pay your way—but better a few real themes to study by means of a schedule of interviews and discussions. From the trips I've made in this way (beginning back in 1945 with research trip for a Senate Committee on Small Business), I have gotten so much that usually it takes a month or so, after getting home, for every week on the road just to get a first draft of it done.

On Interviewing

Apart from mere sightseeing, short visits to another country amount to a series of interviews one has with a small and highly selected number of its inhabitants. That is the major basis of one's "observation." The selection of these people is obviously of the first importance. In two visits to Poland and one tour of Yugoslavia, as well as in interviewing in the United States, Western Europe and Latin America, the rules I try to follow when on the road are, roughly and briefly, as follows:

1) Don't try to cover a great range of topics and of people. You cannot do it. Focus on one or two problems about which you've read a good deal. Next month in the Soviet bloc, for example, my topics are going to be: a) the position and role of the intelligentsia and changes in these respects since the death of Stalin; b) Marxist theory and changes in it since the death of Lenin; and c) an open-ended interest, which I can't yet focus well, on the collective and freedom.

2) Don't just converse at random, at least not all the time. Try to

raise the same or very similar questions with each person interviewed. If you don't do this, you can't very well make comparisons between their views.

3) Don't try to find out the frequency (among the intelligentsia, for example) with which some opinion or some type of person prevails. You can't do it. That requires a technique of sampling beyond the visitor's means. Try instead to find out the full range of opinion on each of your chosen topics of concern. Try to get an interview with at least one or two people who represent each type or each outlook that you come upon. But how do you do this?

4) First select someone who is known (from publication or from reliable informants) to represent one extreme of the range of opinion or of types being studied. Interview him, then ask him to refer you to someone else who might be able to give you an interesting or worthwhile view of the matter under discussion. He will generally refer you to someone rather similar to himself, but start interviews with someone who is known to represent an opposite view or type as well. Ask him also for a referral. Now follow up the chains of these referrals from both extremes of the range. Generally, after about six to eight interviews from either side, you will begin to get a great deal of repetition in your answers and the answers will become more "mixed" in the middle of the range of viewpoint. The chains of referral, in other words, will "meet." When this happens, you'll know that you've gotten about all you can from a short visit on that topic.

5) Sometimes it happens that the answers from everyone you interview are quite uniform. That can mean one of three things. a) Opinion on the point is official and everyone, regardless of their true belief, is putting out the same line. The only safeguards against this are skill in interviewing and playing off facts previously known by you against what the person is saying in the interview. b) You have not gotten hold of people who hold "extreme" views; you've not covered the range. In this case, all you can do is to try again to find the other end of the range of opinion. c) There really *is* uniformity on the point in question; the range is quite narrow. In that case, if you're sure, then you've made a finding, but be very careful about this point.

In the case of my topics for the Soviet bloc, one obvious scale is the Diehard Stalinists versus the New Beginners. The latter, in 1957 in Poland, for example, were easy to spot and to talk with. They'd had publicity in the non-Communist world and they were more likely to speak a western European language. The Stalinists were much more difficult for a stranger to find, and also less likely to open up, which made it all the more important that they be found and that they be interviewed well.

Writing on the Road

When one travels seriously, one is working very hard. This reminds me of the difficulties of finding places and times in which to write while on the road. Countries I've been in differ profoundly in this respect. I know it's a rather curious point of view, but I've come to judge a country somewhat on this score. Of course almost anywhere there is a hotel room, but sometimes I don't use hotels. In Europe during 1956 and 1957, for example, I traveled by motorcycle, camping out, and later in a small bus fitted out for sleeping. This was convenient and of course cheap; savings on even the cheaper hotels just about paid for the bus, which was more comfortable than most and much more convenient. I was therefore in need of a place to work several hours each morning, for I was working on several books and had deadlines to meet.

I have never been the kind of writer who requires certain conditions of work. I can work almost anywhere so long as I am fed and kept warm, but there are limits. I find it difficult to imagine a place less well-suited to serious and sustained work than the Latin Quarter of Paris, France. An essential lack of seriousness now marks at least the sidewalk scenes of Paris's Latin Quarter, as well as New York's Greenwich Village. In both one finds types of people who are not—but who wish to appear to be—intellectuals and artists. These semi-intellectuals have taken over: in the Latin Quarter students from abroad, many from the United States; in Greenwich Village, many from the means of distribution of mass culture— well-heeled advertising and promotion men and elaborately casual wives in ponytails.

In Paris there are many cafes with midget tables on the sidewalks and inside. But they are on streets that roar and whine with the bustle of cars and the zip and drone of scooters. They are crowded, like jam in a jar. I do not believe you could take out a notebook, put it on a table, and write. First, the noise, then the stares of everyone, at least in the localities I could find, make it seem impossible.

It is, I think, odd that the open terraces of those cafes on the German Autobahn are better than any place in Paris—during the summer of course. Often they are well placed, with views, and with the edge of the Autobahn traffic far enough away to avoid much noise.

For sidewalk cafes, go to Copenhagen; it is not usual to work there, but no one minds if you do work, and it is altogether pleasant. To work in a cafe in the wintertime, go to Yugoslavia or Austria; those are the places. In Yugoslavia, there are cafes of just the sort one thinks of as places for quiet talk and for work as well. In Zagreb and in Sarajevo there are huge rooms with big windows and *widely* spaced out tables with marble tops, newspapers from the capital cities, and quiet. Such places, no doubt, invite work in a semipublic locale, with just the right kind of stimulating interruptions of one's own choosing. In Salzburg there is the Cafe Mozart, where any waiter will protect you while you work. I wonder where I'll work in the Soviet Union. Are you civilized yet?

Mills kept the following brief statement in his Tovarich notebook, perhaps with the intention of integrating it into a longer essay at some point.

SELF-IMAGES AND AMBITIONS

Here is a summary which I am adding to this account in June of 1960.

I am a politician without a party, and within the American political context, without any talent for real politics, without opportunities to develop them, and with little inclination to do so. The political demands that I put upon myself are now more or less satisfied by writing.

I am a writer without any of the cultural background and without much of the verbal sensibilities of "the born writer"; accordingly I am someone who has worked for twenty years to try to overcome many deficiencies in the practice of my craft and yet remain true to whatever I am and how I got that way, and to the condition of the world as I see it.

I am a man who feels most truly alive only when working—

researching and writing—and who otherwise tends to become an irritable and unpleasant creature.

And I am an impersonal egoist; impersonal because of the craft I try to cultivate; egoist because my ambitions far outrun my capacities. My demands upon myself, in fact, are often downright silly and certainly have interfered and do interfere with my attempts to be "a decent human being." So I am a man who rejects that ideal if it is an ideal, or better yet, I am one who sets up for himself his own ideal of "human being."

To Hans Gerth, from West Nyack, dated July 15, 1960

Dear Gerth:

I have your long letter and your note, and want to let you know three things that you might be aware of: first, that despite my running around so much, I too, am very much isolated and alone; second, that over the last several months especially, I have been going thru a very deep and broad reconsideration of many ideas I have assumed up 'til now; specifically about the world scene and the place within it of the Soviet bloc and the United States; and third, that I take very seriously and will continue to do so whatever you have to say about it.

We must plan a bit about your visit, because I am going to Cuba sometime early in August for about two weeks, and might even be delayed a bit beyond that. I have to go and find out certain things for myself before I write what I feel the need to about the place. So I've arranged to be invited there by the foreign minister. His son, the UN delegate, tells me that Castro sat up in the Oriente reading and discussing with his band *The Power Elite!* My God, and this sort of thing is coming about more and more with that book, and some of the others too. Had a big talk the other day with a wonderful fellow from Yugoslavia, who asks me to come there and study the intelligentsia. Well, we'll see, but I must somehow relax a bit somehow, sometime, for I've been wound up and the words have been simply flowing out of me. I know it is ridiculous but I am actually at work on six books, all of them at least halfway written, and two almost ready for the printer. One pays a price for this sort of moral and psychic energy; I am sure I am not aware of the full price, intellectually I mean. And that is why

I need to talk with you. For although certainly we have not always
agreed and certainly I do not always think your judgment correct, still
you are—as you must know—one of the very few men whose judgment I respect in an active way: that is I won't act, won't publish,
without taking it very seriously into account. [. . .]

Next morning: had to break off letter yesterday; now it's 5:30 A.M.
and am beginning to work. Besides, no good writing letters like this.
Must talk. Just one comment on your letter, which I've earned the
right to say to you by what I wrote above: you . . . like me . . . tend
too readily to scatteration. That will surprise you: my saying that I tend
that way. But it's true. But Gerth you don't fight it enough. I fight
it like hell. I fight it with whiskey sometimes but most of the time I
fight it with work, overly systematic work maybe, but work. Read the
new Thomas Wolfe biography by Elizabeth Nowell.[102] Just out, first
rate. I've never really read Wolfe but my God that man is my brother.

I don't know how to end this except to say I get the impression
that you think it's bad all over. Correct. But not good enough. All
of them, they are murderers and the rest of it. Correct. But not yet
good enough. I think you know what you're doing: you're mixing
up terribly your personal tragedies with public affairs, history with
biography. Well, by God I am solving that; it is something you have
to keep on solving you know, and never let go of.

Please write me right away the date of the meeting and of your
trip here.[103] Will you bring family, etc.? I shan't attend the meetings,
or at least don't think so, but plan to stay out here. Will you drive east?

Yours,
Mills

∽

To Ralph Miliband, from West Nyack, New York, dated July 18, 1960

Dear Ralph:

You are such a funny man! Of course you are going to Moscow. Be
an idiot not to. Go this summer: it will help the book.[104] Make it

---

102. *Thomas Wolfe: A Biography* (New York: Doubleday, 1960).
103. The meeting was a sociology convention to be held in New York in September 1960.
104. *Parliamentary Socialism: A Study in the Politics of Labour* (London: George Allen and

help: never lose anything. No matter who or what invited you to Russia, you will have, the second day you're there, a meeting at which you'll be able to tell them what you want. *Before* that meeting if possible, get them to take you to the Soviet Friendship Societies, Kalinin Street 14, Moscow, and see my pal Igor Alexandrov there:[105] give him my best, and tell him you and I are close friends and went to Poland together, etc. Tell him who invited you and that this is what you want to do: focus upon one or two themes and not run all over the place just sight seeing: your themes are of course: Trade Unions in the Soviet Union . . . all about them, then maybe one or at most two additional themes. Don't try to do more. Tell him by the way about our evening's talk in London (he'll like that: it's his business). Then be firm with your hosts, and get them to line up a series of interviews with appropriate people for your themes: don't let them have you talk with more than 3 at most at a time. Tell Alexandrov that and he'll phone for you and make it clear.

The trade union stuff you pick up there you will not of course use in any direct way in your book. But no matter how horrible or how wonderful Soviet Trade Unions turn out to be, it will be most helpful; there is nothing, repeat nothing, so powerful as *comparative* stuff. And here's the chance to get some of it, don't you see? Please do let me know all about the setup as soon as it's fixed. I give you no more names because Alexandrov is truly all you need and he's back from vacation now. I seem to have worn him out and he was given a month's vacation!

As for me: I work. The Soviet Diary came to 300 typed pages.[106] Cuba [*Listen, Yankee*] is almost one-fourth drafted, all I can do here: just the clips and books available: all that is done with; now I've got my questions ready for them. "The Marxians: Thinkers & Politicians" is about 85% done now. Looking quite neat, on the whole. Still got a mess with "the second revisionists": they really haven't done anything, you know. Really nothing at all. Sent a day ago, or

---

Unwin, 1961). Miliband did not visit the Soviet Union while working on that book, but he did go there in the spring of 1961.

105. The guide who had been assigned to facilitate interviews and make other arrangements during Mills's visit.

106. An unpublished manuscript, also entitled "On Observing the Russians," which consists mainly of transcripts from Mills's interviews in the Soviet Union in April 1960.

so, the thing for the NL.[107] Hope they like it. Hope you do. Tried to do a bit with these "students" towards the end of it. Let me know if you see it around. I rather think the ending is the nuts, but it could be . . . just corn.

Yours as ever,
M
Wright

Mills's "Letter to the New Left" became one of his most well-known essays. The following are his concluding paragraphs for its publication in the British journal New Left Review, *which he discussed above:*

In the Soviet bloc, who is it that has been breaking out of apathy? It has been students and young professors and writers; it has been the young intelligentsia of Poland and Hungary, and of Russia too. Never mind that they've not won; never mind that there are other social and moral types among them. [. . .] We've got to study these new generations of intellectuals around the world as real live agencies of historic change. Forget Victorian Marxism, except whenever you need it; and read Lenin again (be careful)—Rosa Luxembourg, too.

"But it's just some kind of moral upsurge, isn't it?" Correct. But under it: no apathy. Much of it is direct non-violent action, and it seems to be working, here and there. Now we must learn from their practice and work out with them new forms of action.

"But it's all so ambiguous. Turkey, for instance. Cuba, for instance." Of course it is; history-making is always ambiguous; wait a bit; in the meantime, *help* them to focus their moral upsurge in less ambiguous political ways; work out with them the ideologies, the strategies, the theories that will help them consolidate their efforts: new theories of structural changes of and by human societies in our epoch.

"But it's utopian, after all, isn't it?" No—not in the sense you mean. Whatever else it may be, it's not that: tell it to the students in Japan.

Isn't all this, isn't it something of what we are trying to mean by

107. "Letter to the New Left," *New Left Review* 5 (September–October 1960): 18–23.

the phrase, "The New Left?" Let the old men ask sourly, "Out of Apathy—into what?" The Age of Complacency is ending. Let the old women complain wisely about "the end of ideology." We are beginning to move again.

Yours truly,
C. Wright Mills

When "Letter to the New Left" was reprinted in slightly different form in the American journal Studies on the Left, *Mills dropped the last paragraph.*[108]

108. "On the New Left," *Studies on the Left,* 1, no. 4 (1961): 72.

VI

THE LAST TWO YEARS
New York and Cuba, 1960–1962

Anybody who is "non-communist left"
today and goes into the hungry nation bloc,
he's got one hell of a set of problems.

> C. Wright Mills, letter to
> E. P. Thompson, late 1960

During his last two years Mills worked at home, visited Cuba, and traveled in Europe and the Soviet Union. He and his wife, Yaroslava, and his two younger children lived for a month in Switzerland and several months in England before returning to New York. He completed work on two mass-market paperbacks (Listen, Yankee: The Revolution in Cuba *and* The Marxists) *and wrote articles for left-wing journals as well as mainstream magazines.*

In August of 1960, Mills spent two weeks in Cuba, doing research for Listen, Yankee, *which was written in the style of a letter from a Cuban revolutionary attempting to communicate with his United States neighbors about Cuban life under Batista, the ill effects of U.S. policies toward Cuba, and the accomplishments of Castro's revolution—especially in the areas of education and health care.*

Mills's visit to Cuba was a pivotal experience for him. He explained its background this way:

> *Until the summer of 1960, I had never been in Cuba nor even thought about it much. In fact, the previous fall, when I was in Brazil, and in the spring of 1960, when I was in Mexico for several months, I was embarrassed not to have any firm attitude towards the Cuban revolution. For in both Rio de Janeiro and Mexico City, Cuba was of course a major topic of discussion.[1] But I did not know what was happening there, much less what I might think about it, and I was then busy with other studies.*
>
> *In the late spring of 1960, when I decided "to look into Cuba," I first read everything I could find and summarized it: partly in the form of questions to which I could find no answers in print. With these questions, and a few ideas on how to go about getting answers to them, I went to Cuba.[2]*

Mills interviewed journalists, soldiers, intellectuals, government officials, and citizens in Cuba; he spent three and a half eighteen-hour days interviewing and touring with Prime Minister Fidel Castro (using a wire recorder) and interviewing most

---

1. Fidel Castro had come to power in January 1959, after leading the revolution that ousted Batista.

2. *Listen, Yankee: The Revolution in Cuba* (New York: Ballantine Books, 1960), 9.

*of the other leaders of the young revolutionary government of Cuba, including Che
Guevara, who was then president of the National Bank of Cuba. Castro told Mills
that he had studied* The Power Elite *during his guerrilla war period (1957–58).[3]*

*When Mills returned home he completed the manuscript in an intense six weeks
of working day and night. He wrote, "My major aim in this book is to present the
voice of the Cuban revolutionary, as clearly and as emphatically as I can, and I have
taken up this aim because of its absurd absence from the news of Cuba available in
the United States today."[4]*

In December of 1960, Harper's Magazine *made Mills's piece criticizing U.S.
policy toward Cuba the cover story; the article was adapted from the book and was
entitled "Listen, Yankee: The Cuban Case against the United States." The FBI
clipped that article and included it in its entirety in the Bureau's file on Mills.*

*In April of 1960, a few months before Mills wrote the following piece, one of the first
civil rights bills in a century passed in the U.S. Senate (despite a Southern filibuster),
but the resulting bill concerning voting rights was so encumbered by federal procedures
for enforcement that the small gains were nullified.[5]*

To Tovarich, from West Nyack, New York, summer 1960

ON RACE AND RELIGION

> Listen! I will be honest with you,
> I do not offer the old smooth prizes,
>   but offer rough new prizes.
>
>   Walt Whitman, from
>   "Song of the Open Road"

Tovarich, every now and then I have to go to the local hospital,
a baby has been born or something. There I see on every wall those
heroically gentle pictures of Jesus Christ—just like the heroic and
not gentle pictures of Lenin on the walls of offices in your country.

---

3. Notation from Saul Landau to K. Mills, April 1998.

4. *Listen, Yankee*, 8.

5. William Miller, *A New History of the United States* (New York: Dell Publishing, 1958,
1962, 1968), 462. Also Gorton Carruth, *What Happened When: A Chronology of Life and Events
in America* (New York: Penguin Books, 1991), 891.

I think it's horrible—in both cases. Still, here it is much better; the Catholics have got only a little piece of this territory, and they haven't got me.

Don't misunderstand me; I know what I am talking about; I was an Irish altar boy before I reached the age of consent, and Tovarich, I never revolted from it; I never had to. For some reason, it never took. It was all a bit too tangible and bloody. Then too, my father was a Catholic only for my mother's sake—and although he was not an educated man, he was and is the most honest man I have ever known. Early on I got the idea he didn't believe in it. He never said so; all he said was, "I just don't know, son, I really don't." He was puzzled and his puzzlement was enough for me; it never took.

The same sort of thing happened on "the racial business." My mother spoke Spanish before English; she was brought up on a ranch by Mexicans and she truly loved them—not like a gringo lady, but as one human being loves another. For her, I think, Mexicans have always formed her ideal images of The Human Being. And I got that from her.

I wasn't really aware of any differences between Jews and Gentiles and Mexicans and Irishmen and Negroes until I was well into my teens. Then it came as a shock to me, and I instantly rejected the idea of racial superiority and inferiority. In fact, maybe I did that a little too instantly. I was driving a truck that summer—I was under twenty—hauling collapsible houses in the East Texas oil fields. I came to the lumberyard where I was to be loaded; two Negroes started to load my truck and I jumped out to help them. A white man came up and hit one of them on the head with a two-by-four. "Don't you be getting that white boy to work alongside you, you black bastard," he said. The other Negro ran; the one hit lay on the ground, blood on his scalp; I was up on the tail of the truck when it happened; I did not think, I just jumped, booted feet first, into the silly man's face. I think he must have been drunk; otherwise it might have ended differently—he was quite large. As it was, he stayed down, and I got out of there with the hit Negro groaning on the passenger seat, holding his head in both hands.

I have never forgotten the blood on that man's head, nor regretted in the slightest trying to kill the white man. Oh yes, Tovarich, that is what I was trying to do. As I've said, I was well under twenty at the time. It may be that this little incident has meant much more to me than I have known. It may be why I cannot feel myself a pacifist. Intellectually and morally, I am of course persuaded; but in my hands and in my heart, I know that I am not a pacifist. Anyway, I got out of there.

The point is I have never been interested in what is called "the Negro problem." Perhaps I should have been and should be now. The truth is, I've never looked into it as a researcher. I have a feeling that if I did it would turn out to be "a white problem" and I've got enough of those on my hands just now.

But that isn't quite good enough, is it? The only answer—I didn't say practical program, feasible plan, etc., I said the answer—is so obvious that it has no intellectual interest, and so in the long-term, as matters now stand, it has no political interest. The answer, of course, is full and complete marriage between members of all races.

Immediately I hear the Southern voices from my late adolescence, drawling, as if to clinch the point once and forever: "You'd want your daughter to marry a Nigger?"

Well, it so happens I have a daughter [Pamela] who is seventeen. If she came to me and said, "I am going to marry so-and-so; he is black"—or brown, or yellow, or red, or pink—"I'm for him and he's for me," I would immediately say three things to her:

1) "You've thought about it—you really are for this boy?"
2) "Then name the first one after me."
3) "How can I help you both get set up outside the USA?"[6]

Number three I think would be wisest, if they wanted to do anything with their lives other than fight racial silliness. Of course, that's a good thing to do with your life, but I'd want them to realize fully that *is* what they'd be choosing. I know that the "Negro in America" has made Great Progress, etc., etc. That's all true. Yet still, as of now, the US of A is a white tyranny. It will remain so until there is no distinction whatsoever drawn in marriages between the races.

Now I have a question for you, Tovarich. Why haven't you

6. As it turned out, Pamela married a Brazilian of Russian and Romanian Jewish parents, named their first son Carlos, the Portuguese equivalent of Charles, in honor of her father, and settled in Rio de Janeiro, Brazil.

answered me? Perhaps you are not used to speaking concretely about your real feelings and beliefs, certainly not to strangers and out-landers. Nowadays many people, including me, don't ordinarily do this. I have never before written as I have written to you.

In a sense, Mills's fierce opposition to racism in the South mirrored his defense of the nascent Cuban revolution. Later he reminded his mother of her fondness for the Mexican culture and told her, "The Cubans are my Mexicans."[7]

To Fidel Castro, from West Nyack, New York, dated September 20, 1960

Dear Dr. Castro:

When I was in Cuba last month, Dr. Franz Stettmeier of the University of Oriente asked me to try to get some young professors for him, to teach there and possibly to work with INRA.[8] I have now found one such man and wish to recommend him as strongly as I am able. I have written to Dr. Stettmeier about him but am following that up with this note to you, a copy of which goes to Dr. Stettmeier.

1: The man's name is Edward Thompson; he is an Englishman who now teaches, I believe, at the University of Hull. Address: Holly Bank, Whitegate, Halifax, York, England. If you spent ten minutes with him you would see at once that he is a real thinker. He is, in fact, one of the most brilliant young men of Great Britain. He can teach political theory or sociology of English literature or—given a month or so—anything that needs to be taught. Until the Hungarian affair, he was, I understand, a member of the Communist Party of Great Britain, but now has no political affiliation. He is an editor of the *New Left Review,* a magazine in Britain for which I write. If you should approve "The Cuban Seminar on Varieties of Marxism," about which I am writing to you separately, I'd certainly be glad if Thompson were in it. For there is no nonsense in this man about Communism or anti-Communism. He is an honest observer and straight thinker.

7. See letter on p. 331.
8. Instituto Nacional de Reforma Agraria (National Institute of Agrarian Reform).

2: I write to you about him because it occurs to me that Dr. Stettmeier may run into practical difficulties in getting him. Mr. Thompson is very poor, his wife, Dorothy—who could also teach in the university—would of course come to Cuba with him, and they have two or three children. Their transportation to Cuba would have to be advanced to them in some way. I have found out that he is willing, indeed, eager to take up some work in Cuba.

What else can I say? Do try to get this man.

Sincerely yours,
C. Wright Mills
Professor of Sociology
Columbia University
copy to Edward Thompson

E. P. Thompson and Dorothy Thompson did not receive an invitation to teach in Cuba, much to their disappointment. They understood from two sources that the reason they were not invited was that someone had told the Cubans that Edward Thompson was not politically reliable.[9]

Somehow the FBI obtained a copy of the manuscript for Listen, Yankee prior to its publication.[10] Although the FBI's review of the book's political content was negative, an informant's assessment of its literary merit was actually favorable, which was one reason the Bureau was dismayed at the prospect of its publication. An FBI agent wrote that on October 24, 1960, the informant described his reactions to the manuscript for the book and concluded that as it was "such an artfully written piece of pro-Castro and pro-Communist propaganda, handled in a competent manner and easily readable style, it is highly likely to become a factor in disarming and confusing public opinion in this country. . . . It asserts that the regime in Cuba is not Communist as widely believed here." In a "Note to the Reader" in Listen, Yankee, Mills wrote: "The Cuban revolutionary is a new and distinct type of left-wing thinker and actor. He is neither capitalist nor Communist. He is socialist in a manner, I believe, both practical and humane. And if Cuba is let alone, I believe that Cubans have a good chance to keep the socialist society they are building practical and humane. If Cubans are properly helped—economically, technically, and culturally—I

9. Letter from Dorothy Thompson to K. Mills, dated September 23, 1997.
10. In November 1960.

believe they would have a very *good chance." Mills also wrote that he didn't condone Castro's "virtually absolute power," but that that political situation could, with proper support, be a passing phase. Mills wrote that he believed there was a* chance *that Cuba could develop a society that was both economically just and "politically fluent and free."*[11]

According to the FBI report, the Bureau agent approached Ian Ballantine (the publisher of the book) and attempted to convince him to solicit proposals from other writers who would refute the arguments Mills presented in Listen, Yankee. *Judging from the report, Ian (whose aunt was Emma Goldman) handled the situation with great diplomacy: he told the agent that the FBI would be able to pursue such a project in a more sophisticated and effective way than he could himself, and he asked them to please inform him if they found someone for the task.*

The following letter is addressed to Carlos Fuentes, the internationally recognized Mexican writer, who was in his early thirties at the time. Mills mentions his upcoming debate with A. A. Berle Jr., whom Mills had quoted and argued against within the text of Listen, Yankee. *(And in 1956 Berle had argued against Mills's* The Power Elite *in a review in the* New York Times Book Review.*)*[12]

To Carlos Fuentes, from West Nyack, New York, dated October 19, 1960

Dear Carlos:

Thank you so much for your letter of 15 October; with it came a note from Senor Orfila;[13] I have passed it on to my agent here, who is handling the translations [of *Listen, Yankee*]. I am delighted that Gonzalez and wife would do the job if the Fondo brought it out, and it is exactly a large paperback in cheap edition that I want. I've asked my agent, Brandt and Brandt [. . .] to set it up with Fondo, if they want it.[14] But I write to you to tell you this:

If they do it, they ought to do it very fast; they ought to make

11. *Listen, Yankee,* 181–83, 188–89.

12. "Are the Blind Leading the Blind?" *New York Times Book Review* (22 April 1956): 3, 22.

13. Arnaldo Orfila Reynal, of the Mexican publishing house Fondo de Cultura Economica.

14. Fondo de Cultura Economica did publish the Mexican edition of *Listen, Yankee,* translated by Julieta Campos and Enrique Gonzalez Pedrero.

ready now to get it right out. Second, they must realize that I do not know the Cuban government's attitude towards the book, especially my candid handling of Communism. It's touch and go on that issue inside Cuba. Of course the book is a strong pro-revolution statement.

In the US the following is going on about the book: First, a chapter from it will appear in the December *Harper's* (circulation about 450,000). Second, McGraw-Hill will bring out a hardcover edition. (They are the biggest publishing combine up here.) Third, at the same time, Ballantine Books will bring out a paperbound copy at 50 cents each . . . first printing 160,000 copies. Fourth, on December 10th at 9:30 P.M., Saturday night, I debate for one hour with A. A. Berle Jr. (former ambassador to Brazil) on the full NBC network (20 million viewers). So what started out as a little 60,000 word pamphlet is becoming a big thing, or at any rate so we hope. God knows what will happen, given the monolithic anti-Castro press and opinion in the USA. It is going to be fascinating to see.

Maybe you'll want to let Orfila know all this. I'm not writing to him; my agent is. In about one week, we'll have final page proofs from which translations will be made. Copy will go to Fondo.

Your novel hasn't come yet, but you may be sure I'll get it and read it with attention.

Also I am in touch with *Evergreen Review,* and when they get to me an English draft we'll edit it a bit and let them have it.[15] [. . .]

Salut,
W. M.
Wright Mills

Mills wrote the next letter in response to Frank Freidel's comments about Listen, Yankee. Freidel had said he thought the book would have been more effective if it had been written in Mills's voice instead of the voice of a Cuban revolutionary. Freidel had also commented that Mills didn't acknowledge the Cuban revolution's "excesses and unpleasantness."

15. Published as "C. Wright Mills on Latin America, the Left, and the U.S.: An Interview with Victor Flores Olea, Enrique Gonzales Pedrero, Carlos Fuentes, and Jaime Garcia Terres in Mexico City," *Evergreen Review* 5, no. 16 (January–February 1961).

To Frank Freidel, from West Nyack, New York, dated October 31, 1960

Dear Frank:

Thanks a lot for the quote and for the comment. You may be right about "the choice of voice"—it just wrote itself that way (and I wanted to see if I could write it that way!). In the final manuscript, now in press, I have added a lengthy essay, in my own voice, about "Cuba, Latin America and the USA." I am hopeful the final version of this will help to meet your objection.

Please know that I too see a lot of "unpleasantness" in the Cuban possibilities—but most of them, I think are being brought on by US action and inaction. And that's the point for us, isn't it?

Yours as ever,
Wright
C. *Wright Mills*

∾

To James Meisel, from West Nyack, New York, dated November 24, 1960

Dear James Meisel:

Many thanks for your kind note about the books. Kind notes don't come my way often these days! I'm in the middle of this fight over Cuba and have just published a little book, *Listen Yankee: The Revolution in Cuba,* which no doubt is in for much clobbering. Well, no matter. One does what one must, and takes the consequences.

Again, many thanks,
Wright M.
Wright Mills

According to an FBI memo, dated November 29, 1960, Mills had recently received an anonymous letter from someone who warned that, in the words of the FBI, "an American agent disguised as a South American would assassinate him on his next visit to Cuba." The FBI report went on to say that "Mills indicated he would not be surprised if this were true since he does not doubt that the Federal Bureau of In-

vestigation and other similar United States organizations do not approve of his activities. Mills has made several inquiries in regard to purchasing a gun for self-protection." The paragraph immediately following this statement in the FBI report was blacked out by the FBI.

Saul Landau remembers Mills discussing the warning, and Mills's worry that he might be attacked in his home. Mills told Saul not to tell Yaroslava about the warning, because he did not want to alarm her. In 1961 Mills made it clear to friends that he was concerned for his safety; he showed a pistol he kept by his bedside to Dan Wakefield and another friend and former student, Walter Klink.

The following is an excerpt from a letter from Mills to E. P. Thompson, written in late 1960, as it was quoted by Thompson is his essay "Remembering C. Wright Mills" in the British edition of The Heavy Dancers.[16] *(The complete letter is no longer available, so we were unable to include it in this collection.)*

To E. P. Thompson, from West Nyack, New York, fall 1960

"I've been running since last February, when I first went to Mexico, then Russia, then Cuba. Too much fast writing, too many decisions of moral and intellectual type, made too fast, on too little evidence. Anybody who is 'non-communist left' today and goes into the hungry nation bloc, he's got one hell of a set of problems . . . Now it looks like I debate A. A. Berle . . . in early December on NBC national TV hook-up (9:30 Sat. night, est. audience 20 million) on 'U.S. policy towards Latin America.' I have to do it: it's my god damned duty, because nobody else will stand up and say shit outloud, but . . . I know little of Latin American and have no help to get me ready for such a thing. But I have to. Then the pressure on me because of Cuba, official and unofficial, is mounting. It is very subtle and very fascinating. But also worrisome and harassing. I want to escape to reality, I want to escape to my study, I want 6 months to think and not to have to talk or write."

In a letter to Hans Gerth, dated October 13, 1960, Mills had expressed similar sentiments: "Forgive my haste but I am under quite some pressure because of the Cuba

16. (London: Merlin Press, 1985), 268–69.

book, from all sides, official and unofficial, Yankee and Cuban. The truth is I am on the edge of exhaustion from it."

Saul Landau was in touch with Mills during Mills's preparation for the televised debate. Landau later wrote of Mills during this time, "He was the only radical with a national reputation and a clean record (no Red connections). He was burdened by this responsibility; he worked harder as the debate neared. By early December his preparation was complete. He had enough material to write a definitive work on modern Latin America."[17]

The night before the television debate with A. A. Berle Jr.—or perhaps two nights before—Mills was at home watching The Wizard of Oz with Katie on his recently acquired first television set when he felt ill; he walked across the room and halfway upstairs before he had to stop and sit down, suffering from a severe heart attack.

Congressman Porter took Mills's place in the debate and Mills spent four days in an oxygen tent in a coma. While he was unconscious, Columbia University asked Yaroslava for permission to assign a heart specialist to give a second opinion about the treatment Mills was receiving; the specialist hired by Columbia approved of the care given by Mills's physician. Although at one point during this period the hospital staff believed that Mills was about to die, he survived. After a two-week stay, he checked himself out of the hospital against medical advice, preferring to convalesce at home.[18]

After this heart attack, Mills's doctor informed him that there were two scars on his heart and that, if he had another heart attack, he probably would die. The doctor urged him to try to avoid stress. "That's like telling me to avoid eating or breathing," Mills joked.[19]

For the first time in Mills's life, he knew there was a good chance he would not live for many more years. For the remaining fifteen months of his life, the state of his health was an issue for him; in the past he had usually ignored his hypertension, or "heart nonsense" as he called it. Although he recovered enough to live and work quite actively, he did not recover all of his former strength and energy.

Several weeks after Mills's heart attack, a lawsuit was brought against him, Ballantine Books, and McGraw-Hill Book Company, alleging defamation of character and libel in a passage of Listen, Yankee: The Revolution in Cuba. The plaintiffs objected to Mills's description of their business activities in Cuba under Batista. Mills mentioned no names in his description of a financial empire allegedly

17. Saul Landau, "C. Wright Mills: The Last Six Months," *Ramparts* (August 1965): 47.
18. Personal communication from Yaroslava to K. Mills, September 14, 1997.
19. Notation from Saul Landau to K. Mills, April 1998.

involved in drug dealing and other illegal activities. According to the FBI report, the complaint sought a total judgment of $25 million.

The FBI report also mentioned that in February of 1961 a person whom the House Un-American Activities Committee identified as an active member of the Fair Play for Cuba Committee had applied for a passport to Cuba in order to gather facts and documents on behalf of Mills and his publishers for their defense in the court action. The U.S. Passport Office refused to grant permission for the trip.

On January 11, 1961, FBI agents watched Mills's home as Igor Aleksandrov, from the Union of Soviet Societies for Friendship and Cultural Relations with Foreign Countries, and a companion, visited from 11:01 A.M. to 2:04 P.M. The next day, Mills wrote the following note to Carlos Fuentes, in which he referred to a letter to the editor (which appeared in the January 21, 1961, issue of the Saturday Review*) written by Carlos Fuentes, Enrique Gonzales Pedrero, Arnaldo Orfila Reynal, Pablo Gonzalez Casanova, and four other Mexican writers and intellectuals, who strongly defended Mills and his book* Listen, Yankee *in response to an extremely negative review by the journalist Jules Dubois.*

To Senor Carlos Fuentes, from West Nyack, New York, dated January 12, 1961

Dear Carlos:

Forgive the brevity of this note which I am dictating; this is the first time they have let me write to anyone. Know how very grateful I am to all of you in Mexico for the wonderful letter you sent to the *Saturday Review,* and please convey my greetings to all.

I write to tell you that the editor of *Harper's Magazine* wants to consider an article by you on "The Intellectual Climate of Latin America." This might well be a real chance to get over to the half million readers of *Harper's* what Latin America looks like from the standpoint of our New Left. May I suggest the following: write a letter addressed to Mr. John Fischer, Harper & Brothers [. . .] outlining in about a page or so what you think should go into a 5,000–6,000 word article on this subject. Don't pull any punches. Mail a copy of this to me and another copy to my agent, who is handling the whole deal. His name is Carl Brandt, of Brandt & Brandt. [. . .][20]

By the way, Carl should be your agent for all sorts of things up

20. Mills supplied the addresses of Harper and Brothers and Brandt and Brandt.

here because I think that at just this point all kinds of Mexican writers, as well as writers from other Latin American countries (at least outside Cuba!) can find an audience.[21]

Venceremos![22]
Wright
Wright Mills

P.S. I hope that Orfila will send copies of the Spanish edition of *Listen, Yankee* to various U.N. people from Latin America.

ॐ

To Ralph Miliband, from West Nyack, New York, dated January 25, 1961

Dear Ralph:

Forgive my long delay in responding to your letters, but this is the first day they've allowed me to use [the] typewriter; Yaro has had so much to do that I've not wanted to dictate letters to her; and to get a secretary of some sort is just too much trouble. Besides weather here has been fearful so people can't move about much with ease in suburbs.

I seem to remember that your brother-in-law or someone like that is a medical man, yes? So he can tell you as much as I once he knows the following: in mid December what hit me is known as a myocardial infarction (death of heart muscle). I suppose it was close; anyway shock and all that for a couple of days. Studies of my cardiograms, however, reveal that I must have had one previous attack which definitely caused some injury to the heart . . . possibly in Copenhagen in 56 or Austria in fall of 57. [. . .]

The physical outlook then is about like this: I've two scars on the heart, the old one and the new and more serious one that is now healing. It would be best not to pick up a third. Everything goes as expected. I can now handle the stairs in the house if I take them slowly, but not allowed of course to drive a car yet. [. . .] In two months or so, I should be quite O.K. physically: I'm not ever going to be a track star; probably can't really get into any revolutionary

21. Carlos Fuentes followed up on this advice, and Carl Brandt became his agent.
22. "We will win" or "we shall overcome."

action in anybody's mountains, but with a little carefulness, on the physical side, I shouldn't be handicapped much at all. But of course that's only medicine, which is about living and dying, not about *how* one might live, or even must live. That's well beyond medicine and well into one's own morality.

What we do not know as yet is how much intellectual and moral tension I can stand without the silly heart blistering out again (think of it physically as like an inner tube of a tire). I could of course, to take the extremes: ONE, set up as a very scholarly boy, write and think and act narrowly with reference to, say, the society of knowledge or any number of quite useful things to study which could be studied in a scholarly and apolitical manner. The other extreme is that, for instance, Fidel keeps cabling me to come on down and convalesce in Cuba, and my friend Vallejo . . . a medical man of real ability, as well as head of INRA in the Oriente, says that just to step on the island will cure me! and that he has some things to talk over anyway! That's TWO. Of course I'll not take either one, not just yet at least, and will try over long run to become more deliberate and even-paced in work, less frenzied. In short, I can still go hunting with Tito, but I really must allow 6 months rather than 3 weeks to complete the book about it.

So we don't have to talk any more about this other than one point that bothers me greatly: I'm afraid there is going to come about a very bad time in my country for people who think as I do; and there is some reason to expect that I personally am in for quite a time. What bothers me is whether or not the damned heart will stand up to what must then be done, by way of writing and lecturing and debating. I won't here go into the reasons for my thinking I'm "going to be in for it."

In a week or so, a friend who's also a publisher and one of the best editors I know, name of Dick Fisher, will try to get into touch with you in London. Do see him. [. . .] Dick has been the editor etc. of *The Marxians*. (Alas! Delayed a bit now.) Trust him and know that his word about US publishing is also well worth listening to.

I'm delighted that you may well go to the USSR in late March, except please do keep me closely informed about dates of any trips from England you take. Point is: I am probably going to come to Europe some time in late spring. [. . .] I do not yet know. Depends in part upon [my] condition and in part upon things out of my hands at the moment. Also money. I am not teaching this spring of course and do not yet know if Columbia will pay my salary for the semester or not. I have no "hospitalization" or such insurance (which anyway is a racket) and my first week (in a local suburban hospital mind you) cost 1,100 dollars . . . that's just hospital, no doctors or surgery (deep cuts were needed in both ankles, etc. to insert all kinds of plumbing equipment into me). Only one prof. of sociology at Columbia has sent me as much as a sorry you're sick card: Robt Lynd.

But the really great mail is in connection with *Listen, Yankee.* They ask whom to contact in order to take up work in Cuba! The book in paperback has now sold about 275,000 copies, and 350,000 are in print. The Mexicans are about to come out with the Spanish edition. (My friend Carlos Fuentes, the novelist, checked the translation and writes that it really is a superb job of translation.) Feltrinelli of Italy is bringing out a routrogavure (sp?) [rotogravure] thing with it; very cheaply with pictures etc. West Germans bring out small edition. Poles are translating. The French as usual won't do nothing, but my friend, K. S. Karol, did a two-page spread in *The Express* of Paris and the agent there is as good as they come. Maybe the French have been busy with troubles of their own to their south; also their boy Sartre has written much on Cuba.

Anyway, let us each tell the other immediately of any hard decisions on travel.

As ever,
Mills

The following was written at the bottom of a short form letter from Yaroslava: "Thank you for your recent letter to my husband, Wright Mills, who last December suffered a myocardial infarction. Although now past any immediate crisis, he must remain at rest, and will not return to Columbia University until September 1961. Meanwhile, please forgive his not answering your letter."

To Frances and Charles Grover Mills, from West Nyack, New York, dated March 18, 1961

Dear Mother and Father:

The above is a form letter we have been using, because I just can't handle the mail I've been getting about my illness and about *Listen,*

Yankee. You must not pay any attention to what the gutter newspapers and TV say about my book and about Fidel. They lie. This book is the truth, and it has now sold in the USA about 400,000 copies in paperback, and still going strong; it is about to appear in translations in all major languages of the world: Japan, Italy, Great Britain has a separate edition, Poland, Yugoslavia, Russia, France, West Germany, etc. I get from 7 to 10 letters a day from people all over the world thanking me for having written the book and many asking, "How can you help me to get to Cuba so I can help Fidel?" [. . .] In sum, every US ambassador to every Latin American country is going to have to argue with my book and answer it. And that is exactly as it should be because these Yankee idiots are wrong.

I write you, Mother, to make a request. You remember that long letter you wrote me about my own childhood? Of course I still have it and I need another one from you about my grandfather, your father. I want to know the facts of his life as you remember them and I want to know the exact circumstances of his death. Also his relations with your mother. If there is someone in Lareda to whom you could write who would copy out or have Photostatted anything from the newspaper file there, perhaps an obituary notice, write to them and have them do that. I am going to use some of this stuff in a book I am going to write sometime in the next two years. A very bright idea I've had for years but guess until now didn't have the guts to do it; in the form of a series of sorta autobiographical letters to an unknown Russian intellectual, explaining to him who I am and how I got that way; and so what freedom means, because lying here these weeks and having damned near died, because this thing was pretty damned close, well it's made me much stronger and made me think about myself, which I'd not had the chance to do before. I know now that I have not the slightest fear of death; I know also that I have a big responsibility to thousands of people all over the world to tell the truth as I see it and to tell it exactly and with drama and quit this horsing around with sociological bullshit.

Anyway, you write up your father for me, will you? And don't you bullshit me. Get it straight.

C. G.: I've now got a .30-30 Winchester; a .22 squirrel gun with a 4-power scope on it; and a wonderful MI 30 carbine . . . like was used in the Pacific war . . . weighs only 4 pounds and throws a slug about like a .45 caliber pistol: semiautomatic, it holds clips of any size you want made. (Although for hunting, you've got to use only 5 or 6 clips.)[23] Am in the market for a shotgun now or maybe two or three of them. Do you ever use yours? What kind is it? Do you want to sell it? If so, how much [do] you want?

Your son,
Charleswright

∾

To Harvey and Bette Swados, from West Nyack, New York, undated (early 1961)

Dear Harvey and Bette:

Forgive my not writing to you for so long but first I was busy breaking my heart and then allowing the silly thing to mend. Things still in slow motion as it were but I feel very virtuous now: weight is of the sort one might call controlled appearance; I do not smoke and feel no need to do so. Just a matter of keeping deliberate rather than frenzied, and being protected from the world for a bit longer. Should be quite OK by late April to do damned near anything or rather face damned near anything, although heart has two scars: one from fall of 1957 in Austria. Must have occurred in sleep.

But what I write to say is that Harvey is not to allow the shitliberal types of reviews [. . .] to bother him or hurt him. They are inevitable: would be same if book being reviewed were half blank paper or great American novel. It is a good book [*Nights in the Gardens of Brooklyn* (1961)],[24] especially the title story, so fuck them all.

good bye,
Wright

[P.S.] Everything goes well. Venceremos.
W.

23. When Mills was young, he and his father used to go hunting together in Texas.

24. When the collected short stories of Harvey Swados were published in 1986, with an introduction by Robin Swados, the title was also *Nights in the Gardens of Brooklyn*.

∾

To Walter Klink, from West Nyack, New York, dated March 13, 1961

Dear Walter:

Do, by all means, plan to come out when you can, phoning Yaro a day or so ahead.

Yes, perhaps more people than one might believe share my view of Cuba, or at least are capable of listening to it with attention; we've sold over 370,000 now and are considering another large printing.

But the one thing I have learned from the entire experience is a terrible thing: that the moral cowardice of the American intelligentsia is virtually complete. I don't of course mean that they should agree with me, but I do demand that they face the moral ambiguity, indeed agony is not too strong a word, which any violence involves. This is what you are talking about in your letter: I agree with you fully about that, even tho I have never to my knowledge killed anyone. In LY, which more and more I come to see as a pivotal book for me, and not merely a pamphlet, I do confront this ambiguity. The critics, as in *Dissent* and in *Encounter,* are cowards: they will not even confront it; they take the easy way out. I am extremely embittered at this, and even more embittered that I should allow such cowards to waste my energy in mere bitterness when there are so many real problems to solve.

My heart disease "comes and goes" in a rather irritating way, and I have not been able even to read in any systematic way, much less write. Often I can only lie all day and think in unsystematic ways . . . which hasn't happened since 1934 at Texas A and M after I'd contracted out of the whole freshman class. But then, in the end, one way or another, time is an enormous force.

See you soon as you like and have the time.

W
Wright

P.S.: The International Sociological Association meeting at Washington in Sept. 62 has asked me to give an address to the First Plenary Session, and I have agreed to do so. Since there are only two such papers, and I'm [the] only American, you can see what this means!

During the week before the next letter was written, the New York Times *ran the following front-page headlines about Cuba: "US Urges Castro to Cut His Ties with Communism; Would Aid a Free Regime: Cuba Is Warned" (April 4, 1961); "Castro Minister Says US Wages Undeclared War" (April 6, 1961); "Anti-Castro Units Trained to Fight at Florida Bases· Force There and in Central America Is Reported to Total 5,000 to 6,000" (April 7, 1961); and "Top US Advisors in Dispute on Aid to Castro's Foes: Kennedy Getting Conflicting Views from CIA, Rusk, and Pentagon Aides; Intervention Is Feared; Some Urge Military Help, but President Bars Use of American Troops" (April 11, 1961). The important point was that groups of Cuban exiles were being recruited and trained in the United States for the invasion at the Bay of Pigs, and, as I. F. Stone pointed out, this was a violation of neutrality laws.*[25]

When Fidel Castro's foreign minister, Raul Roa, stated that the United States was formalizing its undeclared war against Cuba, he was referring to the support and training of troops as well as a pamphlet released by the State Department. The pamphlet promised full support for "future democratic governments in Cuba," urging the Castro regime to break links with Communist countries and warning that if this were not done, the United States felt confident that the Cuban people would fight for a free Cuba in keeping with a vision of "inter-American unity."[26]

In the next letter, Mills responds to a comment from Hazel Erskine about a morale problem. Hazel had been active in civil rights and social reform issues since she moved to Nevada in 1947. She was a founder of the Nevada chapter of the American Civil Liberties Union.

To Hazel Gaudet Erskine, from West Nyack, New York, dated April 11, 1961

Dear Hazel:

Thanks for your letter. I've secured a leave from the university for the next academic year and with all the family will spend it wandering in Europe: north and south, east and west.

---

25. "The Press on the New Frontier," *I. F. Stone's Weekly* 9, no. 26 (10 July 1961): 2. All of the issues of *I. F. Stone's Weekly* that are quoted in this volume were among the periodicals Mills had saved in his personal papers.

26. "Text of the State Department's Document Denouncing Castro Regime in Cuba," *New York Times*, 4 April 1961, late ed., p. 14.

I have begun a play, "The Fey Tiger," I call it now; it is set in Yugoslavia and my ambition is to go goat hunting with Tito.

We are well over 450,000 copies in paper of *Listen, Yankee*. Huge Spanish edition is now out, and I am happy to say, in Spanish there are several pirated editions floating around. As you will know if you've read most recent reports on the matter, *Listen Yankee* is still right on the ball. [. . .] It does help now and then to have a little bit of historical reality on your side, doesn't it now?

The morale problem you refer to is damned real; that's why, in all truth, I wander in Europe next year—to keep from thinking about what's happening in the world. But with me you know the morale problem is also a moral problem. I'd much rather be dead than to have to live in half a dozen ways of which I can think. I know that now. Anyway, in the end, everyone who's free has to live, and die, as he must. No one can do much about it.

Yours as ever,
Wright

On April 17, 1961, Cuban exile troops, supported by the United States, invaded the Bay of Pigs, Cuba. Cuban residents did not join them in an uprising, and Castro's forces defeated the invaders in seventy-two hours. After this debacle, U.S. Representative Frank Kowalski (D-Conn.) proposed negotiating with Castro. In comments largely ignored by the national press, but faithfully reported by I. F. Stone's Weekly, Representative Kowalski said, "The counterrevolution failed because it had no roots in Cuba. It failed because it had no appeal for the farmer and the worker. . . . Whatever Americans may think of Castro, he is nonetheless a living example of a successful revolutionist. . . . He has maintained himself in Cuba because he fans the great pride of Cubans in Cuba and in themselves."[27]

Six days after the Bay of Pigs invasion, Mills wrote the next letter to his parents, referring to his mother's image of Mexicans. When Frances was a child on a ranch in Texas, Mexican domestic workers helped to take care of her and taught her to speak Spanish; she had fond memories of them and a continuing respect for Mexican culture.

27. *I. F. Stone's Weekly* 9, no. 17 (8 May 1961): 3.

To Frances and Charles Grover Mills, from West Nyack, New York, dated April 23, 1961

Dear Mother and Dad,

I have your letters of April 18 and April 21. You must forgive me for not having answered you sooner or writing more frequently. But I have been ill and full of spleen and also in the middle of fighting the criminal activities of the Kennedy administration against Cuba. My mother will understand this, for although she has never seen Cuba I know that she has—as her image of the human being—the men and women of Mexico. The Cubans are my Mexicans.

I leave early in the morning with Katy to address a rally in London. Yaroslava and Nikolas follow me on 15 May.

I am mailing to you the picture of the "Old Maid." You may, of course, keep it. In return you must write as soon as you possibly can your memories of my grandfather Bragg Wright. I have three pictures of him now, which I have turned over to a trusted friend who is having them reproduced by expert photographers, and you will receive good copies of all three very shortly. Probably I shall use one of them as the jacket for a book I am writing called "Contacting the Enemy."

You must not worry merely because your son, your daughter, and your grandchildren are in Europe and Asia for the year. We have many friends and we shall be well taken care of. Also you should plan to visit us for two or three weeks—perhaps in December. Would you prefer Italy or Tashkent? Let me know. [. . .]

Con un abrazo revolucionario,[28]
Wright Mills

Meanwhile the FBI was watching Mills's movements. In a memo in the FBI file on Mills, dated April 25, 1961, a federal agent noted Mills's plan to participate in the rally in London about the Cuban situation. As far as we know he did speak at the rally after arriving in London.

By June the Millses and Saul Landau were in the Swiss Alps, in a chalet called La Violette, where they stayed for a month.

28. "With a revolutionary embrace."

Harvey and Bette Swados and their three children, Marco, Felice, and Robin, were living in the south of France when Mills wrote the next letter.

To Harvey and Bette Swados, from Switzerland, dated June 13, 1961

Dear Harvey and Bette:

It's extraordinary that you should be talking about staying in Europe "forever" just when we are very seriously considering just that. Please keep this absolutely confidential for the time being but I have been offered two professorships in England[29] and I am considering them very seriously.

Our plans are not yet definite, although we will be at this address until July 2 or 3. [. . .] After early July, we will probably wander slowly through Berlin and Warsaw to Moscow in our caravan/bus and I will spend a month or so in a Soviet heart clinic. I feel generally okay physically except that I must "push" myself to get anything done: I seem to have "stabilized" at a rather mediocre level, and on the basis of a lot of dope for my heart, which I would like to kick.

Perhaps in September or early October we will settle for a while in England. [. . .]

Sometime in the winter I am going for a month to Cuba;[30] meanwhile I have just mailed a 60-page update of *Listen, Yankee* for the 5th American printing and the 3rd Mexican printing in September. We are touching the ½ million mark [of copies sold] in the USA and want to give the thing a shot in the arm. I am hard at work now on the Marxians,[31] and hope to have it out of the way in 10 days or so. Then everything will be clear for the "Contacting the Enemy" book,[32] on which I will be at work until about Xmas. (No data! No files!)

Meanwhile: I have never been so depressed about the obfuscation and the apparent realities of the USA. I think it's time for all of us to move out.

Yours as ever,
Mills

29. One offer was from the University of Sussex at Brighton; we don't have information about the other.
30. As it turned out, he did not take that trip.
31. Published as *The Marxists* (New York: Dell, 1962).
32. "Tovarich: Contacting the Enemy" (see selected letters to Tovarich in this book).

Here's Yara:

We're in a fantastic Swiss-Victorian villa with a spectacular view
(when the fog lifts) that a friend of W's [Wright's] loaned us pre-
season. It's 2 miles up a cowpath from the road; what a din the cows'
bells make on their way to summer pasture. The other day the Swiss
army marched by and said something to me in French and began
firing big guns nearby. Otherwise things are very peaceful. [. . .]
I have learned to tend fires (there's still skiing up here) and at 6 A.M.
I start the kitchen woodstove. There's a big boiler always going, full
of diapers.[33] [. . .] Katie is beaming with health, having acquired
Swiss red cheeks. There are 5 kids who belong to the caretaker (ages
9 months to 7) and they have absolutely no trouble despite language
difference. The fields are full of such wonderful flowers; Katie keeps
our house filled with color. It's really an ideal resting place, if one
was the type to be able to do so . . . [. . .]

Sincerely hope we will be seeing you, if W can be convinced
to visit the "decadent coast." Right now we all long for a bit of warm
sun . . .

Much much love to all,
Yara

*According to Saul Landau, who assisted Mills on the project, Mills reworked the manu-
script for* The Marxists *three times during his month in the Swiss Alps.*

*In June 1961, Mills and Landau went to Paris and had lunch with Jean Paul
Sartre, Simone de Beauvoir,[34] and K. S. Karol, who translated for Mills and Sartre.
De Beauvoir spoke English. In de Beauvoir's memoir she wrote about their meeting:*

---

33. Nik was one year old at the time.

34. In a posthumously published review of Simone de Beauvoir's book *Second Sex* (1953),
Mills wrote, "Mlle. de Beauvoir's solution to the man-woman problem, put in its briefest
form, is the elimination of woman as we know her—with which one might agree, but to
which one must add: and the elimination of man as we know him. There would then be
male and female and each would be equally free to become an independent human being.
No one can know what new types of human beings would be developed in this historically
unique situation, but perhaps in sharing Mlle. de Beauvoir's passion for liberty we would all
gladly forego femininity and masculinity to achieve it; and perhaps the best types would follow Coleridge's adage and become androgynous characters in an androgynous world."
"Women: The Darling Little Slaves" in *Power, Politics, and People: The Collected Essays of C.
Wright Mills.*

"Mills's book White Collar *had opened the way for all the subsequent studies of American society today.* Les Temps Modernes *had published long extracts from another of his books,* The Power Elite. *Bright-eyed, bearded, he said to me gaily: 'We have the same enemies,' reeling off the names of certain American critics who didn't have much use for me. [. . .] C. Wright Mills was popular in Cuba. [. . .] Like us, he was wondering what was happening there at the moment. The Communist Party was providing the regime with an administrative framework that it had lacked, true enough; unfortunately, it contained within its ranks a clique, led by Anibal Escalante—whom we had thought a pompous imbecile in February 1960—whose sectarianism and opportunism were threatening to force the Castroist revolution into a blind alley."* [35]

Landau wrote that, although Mills agreed that the direction of Cuba's future would be toward the Soviet bloc, he held out some hope that Cuban leaders would be able to preserve a measure of originality. The discussion ended with general agreement that the antagonistic U.S. Cold War policies were to be damned for forcing Cuba into the Soviet camp. [36]

In the following hurried letter to Ian Ballantine, Mills referred to his trip to Paris, without mentioning his meeting with Sartre and de Beauvoir.

To Ian Ballantine, from Switzerland, dated June 27, 1961

Dear Ian:

I have just returned from Paris, for a brief rest, to find your letter of 22 June—rather than a clean draft of the update material for *Listen, Yankee*. This is very disappointing. [. . .] The Mexican printers are literally waiting, having delayed one month to receive it before printing. Such details as exactly when you print, or whether it should be cut in half, or whether it should be put in question and answer form vs. straight prose—all that is a detail. It can be fixed, or rather could have been fixed, in one morning's work, once I saw it clean. Now I do not know what to do if copies don't come by the third of July. I leave here about then. I tried hard to get an English language secretary in Geneva, but can't. So:

The only thing I can do is ask you once more: *please send to me as soon as you can copies of the material I sent to you.* Follow it with any

35. *Force of Circumstance,* translated from the French by Richard Howard (New York: G. P. Putnam's Sons, 1964), 589–90.

36. Landau, "C. Wright Mills," 49–50.

editorial stuff you want to suggest for the Ballantine edition, whenever that may be. Bill me for cost of copies.

Here, so far as I know them, are [my] addresses. None of them is reliable after I leave here. That is why I wrote you such an urgent letter and that is why I worked my ass off finishing up a rough draft during the month of June.

Between 24th and 30th of July:

Care Adam Schaff
    Univerisytetu, Warszawaskiego
    Warszaw, [. . .]
    Poland
    Month of August:

Care Igor Alexandrov
    Soviet Friendship Societies
    [. . .]
    Moscow USSR

[. . .]

Wright Mills

In August 1961 Mills, Saul Landau, Yaroslava, Kate, and Nik spent several weeks traveling by Volkswagen camping bus. The trip took them from Switzerland to Austria and Germany. After a week in Poland they made the risky three-day drive to Moscow, with Landau at the wheel, taking the undulating highway through mostly unpopulated areas in Byelorussia. Few people drove that route in those days.

Mills was highly ambivalent about what he found in Russia. Landau quotes Mills as saying that the Soviets "have done away with some of the state machinery and replaced it by perhaps even more rigid societal controls, an old technique. [. . .] They have started to organize an industrially advanced, technologically based society, and returned to a primitive kind of law and control." At a dinner party in Moscow that included many Soviet officials and many toasts with vodka, Mills upset his host when he said, "Here is to the day when the complete works of Trotsky are published and widely distributed in the Soviet Union. On that day the USSR will have achieved democracy."[37]

Landau (who left Moscow before the Millses) commented that Soviet society both inspired and depressed Mills. Some progress was being achieved, but Mills

37. Ibid., 52.

found many aspects of Soviet life repugnant or just plain backward. His reaction was not surprising; to borrow Landau's phrase, Mills was, after all, a cosmopolitan Texan.

When Mills visited the publishers of the Russian translation of The Power Elite, *he asked for royalties from that edition. The Russian publishers initially refused, but Mills energetically insisted on receiving payment, and he succeeded in obtaining a sum of rubles.[38]*

Mills's American doctor had told him about a Soviet sanitarium in Crimea[39] that specialized in heart disease and might offer hope for Mills's own scarred heart. For more information, Mills visited a polyclinic in Moscow but was not pleased with what he found out. As a patient his diet would be severely restricted. Smoking, alcohol, and lovemaking were prohibited. He would be isolated from his family, who would be allowed in only for visits. After the Soviet doctors explained their rules, Mills quickly made his exit and drove to Leningrad, where he and the family boarded a ship, the Baltika,[40] sailing to London. While onboard they stayed in a private suite with their VW camping bus secured to the deck nearby—accommodations obtained with the rubles from the Russian publisher of The Power Elite.

The Millses were settled, temporarily at least, in London by September.

To Ian Ballantine, from London, England, dated October 2, 1961

Dear Ian:

I have your good letter of 29 Sept. with the enclosure from Deutscher, for which many thanks. The present letter does not require any answer, as we'll be meeting soon. You may show it to Carl Brandt if you should see him before coming over. I want, as it were, to think out loud on paper a little bit, in order to let you know how matters stand, and thus to impose upon you once more.

Usually when you are confronted with a decision, you don't really decide if you take very long about it. You've begun to drift to one side or the other and in the back of your mind, somewhere, you know what the answer is going to be. You seek advice and look for evidence merely to firm up this already-made decision. But about moving to England this is not the case. For a day or so at a time, I'll "really" decide

---

38. Personal communication from Yara Mills to K. Mills, March 1996.
39. On a peninsula in the Black Sea.
40. A turboelectric ship run by the USSR Baltic state steamship line.

yes and rest more or less content with that rather secret knowledge; then for a day or so, the answer will be no, with same result. In brief, I am genuinely undecided. And the reason for this is twofold: First, I understand it as a rather total decision, involving everything from the most intimate and moral questions to the most public conception of my own self which I am capable of assuming. Second, because there are so many unknowns in it both here in England and in the USA.

There are two broad levels of consideration: First, the personal, which at least in the past has always boiled down to: what are the conditions under which I can do the best work? Second, the practical, which in this case means such things as the financial question, the difficulty of moving, and so on. On each of these levels there are many factors, and each is full of unknowns. Fortunately for us all, Yaroslava does not enter into it one way or the other, as she has already demonstrated that she can be happy in either place, or in any place, with the minimum amenities, and she is capable of coping without undue strain with the practical side of things.

On the practical side, which is less important but nonetheless there, there is little doubt now that we should lose quite a bit in standard of living by moving. Not only would I make less money, after taxes and before, but the chances to earn money would be less here, and I would take a really bad financial beating by the move itself.

On the personal side: the risk of not doing good work in the US has to do with unmanageable tensions arising there for me. In England it has to do with a whole set of unknowns. The fact that I've not settled down to work here yet means little or nothing in view of the decision to be made and the fact that I've not got my library and files, my little apparatus for thinking, here with me. So England really is an unknown. One thing is clear to me: the similarity of the language is misleading. This *is* a foreign country to me.

But enough. Will be seeing you soon, and will not make any decision until after we have a talk.

My best to all.
[unsigned copy]

Mills's physical distance from the United States was not creating a sense of detachment or calm. Saul Landau later wrote that when he bought the New York Times *during his visit to London, he and Mills "would sit down and discuss it, and clip and laugh, and then he [Mills] would get a pain in his chest when he read that Kennedy was planning new evil against Cuba, or that Marines were being sent to Southeast Asia."*[41]

To Frances and Charles Grover Mills, from London, England, dated October 17, 1961

Dear Mother and Dad:

I have decided to return to the United States and to Columbia, probably sailing around the first of the year, although not teaching again until next Sept. The decision has less to do with the many attractions of England than with the fact that my argument lies in America and has to be worked out there. You carry it with you and after all it is your damned duty. [. . .]

Maybe, I don't know, I may go along for a short visit to Mexico in the spring. Lonesome for it somehow.

M.

In December 1961, the Millses went to Haut de Cagnes, Cagnes-sur-Mer, France, renting an apartment for a month and visiting the Swados family. Mills and Harvey Swados took long walks and had long arguments—mostly about Cuba.

When Mills left France and returned to the United States in January 1962, he faced a number of problems. The multimillion-dollar libel lawsuit concerning a passage in Listen, Yankee *could not be postponed forever. The New York Office of the FBI reported that the time for Mills and his publishers to answer the complaint had been extended repeatedly since April 1961 through the date of the FBI memo, December 11, 1961. The FBI file also documented that the defense efforts had been hampered by lack of cooperation from the U.S. Passport Office. The lawsuit had the potential of ruining Mills financially. (He was already flat broke due to his travels in Europe the previous year, when he had spent advances for books he had not yet written.)*

In the public arena, the issue Mills faced was the course of the Cuban revolution. On December 1, 1961, Fidel Castro had given a five-hour speech in which he declared himself a Marxist-Leninist and praised the accomplishments of the Soviet Union. At a conference in Uruguay, the Organization of American States responded

41. Landau, "C. Wright Mills," 53.

to these declarations—and the urging of the U.S. Secretary of State, Dean Rusk—by excluding Cuba from participation in its activities. And in February 1962 the United States stepped up its economic boycotts against Cuba. Most exports to Cuba had been banned since 1960; in the wake of Castro's statements in late 1961, the United States added an embargo against imports from Cuba (with the exception of some foods and medicines), thus effectively ending the two-way trade that had once amounted to about $1 billion each year.[42]

On one level Mills was not surprised by Fidel Castro's statements in response to offers of friendship from the USSR—in the face of consistent hostility from the United States—but Mills had gone out on a political limb to present the Cuban revolutionaries' viewpoint to American readers, partly because he believed that, given favorable circumstances, Cuba could develop an independent type of socialism. Using information obtained from personal interviews with Castro and other Cuban leaders in August 1960, Mills had written in Listen, Yankee that, as of mid-1960, the leading men of the Cuban government were not Communists in the sense of the word—party members—in which Mills understood it.[43] Although the degree of political independence that Castro expressed vis-à-vis the USSR waxed and waned in subsequent years, he seemed to be clearly in the Soviet camp as of early 1962. Mills remained irate about U.S. policies toward Cuba, but with the Cold War raging, Castro's declarations of allegiance to Marxism-Leninism and admiration for the Soviet Union put Mills in an increasingly difficult position in the United States.

In addition to Mills's increased political isolation and the multimillion-dollar libel lawsuit against him, he had to cope with his worsening heart disease.

To Ralph and Marion Miliband, from West Nyack, New York, dated March 16, 1962

Dear Ralph and Marion:

This is the first day I've written anything to anybody but now I begin to answer some mail. I am quite all right. I do not drink at all; it turns out that had something to do with a very heavy deficiency in vitamin B something or other, which has now been corrected. They still fool around a bit with my blood chemistry. But please do not worry about

42. "President Orders a Total Embargo on Cuban Imports," *New York Times,* 4 February 1962, sec. 1, p. 1.

43. Ballantine edition, 180.

me. I am slowly acquiring the kind of patience that is required for one in my condition.

Let us know ahead of time when you are in NY and where and when I can pick you up to come out for as long as you have available. I am sorry to say that I don't feel up to attending meetings of any sort, although perhaps Leo and Paul would care to come out some afternoon or for lunch as well.[44]

See you soon.
As ever,
Wright

On March 20, 1962, at the age of forty-five, Mills died of a heart attack in his home.

A memorial service was held at a Quaker Meeting at the Fellowship of Reconciliation in Nyack. Mills had had a strong respect for the Quakers and the Fellowship of Reconciliation, an international, interfaith organization dedicated to fostering active nonviolence, peace, and justice. At the memorial service mourners shared a meditative silence; some kept the silence throughout the service and others rose to speak of Mills or to read aloud from his books. At the request of Mills's mother, Frances, a memorial service was held in a local Roman Catholic church.

At a memorial meeting held at Columbia University, Hans Gerth said that Mills

packed several lives into one. [. . .] His was an open ended "vie experimentale," a way of life, of risks and ventures, of essays and of thrusts held together by extraordinary hard and sustained work of mind and body under stress. [. . .]

His impressive and imaginative trilogy on labor and middle classes, old and new, and on the decision makers in world affairs was the first attempt of an American sociologist to answer the question, whence did we come, where are we going, who are we? [. . .]

He has traversed the course of his life with the tempestuousness of a swift runner. Death struck him down. I have lost my friend, as the Romans used to say, my "alter ego." Requiescas in Pace.[45]

Messages of condolence and grief arrived by the dozens from readers, colleagues, and friends. I. F. Stone telegrammed Yaroslava Mills to say, "Terribly sorry. We are all impoverished by the death of your wonderful and courageous husband." Erich

44. Leo Huberman and Paul Sweezy coauthored a book entitled *Socialism in Cuba* (New York: Monthly Review Press, 1969).

45. "On the Passing of C. Wright Mills," *Berkeley Journal of Sociology* 7, no. 1 (spring 1962): 1, 4, 5.

Fromm telegrammed the following message: "Deeply saddened by death of C. Wright Mills. His courage, forcefulness and intellectual penetration will be sadly missed in America and the world."

A reader of Mills's work wrote that Mills's death gave him "a feeling of great personal loss. Although I never met him, I had always looked forward to the possibility of doing so, and he has exercised considerable influence upon my intellectual development. . . . [He was] a representative of the best tradition of American scholarship and intellectual independence."[46]

Harvey Swados, who was still in Cagnes-sur-Mer, France, at the time, and who had known Mills for twenty-one years, wrote, "What can I say. I have nobody to argue with now. Mills knew always that there was something that held us together no matter how we argued. Or maybe because we argued. This foolish little town will never be the same. Nor will any place that Mills was, even briefly."[47]

Mills's grave is in the shade of an enormous oak tree in the Oak Hill Cemetery in Nyack, New York. When Ralph and Marion Miliband visited Yaroslava after Mills's death, Ralph helped choose the epitaph for the gravestone—words written by Mills:

I have tried to be objective. I do not claim to be detached.[48]

Later that spring Miliband wrote the following about his American friend:

C. Wright Mills cannot be neatly labeled and cataloged. He never belonged to any party or faction; he did not think of himself as a "Marxist"; he had the most profound contempt for orthodox Social Democrats and for closed minds in the Communist world. He detested smug liberals and the kind of radical whose response to urgent and uncomfortable choices is hand wringing. He was a man on his own, with both the strength and also the weakness which go with that solitude. He was on the Left, but not of the Left, a deliberately lone guerrilla, not a regular soldier. He was highly organized, but unwilling to be organized, with self-discipline the only discipline he could tolerate. He had friends rather than comrades. Despite all this, perhaps because of it, he occupied a unique position in American radicalism [. . .] and his death leaves a gaping void. In a trapped and inhumane world, he taught what it means to be a free and humane intellect. "Get on with it," he used to say. "Work." So, in his spirit, let us.[49]

46. Letter from Louis Jones to Mrs. [Yara] Mills, dated March 22, 1962.

47. Letter from Harvey Swados to Yara Mills, dated March 21, 1962.

48. *The Marxists* (New York: Dell Publishing, 1962), 10.

49. Ralph Miliband, "C. Wright Mills," *New Left Review* (May–June 1962). Reprinted in G. William Domhoff and Hoyt B. Ballard, comps., *C. Wright Mills and the Power Elite* (Boston: Beacon Press, 1968), 11.

CHRONOLOGY

August 28, 1916	Charles Wright Mills is born in Waco, Texas.
1934	He graduates from Dallas Technical High School.
1934–1935	Attends Texas Agricultural & Mechanical College.
September 1935	Enters the University of Texas at Austin.
October 1937	Mills marries Dorothy Helen Smith (Freya).
1937–38	A Charles D. Oldright Fellowship in Philosophy aids Mills's graduate work.
1939	Mills obtains both a bachelor's degree in sociology and a master's degree in philosophy from the University of Texas (Phi Beta Kappa).
September 1939	Mills and Freya move to Madison, Wisconsin, where Mills has a research fellowship and enters the doctoral program in sociology at the University of Wisconsin.
Summer 1940	Freya and Mills separate and obtain a divorce, which becomes final the following February.
March 1941	Freya and Mills remarry.
May 1941	Mills completes his course work at the University of

	Wisconsin and passes his preliminary examination for a doctorate.
1941	Mills is appointed associate professor of sociology at the University of Maryland at College Park. He and Freya move to Greenbelt, Maryland.
September 26, 1942	Mills receives a Ph.D. in sociology from the University of Wisconsin after completing his thesis, "A Sociological Account of Pragmatism: An Essay on the Sociology of Knowledge."
January 15, 1943	Mills and Freya's daughter, Pamela, is born.
Early 1945	Mills takes a leave from the University of Maryland and is hired as a research associate at Columbia's Bureau of Applied Social Research (BASR), with summer teaching responsibilities at Columbia University. Mills, Freya, and Pam move to an apartment on East 11th Street in New York City.
Spring 1945	Mills travels to middle-sized cities in the course of his research as a special consultant to the Smaller War Plants Corporation for a congressional study.
Summer 1945	Mills and Freya separate, and Mills moves to an apartment on West 14th Street on the outskirts of Greenwich Village.
1946	Publication of *From Max Weber: Essays in Sociology,* translated and edited by Hans Gerth and Mills.
January 1946	Mills begins to divide his time between work at the BASR and work on his manuscript in progress for *White Collar,* which was supported by a grant from the John Simon Guggenheim Foundation.
April 1946	Mills is appointed assistant professor of sociology at Columbia College; he formally resigns from the University of Maryland and continues working at the BASR.
Mid-1946	Mills is appointed director of the Labor Research Division of the BASR.
February 1947	Mills begins teaching at Columbia College.
July 1947	Mills and Freya obtain a divorce. Mills marries Ruth Harper,

and they take a camping trip, mainly in Nevada and California.

1948	Publication of *New Men of Power,* written with the assistance of Helen Schneider.
Summer 1948	Mills and Ruth take a cross-country trip to California. On the way home they purchase two small islands in Lake Temagami, Ontario, Canada, for $175.
Late 1948	Mills formally withdraws from work at the BASR.
Spring 1949	Mills is a visiting professor of sociology at the University of Chicago.
Summer 1949	Mills and Ruth build a cabin on an island in Lake Temagami, Ontario, where they also stay the following summer.
1950	Publication of *Puerto Rican Journey: New York's Newest Migrants* by Mills, Clarence Senior, and Rose Kohn Goldsen.
July 1, 1950	Effective date of Mills's promotion to associate professor of sociology at Columbia.
Early 1951	Mills and Ruth purchase an old farmhouse in Pomona, New York, and begin to rebuild it.
June 1951	Mills and Ruth take up permanent residence in Pomona, New York.
Late summer 1951	Mills and Ruth drive cross-country to California and also visit Hans and H I Gerth in Madison, Wisconsin.
September 1951	*White Collar* is published.
Spring 1953	Mills is a visiting professor of human relations at Brandeis University.
September 1953	Publication of *Character and Social Structure: The Psychology of Social Institutions,* by Gerth and Mills.
Summer 1954	Mills and Ruth drive cross-country and work on *The Power Elite* as resident fellows at the Huntington Hartford Foundation in Pacific Palisades, California.
1954–55	Mills lectures at the William Alanson White Institute of Psychiatry, New York City.
July 14, 1955	Mills and Ruth's daughter, Kathryn, is born.

January 1956	Mills visits Europe for the first time, learning about motorcycle mechanics at a BMW factory in Munich, Germany.
April 1956	*The Power Elite* is published.
July 1, 1956	Effective date of Mills's promotion to professor of sociology at Columbia College.
1956–57	Mills, Ruth, and Katie move to Copenhagen, where Mills is a Fulbright lecturer at the University of Copenhagen. Mills and Ruth, sometimes with Katie, travel throughout Europe. Mills goes alone to England and Norway, and with Ralph Miliband to Poland.
December 1957	Mills and Ruth separate. Mills returns alone to New York City, leasing an apartment from Columbia University.
1958	*The Causes of World War Three* is published.
Early 1959	*The Sociological Imagination* is published.
May 1959	Ruth obtains a divorce from Mills.
June 1959	Mills marries Yaroslava Surmach, and they move into their new home with Katie in Rockland County, New York. Mills helped design and build the house.
September 1959	Mills attends an international sociology conference in Stresa, Italy, and tours briefly through Austria, Munich, and London with Yara.
January–March 1960	Mills teaches a seminar on Marxism at the University of Mexico, living in Cuernavaca, Mexico, with Yara and Katie.
April 20– May 20, 1960	Mills travels to the Soviet Union at the invitation of the publisher of the Russian translation of *The Power Elite,* and stops in Copenhagen and London. He interviews Soviet professors and gathers material for "Contacting the Enemy: Tovarich."
June 19, 1960	Mills and Yaroslava's son, Nikolas Charles, is born.
August 8–24, 1960	Mills visits Cuba; he interviews Fidel Castro, Che Guevara, and many others.
November 1960	*Listen, Yankee: The Revolution in Cuba* is published.

December 1960	*Harper's Magazine* cover story is an article based on excerpts from *Listen, Yankee.*
Late 1960	Mills receives at least one death threat in response to his defense of the Cuban revolution.
December 1960	A day or two before he is scheduled to debate A. A. Berle Jr. on the topic of U.S. policy toward Cuba on national TV, Mills has a major heart attack.
January 1961	A lawsuit is filed against Mills and the publishers of *Listen, Yankee,* alleging libelous comments about certain Cuban businessmen and seeking $25 million in damages.
April–August 1961	Mills, Yara, Kate, and Nik visit London and tour Europe, especially Switzerland and the Soviet Union, where Mills considers entering a special clinic for heart patients but decides against it.
September–December 1961	The Millses return to London while considering a permanent move to England. They spend a month in an apartment near the Swados family in Haut de Cagnes, Cagnes-sur-Mer, France.
January 27, 1962	The Millses return to West Nyack, New York.
March 20, 1962	Mills dies of a heart attack in his home.
Late March/early April 1962	*The Marxists,* Mills's critical assessment of Marxism, is published.

BOOKS BY C. WRIGHT MILLS

AMERICAN AND FOREIGN EDITIONS

The New Men of Power: America's Labor Leaders (1948)
By C. Wright Mills, with the assistance of Helen Schneider
Harcourt, Brace, and Company
Reprinted by Augustus M. Kelley Publishers

White Collar: The American Middle Classes (1951)
Oxford University Press
Translated into:
   Croat, Biblioteka naprijed, Zagreb, Yugoslavia
   Danish, Fremads Fokusboger, Denmark
   French, Francois Maspero, Paris
   German, Bund-Verlag GMBH, Koln-Deutz
   Hungarian, Kozgazdasagi, Budapest (extracts published in *Hatalom Politika Tecnokratek*)
   Italian, Giulio Einaudi editore, Turin
   Japanese, Tokyo Sogen-sha, Tokyo
   Polish, Ksiazka i Wiedza, Warsaw
   Portuguese, Zahar Editores, Rio de Janeiro
   Spanish, Aguilar, Madrid

The Power Elite (1956)
Oxford University Press; new edition with an afterword by Alan Wolfe (2000)

In some cases, our information about foreign editions may not be complete.

British edition: Secker and Warburg
Translated into:
    Czech, Orbis, Prague
    French, Francois Maspero, Paris
    German, Holsten-Verlag, Hamburg
    Greek, Arsenides, Athens
    Hebrew, Sifriath Poalim, Tel Aviv
    Hungarian, Gondolat, Budapest
    Italian, Feltrinelli Editore, Milan
    Japanese, Tokyo Shogen-Sha, Tokyo
    Polish, Ksiazka i Wiedza, Warsaw
    Portugese, Zahar Editores, Rio de Janeiro
    Russian, Foreign Literature, Moscow
    Serbo, Kultura, Belgrade, Yugoslavia
    Slovenian, Drzavna Zalozba Slovenije, Ljubljana, Yugoslavia
    Spanish, Fondo de Cultura Economica, Mexico City
    Swedish, Raben and Sjogren, Stockholm

The Causes of World War Three (1958)
Simon and Schuster and Ballantine Books
Reprinted by Greenwood Press and M. E. Sharpe, Inc.
British edition: Secker and Warburg
Translated into:
    French, Calmann-Levy, Paris
    German, Kindler Verlag, Munchen
    Italian, Feltrinelli Editore, Milan
    Japanese, Mizo Shobo
    Portuguese, Zahar Editores, Rio de Janeiro
    Spanish, Editorial Palestra

The Sociological Imagination (1959)
Oxford University Press; new edition with an afterword by Todd Gitlin (2000)
British edition: Penguin
Translated into:
    Catalan, Editorial Herder, Barcelona
    Czech, Mlada Fronta, Prague
    Dutch, Het Spectrum, Utrecht (extract in *The Promise*)
    Finnish, Gaudeamus, Helsinki
    Flemish, Utrecht, Aula-Boeken, Antwerpen, Belgium
    French, Francois Maspero, Paris
    German, Hermann Luchterhand Verlag, Darmstadt, Germany
    Greek, Papzissis Publishers, Athens
    Hungarian, Kozgazdasagi, Budapest (extracts published in *Hatalom Politika Tecnokratek*)
    Italian, Il Saggiatore, Milan
    Japanese, Books Kinokuniya, Tokyo Shinjuku, Tokyo
    Norwegian, Pax Forlag, Oslo (extracts)
    Portugese, Zahar Editores, Rio de Janeiro

Romanian, Editura Politica, Bucharest
Serb, Savremena Skola, Belgrade
Spanish, Fondo de Cultura Economica, Mexico City, and Herder, Barcelona
Swedish, Bokforlaget Prisma, Stockholm, and Arkiv, Lund

Listen, Yankee: The Revolution in Cuba (1960)
Ballantine Books and McGraw-Hill Book Company
British edition: Secker and Warburg
Translated into:
  Greek, Dalkafoukis
  Italian, Messus Feltrinelli
  Japanese, Misuzu Shobo
  Polish, Ksiazka i Wiedza, Warsaw
  Portugese, Zahar Editore, Rio de Janeiro
  Spanish, Fondo de Cultura Economica, Mexico City
    Ediciones Grijalbo, S.A., Barcelona

The Marxists (1962)
Dell Publishing
British edition: Penguin
Translated into:
  Italian, Giangiacomo Feltrinelli Editore
  Japanese, Charles E. Tuttle, Tokyo
  Portugese, Zahar Editores, Rio de Janeiro
  Spanish, Ediciones ERA, S.A. Mexico

COLLABORATIONS OR EDITED VOLUMES

From Max Weber: Essays in Sociology (1946)
Edited and translated by Hans Gerth and C. Wright Mills
Oxford University Press

The Puerto Rican Journey: New York's Newest Migrants (1950)
by C. Wright Mills, Clarence Senior, and Rose Kohn Goldsen
Harper and Brothers

Character and Social Structure (1953)
by Hans Gerth and C. Wright Mills
Harcourt, Brace, and World, Inc.

Images of Man: The Classic Tradition in Sociological Thinking (1960)
Edited and with an introduction by C. Wright Mills
George Braziller

POSTHUMOUS PUBLICATIONS

Power, Politics, and People: The Collected Essays of C. Wright Mills (1963)
Edited and with an introduction by Irving Louis Horowitz
Oxford University Press and Ballantine Books
Translated into:
   Dutch, Kritiese Biblioteck, Van Gennep, Amsterdam
   Hungarian, Kozgazdasagi, Budapest (extracts published in *Hatalom Politika Tecnokratek*)
   Italian, Valentino Bompiani, Milan
   Japanese, Misuru Shobo
   Norwegian, Pax Forlag, Oslo
   Portuguese (shorter version), Zahar Editores, Rio de Janeiro
   Spanish, Fondo de Cultura Economica, Mexico City

Sociology and Pragmatism: The Higher Learning in America (1964)
(Mills's dissertation)
   Edited and with an introduction by Irving Louis Horowitz
   Paine-Whitman Publishers and Oxford University Press

NOTES ON SELECTED CORRESPONDENTS

Alinsky, Saul (1909–72)

The social activist and professional organizer whose most well-known books are *Reveille for Radicals* (1946) and *Rules for Radicals* (1971). Alinsky initiated a brief correspondence with Mills in 1943 after hearing about Mills from Robert S. Lynd. At the time, Alinsky was working as a criminologist in Chicago and Mills was teaching at the University of Maryland. As far as we know, Alinsky and Mills never met.

Ballantine, Ian (1916–95)

The founder (with his wife, Betty) of three important paperback houses: Penguin USA in 1935, Bantam Books in 1945, and Ballantine Books in 1952. The Ballantines were given the Literary Market Place's Lifetime Achievement Award a month before his death. Although widely known for their classic science-fiction list, the Ballantines also published commentary on environmental, political, and social issues, including Mills's *The Causes of World War Three* (1958, 1960) and *Listen, Yankee* (1960).

Bell, Daniel (1919–)

The sociologist who was managing editor of *New Leader* (1941–44) and labor editor of *Fortune* magazine (1948–58). Bell taught at the University of Chicago (1945–48) and Columbia University (1952–69) before going to Harvard in 1969, where he has remained. He was named Henry Ford II Professor of Social Sciences in 1980 and has been professor emeritus since 1990. Bell's books include *Marxian Socialism in the United States* (1952, 1967, 1996, ed. with Michael Kazin), *The End of Ideology: On the Exhaustion of Political Ideas in the Fifties* (1960, 1965, 1988), *The Coming of Post-Industrial Society* (1973), *The Cultural Contradictions of Capitalism* (1976), and *The Winding Passage: Essays and Sociological Journeys, 1960–1980* (1980, 1991).

He also edited *The New American Right* (1955), revised as *The Radical Right: The New American Right* (1963, 1977). Mills and Bell met in the early 1940s and were on friendly terms until 1945.

Birnbaum, Norman (1926–)

A sociologist educated at Williams College and Harvard University, Birnbaum taught at the London School of Economics, Oxford University, the University of Strasbourg, the Graduate Faculty of the New School for Social Research, and Amherst College. He is presently a university professor at Georgetown University Law Center. His books include *The Crisis of Industrial Society* (1969), *Towards a Critical Sociology* (1971), *The Radical Renewal: The Politics of Ideas in Modern America* (1988), *and Searching for the Light* (1993). He was on the editorial board of *Partisan Review* and is now on the board of *The Nation*. In the United Kingdom he was an early editor of *Universities and Left Review* and a founding editor of the *New Left Review*. Birnbaum was Mills's host at the London School of Economics, and, with Ralph Miliband, he introduced Mills to members of the nascent New Left group in Great Britain. Among many public activities throughout his career, Birnbaum is currently working with leaders of the AFL-CIO and the Congressional Progressive Caucus.

Bottomore, Tom (1920–92)

British sociologist whose work concentrated on Marxist social theory. His books include *Classes in Modern Society* (1955), *Elites and Society* (1964, 1966, 1993), *Marxist Sociology* (1975), *A History of Sociological Analysis,* with Robert Nisbet (1978), and *Theories of Modern Capitalism* (1985). Bottomore was on the faculty of the London School of Economics and Political Science (1952–65) when he and Mills met. Bottomore also taught at Simon Fraser University in Vancouver, Canada (1965–67), and the University of Sussex (1967–85). When Mills stayed in London in 1961, he visited Bottomore.

Coser, Lewis A. (1913–)

German-born sociologist who studied at the Sorbonne in Paris (1935–38) and received a Ph.D. from Columbia University in 1954. Among many books he authored or edited are the following: *The Functions of Social Conflict* (1956), *Sociological Theory: A Book of Readings,* ed. with Bernard Rosenberg (1957), *Masters of Sociological Thought: Ideas in Historical and Social Context* (1971), *Refugee Scholars in America: Their Impact and Their Experiences* (1984), and *A Handful of Thistles: Collected Papers in Moral Conviction* (1988). Coser and Mills met in the mid-1940s, when they both wrote articles for Dwight Macdonald's journal *politics*. At the time, Coser used the pen name Louis Clair. In 1949, Coser was teaching at the University of Chicago during the semester that Mills spent at that institution. In 1953, as a member of the faculty of Brandeis University, Coser helped arrange for Mills's semester of teaching there.

Erskine, Hazel Gaudet (1908–75)

A social psychologist who became an authority on public opinion research. In addition to coauthoring two books, *The Invasion from Mars,* with H. Contril (1940) and *The People's Choice,* with Paul Lazarsfeld and Bernard Berelson (1944), Erskine was the polls editor of *Public Opinion Quarterly* from 1960 to 1975. She and Mills met in New York in the mid-1940s, when they both worked for the Bureau of Applied Social Research. Besides writing two articles together, Erskine and Mills collaborated occasionally after she left New York in 1947.

Freidel, Frank (1916–93)

The historian who is best known for the six volumes of biography he wrote about Franklin Delano Roosevelt. *Franklin Delano Roosevelt: The Apprenticeship* (1952), *Franklin Delano Roosevelt: The Ordeal* (1954), *Franklin Delano Roosevelt: The Triumph* (1956), *F. D. R. and the South* (1966), *Franklin Delano Roosevelt: Launching the New Deal* (1973), and *Franklin Delano Roosevelt: A Rendezvous with Destiny* (1990). Freidel was on the faculty of Harvard University from 1955 to 1981. Mills and Freidel met in the early 1940s when they were both on the faculty of the University of Maryland.

Fuentes, Carlos (1928–)

The internationally acclaimed Mexican author of many novels, short stories, plays, and works of nonfiction, Fuentes has taught at several universities, including Cambridge, Columbia, Harvard, the University of California, University of Paris, and University of Pennsylvania. Over a dozen of his novels have been published in English, and one, *The Old Gringo,* was made into a Hollywood film. Fuentes and Mills apparently met in 1960, as the result of contacts Mills made during his stay in Mexico that same year. When Mills was recovering from his December 1960 heart attack, Fuentes paid him a two-day visit at his home in West Nyack, New York.

Gerth, Hans H. (1908–78)

German-born and educated sociologist who collaborated with Mills on two books: *From Max Weber: Essays in Sociology* (1946) and *Character and Social Structure* (1953). Gerth and Mills met in 1940 at the University of Wisconsin at Madison, where Gerth taught sociology and Mills was studying for his Ph.D. They kept in contact for over two decades in spite of the physical distance between them during all but a few years. Gerth was a collaborator and friend to whom Mills wrote hundreds of letters.

Hofstadter, Richard (1916–70)

The historian who wrote *Social Darwinism in American Thought* (1944), *The American Political Tradition and the Men Who Made It* (1948), *The Age of Reform* (1955), *Anti-Intellectualism in American Life* (1963), and *The Paranoid Style in American Politics* (1965), among other titles. (*The Age of Reform* and *Anti-Intellectualism in American Life* were both awarded the Pulitzer Prize.) Hofstadter and Mills met in the early 1940s, when they both taught at the University of Maryland. In September 1946, the year after Mills's arrival in New York, Hofstadter joined the faculty of Columbia University.

Howe, Irving (1920–93)

Author, historian, and critic who was the cofounder and longtime editor of *Dissent* magazine. Howe taught at Brandeis University (1953–61), Stanford University (1961–63), and CUNY's Hunter College (1963–86), where he was Distinguished Professor from 1970 to 1986. His books include *The UAW and Walter Reuther,* with B. J. Widick (1949), *Sherwood Anderson: A Critical Study* (1951), *Politics and the Novel: A World More Attractive* (1963, 1977, 1992), *World of Our Fathers: The Journey of the Eastern European Jews to America and the Life They Found and Made* (1976, 1989, 1990, 1994), which won the National Book Award in 1976, *Socialism and America* (1985), *The American Newness: Culture and Politics in the Age of Emerson* (1986), and *William Faulkner: A Critical Study* (4th ed., 1991).

Lowenthal, Leo (1900–93)

German-born and educated sociologist who worked at the Institute of Social Research in Frankfurt and the Bureau of Applied Social Research in New York from 1926 to 1949. He was also a lecturer at Columbia University from 1940 to 1956, and worked for the U.S. Department of State in the 1940s and 1950s. He began a long career at University of California at Berkeley in 1956. Lowenthal was the managing editor of *Studies in Philosophy and Social Sciences* from 1932 to 1941. His books in English include *Literature and the Image of Man: Sociological Studies of the European Drama and Novel, 1600–1900* (1957) and *Literature, Popular Culture, and Society* (1961). He and Mills met after Mills wrote him a letter in May 1944 praising Lowenthal's "piece on biography in radio research" and suggesting a meeting.

Macdonald, Dwight (1906–82)

Journalist and critic who was an editor of *Partisan Review* from 1937 to 1943 and who founded and edited the journal *politics*, published from 1944 to 1949. He later wrote for the *New Yorker* and was a film critic for *Esquire*. In addition to authoring books of criticism, Macdonald wrote *Henry Wallace: The Man and the Myth* (1948) and *Memoirs of a Revolutionist* (1957). Macdonald and Mills met in the early 1940s, through Daniel Bell, when Mills was teaching at the University of Maryland.

Merton, Robert K. (1910–)

A sociologist on the faculties of Harvard and Tulane Universities before going to Columbia in 1941, where he has remained ever since. Associate director of the Columbia Bureau of Applied Social Research from 1942 to 1971, he was named Giddings Professor of Sociology from 1963 to 1974 and then a university professor until he became university professor emeritus in 1979. His books include *Science, Technology, and Society in 17th-Century England* (1938), *Social Theory and Social Structure* (1949, 1957, 1968), *On the Shoulders of Giants* (1965, 1985, 1993), *The Sociology of Science: Theoretical & Empirical Investigations* (1973), *Sociological Ambivalence* (1976), *Social Research and the Practicing Professions* (1982), and *On Social Structure and Science* (1996). Mills wrote to Merton as early as 1939, and they had met before Mills began to work at the Columbia Bureau of Applied Social Research in 1945.

Miliband, Ralph (1924–94)

London-based political scientist and coeditor of *The Socialist Register* from its foundation in 1964 until his death. He wrote *Parliamentary Socialism* (1961, 1973), *The State in Capitalist Society* (1969), *Marxism and Politics* (1977), *Capitalist Democracy in Britain* (1981), *Class Power and State Power* (1983), *Divided Societies: Class Struggle in Contemporary Capitalism* (1989), and *Socialism for a Skeptical Age* (published posthumously in 1994). Miliband and Mills met when Mills went to England in 1957; at the time, Miliband was a lecturer at the London School of Economics and Political Science. For the rest of Mills's life, they kept in touch through correspondence and visits.

Miller, William (1912–92)

A historian who had a varied career as university teacher, journalist, editor, and consultant to government and industry. His books include *The Age of Enterprise,* with Thomas Cochran (1942) and, in collaboration with Richard Hofstadter and Daniel Aaron, *The United States: The History of a Republic* (1957), *The American Republic* (1959), and *The Structure of American*

History (1964). Miller's *A History of the United States* (1958) was reissued as *A New History of the United States* (1962). He also authored *Readings in American Values* (1964). Miller and Mills, who met in the early 1940s through their mutual friend Richard Hofstadter, kept in contact through visits and correspondence throughout the rest of Mills's life. In Mills's will, he named Miller executor of his estate.

Riesman, David (1909–)

Lawyer and social scientist whose best-known book is *The Lonely Crowd: A Study of the Changing American Character,* written in collaboration with Nathan Glazer and Revel Denny (1950). Riesman also wrote *Faces in the Crowd* (1952), *Individualism Reconsidered and Other Essays* (1954), *Abundance for What? and Other Essays,* with Evelyn Thompson Riesman (1963, 1993), and *The Academic Revolution,* with Christopher Jencks (1968), among others. Professor of social science at the University of Chicago from 1949 to 1958, Riesman became Henry Ford II Professor of Social Science at Harvard in 1958. We do not know how Riesman and Mills met.

Swados, Harvey (1920–72)

The author of novels including *Out Went the Candle* (1955), *False Coin* (1959), *Standing Fast* (1970), and *Celebration* (1972); collections of short stories including *On the Line* (1957) and *Nights in the Gardens of Brooklyn* (1961); and works of nonfiction, such as *A Radical's America* (1962). Swados and Mills met in Maryland in the early 1940s, when Swados was a merchant marine and Mills taught at the University of Maryland. During most of the last decade of Mills's life, he and Swados both lived in Rockland County, New York.

Thompson, E. P. (1924–93)

British historian whose major historical publications include *William Morris: Romantic Revolutionary* (1955, 1977), *The Making of the English Working Class* (1963), *Whigs and Hunters: The Origins of the Black Act* (1975), *Customs in Common* (1991), and *Witness against the Beast: William Blake and the Moral Law* (1993). He was one of the founders of the journal the *Reasoner,* which became the *New Reasoner* in 1957 before merging with *Universities and Left Review* in 1959. Thompson was also a regular contributor to the *New Left Review.* A political activist, he was the acknowledged leader of the Campaign for Nuclear Disarmament in the early 1980s. Mills visited Thompson at his home on at least one occasion, accompanied by Ian Ballantine, in 1961.

Wakefield, Dan (1932–)

Author and screenwriter whose best-selling novel *Going All the Way* (1970, 1997) was made into a film. Other novels include *Starting Over* (1973), *Under the Apple Tree* (1982), and *Selling Out* (1985). His works of nonfiction include *Island in the City: The World of Spanish Harlem* (1959), *Returning: A Spiritual Journey* (1988), *The Story of Your Life: Writing a Spiritual Autobiography* (1990), *New York in the Fifties* (1993), and *Expect a Miracle: The Miraculous Things That Happen to Ordinary People* (1995). Wakefield met Mills in the mid 1950s when he took a seminar Mills was teaching at Columbia College. He wrote his impressions of Mills both in *New York in the Fifties* and in an article on Mills for *Atlantic Monthly* (September 1971) entitled "Taking It Big: A Memoir of C. Wright Mills."

ABOUT THE EDITORS

KATHRYN MILLS

Kate graduated from Hampshire College (Amherst, Massachusetts) with a B.A. in political economics. After attending Boston University Law School for one year, she spent four years working as a community organizer and advocate. She has been working for a Boston publisher since 1982 in various aspects of trade and school publishing and currently leads a department that drafts, negotiates, and vets trade and reference publishing contracts. She lives with her husband and son.

PAMELA MILLS

After two years at Oberlin College, Pamela transferred to Barnard College, from which she received a B.A. in American studies. She then moved to Rio de Janeiro, Brazil, where she has since resided. As an English teacher at a large binational center, she received first an M.A. and then a Ph.D. in English and American literature from the Universidade Federal do Rio de Janeiro. Besides teaching, she heads the center's college-level English program and has published several articles in her field in Brazilian journals. She is married and has three Brazilian-American sons.

GLOSSARY OF ABBREVIATIONS

C & SS	*Character and Social Structure* by Hans Gerth and C. Wright Mills
DAB	Dictionary of American Biography
INRA	Instituto Nacional de Reforma Agraria (National Institute of Agrarian Reform) in Cuba
LY	*Listen, Yankee: The Revolution in Cuba* by C. Wright Mills
PE	*The Power Elite* by C. Wright Mills
SANE	The National Committee for a Sane Nuclear Policy
WC	*White Collar* by C. Wright Mills

INDEX

Text:	Bembo
Display:	Futura Heavy, Bembo
Composition:	Integrated Composition Systems, Inc.
Printing and binding:	Edwards Brothers
Index:	Patricia Deminna